SECOND EDITION

LANGUAGE ASSESSMENT

Principles and

Classroom Practices

PEARSON
Longman

H. DOUGLAS BROWN
PRIYANVADA ABEYWICKRAMA

Language Assessment, Principles and Classroom Practices, Second Edition

Pearson Education, 10 Bank Street, White Plains, NY 10606

Staff credits: The people who made up the **Language Assessment, Principles and Classroom Practices, Second Edition** team, representing editorial, production, design, and manufacturing, are Danielle Belfiore, John Brezinsky, Tracey Munz Cataldo, Nancy Flaggman, Jaime Lieber, Lise Minovitz, Kim Steiner, and Jennifer Stem.

Cover design: Tracey Munz Cataldo
Text design: Wendy Wolf, TSI Graphics
Text composition: TSI Graphics
Text font: Garamond Book
Text art: Don Martinetti
Text credits: See page xiv.

Library of Congress Cataloging-in-Publication Data
Brown, H. Douglas, 1941–
        Language assessment: principles and classroom practices/H. Douglas Brown; Priyanvada Abeywickrama.
                p. cm.
        ISBN 0-13-814931-3
            1. Language and languages—Study and teaching. 2. Language and languages—Examinations.
3. Language acquisition. I. Abeywickrama, Priyanvada. II. Title.

    P53.4.B76 2010
    418.0076—dc22

                                                                            2009039195

ISBN-13: 978-0-13-814931-4
ISBN-10: 0-13-814931-3

Printed in the United States of America
    2 3 4 5 6 7 8 9 10—V056—15 14 13 12 11

CONTENTS

Chapter 7   Assessing Listening   **156**

Chapter 8   Assessing Speaking   **183**

Chapter 9 Assessing Reading 224

Chapter 10   Assessing Writing   259

Chapter 11   Assessing Grammar and Vocabulary   292

Chapter 12   Grading and Student Evaluation   318

PREFACE

As this second edition of *Language Assessment: Principles and Classroom Practices* goes to press, we are embarking on the second decade of this new millennium. In that first ten-year period alone, the field of second language acquisition and pedagogy saw remarkable advances in our stockpile of methodological options for teaching languages. The subdiscipline of language assessment kept pace with this growth. In this second edition, we have almost doubled the number of bibliographic entries found in the first edition, a sign of a full research agenda. Also, in that period of time several new journals—exclusively devoted to language assessment—have been published, a further index of academic prosperity.

Assessment in general, but in particular *language* assessment, is an area of intense fascination. No longer a field exclusively relegated to psychometricians and testing "experts," assessment has caught the interest of classroom teachers, students, parents, and political action groups. How can I (a teacher) design an effective classroom test? What can I (a student) do to prepare for a test and to make assessments of all kinds enhancing, learning experiences? Are the standardized tests of language (that my child has to take) accurate measures of ability? And do I (as an advocate for fair testing practices) believe that the plethora of tests that students are exposed to are culture-fair, free from bias, and not instruments of a powerful elite designed to further the gap between the haves and the have-nots?

All of these and many more questions now being addressed by teachers, researchers, and specialists can be overwhelming to the novice language teacher, who is already baffled by linguistic and psychological paradigms and a multitude of methodological options. This book provides teachers—and teachers-to-be—with a clear, reader-friendly presentation of the essential foundation stones of language assessment, with ample practical examples to illustrate their application in language classrooms. It is a book that simplifies the issues without oversimplifying. It doesn't dodge complex questions, and it treats them in ways that classroom teachers can comprehend. Readers do not have to become testing experts—or statisticians adept in manipulating mathematical equations and advanced calculus—to understand and apply the concepts in this book.

PURPOSE AND AUDIENCE

This book is designed to offer a comprehensive survey of essential principles and tools for second language assessment. It has been successfully used in its first edition in teacher-training courses, teacher certification curricula, and TESOL master of arts programs. As the third in a trilogy of teacher education textbooks, it is designed to follow H. Douglas Brown's other two books, *Principles of Language Learning and Teaching* (fifth edition, Pearson Education, 2007) and *Teaching by Principles* (third edition, Pearson Education, 2007). References to those two books are sprinkled throughout the current book. In keeping with the tone set in the previous two books, this one features uncomplicated prose and a systematic, spiraling organization. Concepts are introduced with a maximum of practical exemplification and a minimum of weighty definition. Supportive research is acknowledged and succinctly explained without burdening the reader with ponderous debate over minutiae.

The testing discipline sometimes possesses an aura of sanctity that can cause teachers to feel inadequate as they approach the task of mastering principles and designing effective instruments. Some testing manuals, with their heavy emphasis on jargon and mathematical equations, don't help to dissipate that mystique. By the end of *Language Assessment*, readers will have gained access to this not-so-frightening field. They will have a working knowledge of a number of useful, fundamental principles of assessment and will have applied those principles to practical classroom contexts. They will also have acquired a storehouse of useful, comprehensible tools for evaluating and designing practical, effective assessment techniques for their classrooms.

PRINCIPAL FEATURES

Notable features of this book include the following:

- Clearly framed **fundamental principles** for evaluating and designing assessment procedures of all kinds
- Focus on the most common pedagogical challenge: **classroom-based assessment**
- Many **practical examples** to illustrate principles and guidelines
- Concise but comprehensive treatment of assessing all **four skills** (listening, speaking, reading, writing)
- In each skill, **classification of assessment techniques** that range from controlled to open-ended item types on a specified continuum of micro- and macroskills of language
- Explanation of **standards-based assessment**: what it is, why it is so popular, and its pros and cons
- Thorough discussion of large-scale **standardized tests**: their purpose, design, validity, and utility

- Consideration of the **ethics of testing** in an educational and commercial world driven by tests
- A comprehensive presentation of **alternatives in assessment**, namely, portfolios, journals, conferences, observations, interviews, and self- and peer-assessment
- A systematic discussion of letter **grading** and overall **evaluation** of student performance in a course
- **End-of-chapter exercises** that suggest whole-class discussion and individual, pair, and group work for the classroom
- Suggested **additional readings** at the end of each chapter

IMPROVEMENTS IN THE SECOND EDITION

In this second edition of *Language Assessment*, a number of changes are present, reflecting advances in the field as well as enhancements based on feedback from the first edition. Some of those changes are as follows:

- **Advance organizers at the beginning of each chapter.** Each chapter now begins with a brief list of objectives, which serve as pre-reading organizers for students and instructors.
- **A new chapter.** The domain of form-focused assessment is now addressed in a separate chapter (Chapter 11). Although assessing the four skills involves, in some cases, assessing pertinent grammar and vocabulary, it is appropriate to treat such focus as a separate issue. Background information and a survey of research are presented along with practical examples of techniques for assessing grammar and vocabulary.
- **Updated references and new information.** The six years of research and practice that have transpired since the first edition of this book create the obvious need to encapsulate that progress in the form of reports of new research, updated references, and the insertion of new information. The latter includes the following:
  - Reorganization of the first three chapters for a more logical progression of steps toward understanding classroom-based assessment
  - A slimmer and more incisive discussion of the history of language assessment
  - Updated descriptions of current issues and challenges throughout
  - Recent research and practice with regard to standards-based assessment, in a completely redesigned chapter (Chapter 4)
  - A discussion of rubrics in the chapter on "alternatives" (Chapter 6)
  - The aforementioned treatment of assessing grammar and vocabulary, now with the attention it deserves in a separate chapter (Chapter 11)
  - An additional section in the chapter on grading and evaluation (Chapter 12) on calculating grades with references to Web-based resources

- **Glossary of terminology.** In this edition you will find a glossary of assessment terms and concepts, all of which have been boldfaced in the text of the book. We hope this will be a useful way to quickly clarify the meaning of the myriad of terms introduced in this book.
- **Appendix listing commercially available tests.** Current data on widely marketed tests is now presented in an appendix that lists pertinent information, specifications, and Internet references.

PERSONAL WORDS OF APPRECIATION

First, I want to welcome my coauthor for this edition, Dr. Priyanvada Abeywickrama, professor of English at San Francisco State University. It has been my pleasure to work with Priya in writing this second edition, as she has been especially helpful in identifying new, cutting-edge research in the field as well as in offering insights on standards-based and form-focused assessment.

We can both heartily assert that this book is very much the product of our own teaching of language assessment. Our students have collectively taught us more than we have taught them, which prompts us to thank them all, everywhere, for these gifts of knowledge. And of course the embracing support of the MATESOL faculty at San Francisco State University is an uplifting source of stimulation and affirmation.

I'm further indebted to teachers in many countries around the world where I have had the honor of offering workshops and seminars on language assessment. I have memorable impressions of such sessions in Brazil, Canada, Chile, the Dominican Republic, Egypt, Japan, Korea, Mexico, Peru, Spain, Taiwan, Thailand, Turkey, Uruguay, and the former republic of Yugoslavia, where cross-cultural issues in assessment have been especially stimulating.

Finally, we wish to thank our respective partners, Scott and Mary, for tolerating authors in their home who need all too many hours of uninterrupted focus during periods of book writing. Their love and support is a marvelous affirmation of our work.

We would like to thank the following reviewers who offered invaluable insights about the first edition and early drafts of the revised edition: **Jorge H. Cubillos**, University of Delaware, Newark, Delaware; **Fernando Fleurquin**, University of Maryland Baltimore County, Baltimore, Maryland; **Vasie Kelos**, Seneca College, Toronto, Canada; **Suzanne Medina**, California State University, California; (the late) **Lynn Stafford-Yilmaz**, Bellevue Community College, Bellevue, Washington; **Diane Strong-Krause**, Brigham Young University, Provo, Utah; **Latricia Trites**, Murray State University, Kentucky.

Dr. H. Douglas Brown
September 2009

TEXT CREDITS

Grateful acknowledgment is made to the following publishers and authors for permission to reprint copyrighted material.

American Council on Teaching Foreign Languages (ACTFL), for material from *ACTFL Proficiency Guidelines: Speaking* (1986); *Oral Proficiency Inventory (OPI): Summary Highlights.*

Blackwell Publishers, for material from Brown, James Dean & Bailey, Kathleen M. (1984). A categorical instrument for scoring second language writing skills. *Language Learning, 34,* 21–42.

California Department of Education, for material from *California English Language Development (ELD) Standards: Listening and Speaking.*

Educational Testing Service (ETS), for material from *Test of English as a Foreign Language (TOEFL® Test); Test of Spoken English (TSE® Test); Test of Written English (TWE® Test).*

English Language Institute, University of Michigan, for material from *Michigan English Language Assessment Battery (MELAB).*

Georgetown University Press, for material from Swain, Merrill. (1990). The language of French immersion students: Implications for theory and practice. In James E. Alatis (Ed.), *Georgetown University round table on languages and linguistics.* Washington: Georgetown University Press.

Oxford University Press, for material from Bachman, Lyle F. (1990). *Fundamental considerations in language testing.* New York: Oxford University Press.

Pearson Education, for material from *Versant® Test.*

Pearson Longman ESL, and Deborah Phillips, for material from Phillips, Deborah. (2001). *Longman Introductory Course for the TOEFL® Test.* White Plains, NY: Pearson Education.

Second Language Testing, Inc. (SLTI), for material from *Modern Language Aptitude Test.*

University of Cambridge Local Examinations Syndicate (UCLES), for material from *International English Language Testing System.*

Yasuhiro Imao, Roshan Khan, Eric Phillips, and Sheila Viotti, for unpublished material.

CHAPTER 1

ASSESSMENT CONCEPTS

AND ISSUES

OBJECTIVES: After reading this chapter, you will be able to

- understand differences between *assessment* and *testing*, along with other basic assessment concepts and terms
- distinguish among five different types of language tests, cite examples of each, and apply them for different purposes and contexts

- appreciate historical antecedents of present-day trends and research in language assessment
- grasp some of the major current issues that assessment researchers are now addressing

Tests have a way of scaring students. How many times in your school days did you feel yourself tense up when your teacher mentioned a test? The anticipation of the upcoming "moment of truth" provoked feelings of anxiety and self-doubt along with a fervent hope that you would come out on the other end with at least a sense of worthiness. The fear of failure is perhaps one of the strongest negative emotions a student can experience, and the most common instrument inflicting such fear is the test. You are not likely to view a test as positive, pleasant, or affirming, and, like most ordinary mortals, you intensely wish for a miraculous exemption from the ordeal.

And yet, tests seem as unavoidable as tomorrow's sunrise in virtually all educational settings around the world. Courses of study in every discipline are marked by these periodic milestones of progress (or sometimes, in the perception of the learner, confirmations of inadequacy) that have become conventional methods of measurement. The gate-keeping function of tests—from classroom achievement tests to large-scale standardized tests—has become an acceptable norm.

Now, just for fun, take the following quiz. All five of the words are found in standard English dictionaries, so you should be able to answer all five items easily, right? Okay, go for it.

Directions: In each of the five items below, select the definition that correctly defines the word. You have two minutes to complete this test!

1. onager
    a. a large specialized bit used in the final stages of oil well drilling
    b. in cultural anthropology, an adolescent approaching puberty
    c. an Asian wild ass with a broad dorsal stripe
    d. a phrase or word that quantifies a noun

2. shroff
    a. (Yiddish) a prayer shawl worn by Hassidic Jews
    b. a fragment of an ancient manuscript
    c. (Archaic) past tense form of the verb *to shrive*
    d. a banker or money changer who evaluates coin

3. hadal
    a. relating to the deepest parts of the ocean below 20,000 feet
    b. one of seven stations in the Islamic *hajj*, or pilgrimage, to Mecca
    c. a traditional Romanian folk dance performed at spring festivals
    d. pertaining to Hades

4. chary
    a. discreetly cautious and vigilant about dangers and risks
    b. pertaining to damp, humid weather before a rainstorm
    c. optimistic, positive, looking on the bright side
    d. expensive beyond one's means

5. yabby
    a. overly talkative, obnoxiously loquacious
    b. any of various burrowing Australian crayfishes
    c. a small horse-drawn carriage used in Victorian England for transporting one or two persons
    d. in clockwork mechanisms, a small latch for calibrating the correct time

---

Now, how did that make you feel? Probably just the same as many learners feel when they take multiple-choice (or shall we say multiple-guess?), timed, "tricky" tests. To add to the torment, if this were a commercially administered standardized test, you would probably get a score that, in your mind, demonstrates that you did *worse* than hundreds of people! If you're curious about how you did on the quiz, check your answers by turning to page 22 at the end of this chapter.

Of course, this little quiz on obscure, infrequently used English words is not an appropriate example of classroom-based achievement testing, nor is it intended to be. It was designed to be overly difficult, to offer you no opportunity to use contextual clues, and to give you little chance of deciphering the words from your knowledge of English. It's simply an illustration of how tests make us feel much of the time.

Here's the bottom line: Tests need *not* be degrading or threatening to your students. Can they build a person's confidence and become learning experiences? Can they become an integral part of a student's ongoing classroom development? Can they bring out the best in students? The answer is yes. That's mostly what this book is about: helping you as a teacher create more authentic, intrinsically motivating assessment procedures that are appropriate for their context and designed to offer constructive feedback to your students.

To reach this goal, it's important to understand some basic concepts: What do we mean by *assessment*? What is the difference between assessment and a test? And how do various categories of assessments and tests fit into the teaching-learning process?

ASSESSMENT AND TESTING

Assessment is a popular and sometimes misunderstood term in current educational practice. You might be tempted to think of *assessing* and *testing* as synonymous terms, but they are not. Let's differentiate the two concepts.

Assessment is "appraising or estimating the level or magnitude of some attribute of a person" (Mousavi, 2009, p. 36). In educational practice, assessment is an ongoing process that encompasses a wide range of methodological techniques. Whenever a student responds to a question, offers a comment, or tries out a new word or structure, the teacher subconsciously makes an appraisal of the student's performance. Written work—from a jotted-down phrase to a formal essay—is performance that ultimately is "judged" by self, teacher, and possibly other students. Reading and listening activities usually require some sort of productive performance that the teacher observes and then implicitly appraises, however peripheral that appraisal may be. A good teacher never ceases to assess students, whether those assessments are incidental or intended.

Tests, on the other hand, are a subset of assessment, a genre of assessment techniques. They are prepared administrative procedures that occur at identifiable times in a curriculum when learners muster all their faculties to offer peak performance, knowing that their responses are being measured and evaluated.

In scientific terms, a test is a method of measuring a person's ability, knowledge, or performance in a given domain. Let's look at the components of this definition. A test is first a *method*. It's an instrument—a set of techniques, procedures, or items—that requires performance on the part of the test-taker. To qualify as a test, the method must be explicit and structured: multiple-choice questions with prescribed correct answers, a writing prompt with a scoring rubric, an oral interview based on a question script, or a checklist of expected responses to be filled in by the administrator.

Second, a test must *measure,* which may be defined as a process of quantifying a test-taker's performance according to explicit procedures or rules (Bachman, 1990, pp. 18–19). Some tests measure general ability, whereas others focus on very specific competencies or objectives. A multiskill proficiency test determines a general ability level; a quiz on recognizing correct use of definite articles measures specific knowledge. The way the results or measurements are communicated may vary. Some tests, such as a classroom-based, short-answer essay test, may earn the test-taker a letter grade accompanied by the instructor's marginal comments. Others, particularly large-scale standardized tests, provide a total numerical score, a percentile rank, and perhaps some subscores. If an instrument does not specify a form of reporting measurement—a means for offering the test-taker some kind of result—then that technique cannot appropriately be defined as a test.

Next, a test measures an *individual's* ability, knowledge, or performance. Testers need to understand who the test-takers are. What are their previous experiences and backgrounds? Is the test appropriately matched to their abilities? How should test-takers interpret their scores?

A test measures **performance**, but the results imply the test-taker's ability or, to use a term common in the field of linguistics, **competence**. Most language tests measure one's ability to perform language, that is, to speak, write, read, or listen to a subset of language. On the other hand, it is not uncommon to find tests designed to tap into a test-taker's knowledge about language: defining a vocabulary item, reciting a grammatical rule, or identifying a rhetorical feature in written discourse. Performance-based tests sample the test-taker's actual use of language, but from those samples the test administrator infers general competence. A test of reading comprehension, for example, may consist of several short reading passages each followed by a limited number of comprehension questions—a small sample of a second language learner's total reading behavior. But from the results of that test, the examiner may infer a certain level of general reading ability.

Finally, a test measures a given *domain*. For example, in the case of a proficiency test, even though the actual performance on the test involves only a sampling of skills, the domain is overall proficiency in a language—general competence in all skills of a language. Other tests may have more specific criteria. A test of pronunciation might well be a test of only a limited set of phonemic minimal pairs. A vocabulary test may focus on only the set of words covered in a particular lesson or unit. One of the biggest obstacles to overcome in constructing adequate tests is to measure the desired criterion and not include other factors inadvertently, an issue that is addressed in Chapters 2 and 3.

A well-constructed test is an instrument that provides an accurate measure of the test-taker's ability within a particular domain. The definition sounds fairly simple, but, in fact, constructing a good test is a complex task involving both science and art.

Measurement and Evaluation

A couple other potentially confusing terms often appear in discussions of assessment and testing: *measurement* and *evaluation.* Because the terms lie somewhere in between assessment and testing, they are at times mistakenly used as synonyms of one or the other concept. Let's take a brief look at these two processes.

Measurement is the process of quantifying the observed performance of classroom learners. Bachman (1990) cautioned us to distinguish between quantitative and qualitative descriptions of student performance. Simply put, the former involves assigning numbers (including rankings and letter grades) to observed performance whereas the latter consists of written descriptions, oral feedback, and other nonquantifiable reports.

There are clear advantages to quantification. Numbers allow us to provide exact descriptions of student performance and to compare one student to another more easily. They also can spur us to be explicit in our specifications for scoring student responses, thus leading to greater objectivity. On the other hand, quantifying student performance can work against the teacher or tester, perhaps masking nuances of performance or giving an air of certainty when scoring **rubrics** may actually be quite vague. Verbal or qualitative descriptions may offer an opportunity for a teacher to individualize feedback to a student, such as in marginal comments on a student's written work or oral feedback on pronunciation.

Yet another potentially confusing term that needs explanation is **evaluation**. Is evaluation the same as testing? Evaluation does not necessarily entail testing; rather, evaluation is involved when the results of a test (or other assessment procedure) are used for decision making (Bachman, 1990, pp. 22–23). Evaluation involves the interpretation of information. Simply recording numbers or making check marks on a chart does not constitute evaluation. You evaluate when you "value" the results in such a way that the worth of the performance is conveyed to the test-taker, usually with some reference to the consequences—good or bad—of the performance.

Test scores are an example of measurement, and conveying the "meaning" of those scores is evaluation. If a student achieves a score of 75 percent (measurement) on a final classroom examination, he or she may be told that the score resulted in a failure (evaluation) to pass the course. Evaluation can take place without measurement, as in, for example, a teacher's appraisal of a student's correct oral response with words like "excellent insight, Fernando!"

Assessment and Learning

Returning to our contrast between tests and assessment, we find that tests are a subset of assessment, but they are certainly not the only form of assessment that a teacher can make. Although tests can be useful devices, they are only one among many procedures and tasks that teachers can ultimately use to assess (and measure) students. But now, you might be thinking, if you make assessments every time you teach something in the classroom, does all teaching involve assessment? Are teachers constantly assessing students with no interaction that is assessment-free?

The answer depends on your perspective. For optimal learning to take place, students in the classroom must have the freedom to experiment, to try out their own hypotheses about language without feeling that their overall competence is being judged in terms of those trials and errors. In the same way that tournament tennis players must, before a tournament, have the freedom to practice their skills with no implications for their final placement on that day of days, so also must learners have ample opportunities to "play" with language in a classroom without being formally graded. Teaching sets up the practice games of language learning: the opportunities for learners to listen, think, take risks, set goals, and process feedback from the "coach" and then recycle through the skills that they are trying to master.

At the same time, during these practice activities, teachers (and tennis coaches) are indeed observing students' performance, possibly taking measurements, offering qualitative feedback, and making strategic suggestions. How did the performance compare to previous performance? Which aspects of the performance were better than others? Is the learner performing up to an expected potential? What can the learner do to improve performance the next time? How does the performance compare to that of others in the same learning community? In the ideal classroom, all these observations feed into the way the teacher provides instruction to each student. (See Clapham, 2000, for a discussion of the relationship among testing, assessment, and teaching.)

Our discussion of all these overlapping concepts is represented in the following diagram (see Figure 1.1) showing the interrelationships among testing, measurement, assessment, teaching, and evaluation.

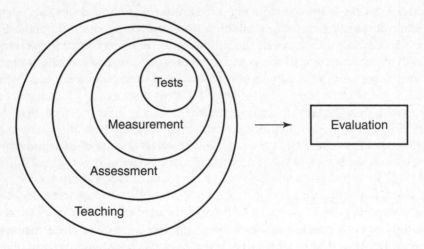

Figure 1.1. Tests, measurement, assessment, teaching, and evaluation

Informal and Formal Assessment

One way to begin untangling the lexical conundrum created by distinguishing among tests, assessment, teaching, and other related concepts is to distinguish between informal and formal assessment. **Informal assessment** can take a number of forms, starting with incidental, unplanned comments and responses, along with coaching and other impromptu feedback to the student. Examples include saying "Nice job!"; "Good work!"; "Did you say *can* or *can't?*"; "I think you meant to say you *broke* the glass, not you *break* the glass"; or putting a smiley face on some homework.

Informal assessment does not stop there. A good deal of a teacher's informal assessment is embedded in classroom tasks designed to elicit performance without recording results and making fixed conclusions about a student's competence. Informal assessment is virtually always nonjudgmental, in that you as a teacher are not making ultimate decisions about the student's performance; you're simply trying to be a good coach. Examples at this end of the continuum are marginal comments on papers, responding to a draft of an essay, offering advice about how to better pronounce a word, suggesting a strategy for compensating for a reading difficulty, or showing a student how to modify his or her notetaking to better remember the content of a lecture.

On the other hand, **formal assessments** are exercises or procedures specifically designed to tap into a storehouse of skills and knowledge. They are systematic, planned sampling techniques constructed to give teacher and student an appraisal of student achievement. To extend the tennis analogy, formal assessments are the tournament games that occur periodically in the course of a regimen of practice.

Is formal assessment the same as a test? We can say that all tests are formal assessments, but not all formal assessment is testing. For example, you might use a student's journal or portfolio of materials as a formal assessment of the attainment of certain course objectives, but it is problematic to call those two procedures "tests." A systematic set of observations of a student's frequency of oral participation in class is certainly a formal assessment, but it too is hardly what anyone would call a test. Tests are usually relatively time-constrained (usually spanning a class period or at most several hours) and draw on a limited sample of behavior.

Formative and Summative Assessment

Another useful distinction to bear in mind is the function of an assessment: How is the procedure to be used? Two functions are commonly identified in the literature: formative and summative assessment. Most of our classroom assessment is **formative assessment**: evaluating students in the process of "forming" their competencies and skills with the goal of helping them to continue that growth process. The key to such formation is the delivery (by the teacher) and internalization (by the student) of appropriate feedback on performance, with an eye toward the future continuation (or formation) of learning.

For all practical purposes, virtually all kinds of informal assessment are (or should be) formative. They have as their primary focus the ongoing development of the learner's language. So when you give a student a comment or a suggestion, or call attention to an error, that feedback is offered to improve the learner's language ability.

Summative assessment aims to measure, or summarize, what a student has grasped and typically occurs at the end of a course or unit of instruction. A summation of what a student has learned implies looking back and taking stock of how well that student has accomplished objectives, but it does not necessarily point the way to future progress. Final exams in a course and general proficiency exams are examples of summative assessment. Summative assessment often, but not always, involves evaluation (decision making).

Ross (2005) cited research to show that the appeal of formative assessment is growing and that conventional summative testing of language-learning outcomes is gradually integrating formative modes of assessing language learning as an ongoing process. Also, Black and William's (1998) analysis of 540 research studies found that formative assessment was superior to summative assessment in providing crucial information to classroom teachers.

One of the problems with prevailing attitudes toward testing is the view that all tests (quizzes, periodic review tests, midterm exams, etc.) are summative. At various points in your past educational experiences, no doubt you've considered such tests summative. You may have thought, "Whew! I'm glad that's over. Now I don't have to remember that stuff anymore!" A challenge to you as a teacher is to change that attitude among your students: Can you instill a more formative quality to what your students might otherwise view as a summative test? Can you offer your students an opportunity to convert tests into "learning experiences"? We will take up that challenge in subsequent chapters in this book.

Norm-Referenced and Criterion-Referenced Tests

Another dichotomy that's important to clarify and that aids in sorting out common terminology in assessment is the distinction between norm-referenced and criterion-referenced testing. In **norm-referenced tests**, each test-taker's score is interpreted in relation to a mean (average score), median (middle score), standard deviation (extent of variance in scores), and/or percentile rank. The purpose of such tests is to place test-takers along a mathematical continuum in rank order. Scores are usually reported back to the test-taker in the form of a numerical score (e.g., 230 out of 300) and a percentile rank (such as 84 percent, which means that the test-taker's score was higher than 84 percent of the total number of test-takers but lower than 16 percent in that administration). Typical of norm-referenced tests are standardized tests such as the Scholastic Aptitude Test (SAT®), the Graduate Record Exam (GRE®), and the Test of English as a Foreign Language (TOEFL® Test), all intended to be administered to large audiences, with results efficiently disseminated to test-takers. Such tests must have fixed, predetermined responses in a format that can be scored mechanically at minimum expense. Cost and efficiency are primary concerns in these tests.

Criterion-referenced tests, on the other hand, are designed to give test-takers feedback, usually in the form of grades, on specific course or lesson objectives. Classroom tests involving students in only one course, and connected to a curriculum, are typical of criterion-referenced testing. A good deal of time and effort on the part of the teacher (test administrator) is sometimes required to deliver useful, appropriate feedback to students, or what Oller (1979, p. 52) called "instructional value." In a criterion-referenced test, the distribution of students' scores across a continuum may be of little concern as long as the instrument assesses appropriate objectives (Brown & Hudson, 2000; Lynch & Davidson, 1994). In *Language*

Assessment, with an audience of classroom language teachers and teachers in training, and with its emphasis on classroom-based assessment (as opposed to standardized, large-scale testing), criterion-referenced testing is of more prominent interest than norm-referenced testing.

TYPES AND PURPOSES OF ASSESSMENT

Assessment instruments, whether formal tests or informal assessments, serve multiple purposes. Commercially designed and administered tests may be used for measuring proficiency, placing students into one of several levels of a course, or diagnosing students' strengths and weaknesses according to specific linguistic categories, among other purposes. Classroom-based teacher-made tests might be used to diagnose difficulty or measure achievement in a given unit of a course. Specifying the purpose of an assessment instrument and stating its objectives is an essential first step in choosing, designing, revising, or adapting the procedure you will finally use.

Tests tend to fall into a finite number of types, classified according to their purpose. Let's take a look at these test types, so that you'll be familiar with them before proceeding with the practical task of creating your own assessments. We'll begin with the most common type for classroom-based assessment.

Achievement Tests

The most frequent purpose for which a classroom teacher will use a test is to measure learners' ability within a classroom lesson, unit, or even total curriculum. Commonly called **achievement tests**, they are (or should be) limited to particular material addressed in a curriculum within a particular time frame and are offered after a course has focused on the objectives in question. Achievement tests can also serve the diagnostic role of indicating what a student needs to continue to work on in the future, but the primary role of an achievement test is to determine whether course objectives have been met—and appropriate knowledge and skills acquired—by the end of a given period of instruction.

Achievement tests are often summative because they are administered at the end of a lesson, unit, or term of study. They also play an important formative role, because an effective achievement test will offer feedback about the quality of a learner's performance in subsets of the unit or course. The specifications for an achievement test should be determined by

- the objectives of the lesson, unit, or course being assessed
- the relative importance (or weight) assigned to each objective
- the tasks employed in classroom lessons during the unit of time
- the time frame for the test and turnaround time
- its potential for formative feedback

Achievement tests range from 5- or 10-minute quizzes to three-hour final examinations, with an almost infinite variety of item types and formats. More will be said in Chapter 3 about choosing assessment methods for achievement tests.

Diagnostic Tests

The purpose of a **diagnostic test** is to diagnose aspects of a language that a student needs to develop or that a course should include. A test in pronunciation, for example, might diagnose the phonological features of English that are difficult for learners and should therefore become part of a curriculum. Usually, such tests offer a checklist of features for the administrator (often the teacher) to use in pinpointing difficulties. A writing diagnostic would elicit a writing sample from students that would allow the teacher to identify those rhetorical and linguistic features on which the course needs to focus special attention.

It's tempting to blur the line of distinction between a diagnostic test and a general achievement test. Achievement tests analyze the extent to which students have acquired language features that have already been taught; diagnostic tests should elicit information on what students need to work on in the future. Therefore, a diagnostic test will typically offer more detailed, subcategorized information on the learner. In a curriculum that has a grammatical form-focused phase, for example, a diagnostic test might offer information about a learner's acquisition of verb tenses, modal auxiliaries, definite articles, relative clauses, and the like. Likewise, a course in oral production might start off with a read-aloud passage (Prator, 1972) or an elicitation of a free speech sample (Celce-Murcia, Brinton, & Goodwin, 1996, p. 346), either of which could give a teacher an advance sense of a learner's ability to produce stress and rhythm patterns, intonation, and segmental phonemes.

Placement Tests

Some achievement tests and proficiency tests (see the next page) can act as **placement tests**, the purpose of which is to place a student into a particular level or section of a language curriculum or school. A placement test usually, but not always, includes a sampling of the material to be covered in the various courses in a curriculum; a student's performance on the test should indicate the point at which the student will find material neither too easy nor too difficult but appropriately challenging.

Some would argue that an effective placement test should be diagnostic as well. If an institution is going to the effort and expense to administer a test for placing students into one of several possible levels of a curriculum, a beneficial side effect of such a test would be a breakdown of strengths and weaknesses that students showed. A tally of correct and incorrect responses, categorized by modules in a curriculum, can provide teachers with useful information on what may or may not need to be emphasized in the weeks to come. Thus a placement test takes on a formative role.

Placement tests come in many varieties—assessing comprehension and production, responding through written and oral performance, open-ended and limited responses, selection (e.g., multiple-choice) and gap-filling formats—depending on the nature of a program and its needs. Some programs simply use existing standardized proficiency tests because of their obvious advantage in practicality: cost, speed in scoring, and efficient reporting of results. Other programs prefer specific course-based assessments that double as diagnostic instruments. Although the ultimate objective of a placement test is to correctly place a student into a course or level, a very useful secondary benefit is diagnostic information on a student's performance, which in turn gives teachers a head start on assessing their students' abilities.

Proficiency Tests

If your aim is to test global competence in a language, then you are, in conventional terminology, testing proficiency. A **proficiency test** is not limited to any one course, curriculum, or single skill in the language; rather, it tests overall ability. Proficiency tests have traditionally consisted of standardized multiple-choice items on grammar, vocabulary, reading comprehension, and aural comprehension. Many commercially produced proficiency tests—the Test of English as a Foreign Language (TOEFL® Test), for example—include a sample of writing as well as oral production performance.

Proficiency tests are almost always summative and norm-referenced. They provide results in the form of a single score (and usually two or three subscores, one for each section of a test), which, to many, is sufficient for the **gate-keeping** role they play of accepting or denying someone passage into the next level of education. Also, because they measure performance against a norm, with equated scores and percentile ranks taking on paramount importance, they are usually not equipped to provide diagnostic feedback.

A key issue in testing proficiency is how the **constructs** of language ability are specified. (See Chapter 2 for further discussion of assessment constructs.) The tasks that test-takers are required to perform must be legitimate samples of English language use in a defined context. Creating these tasks and validating them with research is a time-consuming and costly process. Language teachers should not attempt to create an overall proficiency test on their own. A far more practical method is to choose one of a number of commercially available proficiency tests.

Aptitude Tests

This last type of test no longer enjoys the widespread use it once had. An **aptitude test** is designed to measure capacity or general ability to learn a foreign language *a priori* (before taking a course) and ultimate predicted success in that undertaking. Language aptitude tests were ostensibly designed to apply to the classroom learning of any language.

Two standardized aptitude tests were once used in the United States: the Modern Language Aptitude Test (MLAT; Carroll & Sapon, 1958) and the Pimsleur Language Aptitude Battery (PLAB; Pimsleur, 1966). Both are English language tests and require students to perform language-related tasks such as number learning, distinguishing speech sounds, detecting grammatical functions, and memorizing paired associates. (See Appendix for more information on the MLAT.)

The MLAT and PLAB show some significant correlations with ultimate performance of students in language courses (Carroll, 1981). Those correlations, however, presuppose a foreign language course in which success is measured by similar processes of mimicry, memorization, and puzzle-solving. There is no research to show unequivocally that those kinds of tasks predict communicative success in a language, especially untutored acquisition of the language.

Because of this limitation, standardized aptitude tests are seldom used today, with the exception, perhaps, of identifying foreign language-learning disability (Stansfield & Reed, 2004). Instead, attempts to measure language aptitude more often provide learners with information about their preferred styles and their potential strengths and weaknesses, with follow-up strategies for capitalizing on the strengths and overcoming the weaknesses (Robinson, 2005; Skehan, 2002). Any test that claims to predict success in learning a language is undoubtedly flawed, because we now know that with appropriate self-knowledge, active strategic involvement in learning, and/or strategies-based instruction, virtually everyone can eventually succeed. To pigeon-hole learners *a priori*, before they have even attempted to learn a language, is to presuppose failure or success without substantial cause. (A further discussion of language aptitude can be found in H. D. Brown's [2007a] *Principles of Language Learning and Teaching [PLLT],* Chapter 4.)[1]

ISSUES IN LANGUAGE ASSESSMENT: THEN AND NOW

Before moving on to the practicalities of creating classroom tests and assessments, you will better appreciate the intricacies of the process by taking a brief historical look at language testing over the past half-century and taking note of some current issues in the field.

Historically, language-testing trends and practices have followed the shifting sands of teaching methodology (for a description of these trends, see H. D. Brown [2007b], *Teaching by Principles [TBP],* Chapter 2). For example, in the 1940s and 1950s, an era of behaviorism and special attention to contrastive analysis, language tests focused on specific linguistic elements such as the phonological, grammatical, and lexical contrasts between two languages. In the 1970s and 1980s, communicative theories of language brought with them a more integrative view of testing in which specialists claimed that "the whole of the communicative event

---

[1] Frequent references are made in this book to companion volumes by H. Douglas Brown. *Principles of Language Learning and Teaching (PLLT;* fifth edition, 2007) is a basic teacher reference book on essential foundations of second language acquisition on which pedagogical practices are based. *Teaching by Principles (TBP;* third edition, 2007) spells out that pedagogy in practical terms for the language teacher.

was considerably greater than the sum of its linguistic elements" (Clark, 1983, p. 432). Today, test designers are still challenged in their quest for more authentic, valid instruments that simulate real-world interaction (Leung & Lewkowicz, 2006).

Behavioral Influences on Language Testing

Through the middle of the twentieth century, language teaching and testing were both strongly influenced by behavioral psychology and structural linguistics. Both traditions emphasized sentence-level grammatical paradigms, definitions of vocabulary items, and translation from first language to second language and placed only minor focus on real-world authentic communication. Typically, tests consisted of grammar and vocabulary items in multiple-choice format along with a variety of translation exercises ranging from words to sentences to short paragraphs.

Such **discrete-point** formats still prevail today, especially in large-scale standardized "entrance examinations" used to admit students to institutions of higher education around the world. (See Barnwell, 1996, and Spolsky, 1978, 1995, for a summary.) Essentially, assessments were designed on the assumption that language can be broken down into its component parts and that those parts can be tested successfully. These components are the skills of listening, speaking, reading, and writing and the various units of language (discrete points) of phonology/graphology, morphology, lexicon, syntax, and discourse. It was claimed that an overall language proficiency test, then, should sample all four skills and as many linguistic discrete points as possible.

Discrete-point testing provided fertile ground for what Spolsky (1978, 1995) called the **psychometric-structuralist** approach to language assessment, in which test designers seized the tools of the day to focus on issues of validity, reliability, and objectivity. Standardized tests of language blossomed in this scientific climate, and the language teaching/testing world saw such tests as the Michigan Test of English Language Proficiency (1961) and the Test of English as a Foreign Language (1963) become extraordinarily popular. The science of measurement and the art of teaching appeared to have made a revolutionary alliance.

Integrative Approaches

In the midst of this fervor, language pedagogy was rapidly moving in more communicative directions, and testing specialists were forced into a debate that would soon respond to the changes. The discrete-point approach presupposed a decontextualization that was proving to be inauthentic. So, as the profession emerged into an era of emphasizing communication, authenticity, and context, new approaches were sought. John Oller (1979) argued that language competence was a unified set of interacting abilities that could not be tested separately. His claim was that communicative competence is so global and requires such integration that it cannot be captured in additive tests of grammar, reading, vocabulary, and other discrete points of language. Others (among them Cziko, 1982, and Savignon, 1982) soon followed in their support for what became known as **integrative testing**.

What does an integrative test look like? Two types of tests were, at the time, claimed to be examples of integrative tests: cloze tests and dictations. A **cloze** test is a reading passage (perhaps 150 to 300 words) in which roughly every sixth or seventh word has been deleted; the test-taker is required to supply words that fit into those blanks. (See Chapter 8 for a full discussion of cloze testing.)

Oller (1979) claimed that cloze test results were good measures of overall proficiency. According to theoretical constructs underlying this claim, the ability to supply appropriate words in blanks requires competence in a language, which includes knowledge of vocabulary, grammatical structure, discourse structure; reading skills and strategies; and an internalized "expectancy" grammar (enabling one to predict an item that will come next in a sequence). It was argued that successful completion of cloze items taps into all of those abilities, which were said to be the essence of global language proficiency.

Dictation, in which learners listen to a short passage and write what they hear, is a familiar language-teaching technique that evolved into a testing technique. (See Chapter 6 for a discussion of dictation as an assessment device.) Supporters argued that dictation was an integrative test because it taps into grammatical and discourse competencies required for other modes of performance in a language. Success on a dictation test requires careful listening, reproduction in writing of what is heard, efficient short-term memory, and, to an extent, some expectancy rules to aid the short-term memory. Further, dictation test results tend to correlate strongly with other tests of proficiency. For large-scale testing, the usually classroom-centered dictation technique can be practical and reliable through the design of multiple-choice items.

Proponents of integrative test methods soon centered their arguments on what became known as the **unitary trait hypothesis**, which suggested an "indivisible" view of language proficiency: that vocabulary, grammar, phonology, the "four skills," and other discrete points of language could not be disentangled from each other in language performance. The unitary trait hypothesis argued that there is a general factor of language proficiency such that all the discrete points do not add up to that whole. However, in a series of debates and research evidence (Farhady, 1982; Oller, 1983), the unitary trait hypothesis was abandoned.

Communicative Language Testing

By the mid-1980s, especially in the wake of Canale and Swain's (1980) seminal work on communicative competence, the language-testing field had begun to focus on designing **communicative** language-testing tasks. Bachman and Palmer (1996) included among "fundamental" principles of language testing the need for a correspondence between language test performance and language use: "In order for a particular language test to be useful for its intended purposes, test performance must correspond in demonstrable ways to language use in non-test situations" (p. 9). The problem that language assessment experts faced was that tasks tended to be artificial, contrived, and unlikely to mirror language use in real life. As Weir (1990) noted, "Integrative tests such as cloze only tell us about a candidate's linguistic competence. They do not tell us anything directly about a student's performance ability" (p. 6).

Thus a quest for authenticity was launched, as test designers centered on communicative performance. Following Canale and Swain's (1980) model, Bachman (1990) proposed a model of language competence consisting of organizational and pragmatic competence, respectively subdivided into grammatical and textual components and into illocutionary and sociolinguistic components (see Figure 1.2).

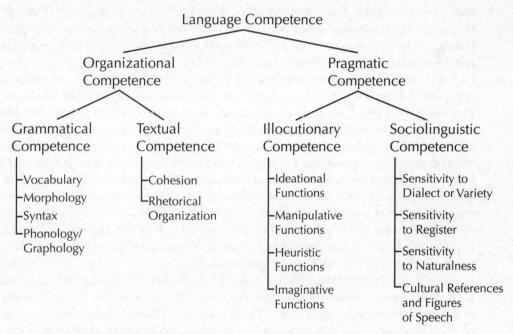

Figure 1.2. Components of language competence (Bachman, 1990, p. 87)

Bachman and Palmer (1996, pp. 70–75) also emphasized the importance of **strategic competence** (the ability to employ communicative strategies to compensate for breakdowns as well as enhance the rhetorical effect of utterances) in the process of communication. All elements of the model, especially pragmatic and strategic abilities, needed to be included in the constructs of language testing and in the actual performance required of test-takers.

Communicative testing presented challenges to test designers, as we will see in subsequent chapters of this book. Test designers began to identify the kinds of real-world tasks that language-learners were called on to perform. It was clear that the contexts for those tasks were extraordinarily widely varied and that the sampling of tasks for any assessment procedure needed to be validated by what language users actually do with language. Weir (1990) reminded his readers that "to measure language proficiency . . . account must now be taken of: where, when, how, with whom, and why language is to be used, and on what topics, and with what effect" (p. 11). The assessment field also became more concerned with the authenticity of tasks and the genuineness of texts. (See Skehan, 1988, 1989, and Fulcher, 2000, for surveys of communicative testing research.)

Performance-Based Assessment

In language courses and programs around the world, test designers are now tackling this new and more student-centered agenda (Alderson & Banerjee, 2001, 2002; Bachman, 2002; Leung & Lewkowicz, 2006; Weir, 2005). Instead of offering paper-and-pencil multiple-choice tests of a plethora of separate items, **performance-based assessment** of language typically involves oral production, written production, open-ended responses, integrated performance (across skill areas), group performance, and other interactive tasks. To be sure, such assessment is time-consuming and therefore expensive, but those extra efforts result in more direct and more accurate testing because students are assessed as they perform actual or simulated real-world tasks. In technical terms, higher content validity (see Chapter 2 for an explanation) is achieved because learners are measured in the process of performing the targeted linguistic acts.

In an English language teaching context, performance-based assessment means you may have a difficult time distinguishing between formal and informal assessment. If you rely a little less on formally structured tests and a little more on evaluation while students are performing various tasks, you will be taking some steps toward meeting the goals of performance-based assessment. (See Chapter 10 for a further discussion of performance-based assessment.)

A characteristic of many (but not all) performance-based language assessments is the presence of interactive tasks, hence the alternative term, **task-based assessment**, for such approaches. In such cases, the assessments involve learners in actually performing the behavior that we want to measure. In interactive tasks, test-takers are measured in the act of speaking, requesting, responding, or in combining listening and speaking, and in integrating reading and writing. Paper-and-pencil tests certainly do not elicit such communicative performance.

A prime example of an interactive language assessment procedure is an oral interview. The test-taker is required to listen accurately to someone else and respond appropriately. If care is taken in the test design process, language elicited and volunteered by the student can be personalized and meaningful, and tasks can approach the authenticity of real-life language use (see Chapter 7).

CURRENT "HOT TOPICS" IN CLASSROOM-BASED ASSESSMENT

Designing communicative, performance-based assessment rubrics continues to challenge assessment experts and classroom teachers alike. In addition, three new issues in the field are shaping our current understanding of effective assessment.

These are: (1) the effect of new theories of intelligence on the testing industry in general, (2) the advent of what has come to be called "alternative" assessment, and (3) the increasing use of computer technology in assessments of various kinds. We briefly explore these issues here.

Multiple Intelligences

Intelligence was once viewed strictly as the ability to perform (a) linguistic and (b) logical-mathematical problem solving. This IQ (intelligence quotient) concept of intelligence has permeated the Western world and its way of testing for almost a century. Because "smartness" in general is measured by timed, discrete-point tests consisting of a hierarchy of separate items, why shouldn't every field of study be so measured? For many years, we have lived in a world of standardized, norm-referenced tests that are timed in a multiple-choice format and consist of a multiplicity of logic-constrained items, many of which are inauthentic.

However, in the last two decades of the twentieth century, research on intelligence began to turn the psychometric world upside down. Howard Gardner (1983, 1999), for example, extended the traditional view of intelligence to eight different components.[2] He accepted the traditional conceptualizations of linguistic intelligence and logical-mathematical intelligence on which standardized IQ tests are based but included other "frames of mind" in his theory of **multiple intelligences**: spatial, musical, kinesthetic, naturalist, interpersonal, and intrapersonal. Robert Sternberg (1988, 1997) also charted new territory in intelligence research in recognizing creative thinking and manipulative strategies as part of intelligence. Likewise, Daniel Goleman's (1995) concept of EQ (emotional quotient) spurred us to underscore the importance of the emotions in our cognitive processing.

These conceptualizations of intelligence were not universally accepted by the academic community (see White, 1998, for example). After all, how does one objectively measure such hypothetical constructs as interpersonal intelligence, creativity, and self-esteem? Nevertheless, their intuitive appeal infused educators with a sense of both freedom and responsibility in their teaching and testing agendas, as evidenced by educational reforms at the time (Armstrong, 1994).

In the language assessment field in particular, the recognition of multiple intelligences has had an indirect effect. On the one hand, communicative classroom activities in textbooks and programs have paid increasing attention to diversity of learning abilities and styles. Christison (2005), for example, offered more than 150 activities for language learners, each emphasizing specific intelligences. On the other hand, in classroom assessment, new views on intelligence have helped to free language instruction programs from relying exclusively on timed, discrete-point, analytical tests in measuring language. Classroom language teachers have been collectively prodded to cautiously combat the potential tyranny of "objectivity" and its

---

[2] For a summary of Gardner's theory of intelligence, see H. D. Brown (2007a, pp. 107–110).

accompanying impersonal approach. Teachers and administrators have also been urged to measure whole language skills, learning processes, and the ability to negotiate meaning. Our challenge continues to be designing assessments that tap into interpersonal, creative, communicative, and interactive skills and in doing so place some trust in our subjectivity and intuition.

Traditional and Alternative Assessment

Implied in some of the earlier description of performance-based classroom assessment is a trend to supplement traditional test designs with alternatives that are more authentic in their elicitation of meaningful communication. Table 1.1 highlights differences between the two approaches (adapted from Armstrong, 1994, and Bailey, 1998, p. 207).

Two caveats need to be stated here. First, the concepts in Table 1.1 represent some overgeneralizations and should therefore be interpreted with caution. It is difficult, in fact, to draw a clear line of distinction between what Armstrong (1994) and Bailey (1998) called traditional and **alternative assessment**. Many forms of assessment fall in between the two, and some combine the best of both.

Second, it is obvious that the table shows a bias toward alternative assessment, and one should not be misled into thinking that everything on the left-hand side is tainted whereas the list on the right-hand side offers salvation to the field of language assessment. As Brown and Hudson (1998) aptly pointed out, the assessment traditions available to us should be valued and utilized for the functions they provide. At the same time, we might all be stimulated to look at the right-hand list and ask ourselves if, among those concepts, there are alternatives to assessment that we can use constructively in our classrooms.

It should be noted here that considerably more time and higher institutional budgets are required to administer and score assessments that presuppose more subjective evaluation, more individualization, and more interaction in the process

Table 1.1. Traditional and alternative assessment

Traditional Assessment	Alternative Assessment
Standardized exams	Continuous long-term assessment
Timed, multiple-choice format	Untimed, open-ended responses
Decontextualized test items	Contextualized communicative tasks
Scores suffice for feedback	Individualized feedback
Norm-referenced scores	Criterion-referenced scores
Focus on discrete answers	Open-ended, creative answers
Summative	Formative
Oriented to product	Oriented to process
Noninteractive performance	Interactive performance
Fosters extrinsic motivation	Fosters intrinsic motivation

of offering feedback. The payoff for the latter, however, comes with more useful feedback to students, the potential for intrinsic motivation, and ultimately a more complete description of a student's ability. (See Chapter 6 for a complete treatment of alternatives in assessment.) More educators and advocates for educational reform are arguing for a de-emphasis of large-scale standardized tests in favor of contextualized, communicative, performance-based assessment that will better facilitate learning in our schools. (In Chapters 4 and 5, issues surrounding standardized testing are addressed at length.)

Computer-Based Testing

Recent years have seen a burgeoning of computer technology and applications of that technology to language learning and teaching. Virtually every language learner worldwide is, to a lesser or greater extent, a user of computers, the Internet, iPods, cell phones, the Web, and other common cybertechnology. It's no surprise, then, that an overwhelming number of language courses utilize some form of **computer-assisted language learning (CALL)** to achieve their goals, as recent publications show (Chapelle, 2005; Chapelle & Jamieson, 2008; de Szendeffy, 2005; H. D. Brown, 2007b).

The assessment of language learning is no exception to the mushrooming growth of computer technology in educational contexts (see Chapelle & Douglas, 2006; Douglas & Hegelheimer, 2008; Jamieson, 2005, for overviews of computer-based second language testing). Some computer-based tests are small-scale, "home-grown" tests available on a plethora of Web sites. Others are standardized, large-scale tests in which tens of thousands of test-takers may be involved. Students receive prompts (or probes, as they are sometimes referred to) in the form of spoken or written stimuli from preprogrammed algorithm and are required to type (or, in some cases, speak) their responses. Most computer-based test items have fixed, closed-ended responses; however, tests such as the Test of English as a Foreign Language (TOEFL® Test) now offer a written essay section and an oral production section, both of which are scored by humans (as opposed to automatic, electronic, or machine scoring).

Recent developments in computer-based assessment include contributions of **corpus linguistics** in providing more authenticity, the design of more complex tasks in computer-delivered tests, the utilization of speech and writing recognition software to score oral and written production (Jamieson, 2005), and some intriguing questions about "whether and how the delivery medium [of computer-based language testing] changes the nature of the construct being measured" (Douglas & Hegelheimer, 2008, p. 116).

A specific type of computer-based test, a **computer-adaptive test (CAT)**, has been available for many years but has recently gained momentum. In a computer-adaptive test, each test-taker receives a set of questions that meet the test specifications and are generally appropriate for his or her performance level. The CAT starts with questions of moderate difficulty. As test-takers answer each question, the computer scores the question and uses that information, as well as the responses to previous questions, to determine which question will be presented next. As long as examinees respond correctly, the computer typically selects questions of greater or equal difficulty. Incorrect answers, however, typically bring questions of lesser or equal difficulty. The computer is programmed to fulfill the test design as it continuously adjusts to find questions of appropriate difficulty for test-takers at all performance levels. In CATs, the test-taker sees only one question at a time, and the computer scores each question before selecting the next one. As a result, test-takers cannot skip questions, and once they have entered and confirmed their answers, they cannot return to questions or to any earlier part of the test.

Computer-based testing, with or without CAT technology, offers these advantages:

- a variety of easily administered classroom-based tests
- self-directed testing on various aspects of a language (vocabulary, grammar, discourse, one or all of the four skills, etc.)
- practice for upcoming high-stakes standardized tests
- some individualization, in the case of CATs
- large-scale standardized tests that can be administered easily to thousands of test-takers at many different stations, then scored electronically for rapid reporting of results
- improved (but imperfect) technology for automated essay evaluation and speech recognition (Douglas & Hegelheimer, 2008)

Of course, some disadvantages are present in our current predilection for computer-based testing. Among them:

- Lack of security and the possibility of cheating are inherent in unsupervised computerized tests.
- Occasional "homegrown" quizzes that appear on unofficial Web sites may be mistaken for validated assessments.
- The multiple-choice format preferred for most computer-based tests contains the usual potential for flawed item design (see Chapter 3).
- Open-ended responses are less likely to appear due to (a) the expense and potential unreliability of human scoring or (b) the complexity of recognition software for automated scoring.
- The human interactive element (especially in oral production) is absent.
- Validation issues stemming from test-takers approaching tasks as test tasks rather than as real-world language use (Douglas & Hegelheimer, 2008).

Some argue that computer-based testing, pushed to its ultimate level, might mitigate recent efforts to return testing to its artful form of (a) being tailored by teachers for their classrooms, (b) being designed to be performance-based, and (c) allowing a teacher–student dialogue to form the basis of assessment. This need not be the case. While "computer-assisted language tests [CALTs] have not fully lived up to their promise, . . . research and development of CALTs continues in interesting and principled directions" (Douglas & Hegelheimer, 2008, p. 127). Computer technology can be a boon to both communicative language teaching and testing (Chapelle & Jamieson, 2008; Jamieson, 2005). Teachers and test-makers now have access to an ever-increasing range of tools to make computer-based testing less formulaic. By using technological innovations creatively, testers will be able to enhance authenticity, increase interactive exchange, and promote autonomy.

OTHER CURRENT ISSUES

A survey of recent articles and books on language assessment yields several other current issues, beyond those mentioned above, that are being probed in assessment circles around the world. They will be discussed in subsequent chapters of this book but deserve some mention now, as you begin this journey into the intricacies of language assessment.

Direct assessment of speaking and writing. Whether by means of human evaluators or automated computer-based software, the testing industry has begun a new era in the direct assessment of productive skills. "Direct" means that test-takers must actually "do" language, not just respond to questions "about" language. In bygone years, test designers shrank from involving test-takers in actual language performance, especially in large-scale assessment, because of the cost and unreliability of the endeavor. Now, with advances in discourse analysis, better accounting of examiner–examinee interaction, improved rubrics, and technology-enhanced scoring, the testing industry is taking on the challenge of direct assessment (Taylor, 2004).

Advances in corpus linguistics. As literally billions of words and sentences are gathered from the real world, logged into linguistic corpora, and catalogued into manageable, retrievable data, the design of assessment instruments is being revolutionized. The old complaint that the language of standardized tests was too "phony" and contrived should no longer hold in the near future as we have access to real language spoken and written in the real world (Conrad, 2005).

Standards-based assessment. In Chapter 4, we go into detail on issues surrounding standards-based assessment or, as the process is known in some circles, establishing **benchmarks** or **frameworks of reference**. Around the world, educational institutions are demanding common criteria for evaluation of students entering into programs, advancing from one course to another, and graduating from one grade to the next. Such benchmarks are a hotbed of controversy at times as teachers, administrators, and politicians clash over ethical issues (McNamara & Roever, 2006). In more constructive moments, they provide much needed standardization.

Consequential validity (impact). As you will soon read in the next chapter and then again in Chapter 4, according to some researchers, the impact of standardized tests, ubiquitous in many societies, governs and determines people's future education

(Shohamy, 2001). The antithesis of the negative aspects of such impact is the potential for re-examining the **washback** that tests and assessments can provide in the language classroom (Taylor, 2004).

☆   ☆   ☆   ☆   ☆

As you read this book, we hope you will do so with an appreciation for the place of testing in assessment and with a sense of the interconnection of assessment and teaching. Assessment is an integral part of the teaching–learning cycle. In an interactive, communicative curriculum, assessment is almost constant. Tests, which are a subset of assessment, can provide authenticity, motivation, and feedback to the learner. Tests are essential components of a successful curriculum and one of several partners in the learning process. Keep in mind these basic principles:

1. Periodic assessments, both formal and informal, can increase motivation by serving as milestones of student progress.
2. Appropriate assessments aid in the reinforcement and retention of information.
3. Assessments can confirm areas of strength and pinpoint areas needing further work.
4. Assessments can provide a sense of periodic closure to modules within a curriculum.
5. Assessments can promote student autonomy by encouraging students' self-evaluation of their progress.
6. Assessments can spur learners to set goals for themselves.
7. Assessments can aid in evaluating teaching effectiveness.

Answers to the analogies quiz on page 2: 1. c, 2. d, 3. a, 4. a, 5. b

EXERCISES

[Note: **(I)** Individual work; **(G)** Group or pair work; **(C)** Whole-class discussion.]

1. **(G)** In a small group, look at Figure 1.1 on page 6 that shows, among other relationships, tests as a subset of assessment and the latter as a subset of teaching. Consider the following classroom teaching techniques: choral drill, pair pronunciation practice, reading aloud, information gap task, singing songs in English, writing a description of the weekend's activities. In your group, specifically describe aspects of each that could be used for assessment purposes. Share your conclusions with the rest of the class.
2. **(G)** The chart on the next page shows a hypothetical line of distinction between formative and summative assessment and between informal and formal assessment. In a group, reproduce the chart on a large sheet of paper (or four sheets).

Then come to a consensus on which of the four cells each of the following techniques/procedures would be placed in and justify your decision. Share your results with other groups and discuss any differences of opinion.

Placement tests
Diagnostic tests
Periodic achievement tests
Short pop quizzes
Standardized proficiency tests
Final exams
Portfolios
Journals
Speeches (prepared and rehearsed)
Oral presentations (prepared but not rehearsed)
Impromptu student responses to teacher's questions
Student-written response (one paragraph) to a reading assignment
Drafting and revising writing
Final essays (after several drafts)
Student oral responses to teacher questions after a videotaped lecture
Whole-class open-ended discussion of a topic

	Formative	Summative
Informal		
Formal		

3. **(I)** On your own, research the distinction between norm-referenced and criterion-referenced testing and how bell-shaped and other distributions are derived. Then consider this question: If norm-referenced tests typically yield a distribution of scores that resemble a bell-shaped curve, what kinds of distributions are typical of classroom achievement tests in your experience? Report your findings to the class.

4. **(C)** In a whole-class discussion, have volunteers describe personal experiences (tell their own stories) about either taking or administering the five types of

tests described on pages 9–12. In each case, have the volunteers assess the extent to which the test was successful in accomplishing its purpose.

5. **(C)** As a whole-class discussion, brainstorm a variety of test tasks (e.g., multiple-choice, true/false, essay questions) that class members have experienced in learning a foreign language and make a list on the board of all the tasks that are mentioned. Then decide which of those tasks are performance-based, which are communicative, and which are both, neither, or perhaps fall in between.

6. **(G)** Look at the list of Gardner's eight intelligences. Take one or two intelligences, as assigned to your group, and brainstorm some teaching activities that foster that type of intelligence. Then brainstorm some assessment tasks that may presuppose the same intelligence to perform well. Share your results with other groups.

7. **(G)** Table 1.1 lists traditional and alternative assessment tasks and characteristics. In pairs, brainstorm both the positive and the negative aspects of tasks in each list. Share your conclusions—which should yield a balanced perspective—with the rest of the class.

8. **(C)** Ask class members to share any experiences with computer-based testing and evaluate the advantages and disadvantages of those experiences.

9. **(G)** With a partner, visit Dave's ESL Café at http://eslcafe.com/ and look at some of the dozens of "quizzes" that are presented. Can you determine the extent to which such quizzes are useful for a classroom teacher and the extent to which they may present some problems and disadvantages? Report your findings back to the class.

FOR YOUR FURTHER READING

McNamara, Tim. (2000). *Language testing.* Oxford: Oxford University Press.

One of a number of Oxford University Press's brief introductions to various areas of language study, this 140-page primer on testing offers definitions of basic terms in language testing with brief explanations of fundamental concepts. It is a useful little reference book to check your understanding of testing jargon and issues in the field.

Mousavi, Seyyed Abbas. (2009). *An encyclopedic dictionary of language testing* (4th ed.). Tehran: Rahnama Publications.

This is a highly useful, very detailed compilation of virtually every term in the field of language testing, with definitions, background history, and research references. It provides comprehensive explanations of theories, principles, issues, tools, and tasks and an exhaustive 88-page bibliography. A shorter version of this 946-page tome may be found in Mousavi's (1999) *Dictionary of Language Testing* (Tehran: Rahnama Publications).

CHAPTER 2

PRINCIPLES OF

LANGUAGE ASSESSMENT

> **OBJECTIVES:** After reading this chapter, you will be able to
>
> - understand the five major principles of language assessment (practicality, reliability, validity, authenticity, and washback) and the essential subcategories within reliability and validity
> - cite examples that support and/or fail to support each principle
> - analyze the relative, variable importance of each principle, depending on the context and purpose of the assessment
> - apply each principle to classroom-based assessment instruments and make an informed decision on the extent to which a principle is supported in a given instrument

This chapter explores how principles of language assessment can and should be applied to formal tests but with the ultimate recognition that these principles also apply to assessments of all kinds. In this chapter, these principles are defined and discussed with reference to classroom-based assessment in particular. They are then rephrased in the form of a set of "tips" for testing that can be applied to a number of different kinds of classroom assessments. Chapter 3 then focuses on using these principles, step-by-step, in the actual design of classroom-based tests.

How do you know if a test is effective, appropriate, useful, or, in down-to-earth terms, a "good" test? For the most part, that question can be answered by responding to such questions as: Can it be given within appropriate administrative constraints? Is it dependable? Does it accurately measure what you want it to measure? Is the language in the test representative of real-world language use? Does the test provide information that is useful for the learner? These questions help to identify five cardinal criteria for "testing a test": practicality, reliability, validity, authenticity, and washback. We will look at each one here; however, because all five principles are context dependent, there is no priority order implied in the order of presentation.

PRACTICALITY

Practicality refers to the logistical, down-to-earth, administrative issues involved in making, giving, and scoring an assessment instrument. These include "costs, the amount of time it takes to construct and to administer, ease of scoring, and ease of interpreting/reporting the results" (Mousavi, 2009, p. 518). A test that fails to meet such criteria is impractical. Consider the following attributes of practicality:

A PRACTICAL TEST . . .

- stays within budgetary limits
- can be completed by the test-taker within appropriate time constraints
- has clear directions for administration
- appropriately utilizes available human resources
- does not exceed available material resources
- considers the time and effort involved for both design and scoring

REMEMBER

A test of language proficiency that takes a student five hours to complete is impractical—it consumes more time than is available to accomplish its objective. A test that requires individual one-on-one proctoring is impractical for a group of several hundred test-takers and only a handful of examiners. A test that takes a few minutes for a student to take and several hours for an examiner to evaluate is impractical for most classroom situations. A test that can be scored only by computer is impractical if the test takes place a thousand miles away from the nearest computer. A test that relies too heavily on the subjective "hunches" of the scorer might be impractical (as well as unreliable) because it takes too long to score. The value and quality of a test sometimes hinge on such nitty-gritty, practical considerations.

Here's a little horror story about practicality gone awry. An administrator of a six-week summertime short course needed to place the 50 or so students who had enrolled in the program. A quick search yielded a copy of an old English Placement Test from the University of Michigan. It had 20 listening items based on an audio-tape and 80 items on grammar, vocabulary, and reading comprehension, all multiple-choice format. A scoring grid accompanied the test. On the day of the test, the required number of test booklets had been secured, a proctor had been assigned to monitor the process, and the administrator and proctor had planned to have the scoring completed by later that afternoon so students could begin classes the next day. Sounds simple, right? Wrong.

The students arrived, test booklets were distributed, and directions were given. The proctor started the audio recording. Soon students began to look puzzled. By the time the tenth item played, everyone looked bewildered. Finally, the proctor checked a test booklet and was shocked to discover that the wrong audio program was playing; it contained items for another form of the same test! Now what? She decided to randomly select a short passage from a textbook that was in the room and give the students a dictation. The students responded reasonably well. The subsequent 80 non-tape-based items proceeded without incident, and the students handed in their score sheets and dictation papers.

When the red-faced administrator and the proctor got together later to score the tests, they faced the problem of how to score the dictation—a more subjective process than some other forms of assessment (see Chapter 7). After a lengthy exchange, the two established a point system, but after the first few papers had been scored, it was clear that the point system needed revision. That meant going back to the first papers to make sure the new system was followed.

The two faculty members had barely begun to score the 80 multiple-choice items when students began returning to the office to receive their placements. Students were told to come back the next morning for their results. Later that evening, having combined dictation scores and the 80-item multiple-choice scores, the two frustrated examiners finally arrived at placements for all students.

It's easy to see what went wrong here. While the listening comprehension section of the test was apparently highly practical (easily administered and very quickly scored), the administrator had failed to check the materials ahead of time (which, as you will see later, is a factor that touches on unreliability as well). Then the proctor and administrator established a scoring procedure that did not fit into the time constraints. In classroom-based testing, time is almost always a crucial practicality factor for busy teachers with too few hours in the day.

RELIABILITY

A **reliable** test is consistent and dependable. If you give the same test to the same student or matched students on two different occasions, the test should yield similar results. We might capsulate the principle of reliability in the following:

A RELIABLE TEST . . .

- is consistent in its conditions across two or more administrations
- gives clear directions for scoring/evaluation
- has uniform rubrics for scoring/evaluation
- lends itself to consistent application of those rubrics by the scorer
- contains items/tasks that are unambiguous to the test-taker

REMEMBER

The issue of the reliability of tests can be better understood by considering a number of factors that can contribute to their *un*reliability. We look here at four possible factors regarding fluctuations in (a) the student, (b) the scoring, (c) the test administration, and (d) the test itself. (See Bachman, 1990, J. D. Brown, 2005, and Fulcher & Davidson, 2007, for further and more elaborated discussions of reliability, some of which extend well beyond teacher-made classroom assessments.)

Student-Related Reliability

The most common learner-related issue in reliability is caused by temporary illness, fatigue, a "bad day," anxiety, and other physical or psychological factors, which may make an observed score deviate from one's "true" score. Also included in this category are such factors as a test-taker's **test-wiseness**, or strategies for efficient test-taking (Mousavi, 2009, p. 804).

For the classroom teacher, student-related unreliability may at first blush seem to be a factor beyond control. We're accustomed to simply expecting some students to be anxious or overly nervous to the point that they "choke" in a test administration context. But the experience of many teachers suggests otherwise. In the second half of this chapter, some tips will be offered that may help minimize student-related unreliability.

Rater Reliability

Human error, subjectivity, and bias may enter into the scoring process. **Inter-rater reliability** occurs when two or more scorers yield consistent scores of the same test. Failure to achieve intra-rater reliability could stem from lack of adherence to scoring criteria, inexperience, inattention, or even preconceived biases. Lumley (2002) provided some helpful hints on how to ensure inter-rater reliability.

Rater-reliability issues are not limited to contexts in which two or more scorers are involved. **Intra-rater reliability** is an internal factor, a common occurrence for classroom teachers. Violation of such reliability can occur in cases of unclear scoring criteria, fatigue, bias toward particular "good" and "bad" students, or simple carelessness. When I am faced with up to 40 essay tests (for which there is no absolute right or wrong set of answers) to grade in only a week, I know that the standards I apply—however subliminally—to the first few tests will be different from those I apply to the last few. I may be "easier" or "harder" on those first few papers or I may get tired, and the result may be an inconsistent evaluation across all tests. One solution to such intra-rater unreliability is to read through about half of the tests before rendering any final scores or grades, then to recycle back through the whole set of tests to ensure an even-handed judgment. In tests of writing skills, rater reliability is particularly hard to achieve because writing proficiency involves numerous traits that are difficult to define. The careful specification of an analytical scoring instrument, however, can increase both inter- and intra-rater reliability (J. D. Brown, 1991).

Test Administration Reliability

Unreliability may also result from the conditions in which the test is administered. I once witnessed the administration of a test of aural comprehension in which an audio player was used to deliver items for comprehension, but because of street noise outside the building, students sitting next to open windows could not hear the stimuli accurately. This was a clear case of unreliability caused by the conditions of the test administration. Other sources of unreliability are found in photocopying variations, the amount of light in different parts of the room, variations in temperature, and even the condition of desks and chairs.

Test Reliability

Sometimes the nature of the test itself can cause measurement errors. Tests with multiple-choice items must be carefully designed to include a number of characteristics that will guard against unreliability. For example, the items need to be evenly difficult, distractors need to be well designed, and items need to be well distributed to make the test reliable. In this book, these forms of reliability are not discussed because they rarely are appropriately applied to classroom-based assessment and teacher-made tests. (For a full discussion of reliability from a psychometric, statistical perspective, consult the aforementioned Bachman [1990], J. D. Brown [2005], and Fulcher & Davidson [2007].)

In classroom-based assessment, test unreliability can be caused by many factors, including rater bias. This typically occurs with **subjective tests**, with open-ended responses (e.g., essay responses) that require a judgment on the part of the teacher to determine correct and incorrect answers. **Objective tests**, in contrast, have predetermined fixed responses, a format which of course increases their test reliability.

Further unreliability may be caused by poorly written test items—that is, items that are ambiguous or that have more than one correct answer. Also, a test that contains too many items (beyond what is needed for discriminating among students) may ultimately cause test-takers to become fatigued by the time they reach the later items and hastily respond incorrectly. Timed tests may discriminate against students who do not perform well on a test with a time limit. We all know people (and you may be included in this category) who "know" the course material perfectly but who are adversely affected by the presence of a clock ticking away. In such cases, it is obvious that test characteristics can interact with student-related unreliability, muddying the lines of distinction between the two types.

VALIDITY

By far the most complex criterion of an effective test—and arguably the most important principle—is **validity**, "the extent to which inferences made from assessment results are appropriate, meaningful, and useful in terms of the purpose of the assessment" (Gronlund, 1998, p. 226). In somewhat more technical terms, Samuel Messick (1989), who is widely recognized as an expert on validity, defined validity as "an integrated evaluative judgment of the degree to which empirical evidence and theoretical rationales support the adequacy and appropriateness of inferences and actions based on test scores or other modes of assessment" (p. 11).

We might infer from these definitions the following attributes of validity:

A VALID TEST . . .

- measures exactly what it proposes to measure
- does not measure irrelevant or "contaminating" variables
- relies as much as possible on empirical evidence (performance)
- involves performance that samples the test's criterion (objective)
- offers useful, meaningful information about a test-taker's ability
- is supported by a theoretical rationale or argument

REMEMBER

A valid test of reading ability actually measures reading ability—not 20/20 vision, or previous knowledge of a subject, or some other variable of questionable relevance. To measure writing ability, one might ask students to write as many words as they can in 15 minutes, then simply count the words for the final score. Such a test would be easy to administer (practical), and the scoring quite dependable (reliable), but it would not constitute a valid test of writing ability without some consideration of comprehensibility, rhetorical discourse elements, and the organization of ideas, among other factors.

How is the validity of a test established? According to Weir (2005), Broadfoot (2005), and T. McNamara (2006), there is no final, absolute measure of validity, but several different kinds of evidence may be invoked in support. Moreover, as Messick (1989) emphasized, "it is important to note that validity is a matter of degree, not all or none" (p. 33).

In some cases, it may be appropriate to examine the extent to which a test calls for performance that matches that of the course or unit being tested. In other cases, we may be concerned with how well a test determines whether students have reached an established set of goals or level of competence. Statistical correlation with other related but independent measures is another widely accepted form of evidence. Other concerns about a test's validity may focus on the consequences of a test, beyond measuring the criteria themselves, or even on the test-taker's perception of validity. We look at four types of evidence below.

Content-Related Evidence

If a test actually samples the subject matter about which conclusions are to be drawn, and if it requires the test-taker to perform the behavior that is being measured, it can claim content-related evidence of validity, often popularly referred to as **content-related validity** (e.g., Hughes, 2003; Mousavi, 2009). You can usually identify content-related evidence observationally if you can clearly define the achievement that you are measuring. A test of tennis competency that asks someone to run a 100-yard dash obviously lacks content validity. If you are trying to assess a person's ability to speak a second language in a conversational setting, asking the learner to answer paper-and-pencil multiple-choice questions requiring grammatical judgments does not achieve content validity. A test that requires the learner to actually speak within some sort of authentic context does. And if a course has perhaps 10 objectives but only two are covered in a test, then content validity suffers.

Consider the following quiz on English articles for a high-beginner level of a conversation class (listening and speaking) for English-learners.

Directions: The purpose of this quiz is for you and me to find out how well you know and can apply the rules of article usage. Read the following passage and write *a/an, the,* or *0* (no article) in each blank.

Last night, I had (1) _____ very strange dream. Actually, it was (2) _____ nightmare! You know how much I love (3) _____ zoos. Well, I dreamt that I went to (4) _____ San Francisco zoo with (5) _____ few friends. When we got there, it was very dark, but (6) _____ moon was out, so we weren't afraid. I wanted to see (7) _____ monkeys first, so we walked past (8) _____ merry-go-round and (9) _____ lions' cages to (10) _____ monkey section.

The students had had a unit on zoo animals and had engaged in some open discussions and group work in which they had practiced articles, all in listening and speaking modes of performance. This quiz is somewhat content valid because it uses a familiar setting and focuses on previously practiced language forms. The fact that it was administered in written form, however, and required students to read the passage and write their responses makes it quite low in content validity for a listening/speaking class.

There are a few cases of highly specialized and sophisticated testing instruments that may have questionable content-related evidence of validity. It is possible to contend, for example, that standard language proficiency tests, with their context-reduced, academically oriented language and limited stretches of discourse, lack content validity because they do not require the full spectrum of communicative performance on the part of the learner (see Bachman, 1990, for a full discussion). There is good reasoning behind such criticism; nevertheless, what such proficiency tests lack in content-related evidence they may gain in other forms of evidence, not to mention practicality and reliability.

Another way of understanding content validity is to consider the difference between **direct** and **indirect testing**. Direct testing involves the test-taker in actually performing the target task. In an indirect test, learners are not performing the task itself but rather a task that is related in some way. For example, if you intend to test learners' oral production of syllable stress and your test task is to have learners mark (with written accent marks) stressed syllables in a list of written words, you could, with a stretch of logic, argue that you are indirectly testing their oral production. A direct test of syllable production would require that students actually produce target words orally.

The most feasible rule of thumb for achieving content validity in classroom assessment is to test performance directly. Consider, for example, a listening/speaking class that is doing a unit on greetings and exchanges that includes discourse for asking for personal information (name, address, hobbies, etc.) with some form-focus on the verb *be,* personal pronouns, and question formation. The test on that unit should include all of the above discourse and grammatical elements and involve students in the actual performance of listening and speaking.

What all the above examples suggest is that content is not the only type of evidence to support the validity of a test; in addition, classroom teachers have neither the time nor the budget to subject quizzes, midterms, and final exams to the extensive scrutiny of a full construct validation (see the next page). Therefore, teachers should make every effort to ensure that their tests have content validity by examining the extent to which the tests assess real course objectives and by ensuring that they test directly.

Criterion-Related Evidence

A second form of evidence of the validity of a test may be found in what is called criterion-related evidence, also referred to as **criterion-related validity**, or the extent to which the "criterion" of the test has actually been reached. You will recall from Chapter 1 that most classroom-based assessment with teacher-designed tests fits the concept of criterion-referenced assessment. In such tests, specified classroom objectives are measured, and implied predetermined levels of performance are expected to be reached (80 percent is considered a minimal passing grade).

In the case of teacher-made classroom assessments, criterion-related evidence is best demonstrated through a comparison of results of an assessment with results of some other measure of the same criterion. For example, in a course unit whose objective is for students to be able to orally produce voiced and voiceless stops in all possible phonetic environments, the results of one teacher's unit test might be compared with an independent assessment—possibly a commercially produced test in a textbook—of the same phonemic proficiency. A classroom test designed to assess mastery of a point of grammar in communicative use will have criterion validity if test scores are corroborated either by observed subsequent behavior or by other communicative measures of the grammar point in question.

Criterion-related evidence usually falls into one of two categories: concurrent and predictive validity. A test has **concurrent validity** if its results are supported by other concurrent performance beyond the assessment itself. For example, the validity of a high score on the final exam of a foreign language course will be substantiated by actual proficiency in the language. The **predictive validity** of an assessment becomes important in the case of placement tests, admissions assessment batteries, and achievement tests designed to determine students' readiness to "move on" to another unit. The assessment criterion in such cases is not to measure concurrent ability but to assess (and predict) a test-taker's likelihood of future success.

Construct-Related Evidence

A third kind of evidence that can support validity, but one that does not play as large a role for classroom teachers, is construct-related validity, commonly referred to as **construct validity**. A construct is any theory, hypothesis, or model that attempts to explain observed phenomena in our universe of perceptions. Constructs may or may not be directly or empirically measured—their verification often requires inferential data. *Proficiency, communicative competence,* and *fluency* are examples of linguistic constructs; *self-esteem* and *motivation* are psychological constructs. Virtually every issue in language learning and teaching involves theoretical constructs. In the field of assessment, construct validity asks, "Does this test actually tap into the theoretical construct as it has been defined?" Let's say you're assessing a student's oral fluency. To possess construct validity, your test should account for the various components of fluency: speed, rhythm, juncture, (lack of) hesitations, and other elements within the construct of fluency. Tests are, in a manner of speaking, operational definitions of constructs in that their test tasks are the building blocks of the entity that is being measured (see Davidson, Hudson, & Lynch, 1985; T. McNamara, 2000).

For most of the tests that you administer as a classroom teacher, a formal construct validation procedure may seem a daunting prospect. You will be tempted, perhaps, to run a quick content check and be satisfied with the test's validity. But don't let the concept of construct validity scare you. An informal construct validation of virtually every classroom test is both essential and feasible.

Imagine, for example, that you have been given a procedure for conducting an oral interview. The scoring analysis for the interview includes several factors in the final score: pronunciation, fluency, grammatical accuracy, vocabulary use, and socio-linguistic appropriateness. The justification for these five factors lies in a theoretical construct that claims those factors as major components of oral proficiency. So if you were asked to conduct an oral proficiency interview that evaluated only pronunciation and grammar, you could be justifiably suspicious about the construct validity of that test. Likewise, let's suppose you have created a simple written vocabulary quiz, covering the content of a recent unit, which asks students to correctly define a set of words. Your chosen items may be a perfectly adequate sample of what was covered in the unit, but if the lexical objective of the unit was the communicative use of vocabulary, then the writing of definitions certainly fails to match a construct of communicative language use.

Construct validity is a major issue in validating large-scale standardized tests of proficiency. Because such tests must, for economic reasons, adhere to the principle of practicality, and because they must sample a limited number of domains of language, they may not be able to contain all the content of a particular field or skill. For example, many large-scale standardized tests worldwide have until recently not attempted to sample oral production, yet oral production is obviously an important aspect of language ability. The omission of oral production content, however, was ostensibly justified by research that showed positive correlations between oral production and the behaviors (listening, reading, grammaticality detection, and writing) actually sampled on such tests (Duran, Canale, Penfield, Stansfield, & Liskin-Gasparo, 1985). Because of the crucial need to offer financially affordable proficiency tests and the high cost of administering and scoring oral production tests, the omission of oral content was justified as an economic necessity. However, in the last decade, with advances in developing rubrics for scoring oral production tasks and in automated speech recognition software, more general language proficiency tests include oral production tasks, largely stemming from the demands of the professional community for authenticity and content validity.

Consequential Validity (Impact)

As well as these three widely accepted forms of evidence that may be introduced to support the validity of an assessment, two other categories may be of some interest and utility in your own quest for validating classroom tests. Messick (1989), T. McNamara (2000), Brindley (2001), Fulcher and Davidson (2007), and Gronlund and Waugh (2008), among others, underscore the potential importance of the consequences of using an assessment. **Consequential validity** encompasses all the consequences of a test, including such considerations as its accuracy in measuring intended criteria, its effect on the preparation of test-takers, and the (intended and unintended) social consequences of a test's interpretation and use.

Bachman and Palmer (1996), McKay (2000), Davies (2003), and Choi (2008) use the term **impact** to refer to consequential validity, perhaps more broadly encompassing the many consequences of assessment, before and after a test administration. The impact of test-taking and the use of test scores can, according to Bachman and Palmer (p. 30), be seen at both a macro level (the effect on society and educational systems) and a micro level (the effect on individual test-takers). At the macro level, Choi argued that the wholesale employment of standardized tests for such gatekeeping purposes as college admission "deprive students of crucial opportunities to learn and acquire productive language skills," causing test consumers to be "increasingly disillusioned with EFL testing" (p. 58). More will be said about impact and related issues of values, social consequences, ethics, and fairness in Chapter 4.

As high-stakes assessment has gained ground in the last two decades, one aspect of consequential validity has drawn special attention: the effect of test preparation courses and manuals on performance. T. McNamara (2000) cautioned against test results that may reflect socioeconomic conditions such as opportunities for coaching that are "differentially available to the students being assessed (for example, because only some families can afford coaching, or because children with more highly educated parents get help from their parents)" (p. 54).

At the micro level, specifically the classroom instructional level, another important consequence of a test falls into the category of **washback**, to be defined and more fully discussed later in this chapter. Gronlund and Waugh (2008) encouraged teachers to consider the effect of assessments on students' motivation, subsequent performance in a course, independent learning, study habits, and attitude toward school work.

Face Validity

A further facet of consequential validity is the extent to which "students view the assessment as fair, relevant, and useful for improving learning" (Gronlund, 1998, p. 210), or what has popularly been called—or misnamed—**face validity**. "Face validity refers to the degree to which a test *looks* right, and *appears* to measure the knowledge or abilities it claims to measure, based on the subjective judgment of the examinees who take it, the administrative personnel who decide on its use, and other psychometrically unsophisticated observers" (Mousavi, 2009, p. 247).

Despite the intuitive appeal of the concept of face validity, it remains a notion that cannot be empirically measured or theoretically justified under the category of validity. It is purely a factor of the "eye of the beholder"—how the test-taker, or possibly the test-giver, intuitively perceives an instrument. For this reason, many assessment experts (see Bachman, 1990, pp. 285–289) view face validity as a superficial factor that is too dependent on the whim of the perceiver. In Bachman's "postmortem" on face validity, he echoes Mosier's (1947, p. 194) decades-old contention that face validity is a "pernicious fallacy . . . [that should be]purged from the technician's vocabulary."

At the same time, Bachman (1990) and other assessment experts "grudgingly" agree that test appearance does indeed have an effect that neither test-takers nor test designers can ignore. Students may for a variety of reasons feel that a test isn't testing what it's supposed to test, and this might affect their performance and, consequently, create student-related unreliability referred to previously. So student perception of a test's fairness is significant to classroom-based assessment because it can affect student performance/reliability. Teachers can increase student's perception of fair tests by using

- a well-constructed, expected format with familiar tasks
- tasks that can be accomplished within an allotted time limit
- items that are clear and uncomplicated
- directions that are crystal clear
- tasks that have been rehearsed in their previous course work
- tasks that relate to their course work (content validity)
- a difficulty level that presents a reasonable challenge

Finally, the issue of face validity reminds us that the psychological state of the learner (confidence, anxiety, etc.) is an important ingredient in peak performance. Students can be distracted and their anxiety increased if you "throw a curve" at them on a test. They need to have rehearsed test tasks before the fact and feel comfortable with them. A classroom test is not the time to introduce new tasks, because you won't know if student difficulty is a factor of the task itself or of the objectives you are testing.

I once administered a dictation test and a cloze test (see Chapter 9 for a discussion of cloze tests) as a placement test for a group of learners of English as a second language. Some learners were upset because such tests, on the face of it, did not appear to them to test their true abilities in English. They felt that a multiple-choice grammar test would have been the appropriate format to use. A few claimed they didn't perform well on the cloze and dictation because they were not accustomed to these formats. As it turned out, the tests served as superior instruments for placement, but the students did not think so.

As already noted above, validity is a complex concept, yet it is indispensable to the teacher's understanding of what makes a good test. We do well to heed Messick's (1989, p. 33) caution that validity is not an all-or-none proposition and that various forms of validity may need to be applied to a test in order to be satisfied with its overall effectiveness. If in your language assessment procedures you can make a point of primarily focusing on content and criterion validity, then you are well on your way to making accurate judgments about the competence of the learners with whom you are working.

AUTHENTICITY

A fourth major principle of language testing is **authenticity**, a concept that is difficult to define, especially within the art and science of evaluating and designing tests. Bachman and Palmer (1996) defined authenticity as "the degree of correspondence of the characteristics of a given language test task to the features of a target language task" (p. 23) and then suggested an agenda for identifying those target language tasks and for transforming them into valid test items.

As mentioned, authenticity is not a concept that easily lends itself to empirical definition or measurement. (Lewkowicz [2000] discussed the difficulties of operationalizing authenticity in language assessment.) After all, who can certify whether a task or language sample is "real-world" or not? Often such judgments are subjective, and yet authenticity is a concept that language-testing experts have paid a great deal of attention to (Bachman & Palmer, 1996; Fulcher & Davidson, 2007). Further, according to Chun (2006), many test types fail to simulate real-world tasks.

Essentially, when you make a claim for authenticity in a test task, you are saying that this task is likely to be enacted in the real world. Many test item types fail to simulate real-world tasks. They may be contrived or artificial in their attempt to target a grammatical form or a lexical item. The sequencing of items that bear no relationship to one another lacks authenticity. One does not have to look very long to find reading comprehension passages in proficiency tests that do not reflect a real-world passage.

In a test, authenticity may be present in the following ways:

AN AUTHENTIC TEST . . .

- contains language that is as natural as possible
- has items that are contextualized rather than isolated
- includes meaningful, relevant, interesting topics
- provides some thematic organization to items, such as through a story line or episode
- offers tasks that replicate real-world tasks

REMEMBER

The authenticity of test tasks in recent years has increased noticeably. Two or three decades ago, unconnected, boring, contrived items were accepted as a necessary component of testing. Things have changed. It was once assumed that large-scale testing could not include performance of the productive skills and stay within budgetary constraints, but now many such tests offer speaking and writing components. Reading passages are selected from real-world sources that test-takers are likely to have encountered or will encounter. Listening comprehension sections feature natural language with hesitations, white noise, and interruptions. More tests offer items that are "episodic" in that they are sequenced to form meaningful units, paragraphs, or stories.

We invite you to take up the challenge of authenticity in your classroom tests. As we explore many different types of tasks in this book, especially in Chapters 6 through 9, the principle of authenticity will be very much in the forefront.

WASHBACK

A facet of consequential validity discussed above is "the effect of testing on teaching and learning" (Hughes, 2003, p. 1), otherwise known in the language assessment field as **washback**. To distinguish the impact of an assessment, discussed above, from washback, think of the latter as referring almost always to classroom-based issues such as the extent to which assessment affects a student's future language development. Messick (1996, p. 241) reminded us that the washback effect may refer to both the promotion and the inhibition of learning, thus emphasizing what may be referred to as beneficial versus harmful (or negative) washback. Alderson & Wall (1993) considered washback an important enough concept to define a Washback Hypothesis that essentially elaborated on how tests influence both teaching and learning. Cheng, Watanabe, and Curtis (2004) devoted an entire anthology to the issue of washback, and Spratt (2005) challenged teachers to become agents of beneficial washback in their language classrooms.

The following factors comprise the concept of washback:

A TEST THAT PROVIDES BENEFICIAL WASHBACK . . .

- positively influences what and how teachers teach
- positively influences what and how learners learn
- offers learners a chance to adequately prepare
- gives learners feedback that enhances their language development
- is more formative in nature than summative
- provides conditions for peak performance by the learner

REMEMBER

In large-scale assessment, washback often refers to the effects that tests have on instruction in terms of how students prepare for the test. "Cram" courses and "teaching to the test" are examples of washback that may have both negative and positive effects. The current worldwide use of standardized tests for gate-keeping purposes can lead students to focus on simply gaining an acceptable score rather than on language development. On the positive side, many enrollees in test-preparation courses report increased competence in certain language-related tasks (Chapelle, Enright, & Jamieson, 2008).

In classroom-based assessment, washback can have a number of positive manifestations, ranging from the benefit of preparing and reviewing for a test to the learning that accrues from feedback on one's performance. Teachers can provide information that "washes back" to students in the form of useful diagnoses of strengths and weaknesses. Washback also includes the effects of an assessment on teaching and learning prior to the assessment itself, that is, on preparation for the assessment. Informal performance assessment is by nature more likely to have built-in washback effects because the teacher is usually providing interactive feedback. Formal tests can also have positive washback, but they provide no beneficial washback if the students receive a simple letter grade or a single overall numerical score.

The challenge to teachers is to create classroom tests that serve as learning devices through which washback is achieved. Students' incorrect responses can become windows of insight into further work. Their correct responses need to be praised, especially when they represent accomplishments in a student's developing language competence. Teachers can suggest strategies for success as part of their "coaching" role. Washback enhances a number of basic principles of language acquisition: intrinsic motivation, autonomy, self-confidence, language ego, interlanguage, and strategic investment, among others. (See *PLLT* and *TBP* for an explanation of these principles.)

One way to enhance washback is to comment generously and specifically on test performance. Many overworked (and underpaid) teachers return tests to students with a single letter grade or numerical score and consider their job done. In reality, letter grades and numerical scores give absolutely no information of intrinsic interest to the student. Grades and scores alone, without comments and other feedback, reduce the linguistic and cognitive performance data available to student to almost nothing. At best, they give a relative indication of a formulaic judgment of performance as compared to others in the class—which fosters competitive, not cooperative, learning.

With this in mind, when you return a written test or a data sheet from an oral production test, consider giving more than a number, grade, or phrase as your feedback. Even if your evaluation is not a neat little paragraph appended to the test, you can respond to as many details throughout the test as time will permit. Give praise for strengths—the "good stuff"—as well as constructive criticism of weaknesses. Give strategic hints on how a student might improve certain elements of performance. In other words, take some time to make the test performance an intrinsically motivating experience from which a student will gain a sense of accomplishment and challenge.

A little bit of washback may also help students through a specification of the numerical scores on the various subsections of the test. A subsection on verb tenses, for example, that yields a relatively low score may serve the diagnostic purpose of showing the student an area of challenge.

Another viewpoint on washback is achieved by a quick consideration of differences between formative and summative tests, mentioned in Chapter 1. Formative tests, by definition, provide washback in the form of information to the learner on progress toward goals. But teachers might be tempted to feel that summative tests, which provide assessment at the end of a course or program, do not need to offer much in the way of washback. Such an attitude is unfortunate because the end of every language course or program is always the beginning of further pursuits, more learning, more goals, and more challenges to face. Even a final examination in a course should carry with it some means for giving washback to students.

In my courses I never give a final examination as the last scheduled classroom session. I always administer a final exam during the penultimate session then complete the evaluation of the exams in order to return them to students during the last class. At this time, the students receive scores, grades, and comments on their work, and I spend some of the class session addressing material on which the students were not completely clear. My summative assessment is thereby enhanced by some beneficial washback that is usually not expected of final examinations.

Finally, washback implies that students have ready access to you to discuss the feedback and evaluation you have given. Whereas you almost certainly have known teachers with whom you wouldn't dare argue about a grade, an interactive, cooperative, collaborative classroom can promote an atmosphere of dialogue between students and teachers regarding evaluative judgments. For learning to continue, students need to have a chance to feed back on your feedback, to seek clarification of any issues that are fuzzy, and to set new and appropriate goals for themselves for the days and weeks ahead.

APPLYING PRINCIPLES TO THE EVALUATION OF CLASSROOM TESTS

The five principles of practicality, reliability, validity, authenticity, and washback go a long way toward providing useful guidelines for both evaluating an existing assessment procedure and designing one on your own. Quizzes, tests, final exams, and standardized proficiency tests can all be scrutinized through these five lenses.

Are there other principles that should be invoked in evaluating and designing assessments? The answer, of course, is yes. Language assessment is an extraordinarily broad discipline with many branches, interest areas, and issues. The process of designing effective assessment instruments is far too complex to be reduced to five principles. Good test construction, for example, is governed by research-based rules of test preparation, sampling of tasks, item design and construction, scoring responses, ethical standards, and so on. But the five principles cited here serve as an excellent foundation on which to evaluate existing instruments and to build your own.

We will look at how to design tests in Chapter 3. The tips and checklists that follow in this chapter, indexed by the five principles, will help you evaluate existing tests for your own classroom. It is important for you to remember, however, that the sequence of these questions does not imply a priority order. Validity, for example, is certainly the most significant cardinal principle of assessment evaluation. Practicality could be a secondary issue in classroom testing. Or, for a particular test, you may need to place authenticity as your primary consideration. When all is said and done, however, if validity is not substantiated, all other considerations may be rendered useless.

1. Are the test procedures practical?

Practicality is determined by the teacher's (and the students') time constraints, costs, and administrative details and to some extent by what occurs before and after the test. To determine whether a test is practical for your needs, you may want to use the checklist below.

✓ PRACTICALITY CHECKLIST

- ☐ **1.** Are administrative details all carefully attended to before the test?
- ☐ **2.** Can students complete the test reasonably within the set time frame?
- ☐ **3.** Can the test be administered smoothly, without procedural "glitches"?
- ☐ **4.** Are all printed materials accounted for?
- ☐ **5.** Has equipment been pre-tested?
- ☐ **6.** Is the cost of the test within budgeted limits?
- ☐ **7.** Is the scoring/evaluation system feasible in the teacher's time frame?
- ☐ **8.** Are methods for reporting results determined in advance?

As this checklist suggests, after you account for the administrative details of giving a test, you need to think about the practicality of your plans for scoring the test. In teachers' busy lives, time often emerges as the most important factor, one that overrides other considerations in evaluating an assessment. If you need to tailor a test to fit your own time frame, as teachers frequently do, you need to accomplish this without damaging the test's validity and washback. Teachers should, for example, avoid the temptation to offer only quickly scored multiple-choice selection items that may be neither appropriate nor well-designed. Everyone knows teachers secretly hate to grade tests (almost as much as students hate to take them) and will do almost anything to get through that task as quickly and effortlessly as possible. Yet good teaching almost always implies an investment of the teacher's time in giving feedback—comments and suggestions—to students on their tests.

2. Is the test itself reliable?

Reliability applies to the student, the test administration, the test itself, and the teacher. At least four sources of unreliability must be guarded against, as noted in this chapter on pages 27–29. Test and test administration reliability can be achieved by making sure that all students receive the same quality of input, whether written or auditory. The following checklist should help you to determine if a test is itself reliable:

✓ **TEST RELIABILITY CHECKLIST**

❑ **1.** Does every student have a cleanly photocopied test sheet?
❑ **2.** Is sound amplification clearly audible to everyone in the room?
❑ **3.** Is video input clearly and uniformly visible to all?
❑ **4.** Are lighting, temperature, extraneous noise, and other classroom conditions equal (and optimal) for all students?
❑ **5.** For closed-ended responses, do scoring procedures leave little debate about correctness of an answer?

3. Can you ensure rater reliability?

Rater reliability, another common issue in assessments, may be more difficult, perhaps because we too often overlook this as an issue. Because classroom tests rarely involve two scorers, inter-rater reliability is seldom an issue. Instead, intra-rater reliability is of constant concern to teachers: What happens to our fallible concentration and stamina over the period of time during which we are evaluating a test? Teachers need to find ways to maintain their focus and energy over the time it takes to score assessments. In open-ended response tests, this issue is of paramount importance. It is easy to let mentally established standards erode over the hours required to evaluate the test.

Intra-rater reliability for open-ended responses may be enhanced by answering these questions:

✔ **PRACTICALITY CHECKLIST**

☐ **1.** Have you established consistent criteria for correct responses?
☐ **2.** Can you give uniform attention to those criteria throughout the evaluation time?
☐ **3.** Can you guarantee that scoring is based only on the established criteria and not on extraneous or subjective variables?
☐ **4.** Have you read through tests at least twice to check for consistency?
☐ **5.** If you have made "midstream" modifications of what you consider a correct response, did you go back and apply the same standards to all?
☐ **6.** Can you avoid fatigue by reading the tests in several sittings, especially if the time requirement is a matter of several hours?

---

4. Does the procedure demonstrate content validity?

The major source for establishing validity in a classroom test is content validity: the extent to which the assessment requires students to perform tasks that were included in the previous classroom lessons and that directly represent the objectives of the unit on which the assessment is based. If you have been teaching an English language class to students who have been reading, summarizing, and responding to short passages, and if your assessment is based on this work, then to be content valid, the test needs to include performance in those skills. For classroom assessments, content and criterion validity are closely linked, because lesson or unit objectives are essentially the criterion of an assessment covering that lesson or unit.

Several steps might be taken to evaluate the content validity of a classroom test:

✔ **CONTENT VALIDITY CHECKLIST (FOR A TEST ON A UNIT)**

☐ **1.** Are unit objectives clearly identified?
☐ **2.** Are unit objectives represented in the form of test specifications? (See the next page for details on test specifications.)
☐ **3.** Do the test specifications include tasks that have already been performed as part of the course procedures?
☐ **4.** Do the test specifications include tasks that represent all (or most) of the objectives for the unit?
☐ **5.** Do those tasks involve actual performance of the target task(s)?

A primary issue in establishing content validity is recognizing that underlying every good classroom test are the objectives of the lesson, module, or unit of the course in question. So the first measure of an effective classroom test is the identification of objectives. Sometimes this is easier said than done. Too often teachers work through lessons day after day with little or no cognizance of the objectives they seek to fulfill. Or perhaps those objectives are so poorly defined that determining whether they were accomplished is impossible.

A second issue in content validity is test **specifications** (specs). Don't let this word scare you. It simply means that a test should have a structure that follows logically from the lesson or unit you are testing. Many tests have a design that

- divides them into a number of sections (corresponding, perhaps, to the objectives that are being assessed)
- offers students a variety of item types
- gives an appropriate relative weight to each section

Some tests, of course, do not lend themselves to this kind of structure. A test in a course in academic writing at the university level might justifiably consist of an in-class written essay on a given topic—only one "item" and one response, in a manner of speaking. But in this case the specs would be embedded in the prompt itself and in the scoring or evaluation rubric used to grade it and give feedback. We return to the concept of test specs in the next chapter.

The content validity of an existing classroom test should be apparent in how the objectives of the unit being tested are represented in the form of the content of items, clusters of items, and item types. Do you clearly perceive the performance of test-takers as reflective of the classroom objectives? If so (and you can argue this), content validity has most likely been achieved.

5. Has the impact of the test been carefully accounted for?

This question integrates the concept of consequential validity (impact) and the importance of structuring an assessment procedure to elicit the optimal performance of the student. Remember that even though it is an elusive concept, the appearance of a test from a student's point of view is important to consider.

The following factors might help you to pinpoint some of the issues surrounding the impact of a test:

✓ **CONSEQUENTIAL VALIDITY CHECKLIST**

❑ **1.** Have you offered students appropriate review and preparation for the test?
❑ **2.** Have you suggested test-taking strategies that will be beneficial?
❑ **3.** Is the test structured so that, if possible, the best students will be modestly challenged and the weaker students will not be overwhelmed?
❑ **4.** Does the test lend itself to your giving beneficial washback?
❑ **5.** Are the students encouraged to see the test as a learning experience?

---

6. Is the procedure "biased for best"?

A phrase that has come to be associated with consequential validity is "**biased for best**," a term that goes a little beyond how the student views the test to a degree of strategic involvement on the part of student and teacher in preparing for, setting up, and following up on the test itself. According to Swain (1984), to give an assessment procedure that is biased for best, a teacher provides conditions for a student's optimal performance. In such a case, your role is not to be "tricky" or to scare your students but to encourage them and bring out the best in their performance. Cohen (2006) supported Swain's concept in a comprehensive discussion of research that showed the positive effects of students' awareness and utilization of test-taking strategies.

It's easy for teachers to forget how challenging some tests can be, and so a well-planned testing experience will include some strategic suggestions on how students might optimize their performance. In evaluating a classroom test, consider the extent to which before-, during-, and after-test options are fulfilled.

7. Are the test tasks as authentic as possible?

Evaluate the extent to which a test is authentic by asking the following questions:

✓ **AUTHENTICITY CHECKLIST**

❑ **1.** Is the language in the test as natural as possible?
❑ **2.** Are items as contextualized as possible rather than isolated?
❑ **3.** Are topics and situations interesting, enjoyable, and/or humorous?
❑ **4.** Is some thematic organization provided, such as through a story line or episode?
❑ **5.** Do tasks represent, or closely approximate, real-world tasks?

Consider the following two excerpts from tests, and the concept of authenticity may become a little clearer.

Multiple-choice tasks—contextualized

Directions: After answering the questions, click the "Submit" button.

"Going To"

1. Amanda: What _____ this weekend?
   ○ you are going to do
   ○ are you going to do
   ○ your gonna do

2. Gwen: I'm not sure. _____ anything special?
   ○ Are you going to do
   ○ You are going to do
   ○ Is going to do

3. Amanda: Melissa and I _____ a party. Would you like to come?
   ○ are going to
   ○ are going
   ○ go to

4. Gwen: I'd love to! _____?
   ○ What's it going to be
   ○ Who's going to be
   ○ Where's it going to be

5. Amanda: It's _____ to be at Ruth's house.
   ○ go
   ○ going
   ○ gonna

SUBMIT

Adapted from Sheila Viotti, from Dave's ESL Café.

Multiple-choice tasks—decontextualized

"Going To"

1. What _____ this summer?
   A. John is going to do
   B. is John going to do
   C. you're going to do

2. _____ anything special next weekend?
   A. Are you going to do
   B. You are going to do
   C. Is going to do

3. She and I _____ my English class tomorrow.
   A. are going to
   B. are going
   C. going to

4. The Giants are playing baseball on Wednesday. _____
   A. What's it going to?
   B. Who's it going to be?
   C. Where's it going to be played?

5. The ocean's _____ to be at low tide later this morning.
   A. go
   B. going
   C. going to

The sequence of items in the contextualized tasks achieves a modicum of authenticity by contextualizing all the items in a story line. The conversation is one that might occur in the real world, even if with a little less formality. The sequence of items in the decontextualized tasks takes the test-taker into five different topic areas with no context for any, with the grammatical category as the only unifying element. Each sentence is likely to be written or spoken in the real world but only perhaps in five different contexts. Given the constraints of a multiple-choice format, on a measure of authenticity I would say the first excerpt is good and the second excerpt is only fair.

8. Does the test offer beneficial washback to the learner?

The design of an effective test should point the way to beneficial washback. A test that achieves content validity demonstrates relevance to the curriculum in question and thereby sets the stage for washback. When test items represent the various objectives of a unit, and/or when sections of a test clearly focus on major topics of the unit, classroom tests can serve in a diagnostic capacity even if they aren't specifically labeled as such.

The following checklist should help you to maximize beneficial washback in a test:

✓ **WASHBACK CHECKLIST**

☐ **1.** Is the test designed in such a way that you can give feedback that will be relevant to the objectives of the unit being tested?

☐ **2.** Have you given students sufficient pre-test opportunities to review the subject matter of the test?

☐ **3.** In your written feedback to each student, do you include comments that will contribute to students' formative development?

☐ **4.** After returning tests, do you spend class time "going over" the test and offering advice on what students should focus on in the future?

☐ **5.** After returning tests, do you encourage questions from students?

☐ **6.** If time and circumstances permit, do you offer students (especially the weaker ones) a chance to discuss results in an office hour?

Sometimes evidence of washback may be only marginally visible from an examination of the test itself. Here again, what happens before and after the test is critical. Preparation time before the test can contribute to washback because the learner is reviewing and focusing in a potentially broader way on the objectives in question. In what I like to whimsically refer to as "wash forward," students can be aided by strategic efforts to internalize the material being tested. An increasingly common occurrence in student-centered classrooms is the formation of study groups whose task is to review the subject matter of an upcoming test. Sometimes those study groups are more valuable, in terms of measurable washback, than the test itself.

By spending classroom time after the test reviewing the content, students discover their areas of strength and weakness. Teachers can raise the washback potential by asking students to use test results as a guide to setting goals for their future effort. The key is to play down the "Whew, I'm glad that's over" feeling that students are likely to have and play up the learning that can now take place from their knowledge of the results.

Some of the alternatives in assessment referred to in Chapter 1 may also enhance washback from tests. (See also Chapter 6.) Self-assessment may sometimes be an appropriate way to challenge students to discover their own mistakes. This can be particularly effective for writing performance: Once the pressure of assessment has come and gone, students may be able to look back at their written work with a fresh eye. Peer discussion of the test results may also be an alternative to simply listening to the teacher tell everyone what they got right and wrong and why. Journal writing may provide students a specific place to record their feelings, what they learned, and their resolutions for future effort.

✪   ✪   ✪   ✪   ✪

The five basic principles of language assessment have been expanded here into eight essential questions you might ask yourself about an assessment. As you use the principles and guidelines to evaluate various forms of tests and procedures, be sure to allow each one of the five to take on greater or lesser importance, depending on the context. In large-scale standardized testing, for example, practicality is usually more important than washback, but the reverse may be true of most classroom tests. Validity is of course always the final arbiter. Remember, too, that these principles, important as they are, are not the only considerations in evaluating or making an effective test. Leave some space for other factors to enter in.

The next chapter focuses on how to design a test. These same five principles underlie test construction as well as test evaluation, along with some new concepts that expand your ability to apply principles to the practicalities of language assessment in your own classroom.

EXERCISES

[Note: **(I)** Individual work; **(G)** Group or pair work; **(C)** Whole-class discussion.]

1. **(C)** Ask the class to volunteer brief descriptions of tests they have taken or given that illustrate, either positively or negatively, each of the five basic principles of language assessment that are defined and explained in this chapter. In the process, try to come up with examples of tests that illustrate (and differentiate) four kinds of reliability as well as the four types of evidence that support the validity of a test.
2. **(I/C)** Some assessment experts contend that face validity is not a legitimate form of validity because it relies solely on the perception of the test-taker rather than an external measure. Nevertheless, a number of educational assessment experts recognize the perception of the test-taker as a very important factor in test design and administration. What is your opinion? How would you reconcile the two views?
3. **(G)** In the section on washback, it is stated that "Washback enhances a number of basic principles of language acquisition: intrinsic motivation, autonomy, self-confidence, language ego, interlanguage, and strategic investment, among others" (page 38). In a group, discuss the connection between washback and each of the above-named general principles of language learning and teaching. Describe specific examples or illustrations of each connection. If time permits, report your examples to the class.
4. **(G)** In a small group, evaluate the assessment scenarios in the chart on pages 49–50 by ranking the six factors listed there from 1 to 5 (with a score of 5 indicating that the principle is highly fulfilled and a score of 1 indicating very low or no fulfillment). Evaluate the scenarios by using your best intuition in the absence of complete information for each context. Report your group's findings to the rest of the class and compare.

SCENARIO	Practicality	Rater Reliability	Content Validity	Impact	Authenticity
1. Standardized multiple-choice proficiency test, no oral or written production S (Student) receives a report form listing a total score and subscores for listening, grammar, proofreading, and reading comprehension.					
2. Timed impromptu test of written English (TWE® Test) S receives a report form listing one holistic score ranging between 0 and 6.					
3. One-on-one oral interview to assess overall oral production ability S receives one holistic score ranging between 0 and 5.					
4. S gives a five-minute prepared oral presentation in class. T (Teacher) evaluates by filling in a rating sheet indicating S's success in delivery, rapport, pronunciation, grammar, and content.					
5. S listens to a fifteen-minute video lecture and takes notes. T makes individual comments on each of S's notes.					
6. S writes a take-home (overnight) one-page essay on an assigned topic. T reads paper and comments on organization and content only, then returns essay to S for a subsequent draft.					

(continued)

SCENARIO	Practicality	Rater Reliability	Content Validity	Impact	Authenticity
7. S creates multiple drafts of a three-page essay, peer- and T-reviewed, and turns in a final version. T comments on grammatical/rhetorical errors only and returns it to S.					
8. S assembles a portfolio of materials over a semester-long course. T conferences with S on the portfolio at the end of the semester.					

5. **(G)** This chapter gives checklists to help you gauge and apply the five principles of language assessment. In your group, talk about one principle. Describe a test that someone in your group took or gave. Discuss the following question: Did it meet the criteria in the checklist? Report a summary of your discussion back to the class.

6. **(G)** In our discussion of impact in this chapter, the suggestion was made that teachers can prepare students for tests by offering them strategies for preparing, taking, and benefiting from tests. These might be categorized as "before, during, and after" strategies. "Before" strategies could include giving information about what to expect and suggestions for how to review. "During" strategies might involve tips for tackling items and time management. "After" strategies, such as learning from one's mistakes and setting future goals, could also benefit students. In a small group, design a checklist of test-taking strategies, perhaps with each group tackling just one of the three categories. Report your checklist back to the class.

7. **(I/G)** In an accessible language class, ask the teacher to allow you to observe an assessment procedure that is about to take place (a test, an in-class periodic assessment, a quiz, etc.). Do the following:

   a. Conduct a brief interview with the teacher before the procedure to get information on the purpose of the assessment and its place in the curriculum.
   b. Observe (if possible) the actual administration of the assessment.
   c. Arrange for a short interview with the teacher after the fact to ask any questions you might have.

Evaluate the effectiveness of the assessment in terms of (a) the five basic principles of assessment and/or (b) the eight steps for test evaluation described in this chapter. Present your findings either as a written report to your instructor and/or orally to the class.

FOR YOUR FURTHER READING

Leung, Constance. (2005). Classroom teacher assessment of second language development: Construct as practice. In E. Hinkel (Ed.), *Handbook of research in second language teaching and learning* (pp. 869–888). Mahwah, NJ: Lawrence Erlbaum Associates.

This highly informative "state-of-the-art" article summarizes a number of issues in classroom-based language assessment. For a relatively short article, it is exceptionally broad in its treatment of assumptions, claims, and critical responses that have been faced in recent years. Constructs such as validity and reliability are examined and exemplified, and performance-based and alternative assessments are critically discussed, all with some down-to-earth practical examples that teachers can easily identify with.

Weir, Cyril J. (2005). *Language testing and validation: An evidence-based approach.* Basingstoke, England: Palgrave Macmillan.

This book provides a wealth of information on research, issues, controversies, and solutions to problems that have arisen over the concept of validity in language testing. It offers teachers a theoretical and practical base that will enable them to evaluate their own classroom tests as well as commercially available tests. For the beginning student in the field, it could be difficult reading, as it contains technical and complex discussion. However, classroom teachers will appreciate the many real-world examples of tests and test items.

CHAPTER 3

DESIGNING CLASSROOM

LANGUAGE TESTS

OBJECTIVES: After reading this chapter, you will be able to

- go beyond evaluating an existing test to actually designing one on your own
- analyze the purpose of a proposed test
- state in explicit terms the objectives of a proposed test
- create test specifications for a proposed test

- design a variety of items (test methods) for a proposed test
- carry out the administration of a test, after checking a number of essential details involved
- construct a rationale for scoring, grading, and giving feedback on a proposed test

The previous two chapters introduced a number of building blocks for designing language tests. You now have a sense of where tests belong in the larger domain of assessment. You've sorted through differences between formal and informal tests, formative and summative tests, and norm- and criterion-referenced tests. Different types or purposes of assessment have been introduced to you. You've traced some of the historical lines of thought in the field of language assessment. You have a sense of major current trends in language assessment, especially the present focus on communicative and process-oriented testing that seeks to transform tests from anguishing ordeals into challenging and intrinsically motivating learning experiences. By now, certain foundational principles have entered your working vocabulary: practicality, reliability, validity, authenticity, and washback. You should now also possess a few tools with which you can evaluate the effectiveness of an existing classroom test.

In this chapter, you will draw on those foundations and tools to begin the process of designing tests or revising existing tests. As always, the primary focus in this book is on classroom-based assessment, because that's the down-to-earth context in which you are regularly involved. We'll deal directly with issues in large-scale, standardized testing in the next chapter. So for now, for classroom purposes, let's start the process by asking some critical questions.

1. *What is the purpose of the test?* Why are you creating this test, or why was it created by, say, a textbook writer? What is its significance relative to your course (for example, to evaluate overall proficiency or place a student in a

course)? How important is the test compared to other student performance? What will its impact be on you and your students before and after the assessment? Once you have established the major purpose of a test, it then becomes easier to specify its objectives.

2. *What are the objectives of the test?* What exactly are you trying to find out? Establishing appropriate objectives involves a number of issues, from relatively simple ones about forms and functions covered in a course unit to much more complex ones about constructs to be represented on the test. Included here are decisions about what language abilities are to be assessed.

3. *How will the test specifications reflect both the purpose and the objectives?* To design or evaluate a test, you must make sure that the test has a structure that logically follows from the unit or lesson it is testing. The class objectives should be present in the test through appropriate task types and weights, a logical sequence, and a variety of tasks.

4. *How will the test item types (tasks) be selected and the separate items arranged?* The tasks need to be practical (as defined in Chapter 2). To have content validity, they should also mirror tasks of the course, lesson, or segment. They should also be authentic, with a progression biased for best performance. Finally, the tasks must be ones that can be evaluated reliably by the teacher or scorer.

5. *In administering the test, what details should I attend to in order to help students achieve optimal performance?* Once the test has been created and is ready to administer, students need to feel well prepared for their performance. An otherwise effective, valid test might fail to reach its goal if the conditions for test taking are inadequately established. How will you reduce unnecessary anxiety in students, raise their confidence, and help them view the test as an opportunity to learn?

6. *What kind of scoring, grading, and/or feedback is expected?* The appropriate form of feedback on tests will vary, depending on their purpose. For every test, the way results are reported is an important consideration. Under some circumstances a letter grade or a holistic score may be appropriate; other circumstances may require that a teacher offer substantive washback to the learner.

These six questions should form the basis of your approach to designing, administering, and making maximum use of tests in your classroom.

FOUR ASSESSMENT SCENARIOS

For the purposes of making practical applications in this chapter, we will consider four scenarios as we proceed through the six steps for designing an assessment. These common classroom contexts should enable you to identify with real-world assessment situations.

Scenario 1: Reading Quiz

The first context is an intermediate-level class for secondary school students in an English class in Brazil. The students have been assigned a two-page short story to read on their own for homework, and the teacher has decided to begin class the next day with a brief "pop quiz": 10 short-answer written comprehension questions. The quiz will (a) give students a sense of how well they understood the story and (b) act as a starting point for a teacher-led discussion on each of the items. Results of the quiz will not be recorded in the teacher's record book.

Scenario 2: Grammar Unit Test

This test comes at the end of a three-week unit in a grammar-focus course at a high beginning (Level 2) class in an adult school in the United States. Students have completed Level 1 or have been placed into Level 2 by a placement test. All the students are simultaneously taking two integrated-skills classes (listening/speaking and reading/writing), and the grammar class serves to reinforce the grammatical forms that have been encountered in the other two classes.

The grammar unit has covered verb tenses. The curriculum specifies that the 45-minute test is to be divided into three sections: multiple-choice items, fill in the blank (cloze) items, and a grammar editing task (where students must detect errors in several written paragraphs). The test will be handed in, graded by the teacher, and returned to students a few days later.

Scenario 3: Midterm Essay

In a writing course in a university in Thailand, students at the advanced level have been working for half a semester on writing essays, mostly narrative and description essays. In the second half of the course, students will move on to cause/effect, argument, and opinion essays.

The midterm essay is an opportunity for students to demonstrate their ability to write a coherent essay with relatively few grammatical and rhetorical errors. The essay will be given in class (in a 90-minute class period). The students do not know the topic ahead of time but are allowed to use a bilingual dictionary to look up words or spelling. The curriculum specifies quality of writing over quantity. The teacher will read essays over the weekend and make comments but not give a grade or a score. During the next week, there will be peer conferences with the goal of each student to revise his or her essay, followed by a student–teacher conference after a revision has been turned in.

Scenario 4: Listening/Speaking Final Exam

Children in the fifth grade of a private school in Japan have been taking a 15-week course in oral communication skills (listening and speaking). This is their third year of English courses (they began in the third grade), and by now they are able to comprehend simple English sentences, distinguish many phonemic contrasts, orally produce (repeat) sentences that have been modeled for them, and carry on very rudimentary oral exchanges, mostly using words and phrases they have memorized. Their fluency would be described as very low and their grammatical accuracy is perhaps passable with the minimal amount of language they can handle.

The final exam for the class, according to the prescribed curriculum, consists of (a) listening to an audio program with most of the course's grammatical and phonological elements represented in a variety of stimulus types and responding to written multiple-choice items (the suggested time limit for this listening portion is 20 minutes), followed by (b) a three-minute oral interview, one-on-one, with the teacher. (Because this is a private school, the class size is quite small [15 students], which gives the teacher time to complete oral interviews within the allotted time limit for the final examination.) While students are going, one by one, into the oral interview in a separate room, others are doing Internet-based English activities and games in the school's computer lab. Because this is a final examination, the only anticipated follow-up to the two-part exam is a score report by the teacher, which parents and students will see in a few weeks.

Keep these four assessment situations in mind as you read this chapter. All four will be referred to as we look at the five steps in designing an effective test.

DETERMINING THE PURPOSE OF A TEST

You may think that every test you devise must be a wonderfully innovative instrument that impresses your colleagues and students alike. Not so. First, new and innovative testing formats take a lot of effort to design and a long time to refine through trial and error. Second, traditional testing techniques can, with a little creativity, conform to the spirit of an interactive, communicative language curriculum. Your best course of action as a new teacher is to work within the guidelines of accepted, known, traditional testing techniques. Slowly, with experience, you can attempt bolder designs. In that spirit, let's consider some practical steps in constructing classroom tests.

The first and perhaps most important step in designing any sort of classroom assessment (or in determining the appropriateness of an existing test) is to step back and consider the overall purpose of the exercise that your students are about to perform. The purpose of an assessment is what Bachman and Palmer (1996, pp. 17–19) refer to as **test usefulness** or, very simply put, to what use will you put an assessment? Consider the checklist on the next page for determining purpose and usefulness of an assessment:

✓ **PURPOSE AND USEFULNESS CHECKLIST**

❑ **1.** Do I need to administer a test at this point in my course? If so, what purpose will it serve the students and/or me?

❑ **2.** What is its significance relative to my course?

❑ **3.** Is it simply an expected way to mark the end of a lesson, unit, or period of time?

❑ **4.** How important is it compared to other student performance?

❑ **5.** Do I want to use results to determine if my students have met certain predetermined curricular standards?

❑ **6.** Do I genuinely want students to be recipients of beneficial washback?

❑ **7.** Will I use the results as a means to allocate my own pedagogical efforts in the days or weeks to follow?

❑ **8.** What will its impact be on what I do, and what students do, before and after the test?

Now look back at each of the four assessment scenarios described on pages 54–55 and think about the purpose of each. Before reading on, do some personal brainstorming (see Exercise 1 at the end of this chapter) on just how the eight questions in the checklist will be answered for each scenario.

Reading Quiz. To start your thinking process, let's look at the purpose of the first scenario—the reading quiz. The quiz is designed to be an instructional tool to guide classroom discussion for one classroom period. Its significance is minor but not trivial when viewed against the backdrop of the whole course. Because it is a surprise test and a tool for teaching and self-assessment, the results will justifiably not be recorded, and so one student's performance compared to others is irrelevant. It is entirely formative in nature, with the almost exclusive purpose of providing beneficial washback. Forcing students to think independently about the reading passage allows them to see areas of strength and weakness in their comprehension skills.

Can you now consider the other three scenarios and think about the overall purpose of each one, given the context described and the information given? Your understanding of the purpose of an assessment procedure governs, to a great extent, the next steps you take in identifying clear objectives, designing test specifications, constructing tasks, and determining scoring and reporting criteria.

DESIGNING CLEAR, UNAMBIGUOUS OBJECTIVES

In addition to knowing the purpose of the test you're creating, you need to know as specifically as possible what it is you want to test. Sometimes teachers give tests simply because it's Friday in the third week of the course; after hasty glances at the chapter(s) covered during those three weeks, they dash off some test items so that students will have something to do during the class. This is no way to approach a test. Instead, begin by taking a careful look at everything that you think your students should "know" or be able to "do," based on the material that the students are responsible for. In other words, examine the *objectives* for the unit you are testing.

Remember that every curriculum should have appropriately framed, assessable objectives, that is, objectives that are stated in terms of overt performance by students. Thus an objective that states "Students will learn tag questions" or simply names the grammatical focus of "tag questions" is not testable. You don't know whether students should be able to understand them in spoken or written language, or whether they should be able to produce them orally or in writing. Nor do you know in what context (a conversation? an essay? an academic lecture?) those linguistic forms should be used. Your first task in designing a test, then, is to determine appropriate objectives, stated as explicitly as possible.

Grammar Unit Test. If you're lucky, someone will have already stated objectives clearly in performance terms. If you're less fortunate, you may have to go back through a unit and formulate them yourself. Let's say you find yourself teaching the grammar focus class described in Scenario 2, and the objectives given by the course guide simply specify the following for the unit on verb tenses:

> Students will understand
> and produce the following
> verb tenses in appropriate
> oral and written contexts:
>
> 1. simple present
>   (review from Level 1)
> 2. present continuous
> 3. simple past
> 4. present perfect

Elsewhere in the curriculum, "appropriate contexts" are described as a continuation of the material introduced and practiced in the other two (listening/speaking and reading/writing) classes. So you're left with a sketchy but workable set of objectives on which to base your unit test. You will certainly need to flesh these out in more detail before you can be satisfied that you have clear, assessable objectives.

Where do you begin? In this grammar course, students equally use all four skills as they work with the grammar forms/structures. So to achieve content validity, your objectives should reflect all four modes of performance and sample all four verb tenses. Here is a possible set of objectives for you to work from:

Comprehension:

Students will (in contexts already encountered in the other classes) . . .
recognize oral and written forms of the
1. simple present tense
2. present continuous tense
3. simple past tense
4. present perfect tense

Production:

Students will (in contexts already encountered in the other classes) . . .
correctly produce oral and written forms of the
5. simple present tense
6. present continuous tense
7. simple past tense
8. present perfect tense

Although these objectives may seem a bit overstated, it's usually helpful to articulate all the possible elements of both comprehension and production to give you an instant checklist for your test specifications (see next section). Notice that each objective is stated in terms of the performance elicited and the target linguistic domain. You could improve on these statements by including a list of the verbs that have been covered and a statement about regular and irregular verbs; however, for the moment, we're going to assume that information will go into the test specifications. You may find, in reviewing all the possible objectives of a unit or a course, that you cannot possibly test each one. Deciding which ones to include and exclude is also a matter to take up in your design of test specifications.

We have not explicitly discussed objectives for Scenarios 1, 3, and 4. What would those objectives look like? Consider the brainstorming or discussion you did on the three scenarios. Now see if you can jot down objectives for all three.

DRAWING UP TEST SPECIFICATIONS

Test specifications (specs) for classroom use can be an outline of your test—what it will "look like." Think of your test specs as a blueprint of the test that include the following:

- a description of its content
- item types (methods, such as multiple-choice, cloze, etc.)
- tasks (e.g., written essay, reading a short passage, etc.)
- skills to be included
- how the test will be scored
- how it will be reported to students

For classroom purposes (Davidson & Lynch, 2002), the specs are your guiding plan for designing an instrument that effectively fulfills your desired principles, especially validity.

It's important to note here that for large-scale standardized tests (see Chapter 5) that are intended to be widely distributed and therefore are broadly generalized, test specifications are much more formal and detailed (Spaan, 2006). They are also usually confidential so that the institution that is designing the test can ensure the validity of subsequent forms of a test. Such secrecy is not a part of classroom assessment; in fact, one facet of effectively preparing students for a test is giving them a clear picture of the type of items and tasks they will encounter.

Grammar Unit Test. In the case of Scenario 2 (page 54), the test specifications that you design might comprise the following four sequential steps:

1. a broad outline of how the test will be organized (already specified in the curriculum; see above)
2. which of the eight subskills you will test (if not all)
3. what the various tasks and item types will be
4. how results will be scored, reported to students, and used in a future class (washback)

Those decisions are not easy ones to make. Even though steps 1 and 2 could be fairly easy, 3 and 4 present a genuine challenge. How would you assess oral production of the target linguistic forms? Could you make the tasks practical in terms of the time it would take to evaluate and score items? Would taped student responses to a set of prompts offer a reliable method of elicitation? Or might you, for the sake of practicality, forego oral production in this test and consider previous informal classroom assessment as sufficient performance data? In designing test tasks, can you make them as authentic as possible but still practical within the constraints of this test?

Now with a partner or in a small group, brainstorm some possible appropriate item (task) types for the grammar unit test. You will no doubt experience the challenge of such an undertaking.

Midterm Essay. For now, let's look at Scenario 3 (writing a midterm essay) and see what test specifications we might come up with. The curriculum prescribes an in-class administration of an essay on a "surprise" topic (so that students will not memorize their essay in advance). The specifications for this assessment might look like this:

Midterm Essay Specifications:

1. Provide clear directions.
2. Write a prompt on *either* a narrative *or* a description essay.
3. The prompt must be on a familiar topic that students will, with a reasonable level of confidence, be able to write coherently about.
4. Assign an expectation of a full page, handwritten, and no more than two full pages.
5. Students will be allowed a 90-minute time limit.
6. In the prompt, include evaluation criteria: content, organization, rhetorical discourse, and grammar/mechanics.
7. The final grade is to include four subscores: content, organization, rhetorical discourse, and grammar/mechanics.

The more meticulous you are in specifying details of an assessment procedure, the better off you will ultimately be in providing your students with appropriate opportunities to perform well. Other test specs may look more complex. Suppose you have two or more skills that students will perform, as in the listening/speaking final exam for Japanese fifth graders (Scenario 4). In that case, as described below, test specs will involve several elicitation techniques and a number of categories of student responses. In all cases, specifications are not the actual test items or tasks but rather a description of limitations, boundaries, directions, and other details that you will adhere to. The next step is to design tasks and items that fit the specs.

DEVISING TEST ITEMS

At this point it is important to note that test development is not always a clear, linear process. Ideally, you want to proceed through the six steps outlined in this chapter without having to recycle some of your plans. In reality, test design usually involves a number of "loops" as you discover problems and other shortcomings. With that fair warning, let's look at the midterm essay scenario again and this time more specifically in terms of item design.

Midterm Essay. The single test task described in Scenario 3 (page 54) includes the prompt, directions, and evaluation criteria. This could be one of the easiest kinds of test tasks to create, because only one "item" is involved, student responses are open ended, and evaluation criteria have already been covered well in previous instruction. Let's see what the prompt might look like:

Choose one of the following topics. Write an essay of about three paragraphs on the topic you have chosen. Assume that you are writing this to share with your classmates.

A. Based on the changes and future developments we have read about and discussed in class, invent a possible job of the future. Use your imagination. Write an essay that describes this job.
B. Describe your present job (or profession) or the job of a parent or a friend that you know quite well.

You have 90 minutes to complete your work. You may want to begin with a very quick first draft, an outline, or some freewriting and then write a final draft.

For your final draft, do your best to write a legible, neat essay. However, you will have an opportunity to revise, rewrite, and correct this essay, so don't worry about a few words or phrases or sentences that may be crossed out.

The criteria for evaluation will be
   ✗ Content
   ✗ Organization
   ✗ Rhetorical discourse (coherence, cohesion, appropriateness, etc.)
   ✗ Grammar/mechanics

Given the constraints of the curriculum and the context described for Scenario 3, do you feel that this prompt is effective? Does it adhere to the five principles of practicality, reliability, validity (in various forms), authenticity, and washback potential?

Listening/Speaking Final Exam. Before specifically considering test item types for the listening/speaking final exam for Japanese fifth graders (Scenario 4, pages 54–55), let's look for a moment at the options that are available in designing test items. It's surprising that there are a limited number of modes of eliciting responses (that is, prompting) and of responding on tests of all types and purposes. Consider the options: The test prompt can be oral (student listens) or written (student reads), and the student can respond orally or in writing. It's that simple. Some complexity is added when you realize that the types of prompts in each case vary widely, and within each response mode, of course, there are a number of options, all of which are depicted in Figure 3.1.

Elicitation mode:	Oral *(student listens)*	Written *(student reads)*
	administration directions	administration directions
	sentence(s), question	sentence(s), question
	word, pair of words	word, set of words
	monologue, speech	paragraph
	prerecorded conversation	essay, excerpt
	interactive (live) dialogue	short story, book
Response mode:	**Oral**	**Written**
	repeat	mark multiple-choice option
	read aloud	fill in the blank
	yes / no	spell a word
	short response	define a term (with a phrase)
	describe	short answer (2 to 3 sentences)
	role play	essay
	monologue (speech)	
	interactive dialogue	

Figure 3.1. Elicitation and response modes in test construction

As the above figure indicates, an oral elicitation can be matched with either an oral or a written response and likewise for written elicitations. Granted, not all of the response modes correspond to all of the elicitation modes. For example, it is unlikely that a prompt of a minimal pair ("beat, bit") would be matched with a "yes/no" response, nor would a monologue as a prompt elicit spelling a word as a response. A modicum of intuition will eliminate these nonsequiturs.

In Scenario 4, the fifth-grade English class in Japan, the curriculum dictates a listening section of 20 minutes and a three-minute oral interview. This may be a tall order for a final examination that ostensibly covers a semester's work in oral communication skills, but we'll begin with the course objectives. In shortened form, those objectives are as follows:

Students will orally produce and comprehend:

The following functions and topics:

Simple greetings and good-byes
Simple conversations
Descriptions of self and others (gender, height, clothing, etc.)
Numbers 1 to 100, counting objects, calendars
Colors
Objects in the home and classroom
Family members
Time
Seasons, weather, days of the week, holidays
Clothing, food, sports, and activities
Likes and dislikes

Sentences using the following grammatical forms:

Present and present progressive tenses
Contractions
Negatives
Personal pronouns
Articles *a*, *an*, and *the*; *some* and *any*
Demonstratives *this* and *that*; *these* and *those*
Adjectives to describe people and objects
Possessive adjectives
Yes/no and *wh-* questions; correct responses
Regular and irregular plural nouns
Modal *can* (as in "Yes, I can" and "No, I can't")
Prepositions of location

Words and/or sentences using the following phonological forms:

Syllable stress
Rising and falling intonation
Vowel contrasts in minimal pairs (e.g., *sheep* and *ship*)
Consonant contrasts (e.g., /b/ and /v/; /r/ and /l/

As you design your final exam, it's important to consider the age of the students. Fifth graders are approximately 10 years old, and at this age explicit form focus is appropriately not a part of the curriculum. So your objectives, as stated on the previous page, imply the implicit use of the forms indicated but not explicit identification. A great deal of the instruction throughout the year has consisted of auditory input from Internet-based activities, DVDs, and a CD supplied with the textbook for the course. Activities range from games to repetition drills, and most oral production is rehearsed.

Listening Comprehension Section. Because of the constraints of your curriculum, the listening part of the final exam must take no more than 20 minutes, as already noted. The students have become accustomed to taking multiple-choice tests and quizzes in their classwork. So for reasons of practicality and impact, you decide to design a multiple-choice listening comprehension test with three different test tasks. Your school has the latest computer technology available so you can make a good quality audio recording using your voice and that of one other person (a colleague in the school who is native-speaking Japanese but has excellent oral skills in English). Here's the format you decide to use:

Listening comprehension format
Test method: Audio prompts, multiple-choice response
Specification: Each item uses a familiar, rehearsed context/topic.

Part 1 Minimal pairs in words and sentences (10 items: 5 minutes)
Part 2 Vocabulary comprehension of objects, clothing, and colors
　　　　(10 items: 7 minutes)
Part 3 A mix of items testing negatives, contractions, and prepositions of
　　　　location (10 items: 8 minutes)

Scoring: Record the number of correct responses out of 30.

This informal, classroom-oriented outline gives you an indication of

- the implied elicitation and response formats for items
- the objectives you will cover
- the number of items in each section
- the time to be allocated for each

Notice that a number of the possible listening objectives are not directly tested. This decision may be based on the time you devoted to these objectives, the importance you place on each objective, and of course the finite number of minutes available to administer the test. Is this an appropriate decision?

The final item in your test outline specifies scoring. For the listening section, scoring is simple. For the oral interview, it becomes considerably more complex, as we shall see. We'll look again at scoring, grading, and feedback later in this chapter and then much more comprehensively in Chapter 12.

What will those multiple-choice listening comprehension items look like? How will you design appropriate stems (see pages 68–70 for a description of multiple-choice question design), each with a clear, correct response and multiple distractors? Can you ensure enough authenticity and also provide some variety for your students? We'll take up these questions in the next main section of this chapter. Meanwhile, we turn our attention to the oral production section.

Oral Production Section. Your curriculum allows you to design your own oral interview protocol, and so you draft questions to conform to the accepted pattern of oral interviews (see Chapter 8 for information on constructing oral interviews). You have decided to conduct the interviews one-on-one because you have enough time with a small class to do so. You begin and end with nonscored items (warm-up and wind-down) designed to set students at ease and then sandwich between them items intended to test the objectives (*level check*) and a little beyond (*probe*).

Because these are 10-year-old children, you have decided, on the advice of other teachers, to make use of a file of pictures for stimuli. They have responded well to pictures in previous one-on-one situations. Here is the outline you decide to follow:

Oral interview format

A. Warm-up: greetings and setting the child at ease
B. Level-check questions
 1. Identifying objects, singular and plural
 2. Present progressive tense
 3. Adjectives *(big, little)*
C. Probe questions
 1. Talk about this picture.
 2. Ask me a question.
D. Wind-down: comments and reassurance

You're now ready to draft actual test items—with matching pictures—to elicit responses. Here's what you come up with, as a first draft:

Part A

Hi _____ (name). *How are you?*
(Give a compliment to the child. They have practiced giving compliments in class.)
(Briefly explain, in Japanese, the procedure for the interview. Reassure the child.)

Part B-1

Okay, in this picture, what is this? (point to a brown dog)
What color is it?
(The next picture shows two dogs.) *Now there are two. There are two* _____.
(Child knows the routine, to say "dogs.")
(Repeat this procedure with three other colored objects.)

Part B-2

This is a picture of a boy. (The picture shows a boy walking.) *What is the boy doing?*
(Repeat this procedure with three other pictures depicting action.)

Part B-3

Okay, what are these? (Point to two apples, one big and one small.) *Are they the same size?* (They have practiced simple comparisons.)
(Repeat this procedure with three other pictures of familiar fruits.)

Part C-1

(Show the child a picture of a family eating a meal at home.)
Okay, _____, *talk about this picture.*
(Repeat with a picture of kids playing in a park.)

Part C-2

Good job! Now can you ask me a question?
(This routine has been practiced in class many times.)

Part D

Thank you, _____. *You did a good (excellent, nice) job.* In Japanese: *You can go back to the computer lab now and play games on the computer.*

As you continue to put yourself in the place of the teacher in this school in Japan, are there any changes you would make to your protocol for the oral interview?

The final step in the process is to devise a method of scoring. You need to make this as simple and straightforward as possible, so let's say you decide to give two scores for each separate question, one for pronunciation and one for grammar.

Because the course has focused a good deal on grammatical and phonological form, and because students expect such an assessment, you justify the exclusion of such elements as content and social skills. Here's what you come up with:

- virtually perfect pronunciation/grammar: 2
- some error(s) in the response: 1
- wrong or no response: 0

You prepare a card for each student with your list of questions. Beside each question are the numbers 2, 1, and 0. You circle the numbers as the interview proceeds. When all interviews are complete, you can add up the numbers for a total score. Because it's a final examination and the school's policy doesn't offer a means to give more than a score report to the child (and the parents), your numerical scores appear to be sufficient.

DESIGNING MULTIPLE-CHOICE ITEMS

Soon we'll return to the specific task of designing the multiple-choice listening comprehension test for the Japanese fifth graders, but we first need to turn our attention to some important principles and tips for designing **multiple-choice tests**. Multiple-choice items, which may on the surface appear to be simple items to construct, are actually very difficult to design correctly. Hughes (2003, pp. 76–78) cautions against a number of weaknesses of multiple-choice items:

- The technique tests only recognition knowledge.
- Guessing may have a considerable effect on test scores.
- The technique severely restricts what can be tested.
- It is very difficult to write successful items.
- Beneficial washback may be minimal.
- Cheating may be facilitated.

The two principles that stand out in support of multiple-choice formats are, of course, practicality and reliability. With their predetermined correct responses and time-saving scoring procedures, multiple-choice items offer overworked teachers the tempting possibility of an easy and consistent process of scoring and grading. But is the preparation phase worth the effort? Sometimes it is, but you might spend even more time designing such items than you save in grading the test. Of course, if your objective is to design a large-scale standardized test for repeated administrations, then a multiple-choice format does indeed become viable.

As you face the task of designing the listening comprehension section of the fifth-grade English exam, let's first consider some important terminology.

1. Multiple-choice items are all **receptive**, or **selective response**, items in that the test-taker chooses from a set of responses (commonly called a **supply** type of response) rather than creating a response. Other receptive item types include true/false questions and matching lists. (In the discussion here, the guidelines apply primarily to multiple-choice item types and not necessarily to other receptive types.)
2. Every multiple-choice item has a **stem** (the "body" of the item that presents a stimulus) and several (usually between three and five) **options** or **alternatives** to choose from.
3. One of those options, the **key**, is the correct response, whereas the others serve as **distractors**.

Because there will be occasions when multiple-choice items are appropriate, consider the following four guidelines for designing multiple-choice items for both classroom-based and large-scale situations (adapted from Gronlund, 1998, pp. 60–75, and J. D. Brown, 2005, pp. 48–50).

1. Design each item to measure a single objective.

Consider the following item from a secondary school class in English at the intermediate level. The objective is *wh-* questions:

Test-takers hear: Where did George go after the party last night?
Test-takers read: A. Yes, he did.
    B. because he was tired
    C. to Elaine's place for another party
    D. around eleven o'clock

Distractor A is designed to ascertain that the student knows the difference between an answer to a *wh-* question and a yes/no question. Distractors B and D, as well as the key item, C, test comprehension of the meaning of *where* as opposed to *why* and *when.* The objective has been directly addressed.

On the other hand, here is an item that was designed to test recognition of the correct word order of indirect questions:

Excuse me, do you know _____ ?

  A. where is the post office
  B. where the post office is
  C. where post office is

Distractor A is designed to lure students who don't know how to frame indirect questions and therefore serves as an efficient distractor. But what does distractor C actually measure? In fact, the missing definite article (*the*) is what J. D. Brown (2005) calls an "unintentional clue" (p. 48)—a flaw that could cause the test-taker to eliminate C automatically. In the process, no assessment has been made of indirect questions in this distractor. Can you think of a better distractor for C that would focus more clearly on the objective?

2. State both stem and options as simply and directly as possible.

We're sometimes tempted to make multiple-choice items too wordy. A good rule of thumb is to get directly to the point. Here's a negative example:

My eyesight has really been deteriorating lately. I wonder if I need glasses. I think I'd better go to the _____ to have my eyes checked.

  A. pediatrician
  B. dermatologist
  C. optometrist

You might argue that the first two sentences of this item give it some authenticity and accomplish a bit of schema setting. But if you simply want a student to identify the type of medical professional that deals with eyesight issues, those sentences are superfluous. Moreover, by lengthening the stem, you have introduced a potentially confounding lexical item, *deteriorate,* that could distract the student unnecessarily.

Another rule of succinctness is to remove needless redundancy from your options. In the following item, "which were" is repeated in all three options. It should be placed in the stem to keep the item as succinct as possible.

We went to visit the temples, _____ fascinating.

  A. which were beautiful
  B. which were especially
  C. which were holy

---

3. Make certain that the intended answer is clearly the only correct one.

In the test item described earlier, which turned out to be suitable, a draft of the item appeared as follows:

Test-takers hear: Where did George go after the party last night?
Test-takers read: A. Yes, he did.
                    B. because he was tired
                    C. to Elaine's place for another party
                    D. He went home around eleven o'clock.

A quick consideration of distractor D reveals that it is a plausible answer (because of the mention of "home"), along with the intended key, C. Eliminating unintended possible answers is often the most difficult problem of designing multiple-choice items. With only a minimum of context in each stem, a wide variety of responses may be perceived as correct.

4. (Optional) Use item indices to accept, discard, or revise items.

Many classroom-based multiple-choice items will pass muster on the basis of the first three points here in our discussion. If you're mathematically inclined and want to take one further—but somewhat painstaking—step, you might want to try using item indices to further refine your item design. The appropriate selection and arrangement of suitable multiple-choice items on a test can best be accomplished by measuring items against three indices: item facility (or item difficulty), item discrimination (sometimes called item differentiation), and distractor analysis. Although measuring these factors on classroom tests would be useful, you probably will have neither the time nor the expertise to do this for every classroom test you create, especially one-time tests. However, they are a must for standardized norm-referenced tests that are designed to be administered a number of times and/or administered in multiple forms.

1. ***Item facility*** (IF) is the extent to which an item is easy or difficult for the proposed group of test-takers. You may wonder why that is important if in your estimation the item achieves validity. The answer is that an item that is too easy (say 99 percent of respondents get it right) or too difficult (99 percent get it wrong) really does nothing to separate high-ability and low-ability test-takers. It is not really performing much "work" for you on a test.

IF simply reflects the percentage of students answering the item correctly. The formula looks like this:

$$\text{IF} = \frac{\text{\# of students answering the item correctly}}{\text{Total \# of students responding to that item}}$$

For example, if you have an item on which 13 out of 20 students respond correctly, your IF index is 13 divided by 20 or .65 (65%). There is no absolute IF value that must be met to determine if an item should be included in the test as is, modified, or thrown out, but appropriate test items will generally have IFs that range between .15 and .85. Two good reasons for occasionally including a very easy item (.85 or higher) are to build in some affective feelings of "success" among lower-ability students and to serve as warm-up items. Very difficult items can provide a challenge to the highest-ability students.

2. *Item discrimination* (ID) is the extent to which an item differentiates between high- and low-ability test-takers. An item on which high-ability students (who did well on the test) and low-ability students (who did not) score equally well would have poor ID because it did not discriminate between the two groups. Conversely, an item that garners correct responses from most of the high-ability group and incorrect responses from most of the low-ability group has good discrimination power.

Suppose your class of 30 students has taken a test. Once you have calculated final scores for all 30 students, divide them roughly into thirds—that is, create three rank-ordered ability groups including the top 10 scores, the middle 10, and the lowest 10. To find out which of your 50 or so test items were most "powerful" in discriminating between high and low ability, eliminate the middle group, leaving two groups with results that might look something like this on a particular item:

Item 23	No. Correct	No. Incorrect
High-ability students (top 10)	7	3
Low-ability students (bottom 10)	2	8

Using the ID formula ($7 - 2 = 5 \div 10 = .50$), you would find that this item has an ID of .50, or a moderate level.

The formula for calculating ID is

$$\text{ID} = \frac{\text{High group no. correct} - \text{low group no. correct}}{1/2 \times \text{total of your two comparison groups}} = \frac{7 - 2}{1/2 \times 20} = \frac{5}{10} = .50$$

The result of this example item tells you that the item has a moderate level of ID. High discriminating power would approach a perfect 1.0, and no discriminating power at all would be zero. In most cases, you would want to discard an item that scored near zero. As with IF, no absolute rule governs the establishment of acceptable and unacceptable ID indices.

One clear, practical use for ID indices is to select items from a test bank that includes more items than you need. You might decide to discard or improve some items with lower ID because you know they won't be as powerful an indicator of success on your test.

For most teachers who are using multiple-choice items to create a classroom-based unit test, juggling IF and ID indices is more a matter of intuition and "art" than a science. Your best-calculated hunches may provide sufficient support for retaining, revising, and discarding proposed items. But if you are constructing a large-scale test, or one that will be administered multiple times, these indices are important factors in creating test forms that are comparable in difficulty. By engaging in a sophisticated procedure using what is called **item response theory** (IRT), professional test designers can produce test forms whose **equated** test scores are reliable measures of performance. (For more information on IRT, see Bachman, 1990, pp. 202–209.)

3. *Distractor efficiency* is one more important measure of a multiple-choice item's value in a test and one that is related to item discrimination. The efficiency of distractors is the extent to which (a) the distractors "lure" a sufficient number of test-takers, especially lower-ability ones, and (b) those responses are somewhat evenly distributed across all distractors. Those of you who have a fear of mathematical formulas will be happy to hear that there is no formula for calculating distractor efficiency and that an inspection of a distribution of responses will usually yield the information you need.

Consider the following. The same item used in the ID example (item 23) is a multiple-choice item with five choices, and responses across upper- and lower-ability students are distributed as follows:

Choices	A	B	C*	D	E
High-ability students (10)	0	1	7	0	2
Low-ability students (10)	3	5	2	0	0
*Note: **C** is the correct response.					

No mathematical formula is needed to tell you that this item successfully attracts seven of the ten high-ability students toward the correct response, whereas only two of the low-ability students get this one right. As shown above, its ID is .50, which is acceptable, but the item might be improved in two ways: (a) Distractor D doesn't fool anyone. No one picked it, and therefore it probably has no utility. A revision might provide a distractor that actually attracts a response or two; (b) distractor E attracts more responses (two) from the high-ability group than the low-ability group (zero). Why are good students choosing this one? Perhaps it includes a subtle reference that entices the high group but is "over the head" of the low group, and therefore the latter students don't even consider it.

The other two distractors (A and B) seem to be fulfilling their function of attracting some attention from lower-ability students.

Listening/Speaking Final Exam. Now, armed with that information, can you design some items for the listening comprehension test for the Japanese fifth graders? We'll give you a start here toward the process. Looking back at page 54, where the format was presented, you will be reminded of the three parts of the test. In Part 1, minimal pairs, your objectives are to assess comprehension of some of the phonemic contrasts that students have focused on, which gives you a great opportunity to design binary-choice items. Further, because your students are 10-year-olds, your job is facilitated by using pictures as cues. Your plan for the first five items is to present two pictures for every item, each representing a minimal pair, and students respond by choosing the correct picture matching the audio stimulus. So, for example, two items look like this:

Test-takers see:
1. A.   B.

2. A.   B.

Test-takers hear:
   1. I see a ship.
   2. The glass is nice.

Then, because students have also been reading English words and can recognize them well, the last five items use verbal cues, as follows:

Test-takers see:
    5. A. bat   B. mat
    6. A. 13   B. 30

Test-takers hear:
    5. There's a bat on the floor.
    6. *Voice 1:* How old is she? *Voice 2:* She's thirty.

For Part 2, let's say you again choose to use picture-cued items, this time for six items. Pictures allow you to depict objects easily and unambiguously. You have chosen to have four multiple-choice options for each item, so two of those items look like this:

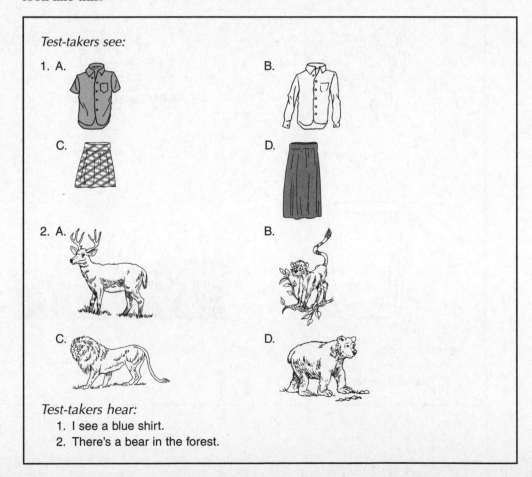

Test-takers see:
1. A.   B.
    C.   D.

2. A.   B.
    C.   D.

Test-takers hear:
    1. I see a blue shirt.
    2. There's a bear in the forest.

For the last four items, you choose to have students do a matching exercise, to test knowledge of objects in the classroom. The item, worth four points for all four objects, looks like this:

Test-takers see:

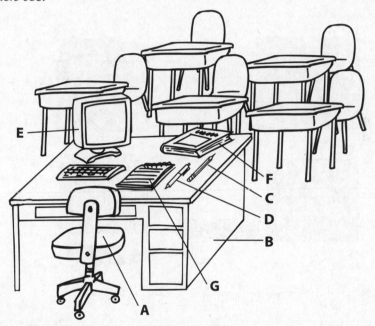

Example: A B Ⓒ D E F G
7. A B C D E F G
8. A B C D E F G
9. A B C D E F G
10. A B C D E F G

Test-takers hear:

In Japanese: Match the correct letters in the picture that you see. For example, when you hear a word, circle the correct <u>letter</u> that matches the word. An example has been done for you.

Example: pencil

The letter "C" has been circled because the letter "C" points to the pencil.

Now listen.
7. desk
8. book
9. computer
10. chair

For Part 3, in which you are to test negatives, contractions, and prepositions of location, once again you have decided to rely on pictures, given the age of your test-takers and what they are accustomed to responding to in your classroom activities. Here's what two of those items look like:

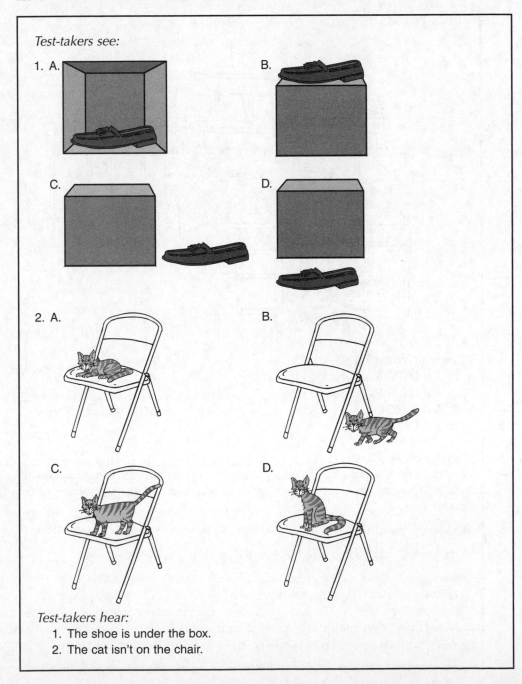

Test-takers see:

1. A.   B.

   C.   D.

2. A.   B.

   C.   D.

Test-takers hear:
   1. The shoe is under the box.
   2. The cat isn't on the chair.

As you can see, these items are quite traditional. The format lends itself to practicality and reliability, paving the way to quick, consistent scoring. The items are all very clearly formulated, within all the expected objectives of the course, and students are accustomed to such testing techniques, so various aspects of validity are accounted for. You might self-critically admit that the format of some of the items is contrived, thus lowering the level of authenticity. But your students are in quite a traditional educational system in which they will need to function in traditional test formats, so these items may help them, in a "friendly" way, to handle such assessments in the future. No washback is built into the system, so you have to be satisfied with what you hope was ample washback in the 15 weeks of classroom activity that led up to this day.

As you look over the items, are there some that need to be revised before you finalize them? In revising your draft, ask yourself the following questions:

Suggestions for revising your test:

1. Are the directions to each section absolutely clear?
2. Is there an example item for each section? If not, are the directions and format so familiar to students that they will clearly understand the tasks they are being asked to perform?
3. Does each item measure a specified objective?
4. Is there a single correct answer for each question?
5. Is each item stated in clear, simple language?
6. Does each multiple-choice item have appropriate distractors; that is, are the wrong items clearly wrong and yet sufficiently "alluring" that they aren't ridiculously easy?
7. Is the difficulty of each item appropriate for your students?
8. Is the language of each item sufficiently authentic?
9. Is there a balance between easy and difficult items?
10. Do the sum of the items and the test as a whole adequately reflect the learning objectives?

Ideally, you would try out all your tests on a sample of students not in your class before actually administering the tests, but in our daily classroom teaching, such a tryout phase is almost impossible. Alternatively, you could enlist the aid of a colleague to look over your test or, better yet, "take" the test as a trial run. You must do what you can to bring to your students an instrument that is, to the best of your ability, practical and reliable.

In the final revision of your test, imagine that you're a student taking the test. Go through each set of directions and all items slowly and deliberately. Time yourself. (Often we underestimate the time students need to complete a test.) If the test should be shortened or lengthened, make the necessary adjustments. Make sure your test is neat and uncluttered on the page and that art is clear and unambiguous, reflecting all the care and precision you have put into its construction. If there is an audio component, as there is in the listening test for Japanese fifth graders, make sure that the script is clear, that your voice and any other voices are clear, and that the audio equipment is in working order before starting the test.

ADMINISTERING THE TEST

The moment has arrived. You have designed your test based on your carefully considered purposes, objectives, and specs. Could anything now go awry in these best-laid plans? Of course, you know the answer is yes. So consider some of the measures you can take to ensure that the actual administration of the test accomplishes everything you want it to. Here's a list of pointers:

Pre-test considerations (the day before the in-class essay):

1. Provide appropriate pre-test information on
    a. the conditions for the test (time limits, no portable electronics, breaks, etc.)
    b. materials that students should bring with them
    c. the kinds of items (item types) that will be on the test
    d. suggestions of strategies for optimal performance
    e. evaluation criteria (rubrics, show benchmark samples)
2. Offer a review of components of narrative and description essays
3. Give students a chance to ask any questions, and provide responses

Test administration details:

4. Arrive early and see to it that the classroom conditions (lighting, temperature, a clock that all can see clearly, furniture arrangement, etc.) are conducive.
5. If audio or video or other technology is needed for administration, try everything out in advance.
6. Have extra paper, writing instruments, or other response materials on hand.
7. Start on time.
8. Distribute the test itself.
9. Remain quietly seated at the teacher's desk, available for questions from students as they proceed.
10. For a timed test, warn students when time is about to run out, and encourage their completion of their work.

This is not an exhaustive list, as it does not cover all possible testing situations, but it should serve as a starting point for you as you attempt to cover all the details involved in an administration.

SCORING, GRADING, AND GIVING FEEDBACK

Scoring

As you design a classroom test, you must consider how the test will be scored and graded. Your scoring plan reflects the relative weight that you place on each section and on the items in each section. In the four scenarios that we have been discussing in this chapter, scoring (in mathematical terms) is a factor in only two of them, the grammar unit test and the final listening/speaking examination for Japanese fifth graders. Let's look at each.

The grammar test has three sections, each with a number of scorable items. Logically, then, you could place equal weight on each section and mathematically calculate a score. However, this may not reflect your own conception of the importance of each task type, and so one decision you might make is to place more weight on, perhaps, the grammar editing section. Your argument might simply be that you feel those tasks represent more general or integrative language ability and therefore are deserving of greater weight.

The listening/speaking final exam for Japanese fifth graders presents a potentially complex challenge, because school policy requires one grade for the final examination to be reported for each student. It's your job to determine the relative weight of the listening section and the oral interview. You could argue that the oral interview involves both comprehension and production and therefore give it more weight, or you might simply consider them equal components. To make a final decision on this issue, you would need to know more about the particular context than has been described here.

As a classroom teacher, after administering a test once, you may decide to revise your scoring plan for the course the next time you teach it. At that point you'll have valuable information about how easy or difficult a test was, about whether the time limit was reasonable, about your students' affective reaction to it, and about their general performance. Finally, you'll have an intuitive judgment about whether a test correctly assessed your students. Take note of these impressions, even though they are not empirical data, and use them for revising a test in another term.

Grading

Your first thought might be that assigning grades to student performance on a test will be easy: Just give an A for 90 to100 percent, a B for 80 to 89 percent, and so on. Not so fast! Grading is such a thorny issue that all of Chapter 12 is devoted to the topic. How you assign letter grades to this test is a product of

- the country, culture, and context of the English classroom
- institutional expectations (most of them unwritten)

(continued)

- explicit and implicit definitions of grades that you have set forth
- the relationship you have established with this class
- student expectations that have been engendered in previous tests and quizzes in the class

For the time being, then, we will set aside issues that deal with grading the four scenarios in particular in favor of the comprehensive treatment of grading in Chapter 12.

Giving Feedback

A section on scoring and grading would not be complete without some consideration of the forms in which you can offer feedback to your students—feedback that you want to become *beneficial washback.* Consider just a few of the many possible manifestations of feedback associated with tests (this is not an exhaustive list):

In general, scoring/grading for a test:

a. a letter grade
b. a total score
c. subscores (e.g., of separate skills or sections of a test)

For responses to listening and reading items:

a. indication of correct/incorrect responses
b. diagnostic set of scores (e.g., scores on certain grammatical categories)
c. checklist of areas needing work and strategic options

For oral production tests:

a. scores for each element being rated
b. checklist of areas needing work and strategic options
c. oral feedback after performance
d. post-interview conference to go over the results

On written essays:

a. scores for each element being rated
b. checklist of areas needing work and suggested strategies/techniques for improving writing
c. marginal and end-of-essay comments, suggestions
d. post-test conference to go over work

Additional/alternative feedback for a test:

a. on all or selected parts of a test, peer conferences on results
b. whole-class discussion of results of the test
c. individual conferences with each student to review a complete test
d. self-assessment in various manifestations

In the four example scenarios that we have been referring to in this chapter, there are a multitude of options for giving feedback:

Reading Quiz. The primary if not exclusive purpose of the reading quiz was to prompt self-assessment and class discussion. With no scoring or grading, feedback was to some degree self-induced through the knowledge of what questions one got right or wrong, but more extensively in the form of whole-class discussion of the reading passage.

Grammar Unit Test. The most salient form of feedback is in a total score and subscores, but perhaps the most useful feedback could come in the form of diagnostic scores, a checklist of areas needing work, and class discussion of the results of the test.

Midterm Essay. All the types of feedback listed are feasible and potentially useful, but perhaps the kind of feedback that would most contribute to beneficial washback would be the subsequent peer conferences and individual conferences between student and teacher.

Listening/Speaking Final Exam. Eventually the children in this class will receive a letter grade for the course, which may include scores and subscores of the final examination, with little else possible within the system. One might venture to say that the teacher could give some minimal oral feedback after the oral interview.

In this chapter, guidelines and tools were provided to enable you to address the five questions posed at the outset: (a) how to determine the purpose of the test, (b) how to state objectives, (c) how to design test specifications, (d) how to design or select test tasks, including evaluating those tasks with item indices, and (e) how to begin to address scoring and grading. This five-part template, shown in Figure 3.2, can serve as a pattern as you design classroom tests.

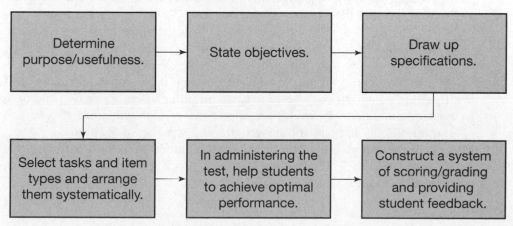

Figure 3.2. Steps to designing an effective test

In the next two chapters (Chapters 4 and 5), you will explore the extent to which many of these principles and guidelines apply to standards-based (and standardized) large-scale testing. You will then consider an array of possibilities of what has come to be called "alternative" assessment (Chapter 6), only because portfolios, conferences, journals, and self- and peer-assessments are not always comfortably categorized among more traditional forms of assessment. Subsequent chapters (7 through 10) will lead you through a wide selection of test tasks in the separate skills of listening, speaking, reading, and writing, as well as provide a sense of how testing for form-focused objectives fits into the picture (Chapter 11). Finally, in Chapter 12 you will take a long, hard look at the dilemmas of grading students.

EXERCISES

[Note: **(I)** Individual work; **(G)** Group or pair work; **(C)** Whole-class discussion.]

1. **(G)** The first issue discussed in this chapter was determining the purpose of a proposed test, and a checklist was offered. In small groups, have one or two members share an experience they had either taking or giving a test, then systematically discuss the probable answers to each item on the checklist. The group may be able to help solve certain problems or dilemmas that came up. Report back to the class any notable surprises or questions that were unresolved.

2. **(G)** Look again at the discussion of objectives (pages 56–58). You will note that we have not explicitly discussed objectives for Scenarios 1, 3, and 4. What would those objectives look like? With a partner or in a small group, see if you can jot down objectives for all three scenarios. Share your thoughts with the rest of the class.

3. **(I/C)** Figure 3.1 depicts various modes of elicitation and response. Are there other modes of elicitation and response that could be included in such a chart? Justify your additions with an example of each.

4. **(G)** With a partner or in a small group, look at the items in each part of the listening comprehension test for Japanese fifth graders (page 64) and design several more items for each part. Share your results with another pair (as a group of four) and talk about strengths and weaknesses of items.

5. **(G)** In the oral interview for Japanese fifth graders discussed earlier in this chapter (pages 65–67), can you justify the decisions made? Would you suggest any changes? Discuss with a partner.

6. **(G)** This exercise could be a challenge, especially those who have never designed test specifications before, so plenty of time and assistance may be necessary. Look at the following nine objectives from a low-intermediate integrated-skills course. In four different groups, draft a set of test specs and sample test items for the objectives your group has been assigned. Report your findings to the rest of the class.

Form-focused objectives (listening and speaking)

Students will
1. recognize and produce tag questions, with the correct grammatical form and final intonation pattern, in simple social conversations
2. recognize and produce *wh-* information questions with correct final intonation pattern

Communication skills (speaking)
Students will
3. state completed actions and events in a social conversation
4. ask for confirmation in a social conversation
5. give opinions about an event in a social conversation
6. produce language with contextually appropriate intonation, stress, and rhythm

Reading skills (simple essay or story)
Students will
7. recognize irregular past tense of selected verbs in a story or essay

Writing skills (simple essay or story)
Students will
8. write a one-paragraph story about a simple event in the past
9. use conjunctions *so* and *because* in a statement of opinion

---

7. **(G)** Select a language class in your immediate environment for the following project: In small groups, design an achievement test for a reasonably short segment of the course (perhaps a lesson or unit for which there is no current test or for which the present test is inadequate). Follow the guidelines in this chapter for developing an assessment procedure. When it is completed, present your assessment project to the rest of the class.
8. **(G)** If possible, locate an existing, recently used standardized multiple-choice test for which there is accessible data on student performance. Calculate the item facility (IF) and item discrimination (ID) index for selected items. If there are no data for an existing test, select some items on the test and analyze the structure of those items in a distractor analysis to determine if they have (a) any bad distractors, (b) any bad stems, or (c) more than one potentially correct answer.

9. **(I/C)** On page 80, ten different options are listed for giving feedback to students on assessments. Review the practicality of each and determine the extent to which practicality (principally, more time expended) is justifiably sacrificed in order to offer better washback to learners.

FOR YOUR FURTHER READING

Bachman, Lyle F., & Palmer, Adrian S. (1996). *Language testing in practice*. New York: Oxford University Press.

Bachman and Palmer's book remains a standard in the field of language assessment. More practically oriented than Bachman's (1990) seminal theoretical exposition on language testing, this one is aimed at providing a comprehensive set of tools for the development of language tests. It's difficult reading for the beginning level graduate student or novice teacher, but others will appreciate its thoroughness, theoretical soundness, and practical examples.

Gronlund, Norman E., & Waugh, C. Keith. (2008). *Assessment of student achievement* (9th ed.). Boston: Allyn & Bacon.

This widely used general manual of testing across educational subject matter provides useful information for language assessment. In particular, Chapters 5, 6, 7, and 8 describe detailed steps for designing tests and writing multiple-choice, true/false, and short-answer items.

Brown, James Dean. (2005). *Testing in language programs* (2nd ed.). New York: McGraw-Hill.

Chapters 3 and 4 of this language-testing manual offer some further information on developing tests and test items, including formulas for calculating item facility and item discrimination.

CHAPTER 4

STANDARDS-BASED

ASSESSMENT

OBJECTIVES: After reading this chapter, you will be able to

- understand the crucial role of standards in educational instruction and assessment, especially in standardized testing
- examine a set of standards for a specified age, level, and context and apply them to contexts of your own
- analyze the purpose, advantages, and disadvantages of standards-based assessment

- apply principles of standardization to the construction of teacher-based standards
- appreciate the two-edged sword of large-scale standards-based testing—its social, political, and ideological consequences
- be prepared to take action in your own teaching and assessing to ensure fairness and openness for your students

Throughout history, people have been tested to prove their capabilities or qualifications. Some of the earliest formal examinations or tests have been traced back almost 2,000 years to the Han Dynasty in China where they were used to select the highest officials in the country (Cheng, 2008). Even earlier, in the Bible (Judges 12:5–6), we have a recorded instance of the use of the so-called "shibboleth test," by means of which two ethnically and linguistically different groups of people were distinguished. When an Ephraimite was ordered to pronounce the word "shibboleth," his language caused him to say "sibboleth," with an /s/, as opposed to the Gileadites' pronunciation that used a /sh/. The consequences were dire: Ephraimites were thus exposed and killed. In another example, before World War II, the Australian government used language tests as a method to keep out immigrants from other countries (T. McNamara, 2000). The government officer could select any language for the dictation test that the immigrant had to take.

Today, we arc all still deeply affected by tests and examinations, especially high-stakes standardized tests. For almost a century, schools, universities, businesses, and governments have looked to standardized measures for economical, reliable, and valid assessments of those who would enter, continue in, or exit their institutions. Proponents of these large-scale instruments make strong claims for their usefulness when great numbers of people must be measured quickly and effectively. Those claims are well supported by reams of research data that comprise construct validations of their efficacy and the specification of **standards** or

benchmarks that are to be incorporated into assessment instruments. We have become a world that abides by the results of standardized tests as if they were sacrosanct, having been blessed by research findings and institutional standards.

In this chapter, we look at just what those standards are that underlie many large-scale standardized tests, where they come from, and whether their validity is sound. Our purpose is to raise your awareness of **standards-based assessment**— measures that are used to evaluate student academic achievement and show that students have reached certain **performance levels** or **standards**. With this backdrop, we will then turn, in Chapter 5, to the issues surrounding the **standardized tests** that such standards are intended to support.

THE ROLE OF STANDARDS IN STANDARDIZED TESTS

Ask non-language specialists what a standardized test is and they are likely to tell you it's a multiple-choice test, and then they will give you an example, such as the SAT or GRE. By now you know that this is not a complete answer. A **standardized test,** among other things, presupposes certain *standard* objectives or performance levels—now better known as **standards** (and also known as **benchmarks**)—that are held constant across one form of a test to another. The standards that underlie standardized tests are usually a set of carefully defined competencies that apply to a course, a curriculum, a year-long program, or even multiple-year objectives for, say, a K–12 program or secondary school graduation criteria. **Standards-based assessment** refers to procedures that have been specifically designed to test such competencies.

Where do these standards come from? Who designs them and how are they incorporated into assessment instruments? The past 30 years have seen a mushrooming of efforts on the part of educational leaders worldwide to base the plethora of school-administered standardized tests on clearly specified criteria within each content area being measured. For example, most departments of education at the state level in the United States have now specified the appropriate standards (that is, criteria or objectives) for each grade level (kindergarten to grade 12) and each content area (math, language, sciences, arts).

The construction of such standards makes possible a concordance between standardized test specifications and the goals and objectives of educational programs. Educational reform goals such as the implementation of standards are efforts to improve education and raise the achievement of all students. By carefully examining existing curricular goals, conducting needs assessments among students, and designing appropriate assessments of those standards, educators have sought to pinpoint desired educational outcomes for students. The intent is for these standards to serve as guidelines for curriculum, assessment, and instructional design that corresponds to what students should know and be able to do as they progress through school, thus enhancing the teacher's knowledge of student achievement and goals.

STANDARDS-BASED EDUCATION

A number of countries have implemented standards-based education, according to a report published in 1993 by the National Education Standards and Improvement Council. For instance, China's standards are set for the entire country and for all levels of the school system by the State Education Commission in Beijing. In England, standards-setting was considered the responsibility of local schools, but in 1988, the Education Reform Act mandated and outlined the process for establishing a national curriculum. Similarly, Japan has created a system of national standards through their Ministry of Education's official curriculum (www.mext.go.jp/english/) which sets standards for the content of instruction in schools and then administers large-scale examinations to test attainment of those standards (Akiyama, 2004).

In many countries, standards are developed specifically for language learning. For example, a goal for making foreign language instruction more communicative in Europe is presented in the formulation of a set of standards known as the Common European Framework of Reference (CEFR) for Languages (Council of Europe, 2001; www.coe.int). Initially, these standards were for transferring language proficiency credentials across national borders in Europe so that recognition could be given to those who need to show language proficiency, such as immigrant workers and professionals. Today CEFR policy goals are well established in European education at all levels. Educational systems must now reflect the standards in both curriculum and assessments and must report to supporting agencies the achievement of students, thereby adding the element of accountability. Another European agency that promotes standards is the European Association for Language Testing and Assessment (www.ealta.eu.org).

In the United States, one particular challenge in constructing standards over the past couple of decades has been in language arts education, with its millions of nonnative users of English. English as a second language (ESL), also known as English for speakers of other languages (ESOL), English language learners (ELLs), and English language development (ELD), have become household terms for elementary and secondary school teachers. The standards movement in the United States has placed a strong emphasis on educational equity. Not only are standards intended to make educational expectations clear and measurable, they also set high expectations for all students—including students who are second language users.

Although the number of schoolchildren from linguistically and culturally diverse backgrounds enrolled in U.S. schools has grown markedly, English as a second language was for many years not a federally designated content area for standards development. To ensure that ELLs would have access to effective educational programs and the opportunity to reach high standards, the Teachers of English to Speakers of Other Languages (TESOL) organization developed ESL standards for education (Gottlieb, Carnuccio, Ernst-Slavit, & Katz, 2006). The standards state what students should know and be able to do as a result of ESL instruction and set goals for students' social and academic language development and sociocultural competence. These ESL standards take a functional approach to language learning and use and allow for maximum flexibility in curriculum and program design. Listed in Table 4.1 are the nine ESL content standards, organized under three educational goals:

Table 4.1. ESL Standards (Short, 2000)

Goal 1: To use English to communicate in social settings
Standard 1: Students will use English to participate in social interactions.
Standard 2: Students will interact in, through, and with spoken and written English for personal expression and enjoyment.
Standard 3: Students will use learning strategies to extend their communicative competence.

Goal 2: To use English to achieve academically in all content areas
Standard 1: Students will use English to interact in the classroom.
Standard 2: Students will use English to obtain, process, construct, and provide subject matter information in spoken and written form.
Standard 3: Students will use appropriate learning strategies to construct and apply academic knowledge.

Goal 3: To use English in socially and culturally appropriate ways
Standard 1: Students will use appropriate language variety, register, and genre according to audience, purpose, and setting.
Standard 2: Students will use nonverbal communication appropriate to audience, purpose, and setting.
Standard 3: Students will use appropriate learning strategies to extend their sociolinguistic and sociocultural competence.

The TESOL standards have been adopted by states such as New Jersey and Florida. In California, New Mexico, and Texas, they have been incorporated into standard curricula as descriptions of proficiency levels and benchmarks of performance.

In 2001, the U.S. federal government entered the usually state-governed setting of standards with the now infamous No Child Left Behind (NCLB) Act, which set into motion the development of new state standards in an attempt to close the achievement gap among all students. Despite its good intentions, NCLB has left teachers and administrators in a quagmire of political, economic, educational, and assessment wrangling (Blake, 2008; Meier & Wood, 2006).

DESIGNING ENGLISH LANGUAGE STANDARDS

The process of designing and conducting appropriate periodic reviews of English language standards involves dozens of curriculum and assessment specialists, teachers, and researchers (Bailey, Butler, & Sato, 2007; Fields, 2000; Kuhlman, 2001).

In creating such "benchmarks for accountability" (O'Malley & Valdez Pierce, 1996), there is a responsibility to carry out a comprehensive study of a number of domains:

- literally thousands of categories of language ranging from phonology at one end of a continuum to discourse, pragmatics, functional, and sociolinguistic elements at the other end
- specification of what ELD students' needs are, at thirteen different grade levels, for succeeding in their academic and social development
- a consideration of what is a realistic number and scope of standards to be included within a given curriculum
- a separate set of standards (qualifications, expertise, training) for teachers to teach ELD students successfully in their classrooms
- a thorough analysis of the means available to assess student attainment of those standards

It has already been noted that standards-setting for English-language courses is a global challenge. In many non-English-speaking countries, English is now a required subject starting as early as the first grade in some countries and by the seventh grade in virtually every country. With the worldwide increase in demand for English, a "communicative" curriculum in English is often required as of the early elementary school grades. Such mandates from ministries of education require the specification of standards, or **benchmarks**, on which to base curricular objectives. Sometimes, such standards are not reasonable due to the English proficiency level of teachers and the practical uses for English in the real world outside the classroom (Akiyama, 2004; Chinen, 2000; Sakamoto, 2002; Yoshida, 2001).

In Japan, the lack of spoken English skills prompted the Ministry of Education to include an oral skills component in their senior high school exit examination. However, these efforts revealed competing social, cultural, and education values of the stakeholders affected by the examination. A study by Akiyama (2004) found that whereas junior high school teachers and students welcomed the addition of the oral skills to the test, many senior high school teachers were against it on the grounds of practicality. Furthermore, in the Japanese merit-based system of examinations in which test-takers are judged purely on test scores, they felt that adding an oral skills component to the senior high school examination gave an unfair advantage to students who had lived in an English-speaking country. Therefore, they argued, the test scores would not reflect the effort put forth by a hardworking student. Thus the proposed changes raised questions about the actual purpose of the Japanese senior high school examination in English and its validity in terms of the curriculum.

A comparable example can be found in language examinations in the final year of high school in Australia. At one time university admission authorities overlooked the language test scores because, according to them, a candidate who may have been exposed at home or elsewhere to the "language" did not count as a true second language learner. Authorities felt that the test did not reflect the effort of the student, again questioning the validity of the test's construct (Elder, 1997).

In the United States, the state of California, with one of the largest populations of second language learners in the United States, was one of the first states to generate standards for English language learners. Other states follow analogous sets of standards. The first paragraph of the preamble to about 70 pages of "strategies and applications" of the California standards sets the tone:

> The Listening and Speaking standards for English language learners (ELLs) identify a student's competency to understand the English language and to produce the language orally. Students must be prepared to use English effectively in social and academic settings. Listening and speaking skills provide one of the most important building blocks for the foundation of second language acquisition and are essential for developing reading and writing skills in English. To develop proficiency in listening, speaking, reading, and writing, students must receive instruction in reading and writing while developing fluency in oral English. (California Department of Education, 2002)

An example of standards for listening and speaking at the beginning level is reproduced in Table 4.2 on the next page. These can give you a general picture of how standards are stated at the broadest level. As standards become more grade-specific, they of course are more detailed. TESOL, for example, lists hundreds of standards for pre-K through 12, not only for social, intercultural, and instructional purposes, but also including specific standards for language arts, mathematics, science, and social studies for each grade level (Gottlieb, et al., 2006).

Assessing the academic achievement of every student is an essential part of educational reform but one that presents a challenge for most schools, school districts, states, and countries. Further, in addition to the careful specification and development of standards, educators also need to design assessment instruments that are aligned to the standards.

STANDARDS-BASED ASSESSMENT

The development of standards obviously implies the responsibility for correctly assessing their attainment. As standards-based education became more accepted in the last decade or so of the twentieth century, many educational systems around the world found that the standardized tests of past decades were not in line with newly developed standards. Thus began the interactive process not only of developing standards but also of creating **standards-based assessments**. The comprehensive process of developing such assessment in California still continues as curriculum and assessment specialists design, revise, and validate numerous tests (Kuhlman, 2001; Stack, Stack, & Fern, 2002).

Table 4.2. California English language development standards for listening and speaking, beginning ELD level (© 2002, California Department of Education, p. 17)

	Listening and Speaking, Beginning ELD Level			
ELA Categories	**Grades K–2**	**Grades 3–5**	**Grades 6–8**	**Grades 9–12**
Comprehension	Begin to speak with a few words or sentences, using some English phonemes and rudimentary English grammatical forms (e.g., single words or phrases).	Begin to speak with a few words or sentences, using some English phonemes and rudimentary English grammatical forms (e.g., single words or phrases).	Begin to speak with a few words or sentences, using some English phonemes and rudimentary English grammatical forms (e.g., single words or phrases).	Begin to speak with a few words or sentences, using some English phonemes and rudimentary English grammatical forms (e.g, single words or phrases).
	Answer simple questions with one- to two-word responses.	Answer simple questions with one- to two-word responses.	Ask and answer questions using simple sentences or phrases.	Ask and answer questions using simple sentences or phrases.
	Respond to simple directions and questions using physical actions and other means of nonverbal communication (e.g., matching objects, pointing to an answer, drawing pictures).	Retell familiar stories and participate in short conversations by using appropriate gestures, expressions, and illustrative objects.	Demonstrate comprehension of oral presentations and instructions through nonverbal responses (e.g., gestures, pointing, drawing).	Demonstrate comprehension of oral presentations and instructions through non-verbal responses.
Comprehension, Organization & Delivery of Oral Communication	Independently use common social greetings and simple repetitive phrases (e.g., "Thank you." "You're welcome.").	Independently use common social greetings and simple repetitive phrases (e.g., "May I go and play?").	Independently use common social greetings and simple repetitive phrases (e.g., "Good morning. Ms. _____.").	
Analysis & Evaluation of Oral & Media Communications, Comprehension				Respond with simple words or phrases to questions about simple written texts.
				Orally identify types of media by name (e.g., magazine, documentary film, news report).

Between 1999 and 2002, the California English Language Development Test (CELDT) was developed. The CELDT is a battery of instruments designed to assess the attainment of ELD standards across grade levels. (For reasons of test security, specifications for this test are not available to the public.) Llosa (2007) examined the extent to which the English Language Development (ELD) Classroom Assessment used in a large urban school district in California measures the same constructs as the CELDT and concluded that that the evidence gathered via the ELD Classroom Assessment is consistent with that provided by the CELDT, the standardized measure. For more information on the CELDT, consult the appendix at the end of this book.

The process of administering a comprehensive, valid, and fair assessment of ELD students continues to be perfected. Stringent budgets within departments of education worldwide predispose many in decision-making positions to rely on traditional standardized tests for ELD assessment, but rays of hope lie in the exploration of more student-centered approaches to learner assessment. Stack and colleagues (2002), for example, reported on a portfolio assessment system in the San Francisco Unified School District called the Language and Literacy Assessment Rubric (LALAR), in which multiple forms of evidence of students' work are collected. Teachers observe students year-round and record their observations on scannable forms. The use of the LALAR system provides useful data on students' performance at all grade levels for oral production and for reading and writing performance in elementary and middle school grades (1–8). Further research is ongoing for high school levels (grades 9–12).

We can find similar standards-based assessments in other countries such as Hong Kong, China, which recently moved from norm-referenced to standards-based assessments in the Hong Kong Certificate of Education Examination (Davison, 2004). In Brazil, Peru, and Ecuador, standards-based assessment is now commonplace, with all the advantages and disadvantages that come with such educational reform (S. Godoy, P. Leon, & M. Magdany, personal communication, 2008). Advantages include common criteria nationwide for teachers to pursue in their curricula, whereas the most obvious disadvantage is the temptation to "teach to the test." In the United States, a perennial complaint of school teachers is the potential loss of the "art" of teaching—the freedom of the teacher to emphasize what he or she judges to be important—and instead having to give equal attention to 193 different competencies in a course unit (S. Brown, personal communication, 2008). These shortcomings notwithstanding, standards, in their best intent, are of course designed to be anchors, aligning curriculum, instruction, and assessment.

CASAS and SCANS

At the higher levels of education (colleges, community colleges, adult schools, language schools, and workplace settings), standards-based assessment systems have also had an enormous impact. The Comprehensive Adult Student Assessment System (CASAS), for example, is a program designed to provide broadly based assessments of ESL curricula across the United States. The system includes more than 80 standardized assessment instruments used to place learners in programs, diagnose learners' needs, monitor progress, and certify mastery of functional basic skills. CASAS assessment instruments are used to measure functional reading, writing, listening, and speaking skills, as well as higher-order thinking skills. CASAS scaled scores report learners' language ability levels in employment and adult life skills contexts. For a review of the CASAS test, see Gorman and Ernst (2004); some details are also provided in the appendix at the end of this book.

A similar set of standards compiled by the U. S. Department of Labor, now known as the Secretary's Commission in Achieving Necessary Skills (SCANS), outlines competencies necessary for language in the workplace. The competencies cover language functions in terms of standards:

- resources (allocating time, materials, staff. etc.)
- interpersonal skills, teamwork, customer service. etc.
- information processing, evaluating data, organizing files, etc.
- systems (e.g., understanding social and organizational systems)
- technology use and application

These five competencies are acquired and maintained through training in the basic skills (reading, writing, listening, speaking); thinking skills such as reasoning and creative problem solving; and personal qualities, such as self-esteem and sociability. For more information on SCANS, see Barron, Henley, & Thompson (2000).

Teacher Standards

In addition to the movement to create standards for learning, an equally strong movement has emerged to design standards for teaching. Cloud (2001) noted that a student's "performance [on an assessment] depends on the quality of the instructional program provided, . . . which depends on the quality of the professional development" (p. 3) of teachers. Kuhlman (2001) emphasized the importance of teacher standards in three domains:

1. linguistics and language development
2. culture and the interrelationship between language and culture
3. planning and managing instruction

In the education of new teachers, the University of California (2008) advocates attention to six domains, one of which is the assessment of student learning, with emphasis on five factors:

1. establishing and communicating learning goals for all students
2. collecting and using multiple sources of information to assess student learning

(continued)

3. involving and guiding all students in assessing their own learning
4. using the results of assessment to guide instruction
5. communicating with students, families, and other audiences about student progress

Professional teaching standards have also been the focus of several committees in the international association of TESOL (Gottlieb et al., 2006). Correspondingly, the Australian Council of TESOL Associations has developed standards for teachers and outlines the expectations of TESOL practitioners in relation to three orientations: working in a multicultural society, second language education, and the practice of TESOL (Barnett & Antenucci, 2006).

How to assess whether teachers have met standards remains a complex issue. Can pedagogical expertise be assessed through a traditional standardized test? In the first of Kuhlman's (2001) domains—linguistics and language development—knowledge can perhaps be so evaluated, but the cultural and interactive characteristics of effective teaching cannot be so easily assessed in such a test. TESOL's standards committee advocates performance-based assessment of teachers for the following reasons:

- Teachers can demonstrate the standards in their teaching.
- Teaching can be assessed through what teachers do with their learners in their classrooms or virtual classrooms (their performance).
- This performance can be detailed in what are called "indicators": examples of evidence that the teacher can meet a part of a standard.
- The processes used to assess teachers need to draw on complex evidence of performance. In other words, indicators are more than simple "how to" statements.
- Performance-based assessment of the standards is an integrated system. It is neither a checklist nor a series of discrete assessments.
- Each assessment within the system has performance criteria against which the performance can be measured.
- Performance criteria identify to what extent the teacher meets the standard.
- Student learning is at the heart of the teacher's performance.

The standards-based approach to teaching and assessment presents the profession with many challenges. However thorny those issues are, the social consequences of this movement cannot be ignored, especially in terms of student assessment.

THE CONSEQUENCES OF STANDARDS-BASED AND STANDARDIZED TESTING

We have already noted that standards-based assessments are not without their share of problems. Although standards are implemented to improve education, a growing body of research has found a number of unintended or negative consequences of standards-based assessments (Jones, Jones, & Hargrove, 2003; Linn, 2001; Wang, Beckett, & Brown, 2006). Some studies have found that standards-based tests can narrow the curriculum, pushing instruction toward lower-order rather than higher-order cognitive skills. Further, lower test scores result in grade retention, which appears not to improve educational achievement for those students who are held back (Darling-Hammond, 2004).

One of the strongest arguments made against standards-based assessments is the issue of accountability. That is, tests results are used to hold school districts accountable for raising student academic achievement and identifying schools in need of improvement. A prime example in the United States is the aforementioned No Child Left Behind Act. Thus for many schools, government funding and support depend on student performance, which puts pressure not only on the students but also on teachers, school principals, and school district administrators. To avoid being penalized, schools and school districts sometimes push low-scoring students into special education or retain or hold them back a grade (thereby encouraging them to drop out) so that the school's average test scores will look better. In this case, some argue (e.g., Darling-Hammond, 2004) that the standards-based assessments do not improve student achievement but rather prohibit some students from making any progress.

Another major challenge in standards-based education is the close link to the standardized testing "industry" that we all are very familiar with. Stories abound—some of them of blockbuster spy-novel proportions—on the high price test-takers are willing to pay to pass such tests, dramatically illustrating the **gate-keeping** role of those tests. We have already alluded to the widespread global acceptance of standardized tests as valid procedures for assessing individuals in many walks of life. Those tests bring with them certain consequences that fall under the category of **consequential validity** or **impact** discussed in Chapter 2.

Some of those consequences are positive. Standardized tests offer high levels of practicality and reliability and are often supported by impressive construct validation studies. They are therefore capable of accurately placing hundreds of thousands of test-takers onto a norm-referenced scale with high reliability ratios (most ranging between 80 and 90 percent). For decades, university admissions offices around the world have relied on the results of tests such as the Scholastic Aptitude Test (SAT®), the Graduate Record Exam (GRE®), and the Test of English as a Foreign Language (TOEFL® Test) to screen applicants. The respectably moderate correlations between these tests and academic performance are used to justify determining the students' educational future on the basis of one relatively inexpensive sit-down multiple-choice test. Thus has emerged the term **high-stakes testing**, based on the gate-keeping function that standardized tests perform.

Are the institutions that produce and utilize high-stakes standardized tests justified in their decisions? An impressive array of research would seem to say yes. Consider the fact that correlations between "old" TOEFL scores (before the advent of computer-based TOEFLs) and academic performance in the first year of college were impressively high (Henning & Cascallar, 1992), and more recent validation studies continue to verify such correspondences (Powers, Roever, Huff, & Trapani, 2003; Roever & Powers, 2005). Are tests that lack a high level of content validity appropriate assessments of ability? A good deal of research says yes to this question as well. A study of the correlation of TOEFL results with oral and written production, for example, showed that years before TOEFL's current use of an essay and oral production section, significant positive correlations were obtained among all subsections of the TOEFL and independent direct measures of oral and written production (Henning & Cascallar, 1992). Test promoters commonly use such findings to support their claims for the efficacy of their tests.

However, several nagging, persistent issues emerge from the arguments about the consequences of standardized testing (Nichols & Berliner, 2007). Consider the following interrelated questions:

1. Should the educational and business worlds be satisfied with high but not perfect probabilities of accurately assessing test-takers on standardized instruments? In other words, what about the small minority who are not fairly assessed?
2. Regardless of construct validation studies and correlation statistics, should further types of performance be elicited to obtain a more comprehensive picture of the test-taker?
3. Does the proliferation of standardized tests throughout a young person's life give rise to test-driven curricula, diverting the attention of students from creative or personal interests and in-depth pursuits?
4. Is the standardized test industry in effect promoting a cultural, social, and political agenda that maintains existing power structures by assuring opportunity to an elite (wealthy) class of people (Shohamy, 2000)?

Test Bias

It's no secret that standardized tests can involve a number of types of test bias. The concept of test fairness is not new in language testing, but a recent surge of interest in the relationship between validity and fairness (Kunnan, 2000; Liao, 2006; Shohamy, 2000) shows a widespread concern over test bias. Some researchers argue that both test developers and test-users must seek to create fair and unbiased tests as well as use tests in a way that is fair for all test-takers. That bias, they say, can come in many forms: language, culture, race, gender, and learning styles (Kohn, 2000; Medina & Neill, 1990; Ross & Okabe, 2006). The National Center for Fair and Open Testing, in its bimonthly newsletter *Fair Test*, every year offers dozens of instances of claims of test bias from teachers, parents, students, and legal consultants. Likewise, the American Psychological Association's Joint Committee on Testing Practices has published a guide for professionals to promote "tests that are fair to all test-takers regardless of age, gender, disability, race, ethnicity, national origin, religion, sexual orientation, linguistic background, or other personal characteristics" (Code of Fair Testing Practices in Education, 2004, p. 1). For example, reading selections in standardized tests may use a passage from a literary piece that reflects a middle-class, white, Anglo-Saxon norm. Lectures used for listening stimuli can easily promote a biased sociopolitical view. Consider the following prompt for an essay in "general writing ability" on the International English Language Testing System (IELTS):

> You rent a house through an agency. The heating system has stopped working. You phoned the agency a week ago, but it has still not been mended. Write a letter to the agency. Explain the situation and tell them what you want them to do about it.

Although this task favorably illustrates the principle of authenticity, a number of cultural presuppositions are evident in such a prompt. For example, accepted norms for "complaining" to an agency or expressing power relationships between renters and landlords/agents may be unfamiliar discourse for test-takers, calling into question a potential cultural bias.

A further issue extends beyond the fact that a biased item measures features that are irrelevant to the test construct. Bias also can systematically harm one group of test-takers, thereby making the test unfair. In an era when we seek to recognize the multiple intelligences present within every student (Christison, 2005; H. Gardner, 1983, 1999), is it not likely that standardized tests promote logical-mathematical and verbal-linguistic intelligences to the virtual exclusion of the other contextualized, integrative intelligences? Only very recently have traditionally receptive tests begun to include written and oral production in their test battery—a positive sign. But is it enough? It is also clear that many otherwise "smart" people do not perform well on standardized tests. They may excel in cognitive styles that are not amenable to a standardized format. Perhaps they need to be assessed by such performance-based evaluation as interviews, portfolios, samples of work, demonstrations, and observation reports. Perhaps, as Weir (2001, p. 122) suggested, learners and teachers need to be given the freedom to choose more formative assessment rather than the summative assessment inherent in standardized tests.

Expanding test batteries to include such measures would help to solve the problem of test bias (which is extremely difficult to control for in standardized items) and account for the small but significant number of test-takers who are not accurately assessed by standardized tests. Those who are using the tests for gate-keeping purposes, with few if any other assessments, would do well to consider multiple measures before attributing infallible predictive power to standardized tests.

On the surface, such efforts sound laudable, with only beneficial outcomes, as they have the potential for transforming the "gate-keeper" role of tests to that of "door opener" (Bachman & Purpura, 2008). On the other hand, assessment experts also warn that principles of practicality and validity can be threatened by "fairness taken too far" (Wagner, 2006). Efforts to remove all bias from a test and its scoring procedures could prove to be costly as well as harmful to its validity. Further, Gennaro (2006) suggested that fair-test practices may mitigate against a number of practicality issues, all of which must be carefully weighed. We must somehow find appropriate middle ground that satisfies both sides of this theoretical conundrum.

Test-Driven Learning and Teaching

Yet another consequence of standardized testing is the danger of test-driven learning and teaching. When students and other test-takers know that one single measure of performance will have a definitive effect on their lives, they are less likely to take a positive attitude toward learning. The motives in such a context are almost exclusively extrinsic, with little likelihood of stirring intrinsic interests. Test-driven learning is a worldwide issue. In Japan, Korea, and Taiwan, to name just a few, students approaching their last year of secondary school focus obsessively on passing the year-end college entrance examination, a major section of which is English (Choi, 2008; Kuba, 2002). Little attention is given to any topic or task that does not directly contribute to passing that one exam. In the United States, high school juniors and seniors are forced to give almost as much attention to SAT scores.

Teachers also get caught up in the wave of test-driven systems. In Florida, elementary school teachers were recently promised cash bonuses of $100 per student as a reward for their schools' high performance on the state-mandated grade-level test, the Florida Comprehensive Achievement Exam ("Florida: Politically Referenced Tests?" 2002). The effect of this policy was undue pressure on teachers to make sure their students excelled in the exam and, most likely, according to a later report by Rothstein (2009), diverting students from pursuing other objectives in their curricula. A further, ultimately more serious effect was to punish schools in lower-socioeconomic neighborhoods. A teacher in such a school might actually be a superb teacher, and that teacher's students might make excellent progress through the school year, but because of the test-driven policy, the teacher would receive no reward at all.

ETHICAL ISSUES: CRITICAL LANGUAGE TESTING

Some researchers believe that one of the by-products of a rapidly growing testing industry is the danger of an abuse of power. In a special report on "fallout from the testing explosion," Medina and Neill (1990) noted the following:

> Unfortunately, too many policymakers and educators have ignored the complexities of testing issues and the obvious limitations they should place on standardized test use. Instead, they have been seduced by the promise of simplicity and objectivity. The price which has been paid by our schools and our children for their infatuation with tests is high. (p. 36)

Another viewpoint on this issue is expressed by Shohamy (1997): "Tests represent a social technology deeply embedded in education, government, and business; as such they provide the mechanism for enforcing power and control. Tests are most powerful as they are often the single indicators for determining the future of individuals" (p. 2). She and other researchers believe that test designers, and the corporate sociopolitical infrastructure that they ostensibly represent, have an obligation to maintain certain standards as specified by their client educational institutions. These standards bring with them certain ethical issues surrounding the gate-keeping nature of standardized tests.

Shohamy (1997, 2000, 2001) and others (Hamp-Lyons, 2001; Kunnan, 2000; McNamara & Roever, 2006; Nichols & Berliner, 2007; Spolsky, 1997) see the ethics of testing as an extension of what educators call **critical pedagogy**, or more precisely in this case, **critical language testing** (see *TBP,* Chapter 23, for some comments on critical language pedagogy in general). Proponents of a critical approach to language testing claim that large-scale standardized testing is not an unbiased process but rather is the "agent of cultural, social, political, educational, and ideological agendas that shape the lives of individual participants, teachers, and learners" (Shohamy, 1997, p. 3). The issues of critical language testing are numerous:

- Psychometric traditions are challenged by interpretive, individualized procedures for predicting success and evaluating ability.
- Test designers have a responsibility to offer multiple modes of performance to account for varying styles and abilities among test-takers.
- Tests are deeply embedded in culture and ideology.
- Test-takers are political subjects in a political context.

These issues are not new. More than a century ago, British educator F. Y. Edgeworth (1888) challenged the potential inaccuracy of contemporary qualifying examinations for university entrance. In recent years, the debate has heated up: Tests are more prevalent in our lives and are often used to make decisions that are significant. Thus it was not surprising that in 1997, an entire issue of the journal *Language Testing* was devoted to questions about ethics in language testing. More recently, in 2004, *Language Assessment Quarterly* had a special issue on the ethical considerations in language testing. Furthermore, the International Language Testing Association (ILTA; 2000) created a Code of Ethics, which draws on moral philosophy to guide appropriate professional conduct. The code of ethics states that it "is neither a statute nor a regulation and it does not provide guidelines for practice, but it is intended to offer a benchmark of satisfactory ethical behavior by all language testers" (p. 1).

One of the problems highlighted by the push for critical language testing is the widespread conviction, already alluded to above, that carefully constructed standardized tests designed by reputable test manufacturers are infallible in their predictive validity. Too often one standardized test is deemed to be sufficient, and follow-up measures are considered to be too costly.

A further problem with our test-oriented culture, according to some researchers, lies in the agendas of those who design and those who utilize the tests. Tests are used in some countries to deny citizenship (McNamara & Roever, 2006; McNamara & Shohamy, 2008; Shohamy, 1997). These researchers further contend that tests may by nature be culture-biased and therefore may disenfranchise members of a non-mainstream value system. In addition, test-givers are always in a position of power over test-takers and therefore can impose social and political ideologies on test-takers through standards of acceptable and unacceptable items. These researchers further suggest that tests promote the notion that answers to real-world problems have unambiguous right and wrong answers with no shades of gray. A corollary to the latter is that tests presume to reflect an appropriate core of common knowledge, such as the competencies reflected in the standards discussed earlier in this chapter. According to this logic, the test-taker must buy in to such a system of beliefs in order to make the cut.

Language tests, some may argue, are less susceptible than general-knowledge tests to such sociopolitical overtones. The research process that undergirds the TOEFL® Test goes to great lengths to screen out Western cultural bias, monocultural belief systems, and other potential agendas. Nevertheless, even the process of the selection of content alone for the TOEFL involves certain standards that may not be universal, and the very fact that the TOEFL is used as an absolute standard of English proficiency by most universities does not exonerate this particular standardized test.

As a language teacher, you might be able to exercise some influence in the ways tests are used and interpreted in your own milieu. If you're offered a variety of choices in standardized tests, you could choose a test that offers the least degree of cultural bias. Better yet, you might encourage the use of multiple measures of performance (varying item types, oral and written production, and other alternatives to traditional assessment) even though this might cost more money and time. Further, you and your co-teachers might help establish an institutional system of evaluation that places less emphasis on standardized tests and more emphasis on an ongoing process of formative evaluation. In so doing, you might be offering educational opportunity to a few more people who might otherwise be prevented from participating.

EXERCISES

[Note: **(I)** Individual work; **(G)** Group or pair work; **(C)** Whole-class discussion.]

1. **(C)** Standards for assessment have been strongly promoted and harshly criticized in almost every country and context. Review those pros and cons and then evaluate standards-based assessment as a general educational model. What are its advantages and disadvantages? How might one compensate for potential disadvantages?

2. **(I/C/G)** As extra class work, on your own, consult published English language standards such as those found in the State of California Department of

Education English Language Development Standards (www.cde.ca.gov) or any other state (use a search engine), the Council of Europe's (www.coe.int) Common European Framework of Reference for Languages, the European Association for Language Testing and Assessment (www.ealta.eu.org), or the official curriculum of the Ministry of Education of Japan (www.mext.go.jp/english/). Then, in small groups, share what you found and, for your own context (country, county, school system), evaluate the usefulness of the standards. Report your findings back to the class.

3. **(I/C)** Consult the California English Language Development Test Web site (http://celdt.cde.ca.gov/). From what you can glean from that information, how would you evaluate the CELDT in terms of content validity, face validity, and authenticity? Report your findings back to the class.

4. **(I)** Consult the TESOL Web site (www.tesol.org/) and search for the "TESOL/NCATE Standards for P-12 Teacher Education Programs." What would you say are the most important standards, for your own context, that language teachers should measure up to? In your own institutional context, or one that you are familiar with, how would you assess a teacher's attainment of those standards?

5. **(G/C)** Look at the four questions posed on page 96 regarding the consequences of standardized testing. In groups, one question for each group, or as a whole class, respond to those questions.

6. **(I/C)** Log on to the Web site for the National Center for Fair and Open Testing (www.fairtest.org/). Report back to the class on the topics and issues sponsored by that organization and discuss the extent to which the same issues apply to local educational contexts that you are familiar with.

7. **(G)** In small groups, brainstorm some specific examples of ways in which efforts to remove test bias may harm the validity and practicality of a test. Report your examples to the rest of the class.

8. **(G)** Shohamy and other researchers contend that test-takers are political subjects in a political context and that large-scale standardized testing is the agent of cultural, social, political, educational, and ideological agendas. In a small group, share personal experiences with taking or giving a test that had political or ideological ramifications. Then, draw up a list of dos and don'ts through which teachers might overcome the potential political agendas in the use of standardized tests. Share your lists with the rest of the class.

FOR YOUR FURTHER READING

McNamara, Tim, & Roever, Carsten (2006). *Language testing: The social dimension*. Malden, MA: Blackwell Publishing.

Clearly one of the most intriguing of current "hot topics" in language assessment is the ethical dimension. Here, the authors bring readers up-to-date on a number of the social and political issues in language testing world-wide. There are extensive discussions of how validity is a key to main-taining the integrity of language tests amid threats to fairness and educational policies. The book is clearly written for both beginning grad-uate students and experienced teachers.

Shohamy, Elana. (2001). *The power of tests: A critical perspective on the uses of language tests.* London: Pearson Education.

Shohamy has for several decades been an outspoken advocate for social responsibility in testing. In this persuasive book, she applies a critical per-spective to language tests by examining their uses and consequences in edu-cation and society. She establishes the power of tests by echoing the voices of test-takers who have been victimized by tests and by demonstrating how bureaucrats use tests for power and control. At the end of the book is a dis-cussion of responsibilities of test-makers and the rights of test-takers.

Gottlieb, Margoargo; Carnuccio; Lynore, Ernst-Slavit, Gisela; & Katz, Anne (2006). *Pre-K–12 English language proficiency standards*. Alexandria, VA: Teachers of English to Speakers of Other Languages.

If you're not able to consult TESOL's Web-based list of English language standards, this book provides that information in print form. In addition, it contains over 40 pages of discussion of the process that TESOL committee members went through to develop the standards, issues that they faced, such as the definition of language proficiency, and how they applied prin-ciples of second language acquisition.

CHAPTER 5

STANDARDIZED TESTING

OBJECTIVES: After reading this chapter, you will be able to

- appreciate the link between standards-based assessment and standardized testing
- apply your understanding of the pros and cons of standardized testing to evaluating and adapting standardized tests on your own
- develop a standardized test of your own, including designing test specifications and items and defining scoring criteria
- analyze the steps taken to perform a construct validation of a standardized test
- examine constructs underlying various standardized language proficiency tests

---

The preceding discussion of standards-based education and assessment provides an appropriate backdrop for the topic of this chapter: a detailed examination of standardized testing. Actually, the standards-based tests that we discussed in the last chapter do not capture the only means of standardizing. A good standardized test is the product of a thorough process of empirical research and development that may extend beyond simply the establishment of standards or benchmarks. Standardization can also mean the use of systematic procedures for administration and scoring. Further, many standardized tests, especially large-scale tests, are norm-referenced, the goal of which is to place test-takers on a continuum across a range of scores and to differentiate test-takers by their relative ranking.

Characteristics of a standardized test

- standards-based
- product of research and development
- systematic scoring and administration procedures
- norm-referenced

Most elementary and secondary schools around the world have standardized achievement tests to measure students' mastery of the standards or competencies that have been prescribed for specified grade levels, exit requirements, and entrance to further levels. It is not uncommon for secondary schools whose requirements for graduation include English language proficiency to institutionalize countrywide standardized tests to measure such ability (Akiyama, 2004). In Korea and Japan,

English language tests such as the Test of English for International Communication (TOEIC® Test) have been used to select job applicants (Gilfert, 1996).

In English-speaking countries, universities rely on tests such as the Test of English as a Foreign Language (TOEFL® Test) or the International English Language Testing System (IELTS) to determine the language ability of students who apply for admission. In the United States, standards-based tests vary by states, counties, and school districts, but they all share the common objective of economical large-scale assessment. College entrance exams such as the Scholastic Aptitude Test (SAT®) are part of the educational experience of many high school seniors in the United States seeking further education. The Graduate Record Exam (GRE®) is a required standardized test for entry into many graduate school programs. Tests like the Graduate Management Admission Test (GMAT®) and the Law School Aptitude Test (LSAT®) specialize in particular disciplines. Of course you are already familiar with language proficiency tests such as the TOEFL, produced by the Educational Testing Service in the United States and its British counterpart, the IELTS, which features standardized tests in affiliation with the University of Cambridge Local Examinations Syndicate. Another well-known test internationally is University of Michigan's Michigan English Language Assessment Battery (MELAB). These are all standardized because they specify a set of competencies (or standards) for a given domain, and through a process of construct validation they program a set of tasks that have been designed to measure those competencies.

Many people are under the incorrect impression that all standardized tests consist of items that have predetermined responses presented in a multiple-choice format. Although it is true that many standardized tests conform to a multiple-choice format, by no means is multiple-choice a prerequisite characteristic. It so happens that a multiple-choice format provides the test producer with an "objective" means for determining correct and incorrect responses and therefore is the preferred mode for large-scale tests. However, standards are equally involved in many human-scored tests of oral production and writing, such as the Test of Spoken English (TSE® Test), the Test of Written English (TWE® Test), and the writing and speaking sections of the MELAB.

ADVANTAGES AND DISADVANTAGES OF STANDARDIZED TESTS

Advantages of institutionally administered standardized testing include, foremost, a ready-made, previously validated product that frees the teacher from having to spend hours creating a test. Administration to large groups can be accomplished within reasonable time limits. In the case of multiple-choice formats, scoring procedures are streamlined (for either scannable computerized scoring or hand-scoring with a hole-punched grid) for fast turnaround time.

Disadvantages must also be taken into account. In the case of multiple-choice formats, many test-takers blithely assume that such instruments are valid and reliable—they have the appearance of authority, whether or not an appropriate construct validation of the instrument has been performed. Another drawback is the inappropriate use of such tests—for example, using an overall proficiency test as an achievement test simply because of the convenience of the standardization. Not too long ago a colleague of mine who was a course director reported an incident in which he was required to give a last-minute placement test to students who entered a program after instruction had begun. A frantic search uncovered a 30-year-old multiple-choice grammar achievement test, which he reluctantly administered, even though the curriculum was mostly listening and speaking and involved few of the grammar points tested. This instrument had the appearance of a good test when in reality it had no content validity whatsoever, and it was only marginally useful as a placement instrument.

A further disadvantage is the potential misunderstanding of the difference between **direct** and **indirect testing** (see Chapter 2). Some standardized tests include tasks that do not directly specify performance in the target objective. For example, before 1996, the TOEFL® Test included neither a written nor an oral production section, yet statistics showed a reasonably strong correspondence between performance on the TOEFL and a student's written and—to a lesser extent—oral production (Henning & Cascallar, 1992). The comprehension-based TOEFL could therefore be claimed to be an indirect test of production. A test of reading comprehension that proposes to measure ability to read extensively and that engages test-takers in reading only short one- or two-paragraph passages could ostensibly be an indirect measure of extensive reading.

Those who use standardized tests need to acknowledge both the advantages and the limitations of indirect testing. In the pre-1996 TOEFL administrations, the expense of giving a direct test of production was considerably reduced by offering only comprehension performance and showing through construct validation the appropriateness of conclusions about a test-taker's production competence. Likewise, short reading passages are easier to administer, and if research validates the assumption that short reading passages indicate extensive reading ability, then the use of the shorter passages is justified. Yet the construct validation statistics that offer that support never offer a 100 percent probability of the relationship, leaving room for some possibility that the indirect test is not valid for its targeted use.

A more serious issue lies in the assumption (alluded to in the previous section) that standardized tests correctly assess all learners equally well (Kohn, 2000; Phelps, 2005). Well-established standardized tests usually demonstrate high correlations between performance on such tests and target objectives, but correlations are not sufficient to demonstrate unequivocally the acquisition of criterion objectives by all test-takers. Here is a nonlanguage example: In the United States, some driver's license renewals require taking a paper-and-pencil multiple-choice test that covers signs, safe speeds and distances, lane changes, and other "rules of the road." Statistics show a strong correlation between high scores on those tests and good driving records, so people who do well on these tests are a safe bet to relicense. Now an extremely high correlation (of perhaps .80 or above) may be loosely interpreted to mean that a large majority of the drivers whose licenses are renewed by virtue of their having passed the quiz are good behind-the-wheel drivers. What about those few who do not fit the model? That small minority of drivers could endanger the lives of the majority, and is that a risk worth taking? Motor vehicle registration departments in the United States seem to think so, and thus they avoid the high cost of behind-the-wheel driving tests.

The disadvantages that pertain to standardized testing should not deter you from embracing them. You are already informed on the social, political, and ethical issues of using standardized tests, so you should feel well equipped to use, adapt, or create such tests with the confidence that you can avoid certain disadvantages while capitalizing on their advantages. A summary of these advantages and disadvantages are capsulated in Table 5.1.

Table 5.1. Advantages and disadvantages of standardized tests

Advantages	Disadvantages
• readily available product	• possibly inappropriate use of such tests
• easily administered to large groups	• potential test biases
• streamlined scoring and reporting procedures	• indirect testing may not elicit a good sample of performance
• a previously validated product (in many cases)	• multiple-choice formats have the appearance of authority

DEVELOPING A STANDARDIZED TEST

Although it is not likely that a classroom teacher, with a team of test designers and researchers, would be in a position to develop a brand-new standardized test of large-scale proportions, it is a virtual certainty that some day you will be in a position to (a) revise an existing test, (b) adapt or expand an existing test, and/or (c) create a smaller-scale standardized test for a program you are teaching in. Even if none of these three cases should ever apply to you, it is of paramount importance to understand the process of the development of the standardized tests that have become ingrained in our educational institutions.

How are standardized tests developed? Where do test tasks and items come from? How are they evaluated? Who selects items and their arrangement in a test? How do such items and tests achieve consequential validity? How are different forms of tests equated for difficulty level? Who sets norms and cut-off limits? Are security and confidentiality an issue? Are cultural and racial biases (discussed in Chapter 4) an issue in test development? All these questions typify those you might pose in an attempt to understand the process of test development.

In the steps outlined below, five different standardized tests are used to exemplify the process of standardized test design. These are indicated in Table 5.2.

Table 5.2. Five standardized tests

	Test	Web Site
A	Test of English as a Foreign Language (TOEFL® Test), Educational Testing Service	www.ets.org; click on "TOEFL"
B	International English Language Testing System (IELTS), Cambridge Local Examinations Syndicate	www.ielts.org
C	Michigan English Language Assessment Battery (MELAB), University of Michigan	www.lsa.umich.edu/eli/testing/melab
D	Test of Spoken English (TSE® Test), Educational Testing Service	www.ets.org; click on "TSE"
E	English as a Second Language Placement Test (ESLPT), San Francisco State University	www.sfsu.edu/~testing/eslpt.html

Four of the five tests are described in the appendix at the end of this book, which lists a selection of commercially available tests. Briefly, the first three (TOEFL® Test, IELTS, and MELAB) are tests of general language ability or proficiency. The fourth test (TSE® Test) is a speaking test administered by the Educational Testing Service. The fifth (ESLPT) is a placement test at a university. As we look at the steps, one by one, you will see patterns that are consistent with those outlined in Chapter 3 for evaluating and developing a classroom test. Here we illustrate six steps of development using these five tests

1. Determine the purpose and objectives of the test.

Most standardized tests are expected to provide high practicality in administration and scoring without unduly compromising validity. The initial outlay of time and money for such a test is significant, but the test is usually designed for repeated use. It's therefore important for its purpose and objectives to be stated specifically. Let's look at the five tests.

A, B, C. The first two tests are the "giants" of the testing industry, each with more than one million users annually worldwide. The third test, the MELAB, is unique in its sponsorship by a university. The purpose of the first three tests is to evaluate the general English ability of people whose native language is not English, and all three assess the skills of listening, speaking, reading, and writing. All three tests are used to help institutions of higher learning make decisions about the English language proficiency of international applicants for admission. IELTS and MELAB clients also may be businesspeople proposing to work in countries where

English is the language of communication. With various cut-off scores applied by different client institutions, the high-stakes, gate-keeping nature of the tests is obvious.

D. The TSE® Test, produced by the Educational Testing Service and used worldwide, assesses test-takers' spoken English ability. The test is used for employment, graduate assistantships, licensure, and certification purposes.

E. The ESLPT, locally designed and administered at San Francisco State University, is designed to place already admitted students into an appropriate course in academic writing, with the secondary goal of placing students into courses in oral production and grammar-editing. Although the test's primary purpose is to make placements, another desirable objective is to provide teachers with some diagnostic information about their students on the first day or two of class.

As you can see, the objectives of each of these tests are quite clear. The content of each test must be designed to accomplish those particular ends. This first stage of goal-setting might be seen as one in which the consequential validity of the test is foremost in the mind of the developer: Each test has a specific gate-keeping function to perform; therefore the criteria for entering those gates must be specified accurately.

2. Design test specifications.

Now comes the hard part. Decisions need to be made on how to go about structuring the specifications (or specs, as they are popularly called) of the test. Before specs can be addressed, a comprehensive program of research must identify a set of **constructs** underlying the test itself (see Chapter 2, pages 33–34, on construct validation). This stage of laying the foundation stones can occupy weeks, months, or even years of effort. Standardized tests that don't work are often the product of short-sighted construct validation. Let's look at the three tests again.

To illustrate the design of test specs, we focus on the TOEFL® Test. Construct validation for the TOEFL is carried out by the staff at the Educational Testing Service under the guidance of a Policy Council that works with a Committee of Examiners that is composed of appointed external university faculty, linguists, and assessment specialists. Dozens of employees are involved in a complex process of reviewing current TOEFL specifications, commissioning and developing test tasks and items, assembling forms of the test, and performing ongoing exploratory research related to formulating new specs. Reducing such a complex process to a set of simple steps runs the risk of gross overgeneralization, but here we provide an idea of how a TOEFL is created.

Because the TOEFL is a proficiency test, the first step in the developmental process is to define the construct of **language proficiency**. First, it should be made clear that many assessment specialists such as Bachman (1990) and Palmer (Bachman & Palmer, 1996) prefer the term *ability* to *proficiency* and thus speak of **language ability** as the overarching concept. The latter phrase is more consistent, they argue, with our understanding that the specific components of language ability must be assessed separately. Others, such as the American Council on Teaching Foreign Languages (ACTFL), still prefer the term *proficiency* because it connotes more of a holistic, unitary trait view of language ability (Lowe, 1988). Most current views accept the ability argument and therefore strive to specify and assess the many components of language. For the purposes of consistency in this book, the term *proficiency* will nevertheless be retained, with the previously mentioned caveat.

How you view language will make a difference in how you assess language proficiency. After breaking language competence down into subsets of listening, speaking, reading, and writing, each performance mode can be examined on a continuum of linguistic units: phonology (pronunciation) and orthography (spelling), words (lexicon), sentences (grammar), discourse (beyond the sentence level), and pragmatic (sociolinguistic, contextual, functional, cultural) features of language.

How does the TOEFL sample incorporate all these possibilities? Oral production tests can be tests of overall conversational fluency or pronunciation of a particular subset of phonology and can take the form of imitation, structured responses, or free responses. Listening comprehension tests can concentrate on a particular feature of language or on overall listening for general meaning. Tests of reading can cover the range of language units and can aim to test comprehension of long or short passages, single sentences, or even phrases and words. Writing tests can take on an open-ended form with free composition or be structured to elicit anything from correct spelling to discourse-level competence. To add a further complication, the Internet-based TOEFL® iBT presents computer-delivered items, with all of its advantages, but not without some challenges (Sawaki, Stricker & Oranje, 2008).

From the sea of potential performance modes that could be sampled in a test, the developer must select a subset on some systematic basis. To make a very long story short (and leaving out numerous controversies), the TOEFL for many years included three types of performance in its organizational specifications: listening, structure, and reading, all of which tested comprehension through standard multiple-choice tasks. In 1996 a major step was taken to include written production in the computer-based TOEFL by adding a slightly modified version of the already existing Test of Written English (TWE® Test). Since 2005, the iBT has been offering assessment of speaking ability. In doing so, content validity was improved (Tannenbaum & Wylie, 2008) and, of course, administrative expenses significantly increased.

So if you were developing a standardized test and had already stipulated language components, method of delivery, and other factors discussed above, you would now be ready to design the specs for your tests. In the case of the TOEFL, we'll capture just the specs for the listening section on the next page (adapted from the description of the current Internet-based TOEFL at www.toefl.org). Such descriptions are not, strictly speaking, specifications, which are kept confidential by a developing organization. Nevertheless, they can give a sense of many of the constraints that are placed on the design of actual TOEFL specifications.

Table 5.3. TOEFL® Test listening competencies

- utilizes the context of spoken language, in both lectures and conversations, in academic settings
- tests ability to comprehend main ideas, major points, and relevant details supporting the main idea
- requires the test-taker to connect and synthesize information and to recognize the organization of information that is presented
- tests listening for pragmatic understanding of a speaker's function or purpose, attitude, and degree of certainty
- assesses ability to make inferences and draw conclusions from the information that is presented
- tests the ability to recognize introductions and conclusions in lectures
- requires the test-taker to recognize topic changes, digressions, and off-topic statements
- includes the following stimuli: lectures, three to five minutes long; conversations, about three minutes long
- tests ability to comprehend vocabulary and idiomatic expressions
- uses the multimedia capability of the computer by presenting photos and graphics to create context and support the content of the lectures, producing stimuli that more closely approximate real-world situations in which people do more than just listen to voices
- accompanies stimuli with either context-setting or content-based visuals, to establish the setting and role of the speakers

---

Adapted from Educational Testing Service. (2009). *TOEFL® iBT tips: How to prepare for the TOEFL iBT*. Princeton, NJ: Author.

Although we have not spelled out the specs for all five of the tests exemplified here, you can probably imagine a similar process for all. If you were to select one of the other five tests, would you be able to induce the process of constructing specs? Try that with a partner (see Exercise 3 at the end of the chapter).

3. Design, select, and arrange test tasks/items.

Once specifications for a standardized test have been stipulated, the sometimes never-ending task of designing, selecting, and arranging items begins. The specs act much like a blueprint in determining the number and types of items to be created. Let's look at a sample from the IELTS Academic Reading section for an illustration of the construction of tasks and items:

Table 5.4. IELTS Academic reading sample specifications

IELTS Academic Reading

Reading

[A 750-word article on the topic of "Wind Power in the U.S." with a short glossary at the end]

Questions 1–5

Complete the summary below.

Choose your answers from the box below the summary and write them in boxes 1 through 5 on your answer sheet. Note: There are more words or phrases than you will need to fill the gaps. You may use any word or phrase more than once.

Example:

The failure during the late 1970s and early 1980s of an attempt to establish a widespread wind power industry in the United States resulted largely from the . . . (1) . . . in oil prices during this period. The industry is now experiencing a steady . . . (2) . . . due to improvements in technology and an increased awareness of the potential in the power of wind. The wind turbines that are now being made, based in part on the . . . (3) . . . of wide-ranging research in Europe, are easier to manufacture and maintain than their predecessors. This has led wind-turbine makers to be able to standardise and thus minimize . . . (4) . . . There has been growing . . . (5) . . . of the importance of wind power as an energy source.

criticism	stability	skepticism
success	operating costs	decisions
design costs	fall	effects
production costs	growth	decline
failure	recognition	results

Questions 6–10

Look at the following list of issues (Questions 6–10) and implications (A–C). Match each issue with one implication. Write the appropriate letters A through C in boxes 6 through 10 on your answer sheet.

Example:

The current price of one wind-generated kilowatt . . .

Answer:

6. The recent installation of systems taking advantage of economies of scale . . .

7. The potential of meeting one-fifth of current U.S. energy requirements by wind power . . .

8. The level of acceptance of current wind turbine technology . . .

9. A comparison of costs between conventional and wind power sources . . .

10. The view of wind power in the European Union . . .

Implications

A. provides evidence against claims that electricity produced from wind power is relatively expensive.

B. supports claims that wind power is an important source of energy.

C. opposes the view that wind power technology requires further development.

As you can see, this is quite a challenging test! Now let's assume that the specs for this Academic Reading section of the test included (a) an initial reading of approximately 750 words, (b) followed by a summary of about 120 words, with 5 cloze-deletions and a choice of 15 possible words to fill in (with certain specs on vocabulary difficulty and frequency), and (c) a second set of items involving inference and implication based on the original passage.

The designers would then need to select the passage, the cloze items, the 15 possible fill-in words, and the 5 inference items. The reading passage would have to adhere to certain predetermined reading difficulty specs, so one would be forced to work within those parameters. In the above example, with all the cloze deletions being nouns, the principal focus is on vocabulary, with both grammatical and semantic context becoming the key to correct choices. In item 1, for example, the three grammatically possible choices (*fall, growth,* and *decline*) require the reader to have understood the passage and therefore to answer *growth.* In item 5, of the three items that fit grammatically and semantically (*criticism, recognition,* and *skepticism*), again an understanding of the passage enables the reader to choose *recognition.* Would you be able to select such a list of 15 words, at least 12 of which serve as distractors? Would you be able, within the specs, to maintain a specified difficulty level and not create any "give away" items but at the same time avoid items that are too difficult or ambiguous?

The inference tasks require an even more sophisticated ability to read "between the lines" in the passage. Paraphrases of the original passage had to be chosen, each quite cleverly matched with three possible sentence completions. Would you arrange these items in the same order in which they appeared in the passage? How would you choose five possible inferences for this test?

In the case of a test such as the IELTS (or any validated standardized test), before any such items are released in published form, they are pre-tested on sample audiences and scientifically selected to meet difficulty specifications within each subsection, each section, and on the test overall. Furthermore, those items are also selected to meet a desired discrimination index. Both of these indices are important considerations in the design of a computer-adaptive test, where performance on one item determines the next one to be presented to the test-taker. (See Chapter 3 for a complete treatment of multiple-choice item design.)

4. Make appropriate evaluations of different kinds of items.

In Chapter 3 the concepts of item facility (IF), item discrimination (ID), and distractor analysis were introduced. As the discussion there showed, such calculations provide useful information for classroom tests, but sometimes the time and effort involved may not be practical, especially if the classroom-based test is a one-time test. Yet for a standardized multiple-choice test that is designed for a commercial market, and/or administered a number of times, and/or administered in a different form, these indices are a must.

For other types of response formats—namely, oral and written responses— different forms of evaluation become important. The principles of practicality and reliability are prominent, along with the concept of facility. Practicality issues in such items include the clarity of directions, timing of the test, ease of administration, and how much time is required to score responses. Reliability is a major player in instances in which more than one scorer is employed and to a lesser extent when a single scorer must evaluate tests over long spans of time, which could lead to deterioration of standards. Facility is also a key to the validity and success of an item type: unclear directions, complex language, obscure topics, fuzzy data, and culturally biased information may all lead to a higher level of difficulty than one desires.

For an example of this stage in designing a standardized test, let's look at the ESLPT at San Francisco State University. In the case of the open-ended responses on the two written tasks on the ESLPT, a set of judgments must be made. Some evaluative impressions of the effectiveness of prompts and passages are gained from informal student and scorer feedback. In the developmental stage of the most recent version of the ESLPT, both types of feedback were formally solicited through questionnaires and interviews. That information proved to be invaluable in the revision of prompts and stimulus reading passages. After each administration, the teacher-scorers provide informal feedback on their perceptions of the effectiveness of the prompts and readings.

Statistical analysis of the multiple-choice editing passage helped determine the usefulness of items and point administrators toward revisions. The following is a sample of the format used:

Multiple-choice editing passage

---

1. <u>Ever</u> since supermarkets first <u>appeared</u>, they have been <u>take</u> over <u>the</u> world.
   A   B   C   D
2. <u>Supermarkets</u> have changed people's life <u>styles</u>, yet <u>and</u> at the same time, changes in
       A   B   C
people's life <u>styles</u> have encouraged the opening of supermarkets.
              D

The task was to locate the error in each sentence. Statistical tests on the trial version of this section revealed that a number of the 45 items were found to be of zero IF (no difficulty whatsoever) and of inconsequential discrimination power (some IDs of .15 and lower). In other words, many distractors were of no consequence because they lured no one. Such information led to a revision of numerous items and their options. For example, in item 2 above, no one chose distractor A, *supermarkets,* and more than 90 percent of the pilot test-takers correctly chose C, *and.* Test designers found that changing A to the word *People's* and D to the word *opening* rendered a considerably greater IF and ID indices. Such changes eventually strengthened the effectiveness of the entire section.

5. Specify scoring procedures and reporting formats.

A systematic assembly of test items in preselected arrangements and sequences, all of which are validated to conform to an expected difficulty level, should yield a test that can then be scored accurately and reported back to test-takers and institutions efficiently.

For an example of scoring procedures, let's take a look at the University of Michigan's MELAB. The standard form of the test is divided into three parts: (1) written composition; (2) listening comprehension; and (3) four different sub-sections on grammar, cloze, vocabulary, and reading comprehension (GCVR). Score reports provide separate results for each of the three parts, plus a final score that is essentially an average of the three sections. An additional option, available at selected test centers, is a speaking test, and a score is provided for the speaking test where applicable.

How are those scores calculated? Parts 2 and 3 are multiple-choice items and are machine-scored. Part 1 is a composition that involves two (and sometimes three) human scorers who use a rubric to achieve a final result. This rubric, found on the MELAB Web site, is reproduced in Table 5.5.

Table 5.5. MELAB composition scoring descriptions

MELAB COMPOSITION DESCRIPTIONS
97 Topic is richly and fully developed. Flexible use of a wide range of syntactic (sentence-level) structures, accurate morphological (word forms) control. Organization is appropriate and effective, and there is excellent control of connection. There is a wide range of appropriately used vocabulary. Spelling and punctuation appear error free.
93 Topic is fully and complexly developed. Flexible use of a wide range of syntactic structures. Morphological control is nearly always accurate. Organization is well controlled and appropriate to the material, and the writing is well connected. Vocabulary is broad and appropriately used. Spelling and punctuation errors are not distracting.
87 Topic is well developed, with acknowledgment of its complexity. Varied syntactic structures are used with some flexibility, and there is good morphological control. Organization is controlled and generally appropriate to the material, and there are few problems with connection. Vocabulary is broad and usually used appropriately. Spelling and punctuation errors are not distracting.
83 Topic is generally clearly and completely developed, with at least some acknowledgment of its complexity. Both simple and complex syntactic structures are generally adequately used; there is adequate morphological control. Organization is controlled and shows some appropriacy to the material, and connection is usually adequate. Vocabulary use shows some flexibility and is usually appropriate. Spelling and punctuation errors are sometimes distracting.

77 Topic is developed clearly but not completely and without acknowledging its complexity. Both simple and complex syntactic structures are present; in some "77" essays these are cautiously and accurately used while in others there is more fluency and less accuracy. Morphological control is inconsistent. Organization is generally controlled, while connection is sometimes absent or unsuccessful. Vocabulary is adequate but may sometimes be inappropriately used. Spelling and punctuation errors are sometimes distracting.

73 Topic development is present, although limited by incompleteness, lack of clarity, or lack of focus. The topic may be treated as though it has only one dimension, or only one point of view is possible. In some "73" essays both simple and complex syntactic structures are present, but with many errors; others have accurate syntax but are very restricted in the range of language attempted. Morphological control is inconsistent. Organization is partially controlled, while connection is often absent or unsuccessful. Vocabulary is sometimes inadequate and sometimes inappropriately used. Spelling and punctuation errors are sometimes distracting.

67 Topic development is present but restricted and often incomplete or unclear. Simple syntactic structures dominate, with many errors; complex syntactic structures, if present, are not controlled. Lacks morphological control. Organization, when apparent, is poorly controlled, and little or no connection is apparent. Narrow and simple vocabulary usually approximates meaning but is often inappropriately used. Spelling and punctuation errors are often distracting.

63 Contains little sign of topic development. Simple syntactic structures are present, but with many errors; lacks morphological control. There is little or no organization, and no connection apparent. Narrow and simple vocabulary inhibits communication, and spelling and punctuation errors often cause serious interference.

57 Often extremely short; contains only fragmentary communication about the topic. There is little syntactic or morphological control, and no organization or connection are apparent. Vocabulary is highly restricted and inaccurately used. Spelling is often indecipherable and punctuation is missing or appears random.

53 Extremely short, usually about 40 words or less; communicates nothing, and is often copied directly from the prompt. There is little sign of syntactic or morphological control, and no apparent organization or connection. Vocabulary is extremely restricted and repetitively used. Spelling is often indecipherable and punctuation is missing or appears random.

N.O.T. (Not On Topic) indicates a composition written on a topic different from any of those assigned; it does not indicate that a writer has merely digressed from or misinterpreted a topic. N.O.T. compositions often appear prepared and memorized. They are not assigned scores or codes.

For the speaking test, the test-taker participates in a one-on-one conversation with a MELAB examiner for 15 minutes, during which time standard prompts are given (see Chapter 7 for more information on oral interview formats). The test-taker is judged on six criteria: fluency, intelligibility, conversational development, conversational comprehension, vocabulary, and grammar. The examiner uses the rubric found in Table 5.6 on the next page to assign a final score ranging from a high of 4 to a low of 1.

Table 5.6. MELAB speaking rating scale descriptors

MELAB Speaking Test Rating Scale Reference Sheet RATING OVERALL SPOKEN ENGLISH DESCRIPTORS

4   Excellent Speaker

**4-   The examinee is a highly fluent user of the language, is a very involved partici-
pant in the interaction, and employs native-like prosody, with a few hesitations
in speech.** The examinee takes a very interactive role in the construction of the
interaction and sustains topic development at length. Prosody is native-like
though may be accented. Idiomatic, general, and specific vocabulary range is
extensive. There is rarely a search for a word or an inappropriate use of a
lexical item. The examinee employs complex grammatical structures, rarely
making a mistake.

3+ Good Speaker

**3   The examinee is quite fluent and interactive but has gaps in linguistic range and
control.**

3-   Overall, the examinee communicates well and is quite fluent. Accent does not
usually cause intelligibility problems, though there may be several occurrences
of deviations from conventional pronunciation. The examinee is usually quite
active in the construction of the interaction and is able to elaborate on topics.
Vocabulary range is good, but lexical fillers are often employed. There are some
lexical mistakes and/or lack of grammatical accuracy, usually occurring during
topic elaboration.

2+ Marginal/Fair Speaker

2   Talk is quite slow and vocabulary is limited.

2-   Overall, the pace of talk is slow with numerous hesitations, pauses, and false
starts, but fluency may exist on limited topics. Although talk may be highly
accented, affecting intelligibility, the examinee can usually convey communicative intent. However, the discourse flow is impeded by incomplete utterances.
Also, the examinee does not always understand the examiner. Vocabulary
knowledge is limited; there are usually many occurrences of misused lexical
items. Basic grammatical mistakes occur.

1+ Poor/Weak Speaker

**1   Talk consists mainly of isolated phrases and formulaic expressions, and there
are many communication breakdowns between the examiner and examinee.**
The examinee's abilities are insufficient for the interaction. Some basic knowledge of English exists and some limited responses to questions are supplied.
Utterances may not consist of syntactic units, and it is often difficult to understand the communicative intent of the examinee. The examinee also frequently
does not understand the examiner. Accent may be strong, making some of the
examinee's responses unintelligible. Vocabulary is extremely limited and sparse.

The two rubrics above give you an idea of how a standardized test—often thought to be "objective" in its black-and-white answers—can still be standardized but involve some human judgments. It is standardized both because of its adherence to standards and its specific scoring criteria. In the next chapter (Chapter 6) we discuss such rubrics some more and look at their pros and cons.

6. Perform ongoing construct validation studies.

From the above discussion, it should be clear that no standardized instrument is expected to be used repeatedly without a rigorous program of ongoing construct validation. Any standardized test, once developed, must be accompanied by systematic periodic corroboration of its effectiveness and by steps toward its improvement from administration to administration. This rigor is especially true of tests that are produced in **equated forms**, that is, forms that are reliable across several administrations (a score on a subsequent form of a test has the same validity and interpretability as its original).

All of the tests we've examined here include programs of construct validation, especially in view of their need to periodically produce new forms of the test. To give you an example of such construct validation, we look at Educational Testing Service's Test of Spoken English (TSE® Test). In the TOEFL® iBT Test, a form of the TSE is now a standard offering, but to take it as a separate test, one must opt for it at designated test centers along with the TOEFL® Paper-Based Test (PBT®). For years, however, the TSE stood alone as a separate test of oral production offered in audiocassette form through certified test centers or examiners around the world. So the metamorphosis of the TSE from its early beginnings to its now computer-based delivery obviously involved a good deal of construct validation.

The TSE requires test-takers to respond to a number of different tasks. The TSE Web site shows six such prompts: telling the "story" of a series of pictures, commenting on a topic or issue, interpreting information visually depicted on a graph, responding to a coworker or friend, responding to a telephone message, and preparing a voice-mail report based on a conversation between coworkers. Scores are given on what is essentially a five-point scale, ranging from 60 (communication is almost always effective; task is performed very competently) to 20 (no effective communication; no evidence of ability to perform the task). With two (or possibly three) raters, final scores are averaged and reported in increments of five points (60, 55, 50, etc.).

One of the principal issues in research on the TSE was and still is inter-rater reliability. With human scorers involved, specifications for rating test-takers underwent a slow process of improvement. For example, Boldt (1992) examined the interaction effect between examinee and examiner across the six subsections of the TSE and contributed to subsequent revisions of procedures. With a revised TSE in place, Powers, Schedl Wilson-Leung, and Butler (1999) proposed to study the extent to which the judgments of "normal" native speakers of English matched the assessment of "expert" examiners. Their research found a concordance between the two groups, but they were also able to make a few recommendations for changing the scoring procedures. A follow-up study (Myford & Wolfe, 2000) looked at the internal consistency of the tasks on the TSE and found justification for issuing a single score (on what is tantamount to a five-point scale) to examinees but found some minor inter-rater unreliability and suggested further research to improve scorers' judgments.

The process of construct validation of the TSE continues as each form of the test is offered and as data are gathered from the performance of test-takers.

STANDARDIZED LANGUAGE PROFICIENCY TESTING

As we wrap up our discussion of standards-based (in Chapter 4) and standardized language testing, let's take a quick look at just what it means to propose to test language **proficiency** or, better put, language ability. Tests of language ability presuppose a comprehensive definition of the specific competencies that comprise overall language ability. They also affect and are affected by instructional goals (Alderson, 2005). The specifications for the TOEFL® Test provided an illustration of an operational definition of ability for assessment purposes. This is not the only way to conceptualize the concept. Swain (1990) offered a multidimensional view of proficiency assessment by referring to three linguistic traits (grammar, discourse, and sociolinguistics) that can be assessed by means of oral, multiple-choice, and written responses (see Table 5.3 on page 110).

Swain's conception was not meant to be an exhaustive analysis of ability but rather to serve as an operational framework for constructing proficiency assessments.

Another definition and conceptualization of ability is suggested by the ACTFL association, mentioned earlier (Lowe, 1988). ACTFL takes a holistic and more unitary view of proficiency in describing four levels: superior, advanced, intermediate, and novice. Within each level, descriptions of listening, speaking, reading, and writing are provided as guidelines for assessment. As an example, the ACTFL Guidelines for the superior level of speaking are listed below. The other three ACTFL levels use the same parameters in describing progressively lower proficiencies across all four skills.

ACTFL speaking guidelines, summary, superior-level

Superior-level speakers are characterized by the ability to

- participate fully and effectively in conversations in formal and informal settings on topics related to practical needs and areas of professional and/or scholarly interests
- provide a structured argument to explain and defend opinions and develop effective hypotheses within extended discourse
- discuss topics concretely and abstractly
- deal with a linguistically unfamiliar situation
- maintain a high degree of linguistic accuracy
- satisfy the linguistic demands of professional and/or scholarly life

---

Table 5.7. *Traits of second language proficiency (Swain, 1990, p. 403)*

		T r a i t		
M e t h o d		**Grammar** (grammatical accuracy within sentences)	**Discourse** (textual cohesion and coherence)	**Sociolinguistic** (social appropriateness of language use)
	Oral	*structured interview*	*storytelling and argumentation/ persuasion*	*role play of speech acts: requests, offers, complaints*
		scored for accuracy of verbal morphology, prepositions, syntax	detailed rating for identification, logical sequence, and time orientation, and global ratings for coherence	scored for ability to distinguish formal and informal register
	Multiple-choice	*sentence-level "select the correct form" exercise (45 items) involving verb morphology, prepositions, and other items*	*paragraph-level "select the coherent sentence" exercise (29 items)*	*speech act-level "select the appropriate utterance" exercise (28 items)*
	Written composition	*narrative and letter of persuasion*	*narrative and letter of persuasion*	*formal request letter and informal note*
		scored for accuracy of verb morphology, prepositions, syntax	detailed ratings much as for oral discourse and global rating for coherence	scored for the ability to distinguish formal and informal register

Such taxonomies have the advantage of considering a number of functions of linguistic discourse but the disadvantage, at the lower levels, of overly emphasizing test-takers' deficiencies. A further disadvantage is noted by Bachman (1990), who advocates a "communicative" definition of ability that recognizes "a dynamic interaction between the situation, the language user, and the discourse, in which communication is something more than the simple transfer of information" (p. 4). Bachman suggested that the ACTFL model may, in its claim to be able to provide a single global rating of general language ability for a test-taker, mask the dynamic nature of communicative language ability.

★   ★   ★   ★   ★

The construction of a valid standardized test is no minor accomplishment, whether the instrument is large- or small-scale. First, a standardized test should be founded on soundly constructed standards, free of bias (the subject of the previous chapter). This is a tall order and requires careful gathering and analysis of performance data and institutional goals. Second, the designing of specifications alone, as this chapter illustrates, requires a sophisticated process of construct validation coupled with considerations of practicality. Third, the construction of items and scoring/interpretation procedures may require a lengthy period of trial and error with prototypes of the final form of the test. Finally, with cautious and painstaking attention to all the details of construction, the end product can result in a cost-effective, time-saving, accurate instrument. Your use of the results of such assessments can provide informative measures of learners' language abilities.

EXERCISES

[Note: **(I)** Individual work; **(G)** Group or pair work; **(C)** Whole-class discussion.]

1. **(C)** As a warm-up to further discussion, tell the class about the worst experience you ever had taking a standardized test. Briefly analyze what made the experience so unbearable, and try to come up with suggestions for improvement of the test and/or its administrative conditions.
2. **(G)** In pairs or small groups, compile a brief list of pros and cons of standardized testing. Cite illustrations—preferably personal experiences—of as many items in each list as possible. Report your lists and examples to the rest of the class.
3. **(G)** In groups, each assigned to one of the five sample tests discussed in this chapter, find out as much as you can about the test using an Internet search. Then, as a group, try to reconstruct what you think would be the specs for the test or a section of the test.
4. **(I)** Select a standardized test that you are quite familiar with (possibly from a recent experience). Mentally evaluate that test using the five principles of practicality, reliability, validity, authenticity, and washback. Report your evaluation to the class.

5. **(C)** (Note: This question requires knowledge from Chapter 4 on standards-based assessment.) Do you think that the IELTS reading passage about wind power, cited in this chapter, manifests any test bias or fairness issues? If so, what are they and how might the problems be remedied? In other tests that members of the class have taken, were there any such issues that you have noticed? Is it possible to design a test that is completely free of bias?

6. **(C/G)** Compare the differences in conceptualization of language proficiency represented by Swain's model and the ACTFL philosophy as indicated by the list of characteristics of a superior-level speaker. What assumptions are made in each about the components of language ability? What are the strengths and weaknesses of each approach?

FOR YOUR FURTHER READING

Stoynoff, Stephen, & Chapelle, Carol A. (2005). *ESOL tests and testing: A resource for teachers and administrators.* Alexandria, VA: Teachers of English to Speakers of Other Languages.

In this little encyclopedia, twenty-one different English language tests are reviewed, with concise descriptions of each test's purpose, methods, and research behind the test. Standardized tests in this book cover all four skills (speaking, listening, reading, and writing). Of special interest may be the introductory chapters, in which the authors provide and excellent introduction to terms, issues, and testing practices over the past few decades.

Phillips, Deborah. (2005). *Longman preparation course for the TOEFL test: Next generation (iBT).* White Plains, NY: Pearson Education.

A careful examination of this or any other reputable preparation course for a standardized language test is well worth a student's time. Note especially how the book acquaints the user with the specifications of the test and offers a number of useful strategies that can be used in preparation for the test and during its administration. Of course, special attention is given to strategies for taking the Internet-based TOEFL® Test.

CHAPTER **6**

BEYOND TESTS: ALTERNATIVES

IN ASSESSMENT

> **OBJECTIVES:** After reading this chapter, you will be able to
>
> - use, in your classroom, a number of modes of assessment, ranging from formal tests to numerous formal and informal "alternatives"
> - weigh the pros and cons of assessment alternatives against varying levels of potential fulfillment of the five principles
> - examine ways to resolve the dilemma of maximizing both practicality and beneficial washback in classroom-based assessment
>
> - develop your own performance-based assessments with carefully structured rubrics and other scoring procedures
> - analyze the benefits and drawbacks of using portfolios, journals, conferences, interviews, observations, and self- and peer-assessments in the classroom

In the public eye, tests have acquired an aura of infallibility. Everyone wants a test for everything, especially if the test is cheap, quickly administered, and scored instantaneously. However, we saw in the previous two chapters that although the standardized test industry has become a powerful force, it also has come under criticism from the public (Kohn, 2000) and from language assessment experts (McNamara & Roever, 2006; Shohamy, 2001). Putting the controversy in perspective, Bailey (1998) reasoned "one of the disturbing things about tests is the extent to which many people accept the results uncritically, while others believe that all testing is invidious. But tests are simply measurement tools: It is the use to which we put their results that can be appropriate or inappropriate" (p. 204).

It's clear by now that tests are one of a number of possible types of assessment. In Chapter 1, an important distinction was made between testing and assessing. Tests are formal procedures, usually administered within strict time limitations, to sample the performance of a test-taker in a specified domain. Assessment connotes a much broader concept in that most of the time when teachers are teaching, they are also assessing. Assessment includes all occasions from informal impromptu observations and comments up to and including tests.

In the decade of the 1990s, when a number of educators questioned the notion that all people and all skills could be measured by traditional tests, a novel concept emerged that began to be labeled "alternative" assessment. As teachers and students were becoming aware of the shortcomings of standardized tests, "an alternative to standardized testing and all the problems found with such testing" (Huerta-Macías, 1995, p. 8) was proposed. That proposal was to assemble additional measures of students—portfolios, journals, observations, self-assessments, peer-assessments, and the like—in an effort to triangulate data about students. For some, such alternatives held "ethical potential" (Lynch, 2001, p. 228) in their promotion of fairness and in shifting some of the power in the classroom to students. Others (Lynch & Shaw, 2005; Ross, 2005) have since followed with evidence of the efficacy of alternatives that offer stronger formative assessments of students' progress to proficiency.

Why, then, should we even refer to the notion of "alternative" when assessment already encompasses such a range of possibilities? This was the question to which Brown and Hudson (1998) responded in a *TESOL Quarterly* article. They noted that to speak of "alternative assessments" is counterproductive because the term implies something new and different that may be "exempt from the requirements of responsible test construction" (p. 657). They proposed to refer to "alternatives in assessment" instead. Their term is a perfect fit within a model that considers tests as a subset of assessment. Already in this book, you have been reminded that all tests are assessments but that, more importantly, not all assessments are tests.

The defining characteristics of the various alternatives in assessment that have been commonly used across the profession were aptly summed up by Brown and Hudson (1998, pp. 654–655). Alternatives in assessments

1. require students to perform, create, produce, or do something
2. use real-world contexts or simulations
3. are nonintrusive in that they extend the day-to-day classroom activities
4. allow students to be assessed on what they normally do in class every day
5. use tasks that represent meaningful instructional activities
6. focus on processes as well as products
7. tap into higher-level thinking and problem-solving skills
8. provide information about both the strengths and weaknesses of students
9. are multiculturally sensitive when properly administered
10. ensure that people, not machines, do the scoring, using human judgment
11. encourage open disclosure of standards and rating criteria
12. call on teachers to perform new instructional and assessment roles

THE DILEMMA OF MAXIMIZING BOTH PRACTICALITY AND WASHBACK

The principal purpose of this chapter is to examine some of the alternatives in assessment that are markedly different from formal tests. Tests, especially the large-scale standardized tests discussed in the previous chapter, tend to be one-shot performances that are timed, multiple-choice, decontextualized, norm-referenced, and that foster extrinsic motivation. On the other hand, tasks like portfolios, journals, and self-assessment are

- open-ended in their time orientation and format
- contextualized to a curriculum

(continued)

- referenced to the criteria (objectives) of that curriculum
- likely to build intrinsic motivation

One way of looking at this contrast poses a challenge to you as a teacher and test designer. Formal standardized tests are almost by definition highly practical, reliable instruments. They are designed to minimize time and money on the part of test designer and test-taker and to be accurate in their scoring. Alternatives such as portfolios, conferencing with students on drafts of written work, or observations of learners over time all require considerable time and effort on the part of the teacher and the student, as well as greater costs to institutional budgets. Even more time must be spent if the teacher hopes to offer a reliable evaluation within students across time, as well as across students (taking care not to favor one student or group of students). But the alternative techniques also offer markedly greater washback, are superior formative measures, and, because of their authenticity, usually carry greater content validity.

This relationship can be depicted in a hypothetical graph that shows practicality/reliability on one axis and washback/authenticity on the other, as shown in Figure 6.1. Notice the implied negative correlation: As a technique increases in its washback and authenticity, its practicality and reliability tend to be lower. Conversely, the greater the practicality and reliability, the less likely you are to achieve beneficial washback and authenticity. I have placed three types of assessment on the regression line to illustrate.

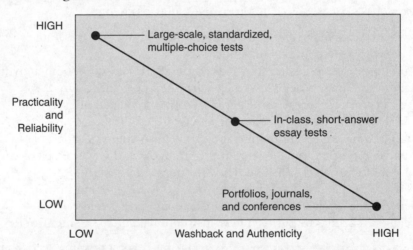

Figure 6.1. Presumed relationship of practicality/reliability to washback/authenticity

The figure appears to imply the inevitability of the relationship: Large-scale multiple-choice tests cannot offer much washback or authenticity, and portfolios and such alternatives cannot achieve much practicality or reliability. This need not be the case. The challenge that faces conscientious teachers and assessors in our profession is to change the position of the line. This can be accomplished by efforts to push traditional test formats on the chart to the right (toward more washback and authenticity) and to raise the practicality and reliability of portfolios, journals, and conferences. The relationship depicted in the chart would thus push the regression line into the right-hand corner, as depicted in Figure 6.2.

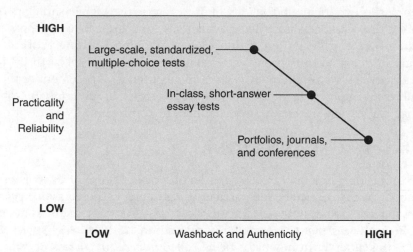

Figure 6.2. Idealized relationship of practicality/reliability to washback/authenticity

Surely we should not sit idly by, accepting the presumably inescapable conclusion that all standardized tests are devoid of washback and authenticity. With some creativity and effort, we can transform otherwise inauthentic and negative-washback-producing tests into more pedagogically fulfilling learning experiences. A number of approaches to accomplishing this end are possible, many of which have already been implicitly presented in this book. They include

- building as much authenticity as possible into multiple-choice task types and items
- designing classroom tests that have both objective-scoring sections and open-ended response sections, varying the performance tasks
- turning multiple-choice test results into diagnostic feedback on areas of needed improvement
- maximizing the preparation period before a test to elicit performance relevant to the ultimate criteria of the test
- teaching test-taking strategies
- helping students to see beyond the test—not "teaching to the test"
- triangulating information on a student before making a final assessment of competence

The flip side of this challenge is to understand that the alternatives in assessment are not doomed to be impractical and unreliable. Administering various alternatives in assessment will not necessarily consume inordinately long hours in our already time-squeezed teaching days. As we look at alternatives in assessment in this chapter, we must remember Brown and Hudson's (1998) admonition to scrutinize the practicality, reliability, and validity of those alternatives while simultaneously celebrating their washback potential, authenticity, and appeal to students' intrinsic motivation. It's easy to fly out of the cage of traditional testing rubrics, but it is tempting in doing so to flap our wings aimlessly and to accept virtually any classroom activity as a viable alternative. Assessments used to supplement or replace traditional tests imply a responsibility to be rigorous in determining objectives, response modes, and criteria for evaluation and interpretation.

PERFORMANCE-BASED ASSESSMENT

Before proceeding to a direct consideration of types of alternatives in assessment, a word about **performance-based assessment** is in order. There has been a great deal of press in recent years about performance-based assessment, sometimes merely called *performance assessment* (Norris, Brown, Hudson, & Yoshioka, 1998; Shohamy, 1995). Is this different from what is being called *alternative assessment*?

The push toward more performance-based assessment is part of the same general educational reform movement that raised strong objections to using standardized test scores as the only measures of student competencies (see, e.g., Shepard & Bliem, 1993; Valdez Pierce & O'Malley, 1992). The argument, as you can guess, was that standardized tests do not elicit actual performance on the part of test-takers. For example, if a child were asked as part of the curriculum to write a description of Earth as seen from space, to work cooperatively with peers to design a three-dimensional model of the solar system, to explain the project to the rest of the class, and to take notes on a videotape about space travel, traditional standardized testing would not be involved. Performance-based assessment, however, would require the performance of the above-named actions, or samples thereof, which would be systematically evaluated through direct observation by a teacher and/or possibly self and peers.

Performance-based assessment, according to Norris et al. (1998), involves test-takers in the performance of **tasks** that are "as authentic as possible" and that are "rated by qualified judges" (p. 8). In order to judge the outcome of such content-valid tasks, productive and observable skills, such as speaking and writing, are almost always implied (Brown, Hudson, Norris, & Bonk, 2002a, 2002b). The criterion of authenticity means that test-takers are engaged in real-world tasks, which in turn usually involve an integration of language skills, and perhaps all four skills in the case of project work. Because the tasks that students perform are consistent with course goals and curriculum, students and teachers are likely to be more motivated to perform them, as opposed to a set of multiple-choice questions about, say, facts and figures on the solar system.

J. D. Brown (2005) noted that a related concept, **task-based assessment**, is perhaps not so much a synonym for performance-based assessment as it is a subset thereof, in which the focus of assessment is explicitly on "particular tasks or task types" (p. 24) in a curriculum. Given our current methodological trend toward task-based teaching, it follows logically that assessment within that paradigm would be most effective if it too is task-based.

For another glimpse of interrelated concepts, note that O'Malley and Valdez Pierce (1996) considered performance-based assessment a subset of authentic assessment. In other words, for them, not all authentic assessment is performance-based. One could infer that reading, listening, and thinking have many authentic manifestations, but because they are not directly observable in and of themselves, they are not performance-based. According to O'Malley and Valdez Pierce (p. 5), the following are characteristics of performance assessment:

1. Students make a constructed response (as opposed to selecting a response from among options given to the students).
2. They engage in higher-order thinking, with open-ended tasks.
3. Tasks are meaningful, engaging, and authentic.
4. Tasks call for the integration of language skills.
5. Both process and product are assessed.
6. Depth of a student's mastery is emphasized over breadth.

Performance-based assessment needs to be approached with caution. It is tempting for teachers to assume that if a student is doing something, then the process has fulfilled its own goal and the evaluator needs only to make a mark in the grade book that says "accomplished" next to a particular competency. In reality, performances as assessment procedures need to be treated with the same rigor as traditional tests. This implies that teachers should

- state the overall goal of the performance
- specify the objectives (criteria) of the performance in detail
- prepare students for performance in stepwise progressions
- use a reliable evaluation form, checklist, or rating sheet
- treat performances as opportunities for giving feedback and provide that feedback systematically
- if possible, utilize self- and peer-assessments judiciously

In sum, performance assessment is not completely synonymous with the concept of alternative assessment. Rather, it is best understood as one of the primary traits of the many available alternatives to assessment.

RUBRICS

Another "hot issue" in language assessment is the movement toward engaging teachers in the use of **rubrics** in their day-to-day classroom-based assessment procedures. Please note that rubrics are *not* a separate alternative in assessment but rather a virtually indispensable tool in effective, responsible, performance-based assessment. A rubric is a device used to evaluate open-ended oral and written responses of learners. It is usually composed of a set of criteria or competencies, each with descriptions of levels of expectation. Some rubrics involve **scaling**, that is, the assignment of numbers (a numerical scale) to the described levels of performance. Others do not, as in Table 6.1 on the next page, which illustrates how a secondary school language arts department in the United States adapted a published rubric for their language arts department. Five criteria are listed, and each criterion is described in terms of the extent to which a student has "completed" the competency.

In recent years, with a marked increase in the use of alternatives in classroom-based assessment, rubrics have taken a front seat in teachers' evaluative tools (Walker, 2004). Andrade and Du's (2005) study of "rubric-referenced assessment" found that not only were rubrics beneficial for teachers but students were also able to better focus their efforts, produce work of higher quality, earn better grades, and feel less anxious about assignments. They echoed Brookhart's (2003) assertion that "classroom assessment information is not merely information 'about' himself or herself. Rather, it forms a major part of his or her learning life, becoming part of the lessons he or she is expected to learn" (p. 6).

It's easy to see the benefits of rubrics in an assessment mode that elicits oral and written responses that may be both lengthy (as in portfolios and journals) and complex. In such circumstances, teachers' responses to learners can be subjective—with a casual comment here and a "nice job" there—without pinpointing students' strengths and weaknesses. Rubrics provide, on an easily comprehended chart, points for students to focus on and goals to pursue.

On the other hand, as Popham (1997, 2007) noted, there are drawbacks to rubrics. It may be all too easy to mark a few points on a chart and consider our job is done. Rubrics, which look very precise and objective to the student, may be less exact in reality and offer students a false sense of where they stand. Their simplicity may mask the depth and breadth of a student's attainment. So with the caveat that rubrics don't provide a magic key to untangle the chaos of performance-based responses, we are wise to use them with some caution. We must, with Andrade (2005), ensure that rubric-referenced assessment is subject to all the rigors of validity and reliability that other assessments are.

Creating effective rubrics requires effort, care, and precision on your part. Consider the following steps (adapted from Andrade, 2005, and Popham, 1997) to ensure the successful design of a rubric:

1. Clearly list the objectives of the assessment instrument.
2. Describe, in a scale from excellent to poor, levels of performance that you expect.

Table 6.1. Secondary school language arts rubric. Adapted from Alternative Assessment Guide (Holt, Rinehart Winston, 2003)

Content	**Complete** Writer uses the appropriate functions and vocabulary for the topic.	**Generally complete** Writer usually uses the appropriate functions and vocabulary for the topic.	**Somewhat complete** Writer uses few of the appropriate functions and vocabulary for the topic.	**Incomplete** Writer uses none of the appropriate functions and vocabulary for the topic.
Comprehensibility	**Comprehensible** Reader can always understand what the writer is trying to communicate.	**Usually comprehensible** Reader can understand most of what the writer is trying to communicate.	**Sometimes comprehensible** Reader can understand less than half of what the writer is trying to communicate.	**Seldom comprehensible** Reader can understand little of what the writer is trying to communicate.
Accuracy	**Accurate** Writer uses language correctly, including grammar, spelling, word order, and punctuation.	**Usually accurate** Writer usually uses language correctly, including grammar, spelling, word order, and punctuation.	**Sometimes accurate** Writer has some problems with language usage.	**Seldom accurate** Writer makes a significant number of errors in language usage.
Organization	**Well-organized** Presentation is logical and effective.	**Generally well-organized** Presentation is generally logical and effective with a few minor problems.	**Somewhat organized** Presentation is somewhat illogical and confusing in places.	**Poorly organized** Presentation lacks logical order and organization.
Effort	**Excellent effort** Writer fulfills the requirements of the assignment and has put care and effort into the process.	**Good effort** Writer fulfills all of the requirements of the assignment.	**Moderate effort** Writer fulfills some of the requirements of the assignment.	**Minimal effort** Writer fulfills few of the requirements of the assignment.

3. In those objectives and levels, use task-specific performance as your criteria—avoid excessively general criteria.
4. Make your statements concise—avoid what Popham (1997) called "dysfunctional detail."
5. If possible, consult other models of rubrics for ideas on how to describe expected performance.
6. After trying out a rubric, consider revisions that will improve your evaluation.

A Web site such as http://rubistar.4teachers.org/index.php might prove to be useful in designing your own rubrics. You will see, in the following sections, a number of examples of rubrics that you can use to evaluate various alternatives in assessment.

PORTFOLIOS

One of the most popular alternatives in assessment, especially within a framework of communicative language teaching, is portfolio development. According to Genesee and Upshur (1996), a portfolio is "a purposeful collection of students' work that demonstrates . . . their efforts, progress, and achievements in given areas" (p. 99). Portfolios include materials such as

- essays and compositions in draft and final form
- reports, projects, and presentations outlines
- poetry and creative prose
- artwork, photos, newspaper or magazine clippings
- audio and/or video recordings of presentations, demonstrations, etc.
- journals, diaries, and other personal reflections
- tests, test scores, and written homework exercises
- notes on lectures
- self- and peer-assessments—comments, evaluations, and checklists

Until recently, portfolios were thought to be applicable only to younger children who assemble a portfolio of artwork and written work for presentation to a teacher and/or a parent. Now learners of all ages and in all fields of study are benefiting from the tangible, hands-on nature of portfolio development.

Gottlieb (1995, 2000) suggested a developmental scheme for considering the nature and purpose of portfolios using the acronym CRADLE to designate six possible attributes of a portfolio:

Collecting
Reflecting
Assessing
Documenting
Linking
Evaluating

As **C**ollections, portfolios are an expression of students' lives and identities. The appropriate freedom of students to choose what to include should be respected, but at the same time the purposes of the portfolio need to be clearly specified. **R**eflective practice through journals and self-assessment checklists is an important ingredient of a successful portfolio. Teacher and student both need to take the role of **A**ssessment seriously as they evaluate quality and development over time. We need to recognize that a portfolio is an important **D**ocument in demonstrating student achievement, and not just an insignificant adjunct to tests and grades and other more traditional evaluation. A portfolio can serve as an important **L**ink between student and teacher, parent, community, and peers; it is a tangible product, created with pride, that identifies a student's uniqueness. Finally, **E**valuation of portfolios requires a time-consuming but fulfilling process of generating accountability.

The CRADLE acronym offers the possibility of constructing a rubric for evaluating students' performance on their portfolios. Each of the six attributes might be listed in a left-hand column, with levels of completion or accomplishment on the horizontal axis. Try sketching out such a rubric.

The advantages of engaging students in portfolio development have been extolled in a number of sources (Brown & Hudson, 1998; Genesee & Upshur, 1996; Lynch & Shaw, 2005; O'Malley & Valdez Pierce, 1996; Weigle, 2002). A synthesis of those characteristics gives us a number of potential benefits. Portfolios

- foster intrinsic motivation, responsibility, and ownership
- promote student-teacher interaction with the teacher as facilitator
- individualize learning and celebrate the uniqueness of each student
- provide tangible evidence of a student's work
- facilitate critical thinking, self-assessment, and revision processes
- offer opportunities for collaborative work with peers
- permit assessment of multiple dimensions of language learning

At the same time, care must be taken lest portfolios become a haphazard pile of "junk," the purpose of which is a mystery to both teacher and student. Portfolios can fail if objectives are not clear, if guidelines are not given to students, if systematic periodic review and feedback are not present, and so on. Sometimes asking students to develop a portfolio seems daunting, especially for new teachers and for those who have never created a portfolio on their own. Successful portfolio development depends on following a number of steps and guidelines.

1. *State objectives clearly.* Pick one or more of the CRADLE attributes named above and specify them as objectives of developing a portfolio. Show how those purposes are connected to, integrated with, and/or a reinforcement of your already-stated curricular goals. A portfolio attains maximum authenticity and washback when it is an integral part of a curriculum, not just an optional box of materials. Show students how their portfolios will include materials from the course they are taking and how that collection will enhance curricular goals.

2. *Give guidelines on what materials to include.* Once the objectives have been determined, name the types of work that should be included. There is some disagreement about how much negotiation should take place between student and teacher over those materials. Hamp-Lyons and Condon (2000) suggested advantages for student control of portfolio contents, but teacher guidance keeps students on target with curricular objectives. It is helpful to give clear directions on how to get started because many students will never have compiled a portfolio and may be mystified about what to do. A sample portfolio from a previous student can help stimulate some thoughts on what to include.

3. *Communicate assessment criteria to students.* This is both the most important aspect of portfolio development and the most complex. Two sources— self-assessment and teacher assessment—must be incorporated for students to receive the maximum benefit. Self-assessment should be as clear and simple as possible. O'Malley and Valdez Pierce (1996) suggested the following half-page self-evaluation of a writing sample (with spaces for students to write) for elementary school English language students.

Portfolio self-assessment questions (O'Malley & Valdez Pierce, 1996, p. 42)

1. Look at your writing sample.
   a. What does the sample show that you can do?
   b. Write about what you did well.
2. Think about realistic goals. Write one thing you need to do better. Be specific.

Genesee and Upshur (1996) recommended using a questionnaire format for self-assessment, with questions such as the following for a project:

Portfolio project self-assessment questionnaire

1. What makes this a good or interesting project?
2. What is the most interesting part of the project?
3. What was the most difficult part of the project?
4. What did you learn from the project?
5. What skills did you practice when doing this project?
6. What resources did you use to complete this project?
7. What is the best part of the project? Why?
8. How would you make the project better?

Asking students to attend to these questions highlights the formative nature of the assessment. Conferences are important checkpoints for both student and teacher. If your own comments include requests for written responses from students, you may need to provide further guidance on how to respond. For example, students may need to be shown how to set future goals or determine certain strategies to follow. Above all, maintain reliability in assessing portfolios so that all students receive equal attention and are assessed by the same criteria.

An option that works for some contexts is to include, at various points during a course, peer-assessment or small-group conferences to comment on one another's portfolios. If the classroom community is relatively closely knit and supportive and students are willing to expose themselves by revealing their portfolios, valuable feedback can be achieved from peer reviews. Such sessions should have clear objectives lest they erode into aimless chatter. Checklists and questions may serve to preclude such an eventuality.

4. *Designate time within the curriculum for portfolio development.* If students feel rushed to gather materials and reflect on them, the effectiveness of the portfolio process is diminished. Make sure that students have time set aside for portfolio work (including in-class time) and that your own opportunities for conferencing are not compromised.

5. *Establish periodic schedules for review and conferencing.* By doing so, you will prevent students from throwing everything together at the end of a term.

6. *Designate an accessible place to keep portfolios.* It is inconvenient for students to carry collections of papers and artwork. If you have a self-contained classroom or a place in a reading room or library to keep the materials, that may provide a good option. At the university level, designating a storage place on campus may involve impossible logistics. In that case, encourage students to create their own accessible location and to bring to class only the materials they need.

7. *Provide positive washback-giving final assessments.* When a portfolio has been completed and the end of a term has arrived, a final summation is in order. Should portfolios be graded? awarded specific numerical scores? Opinion is divided; every advantage is balanced by a disadvantage. For example, numerical scores serve as convenient data to compare performance across students, courses, and districts. For portfolios containing written work, Wolcott (1998) recommended a holistic scoring scale ranging from 1 to 6 based on such qualities as inclusion of out-of-class work, error-free work, depth of content, creativity, organization, writing style, and "engagement" of the student. Such scores are perhaps best viewed as numerical equivalents of letter grades.

One could argue that it is inappropriate to reduce the personalized and creative process of compiling a portfolio to a number or letter grade and that it is more appropriate to offer a qualitative evaluation for a work that is so open-ended. Such evaluations might include a final appraisal of the work by the student, with questions such as those listed on the previous page for self-assessment of a project, and a narrative evaluation of perceived strengths and weakness by the teacher. Those final evaluations should emphasize strengths but also point the way toward future learning challenges.

It is clear that portfolios get a relatively low practicality rating because of the time it takes for teachers to respond and conference with their students. Nevertheless, following the guidelines suggested above for specifying the criteria for evaluating portfolios can raise the reliability to a respectable level, and without question the washback effect, authenticity, and personal consequential validity (impact) of portfolios remain exceedingly high.

In this discussion, we have tried to subject portfolios to the same specifications that apply to more formal tests: You make clear what the *objectives* are, what *tasks* are expected of the student, and how the learner's product will be *evaluated*. Strict attention to these demands is warranted for successful portfolio development to take place.

JOURNALS

Fifty years ago, journals had no place in the second language classroom. When language production was believed to be best taught under controlled conditions, the concept of "free" writing was confined almost exclusively to producing essays on assigned topics. Today, journals occupy a prominent role in a pedagogical model that stresses the importance of self-reflection in a student's education.

A journal is a log (or "account") of one's thoughts, feelings, reactions, assessments, ideas, or progress toward goals, usually written with little attention to structure, form, or correctness. Learners can articulate their thoughts without the threat of those thoughts being judged later (usually by the teacher). Sometimes journals are rambling sets of verbiage that represent a stream of consciousness with no particular point, purpose, or audience. Fortunately, models of journal use in educational practice have sought to tighten up this style of journal in order to give them some focus (Staton, Shuy, Peyton, & Reed, 1987). The result is the emergence of a number of overlapping categories or purposes in journal writing, such as the following (see pages 136–137 for a discussion of each):

- language-learning logs
- grammar journals
- responses to readings
- strategies-based learning logs
- self-assessment reflections
- diaries of attitudes, feelings, and other affective factors
- acculturation logs

Most classroom-oriented journals are what have now come to be known as **dialogue journals**. They imply an interaction between a reader (the teacher) and the student through dialogues or responses. For the best results, those responses should be dispersed across a course at regular intervals, perhaps weekly or biweekly. One of the principal objectives in a student's dialogue journal is to carry on a conversation with the teacher. Through dialogue journals, teachers can become better acquainted with their students, in terms of both their learning progress and their affective states, and thus become better equipped to meet students' individual needs.

The following journal entry from an advanced student from China, and the teacher's response, is an illustration of the kind of dialogue that can take place.

Dialogue journal sample

Journal entry by Ming Ling, China:

Yesterday at about eight o'clock I was sitting in front of my table holding a fork and eating tasteless noodles which I usually really like to eat but I lost my taste yesterday because I didn't feel well. I had a headache and a fever. My head seemed to be broken. I sometimes felt cold, sometimes hot. I didn't feel comfortable standing up and I didn't feel comfortable sitting down. I hated everything around me. It seemed to me that I got a great pressure from the atmosphere and I could not breath. I was so sleepy since I had taken some medicine which functioned as an antibiotic.

The room was so quiet. I was there by myself and felt very solitary. This dinner reminded me of my mother. Whenever I was sick in China, my mother always took care of me and cooked rice gruel, which has to cook more than three hours and is very delicious, I think. I would be better very soon under the care of my mother. But yesterday, I had to cook by myself even though I was sick, The more I thought, the less I wanted to eat. Half an hour passed. The noodles were cold, but I was still sitting there and thinking about my mother. Finally I threw out the noodles and went to bed.

Teacher's response:

This is a powerful piece of writing because you really communicate what you were feeling. You used vivid details, like "eating tasteless noodles," "my head seemed to be broken," and "rice gruel, which has to cook more than three hours and is very delicious." These make it easy for the reader to picture exactly what you were going through. The other strong point about this piece is that you bring the reader full circle by beginning and ending with "the noodles."

Being alone when you are sick is difficult. Now I know why you were so quiet in class.

If you want to do another entry related to this one, you could have a dialogue with your "sick" self. What would your "healthy" self say to the "sick" self? Is there some advice that could be exchanged about how to prevent illness or how to take care of yourself better when you do get sick? Start the dialogue with your "sick" self speaking first.

With the widespread availability of Internet communications, journals and other student–teacher dialogues have taken on a new dimension. With such innovations as "collaboratories" (where students in a class regularly carrying on e-mail discussions with each other and the teacher), on-line education, and distance learning, journals—out of several genres of possible writing—have gained additional prominence.

Journals obviously serve important pedagogical purposes: practice in writing fluently, using writing as a "thinking" process, emphasizing a student's own voice, and communication with the teacher. At the same time, the assessment qualities of journal writing have assumed an important role in the teaching–learning process. Because most journals are—or should be—a dialogue between student and teacher, they afford a unique opportunity for a teacher to offer various kinds of feedback. On the other side of the issue, it is argued that journals are too free a form to be assessed accurately. With so much potential variability, it is difficult to set up criteria for evaluation. For some English language learners, the concept of free and unfettered writing is anathema. Certain critics have expressed ethical concerns: Students may be asked to reveal an inner self, an act that may be virtually unheard of in their own culture. Without a doubt, the assessing of journal entries through responding is not an exact science.

It is important to turn the advantages and potential drawbacks of journals into positive general steps and guidelines for using journals as assessment instruments. The following steps are not coincidentally parallel to those cited above for portfolio development:

1. *Sensitively introduce students to the concept of journal writing.* For many students, especially those from educational systems that play down the notion of teacher–student dialogue and collaboration, journal writing will be difficult at first. University-level students, who have passed through a dozen years of product writing, will have particular difficulty with the concept of writing without fear of a teacher's scrutinizing every grammatical or spelling error. With modeling, assurance, and purpose, however, students can make a remarkable transition into the potentially liberating process of journal writing. Students who are shown examples of journal entries and given specific topics and schedules for writing will become comfortable with the process.

2. *State the objective(s) of the journal.* Integrate journal writing into the objectives of the curriculum in some way, especially if journal entries become topics of class discussion. The following are seven examples of purposes of journals:

    Language-learning logs. In English language teaching, learning logs have the advantage of sensitizing students to the importance of setting their own goals and then self-monitoring their achievement. M. McNamara (1998) suggested restricting the number of skills, strategies, or language categories that students comment on; otherwise students can become overwhelmed with the process. A weekly schedule of a limited number of strategies usually accomplishes the purpose of keeping students on task.

Grammar journals. Some journals are focused only on grammar acquisition. These types of journals are especially appropriate for courses and workshops that focus on grammar. "Error logs" can be instructive processes of consciousness-raising for students: Their successes in noticing and treating errors spur them to maintain the process of awareness of error.

Responses to readings. Journals may have the specified purpose of simple responses to readings (and/or to other material such as lectures, presentations, films, and videos). Entries may serve as precursors to freewrites and help learners to sort out thoughts and opinions on paper. Teacher responses aid in the further development of those ideas.

Strategies-based learning logs. Closely allied to language-learning logs are specialized journals that focus only on strategies that learners are seeking to become aware of and to use in their acquisition process. In H. D. Brown's (2002) *Strategies for Success: A Practical Guide to Learning English,* a systematic strategies-based journal-writing approach is taken in which, in each of 12 chapters, learners become aware of a strategy, use it in their language performance, and reflect on that process in a journal.

Self-assessment reflections. Journals can be a stimulus for self-assessment in a more open-ended way than through using checklists and questionnaires. With the possibility of a few stimulus questions, students' journals can extend beyond the scope of simple one-word or one-sentence responses.

Diaries of attitudes, feelings, and other affective factors. The affective states of learners are an important element of self-understanding. Teachers can thereby become better equipped to effectively facilitate learners' individual journeys toward their goals.

Acculturation logs. A variation on the above affectively based journals is one that focuses exclusively on the sometimes difficult and painful process of acculturation in a nonnative country. Because culture and language are so strongly linked, awareness of the symptoms of acculturation stages can provide keys to eventual language success.

3. *Give guidelines on what kinds of topics to include.* Once the purpose or type of journal is clear, students will benefit from models or suggestions on what kinds of topics to incorporate into their journals.

4. *Carefully specify the criteria for assessing or grading journals.* Students need to understand that journals aren't subjected to the same criteria as an essay or final report, but, at the same time, they need to know the assessment criteria. Once you have clarified that journals will *not* be evaluated for grammatical correctness and rhetorical conventions, state how they *will* be evaluated. This gives you a perfect opportunity to create a rubric for assessing student journals. Usually the purpose of the journal will dictate the major assessment criterion. Effort as exhibited in the thoroughness of students'

entries will no doubt be important. Also, the extent to which entries reflect the processing of course content might be considered. Additional criteria could include creativity and overall comprehensibility. Maintain reliability by adhering conscientiously to the criteria that you have set up.

5. *Provide optimal feedback in your responses.* M. McNamara (1998, p. 39) recommended three different kinds of feedback to journals:

   a. cheerleading feedback, in which you celebrate successes with the students or encourage them to persevere through difficulties
   b. instructional feedback, in which you suggest strategies or materials, suggest ways to fine-tune strategy use, or instruct students in their writing
   c. reality-check feedback, in which you help the students set more realistic expectations for their language abilities

   The ultimate purpose of responding to student journal entries is well captured in McNamara's threefold classification of feedback. Responding to journals is a very personalized matter, but closely attending to the objectives for writing the journal and its specific directions for an entry will focus those responses appropriately.

   Peer responses to journals may be appropriate if journal comments are relatively "cognitive," as opposed to very personal. Personal comments could make students feel threatened by other pairs of eyes on their inner thoughts and feelings.

6. *Designate appropriate time frames and schedules for review.* Journals, like portfolios, need to be esteemed by students as integral parts of a course. Therefore, it is essential to budget enough time within a curriculum for both writing journals and for your written responses. Set schedules for submitting journal entries periodically; return them in short order.

7. *Provide formative, washback-giving final comments.* Journals, perhaps even more than portfolios, are the most formative of all the alternatives in assessment. They are day-by-day (or at least weekly) chronicles of progress whose purpose is to provide a thread of continuous assessment and reassessment, to recognize midstream direction changes, and/or to refocus on goals. Should you reduce a final assessment of such a procedure to a grade or a score? Some say yes; others say no (Peyton & Reed, 1990), but it appears to be in keeping with the formative nature of journals not to do so. Credit might be given for the process of actually writing the journal, and possibly a distinction might be made among high, moderate, and low effort and/or quality, but to accomplish the goal of positive washback, narrative summary comments and suggestions are clearly in order.

How do journals score on principles of assessment? Practicality remains relatively low, although the appropriation of electronic communication increases practicality by offering teachers and students convenient, rapid (and legible) means of responding. Reliability can be maintained by the adherence of journal entries to stated purposes and objectives, but because of individual variations in writing and the accompanying variety of responses, reliability may reach only a moderate level.

Content validity and impact are very high if the journal entries are closely inter-woven with curriculum goals (which in turn reflect real-world needs). In the cate-gory of washback, the potential in dialogue journals is off the charts.

CONFERENCES AND INTERVIEWS

For a number of years, conferences have been a routine part of language class-rooms, especially of courses in writing. Conferencing is a standard part of a process approach to teaching writing, in which the teacher, in a conversation about a draft, facilitates the improvement of the written work. Such interaction has the advantage of one-on-one interaction between teacher and student and the teacher's ability to direct feed back toward a student's specific needs.

Conferences are not limited to drafts of written work. Including portfolios and journals discussed previously, the list of possible functions and subject matter for conferencing is substantial:

- commenting on drafts of essays and reports
- reviewing portfolios
- responding to journals
- advising on a student's plan for an oral presentation
- assessing a proposal for a project
- giving feedback on the results of performance on a test
- clarifying understanding of a reading
- exploring strategies for improving performance
- focusing on aspects of oral production
- checking a student's self-assessment of a performance
- setting personal goals for the near future
- assessing general progress in a course

It must be assumed that the teacher plays the role of a facilitator and guide in a conference and not that of an administrator making a formal assessment. In this intrinsically motivating atmosphere, students need to understand that the teacher is an ally who is encouraging self-reflection and improvement. So that the student will be as candid as possible in self-assessing, the teacher should not consider a confer-ence as something to be scored or graded. Conferences are by nature formative, not summative, and their primary purpose is to offer positive washback.

Genesee and Upshur (1996, p. 110) offered a number of generic kinds of ques-tions that may be useful to pose in a conference:

- What did you like about this work?
- What do you think you did well?
- How does it show improvement from previous work? Can you show me the improvement?

(continued)

- Are there things about this work you do not like? Are there things you would like to improve?
- Did you have any difficulties with this piece of work? If so, where, and what did you do (will you do) to overcome them?
- What strategies did you use to figure out the meaning of words you could not understand?
- What did you do when you did not know a word that you wanted to write?

Discussions of alternatives in assessment usually encompass one specialized kind of conference: an **interview**. This term is intended to denote a context in which a teacher interviews a student for a designated assessment purpose. (We are not talking about a student conducting an interview of others in order to gather information on a topic.) Interviews may have one or more of several possible goals, in which the teacher

- assesses the student's oral production
- ascertains a student's needs before designing a course or curriculum
- seeks to discover a student's learning styles and preferences
- asks a student to assess his or her own performance
- requests an evaluation of a course

One overriding principle of effective interviews centers on the nature of the questions that will be asked. It is easy for teachers to assume that interviews are just informal conversations which need little or no preparation. To maintain reliability, interview questions should be constructed carefully to elicit as focused a response as possible. When interviewing for oral production assessment (see Chapter 8), for example, a highly specialized set of probes is necessary to accomplish predetermined objectives.

Because interviews have multiple objectives, as noted above, it is difficult to generalize principles for conducting them, but the following guidelines may help to frame the questions efficiently:

1. Begin with friendly, anxiety-lowering "small talk."
2. In the warm-up stage, use relatively simple questions.
3. Continue with level-check and probe questions, but adapt to the interviewee as needed.
4. Frame questions simply and directly.
5. Focus on only one factor for each question. Do not combine several objectives in the same question.
6. Be prepared to repeat or reframe questions that are not understood.
7. Wind down with friendly and reassuring closing comments.

How do conferences and interviews score in terms of principles of assessment? Their practicality, as is true for many of the alternatives to assessment, is low because they are time-consuming. Reliability will vary between conferences and interviews. In the case of conferences, it may not be important to have rater reliability because the whole purpose is to offer individualized attention, which will vary greatly from student to student. For interviews, a relatively high level of reliability should be maintained with careful attention to objectives and procedures. Content validity for both can be maintained at a high level due to their individualized nature. As long as the subject matter of the conference/interview is clearly focused on the course and course objectives, content validity should also be upheld. Washback potential and authenticity are high for conferences but possibly only moderate for interviews unless the results of the interview are implemented in subsequent learning.

OBSERVATIONS

All teachers, whether or not they are aware of it, observe their students in the classroom almost constantly. Virtually every question, every response, and almost every nonverbal behavior is, at some level of perception, noticed. All those intuitive perceptions are stored as little bits and pieces of information about students that can form a composite impression of a student's ability. Without ever administering a test or a quiz, teachers know a lot about their students. In fact, experienced teachers are so good at this almost subliminal process of assessment that their estimates of a student's competence are often highly correlated with actual independently administered test scores (see Acton, 1979, for an example).

How do all these chunks of information become stored in a teacher's brain cells? Usually not through rating sheets and checklists and carefully completed observation charts. Still, teachers' intuitions about students' performance are not infallible, and certainly both the reliability and relevance of their feedback to students can be increased with the help of empirical means of observing their language performance. The value of systematic observation of students has been extolled for decades (Flanders, 1970; Moskowitz, 1971; Spada & Frölich, 1995), and its utilization greatly enhances a teacher's intuitive impressions by offering tangible corroboration of conclusions. Occasionally, intuitive information is disconfirmed by observation data.

We are not concerned in this section with the kind of observation that rates a formal presentation or any other prepared, prearranged performance in which the student is fully aware of some evaluative measure being applied and in which the teacher scores or comments on the performance. We are talking here about observation as a systematic, planned procedure for real-time, almost surreptitious recording of student verbal and nonverbal behavior. One of the objectives of such observation is to assess students without their awareness (and possible consequent anxiety) of the observation so that the naturalness of their linguistic performance is maximized.

What kinds of student performance can be usefully observed? Consider the following possibilities:

Potential observation foci

- sentence-level oral production skills (see microskills, Chapter 8)

  —pronunciation of target sounds, intonation, etc.

  —grammatical features (verb tenses, question formation, etc.)

  —correct/appropriate vocabulary use

- discourse-level skills (conversation rules, turn-taking, and other macroskills)

- interaction with classmates (cooperation, frequency of oral production)

- reactions to particular students, optimal productive pairs and groups, which "zones" of the classroom are more vocal, etc.

- frequency of student-initiated responses (whole class, group work)

- quality of teacher-elicited responses

- pauses, silent periods (number of seconds, minutes, etc.)

- length of utterances

- evidence of listening comprehension (questions, clarifications, attention-giving verbal and nonverbal behavior)

- affective states such as self-esteem, extroversion, anxiety, and motivation (but these are only indirectly observable)

- evidence of attention-span issues, learning style preferences, etc.

- students' verbal or nonverbal response to materials, types of activities, teaching styles

- use of strategic options in comprehension or production (use of communication strategies, avoidance, etc.)

- culturally specific linguistic and nonverbal factors (kinesics; proxemics; use of humor, slang, metaphor, etc.)

The list might of course be modified to conform to specific needs of students, the focus of a lesson or module, the objectives of a curriculum, and other factors. The list might expand, as well, to include other possible observed performance. In order to carry out classroom observation, it is of course important to take the following steps:

1. Determine the specific objectives of the observation.
2. Decide how many students will be observed at one time.
3. Set up the logistics for making unnoticed observations.
4. Design a system for recording observed performances.
5. Do not overestimate the number of different elements you can observe at one time—keep them very limited.

6. Plan how many observations you will make.

7. Determine specifically how you will use the results.

Designing a system for observing is no simple task. Recording your observations can take the form of anecdotal records, checklists, or rating scales. Anecdotal records should be as specific as possible in focusing on the objective of the observation, but they are so varied in form that to suggest formats here would be counterproductive. Their very purpose is more notetaking than record-keeping. The key is to devise a system that maintains the principle of reliability as closely as possible.

Checklists are a viable alternative for recording observation results. Some checklists of student classroom performance, such as the COLT observation scheme devised by Spada and Fröhlich (1995), are elaborate grids referring to such variables as

- whole-class, group, and individual participation
- content of the topic
- linguistic competence (form, function, discourse, sociolinguistic).
- materials being used
- skill (listening, speaking, reading, writing)

with subcategories for each variable. The observer identifies an activity or episode, as well as the starting time for each, and checks appropriate boxes along the grid. Completing such a form in real time may present some difficulty with so many factors to attend to at once.

Checklists can also be quite simple, which is a better option for focusing on only a few factors within real time. On one occasion we assigned teachers the task of noting occurrences of student errors in third-person singular, plural, and *-ing* morphemes across a period of six weeks. Their records needed to specify only the number of occurrences of each, across all students in the class and for the whole class period, and whether each occurrence of the error was ignored, treated by the teacher, or self-corrected. Believe it or not, this was not an easy task. Simply noticing errors is hard enough, but making entries on even a very simple checklist required careful attention. The checklist looked like this:

Observation checklist, student errors

Grammatical Feature		
Third person singular	**Plural/s/**	***-ing* progressive**
Ignored	|||	||	||||
Treated by the teacher						
Self-corrected					||

Each of the 30-odd checklists that were eventually completed represented a two-hour class period and was filled in with "ticks" to show the occurrences and the follow-up in the appropriate cell.

Rubrics or rating scales have also been suggested for recording observations. One type of rubric asks teachers to indicate the frequency of occurrence of target performance on a separate frequency scale (from 1 [*never*] to 5 [*always*]). Another is a holistic assessment scale (to be discussed in upcoming chapters on assessing speaking and writing) that requires an overall assessment within a number of categories (e.g., vocabulary usage, grammatical correctness, fluency). Rating scales may be appropriate for recording observations after the fact—on the same day but after class, for example. Specific quantities of occurrences may be difficult to record while teaching a lesson and managing a classroom, but immediate subsequent evaluations can include some data on observations that would otherwise fade from memory in a day or so.

If you scrutinize observations under the microscope of principles of assessment, you will probably find moderate practicality and reliability in this type of procedure, especially if the objectives are kept very simple. Content validity is likely to get high marks, because observations are likely to be integrated into the ongoing process of a course. Washback is only moderate if you do little follow-up on observing. Some observations for research purposes may yield no washback whatever if the researcher simply disappears with the information and never communicates anything back to the student. But a subsequent conference with a student can then yield very high washback as the student is made aware of empirical data on targeted performance. Authenticity is high because, if an observation goes relatively unnoticed by the student, then there is little likelihood of contrived contexts or playacting.

SELF- AND PEER-ASSESSMENTS

A conventional view of language assessment might consider the notion of self- and peer-assessment as an absurd reversal of politically correct power relationships. After all, how could learners who are still in the process of acquisition, especially the early processes, be capable of rendering an accurate assessment of their own performance? Nevertheless, a closer look at the acquisition of any skill reveals the importance, if not the necessity, of self-assessment and the benefit of peer-assessment (Ekbatani & Pierson, 2000). What successful learner has not developed the ability to monitor his or her own performance and to use the data gathered for adjustments and corrections? Most successful learners extend the learning process well beyond the classroom and the presence of a teacher or tutor, autonomously mastering the art of self-assessment. Where peers are available to render assessments, the advantage of such additional input is obvious.

Self-assessment derives its theoretical justification from a number of well-established principles of second language acquisition. The principle of **autonomy** stands out as one of the primary foundation stones of successful learning. The ability to set one's own goals both within and beyond the structure of a classroom curriculum, to pursue them without the presence of an external prod, and to independently monitor that pursuit are all keys to success. Developing **intrinsic motivation** that comes from a self-propelled desire to excel is at the top of the list of successful acquisition of any set of skills.

Peer-assessment appeals to similar principles, the most obvious of which is Cooperative Learning. Many people go through a whole regimen of education from kindergarten up through a graduate degree and never come to appreciate the value of collaboration in learning—the benefit of a community of learners capable of teaching each other something. Peer-assessment is simply one arm of a plethora of tasks and procedures within the domain of learner-centered and collaborative education.

Researchers (such as Brown & Hudson, 1998) agree that the above theoretical underpinnings of self- and peer-assessment offer certain benefits: direct involvement of students in their own destiny, the encouragement of autonomy, and increased motivation because of their engagement. Of course, some noteworthy drawbacks must also be taken into account. Subjectivity is a primary obstacle to overcome. Students may be either too harsh on themselves or too self-flattering, or they may not have the necessary tools to make an accurate assessment (Cheng & Warren, 2005; North, 2000; Strong Krause, 2000). Also, especially in the case of direct assessments of performance (see below), they may not be able to discern their own errors. In contrast, Bailey (1998) conducted a study in which learners showed moderately high correlations (between .58 and .64) between self-rated oral production ability and scores on an oral production interview, which suggests that in the assessment of general competence, learners' self-assessments may be more accurate than one might suppose.

Types of Self- and Peer-Assessment

It is important to distinguish among several different types of self- and peer-assessment and to apply them accordingly. I have borrowed from widely accepted classifications of strategic options to create five categories of self- and peer-assessment: (1) direct assessment of performance, (2) indirect assessment of performance, (3) metacognitive assessment, (4) assessment of socioaffective factors, and (5) student self-generated tests.

1. *Direct assessment of (a specific) performance.* In this category, a student typically monitors him- or herself—in either oral or written production—and renders some kind of evaluation of performance. The evaluation takes place immediately or very soon after the performance. Thus, having made an oral presentation, the student (or a peer) fills out a checklist that rates performance on a defined scale. Or perhaps the student views a video-recorded lecture and completes a self-corrected comprehension quiz. A journal may serve as a tool for such self-assessment. Peer-editing is an excellent example of direct assessment of a specific performance.

Today, the availability of media opens up a number of possibilities for self- and peer-assessment beyond the classroom. Internet sites such as Dave's ESL Café (www.eslcafe.com/) offer many self-correcting quizzes and tests. On this and other similar sites, a learner may access a grammar or vocabulary quiz on the Internet and then self-score the result, which may be followed by comparing with a partner. Television and film media also offer convenient resources for self- and peer-assessment. D. Gardner (1996) recommended that students in non-English-speaking countries access bilingual news, films, and television programs and then self-assess their comprehension ability. He also noted that video versions of movies with subtitles can be viewed first without the subtitles, then with them, as another form of self- and/or peer-assessment.

2. *Indirect assessment of (general) competence.* Indirect self- or peer-assessment targets larger slices of time with a view to rendering an evaluation of general ability, as opposed to one specific, relatively time-constrained performance. Self- and peer-assessments of performance are limited in time and focus on a relatively short performance. Assessments of competence may encompass a lesson over several days, a module, or even a whole term of course work, and the objective is to ignore minor, nonrepeating performance flaws and thus evaluate general ability. A list of attributes can offer a scaled rubric, ranging from 1 (*strongly disagree*) to 5 (*strongly agree*) on such items as the following:

Indirect self-assessment rating scale

I demonstrate active listening in class.	5 4 3 2 1
I volunteer my comments in small-group work.	5 4 3 2 1
When I don't know a word, I guess from context.	5 4 3 2 1
My pronunciation is very clear.	5 4 3 2 1
I make very few mistakes in verb tenses.	5 4 3 2 1
I use logical connectors in my writing.	5 4 3 2 1

In a successful experiment to introduce self-assessment in his advanced intermediate preuniversity English as a second language (ESL) class, E. Phillips (2000) created a questionnaire (see Figure 6.3 on the next page) through which his students evaluated themselves on their class participation. The items were simply formatted with just three options to check for each category, which made the process easy for students to perform. They completed the questionnaire at midterm, which was followed up immediately with a teacher–student conference during which students identified weaknesses and set goals for the remainder of the term.

CLASS PARTICIPATION

Please fill out this questionnaire by checking the appropriate box:

Yes, Definitely   **Sometimes**   **Not Yet**
     ☐   ☐   ☐

1. I attend class.   Y   S   N
I come to class.   ☐   ☐   ☐
I come to class on time.   ☐   ☐   ☐
Comments: _____

2. I usually ask questions in class.
I ask the teacher questions.   ☐   ☐   ☐
I ask my classmates questions.   ☐   ☐   ☐
Comments: _____

**3. I usually answer questions
    in class.**
I answer questions that the teacher   ☐   ☐   ☐
asks.
I answer questions that my   ☐   ☐   ☐
classmates ask.
Comments: _____

4. I participate in group work.
I take equal turns in all three roles   ☐   ☐   ☐
(C, W, and R).
I offer my opinion.   ☐   ☐   ☐
I cooperate with my group   ☐   ☐   ☐
members.
I use appropriate classroom   ☐   ☐   ☐
language.
Comments: _____

5. I participate in pair work.   Y   S   N
I offer my opinion.   ☐   ☐   ☐
I cooperate with my partner.   ☐   ☐   ☐
I use appropriate classroom   ☐   ☐   ☐
language.
Comments: _____

**6. I participate in whole-class
    discussions.**
I make comments.   ☐   ☐   ☐
I ask questions.   ☐   ☐   ☐
I answer questions.   ☐   ☐   ☐
I respond to things someone else   ☐   ☐   ☐
says.
I clarify things someone else says.   ☐   ☐   ☐
I use the new vocabulary.   ☐   ☐   ☐
Comments: _____

7. I listen actively in class.
I listen actively to the teacher.   ☐   ☐   ☐
I listen actively to my classmates.   ☐   ☐   ☐
Comments: _____

8. I complete the peer reviews.
I complete all of the peer-reviews.   ☐   ☐   ☐
I respond to every question.   ☐   ☐   ☐
I give specific examples.   ☐   ☐   ☐
I offer suggestions.   ☐   ☐   ☐
I use appropriate classroom   ☐   ☐   ☐
language.
Comments: _____

Figure 6.3. Self-assessment of class participation (E. Phillips, 2000)

Of course, indirect self- and peer-assessment is not confined to scored rating sheets and questionnaires. An ideal genre for self-assessment is journals, in which students engage in more open-ended assessment and/or make their own further comments on the results of completed checklists.

3. *Metacognitive assessment (for setting goals).* Some kinds of evaluation are more strategic in nature, with the purpose not just of viewing past performance or competence but also setting goals and monitoring one's progress. Personal goal-setting has the advantage of fostering intrinsic motivation and providing learners with that extra-special impetus from having set and accomplished one's own goals. Strategic planning and self-monitoring can take the form of journal entries, choices from a list of possibilities, questionnaires, or cooperative (oral) pair or group planning.

A simple illustration of goal-setting self-assessment was offered by Smolen, Newman, Wathen, and Lee (1995). In response to the assignment of making "goal cards," a middle school student wrote in very simple terms:

> 1. My goal for this week is to stop during reading and predict what is going to happen next in the story.
> 2. My goal for this week is to finish writing my Superman story.

On the back of this same card, which was filled out at the end of the week, was the student's self-assessment:

> The first goal help me understand a lot when I'm reading.
>
> I met my goal for this week.

H. D. Brown's (1999) *New Vistas* series offers end-of-chapter self-evaluation checklists that give students the opportunity to think about the extent to which they have reached a desirable competency level in the specific objectives of the unit. Figure 6.4 shows a sample of this checkpoint feature. Through this technique, students are reminded of the communication skills they have been focusing on and are given a chance to identify those that are essentially accomplished, those not yet fulfilled, and those that need more work. The teacher follow-up is to spend more time on items on which a number of students checked "sometimes" or "not yet," or possibly to individualize assistance to students working on their own points of challenge.

I can . . .	Yes!	Sometimes	Not Yet
say the time in different ways.	☐	☐	☐
describe an ongoing action.	☐	☐	☐
ask about and describe what people are wearing.	☐	☐	☐
offer help.	☐	☐	☐
accept or decline an offer of help.	☐	☐	☐
ask about and describe the weather and seasons.	☐	☐	☐
write a letter.	☐	☐	☐

Figure 6.4. Self-assessment of lesson objectives (H. D. Brown, 1999, p. 59)

4. *Socioaffective assessment.* Yet another type of self- and peer-assessment comes in the form of methods of examining affective factors in learning. Such assessment is quite different from looking at and planning language elements (grammar, vocabulary, etc.). It requires looking at oneself through a psychological lens and may not differ greatly from self-assessment across a number of subject-matter areas or for any set of personal skills. When learners resolve to assess and improve motivation, to gauge and lower their own anxiety, to find mental or emotional obstacles to learning and then plan to overcome those barriers, an all-important socioaffective domain is invoked. A checklist form of such items may look like many of the questionnaire items in H. D. Brown (2002), in which test-takers must indicate preference for one statement over the one on the opposite side:

Self-assessment of styles (H. D. Brown, 2002, pp. 2, 13)

I don't mind if people laugh at me when I speak.	A B C D	I get embarrassed if people laugh at me when I speak.
I like rules and exact information.	A B C D	I like general guidelines and uncertain information.

In the same book, multiple intelligences are self-assessed on a scale of 1 *(definite disagreement)* to 4 *(definite disagreement)*:

Self-assessment of multiple intelligences (H. D. Brown, 2002, p. 37)

4 3 2 1	I like memorizing words.
4 3 2 1	I like the teacher to explain grammar to me.
4 3 2 1	I like making charts and diagrams.
4 3 2 1	I like drama and role plays.
4 3 2 1	I like singing songs in English.
4 3 2 1	I like group and pair interaction.
4 3 2 1	I like self-reflection and journal writing.

The *New Vistas* series (H. D. Brown, 1999) also presents an end-of-unit section on "Learning Preferences" that calls for self-assessment of an individual's learning preferences (see Figure 6.5). This information is of value to both teacher and student in identifying preferred styles and planning strategies for further development.

Learning Preferences

Think about the work you did in this unit. Put a check next to the items that helped you learn the lessons. Put two checks next to the ones that helped a lot.

☐ ☐ Listening to the teacher
☐ ☐ Working by myself
☐ ☐ Working with a partner
☐ ☐ Working with a group
☐ ☐ Asking the teacher questions

☐ ☐ Listening to the tapes and doing exercises
☐ ☐ Reading
☐ ☐ Writing paragraphs
☐ ☐ Using the Internet

Figure 6.5. Self-assessment of learning preferences (H. D. Brown, 1999, p. 59)

5. *Student-generated tests.* A final type of assessment that is not usually classified strictly as self- or peer-assessment is the technique of engaging students in the process of constructing tests themselves. The traditional view of what a test is would never allow students to engage in test construction, but student-generated tests can be productive, intrinsically motivating, autonomy-building processes.

Gorsuch (1998) found that student-generated quiz items transformed routine weekly quizzes into a collaborative and fulfilling experience. Students in small groups were directed to create content questions on their reading passages and to collectively choose six vocabulary items for inclusion on the quiz. The process of creating questions and choosing lexical items served as a more powerful reinforcement of the reading than any teacher-designed quiz could ever be. To add further interest, Gorsuch directed students to keep records of their own scores to plot their progress through the term.

Murphey (1995), another champion of self- and peer-generated tests, successfully employed the technique of directing students to generate their own lists of words, grammatical concepts, and content that they think are important over the course of a unit. Those lists were then synthesized by Murphey into a single list for review, and all items on the test come from the list. Students thereby have a voice in determining the content of tests. On other occasions, Murphey used what he called "interactive pair tests" in which students assess each other using a set of quiz items. One student's response aptly summarized the impact of this technique:

> *We had a test today. But it was not a test, because we could study for it beforehand. I gave some questions to my partner and my partner gave me some questions. And we students decided what grade we should get. I hate tests, but I like this kind of test. So please don't give us a surprise test. I think, that kind of test that we did today is more useful for me than a surprise test because I study for it.*

Many educators agree that one of the primary purposes in administering tests is to stimulate review and integration, which is exactly what student-generated testing does, but almost without awareness on the students' part that they are reviewing the material. I have seen a number of instances of teachers successfully facilitating students in the self-construction of tests. The process engenders intrinsic involvement in reviewing objectives and selecting and designing items for the final form of the test. The teacher of course needs to set certain parameters for such a project and be willing to assist learners in designing items.

Guidelines for Self- and Peer-Assessment

Self- and peer-assessment are among the best possible formative types of assessment and possibly the most rewarding, but they must be carefully designed and administered to reach their potential. Four guidelines will help teachers bring this intrinsically motivating task into the classroom successfully.

1. *Tell students the purpose of the assessment.* Self-assessment is a process that many students—especially those in traditional educational systems—will initially find quite uncomfortable. They need to be sold on the concept. It is therefore essential that you carefully analyze the needs that will be met in offering both self- and peer-assessment opportunities and then convey this information to students.

2. *Define the task(s) clearly.* Make sure the students know exactly what they are supposed to do. If you are offering a rating sheet or questionnaire, the task is not complex, but an open-ended journal entry could leave students perplexed about what to write. Guidelines and models are of great help in clarifying the procedures.

3. *Encourage impartial evaluation of performance or ability.* One of the greatest drawbacks to self-assessment is the inevitable subjectivity of the process. By showing students the advantage of honest, objective opinions, you can maximize the beneficial washback of self-assessments. Peer-assessments, too, are vulnerable to unreliability as students apply varying standards to their peers. Clear assessment criteria can go a long way toward encouraging objectivity.

4. *Ensure beneficial washback through follow-up tasks.* It is not enough to simply toss a self-checklist at students and then walk away. Systematic follow-up can be accomplished through further self-analysis, journal reflection, written feedback from the teacher, conferencing with the teacher, purposeful goal-setting by the student, or any combination of these.

A Taxonomy of Self- and Peer-Assessment Tasks

To sum up the possibilities for self- and peer-assessment, it is helpful to consider a variety of tasks within each of the four skills.

Self- and peer-assessment tasks

Listening Tasks
Listening to TV or radio broadcasts and checking comprehension with a partner
Listening to bilingual versions of a broadcast and checking comprehension
Asking when you don't understand something in pair or group work
Listening to an academic lecture and checking yourself on a "quiz" of the content
Setting goals for creating/increasing opportunities for listening

Speaking Tasks
Filling out student self-checklists and questionnaires
Using peer checklists and questionnaires
Rating someone's oral presentation (holistically—see Chapter 8)
Detecting pronunciation or grammar errors on a self-recording
Asking others for confirmation checks in conversational settings
Setting goals for creating/increasing opportunities for speaking

Reading Tasks
Reading passages with self-check comprehension questions following
Reading and checking comprehension with a partner
Taking vocabulary quizzes
Taking grammar and vocabulary quizzes on the Internet
Conducting self-assessment of reading habits
Setting goals for creating/increasing opportunities for reading

Writing Tasks
Revising written work on your own
Revising written work with a peer (peer-editing)
Proofreading
Using journal writing for reflection, assessment, and goal-setting
Setting goals for creating/increasing opportunities for writing

An evaluation of self- and peer-assessment according to our classic principles of assessment yields a pattern that is quite consistent with other alternatives to assessment that have been analyzed in this chapter. Practicality can achieve a moderate level with such procedures as checklists and questionnaires, whereas reliability risks remaining at a low level, given the variation within and across learners. Once students accept the notion that they can legitimately assess themselves, then the impact can be raised from what might otherwise be a low level. Adherence to course objectives will help ensure a high degree of content validity. Authenticity and washback both have very high potential because students are centering on their own linguistic needs and receiving useful feedback.

Table 6.2 is a summary of all six of the alternatives in assessment with regard to their fulfillment of the major assessment principles. The caveat that must accompany such a chart is that none of the evaluative "marks" should be considered permanent or unchangeable. In fact, the challenge that was presented at the beginning of the chapter is reiterated here: Take the "low" factors in the chart and create assessment procedures that raise those marks.

Table 6.2. Principled evaluation of alternatives to assessment

Principle	Portfolio	Journal	Conference	Interview	Observation	Self/Peer
Practicality	low	low	low	mod	mod	mod
Reliability	mod	mod	low	mod	mod	low
Face validity	high	mod	high	high	high	mod
Content validity	high	high	high	high	high	high
Washback	high	high	high	mod	mod	high
Authenticity	high	high	high	mod	high	high

☆　　☆　　☆　　☆　　☆

We hope that it's now clear why "alternatives in assessment" is a more appropriate phrase than "alternative assessment." To set traditional testing and alternatives against each other is counterproductive. All kinds of assessment, from formal conventional procedures to informal and possibly unconventional tasks, are needed to assemble information on students. The alternatives covered in this chapter may not be markedly different from some of the tasks described in the preceding four chapters (assessing listening, speaking, reading, and writing). When we put all of this together, we have at our disposal an amazing array of possible assessment tasks for second language learners of English. The alternatives presented in this chapter simply expand that continuum of possibilities.

EXERCISES

[Note: **(I)** Individual work; **(G)** Group or pair work; **(C)** Whole-class discussion.]

1. **(C)** Using Brown and Hudson's (1998) 12 characteristics of alternatives in assessment (quoted at the beginning of the chapter), ask the class to name some differences between traditional and alternative assessment. Some performance assessments are relatively traditional (oral interview, essay writing, demonstrations), yet they fit most of the criteria for alternatives in assessment. In this light, identify a continuum of assessments, ranging from highly traditional to alternative.

2. **(G)** In a small group, refer to Figures 6.1 and 6.2, which depict presumed and idealized relationships between practicality/reliability and authenticity/washback. With each group assigned to a separate skill area (L, S, R, W), select 10 or 12 commonly used assessment techniques/tasks and place them into this same graph. Show your graph to the rest of the class and explain. In instances where a task scores low on one or the other axis, how might you modify it to raise its plot on the axis? Report findings back to the class.

3. **(I/C)** Search the Internet for writing or speaking *rubrics.* Select one to examine, and, if possible, print it out to bring to class. Tell the class what you think the validity and reliability of your rubric is and what problems one might encounter in using it.

4. **(I/G)** Assign a few volunteers from the class to procure a sample of a portfolio from a teacher they know or from a school they have some connection with (but make sure that privacy issues are not a problem). Small groups can then evaluate the portfolio on as many of the seven guidelines (pages 131–133) as possible. Present the portfolio and evaluation to the rest of the class.

5. **(G)** In pairs or groups, follow the same procedure as item 3 on the previous page for a journal.
6. **(I/C)** If possible, observe a teacher–student conference or a student–student peer-assessment. The most common type of conference might be over a draft of an essay. Report back to the class on what you observed and offer an evaluation of its effectiveness.
7. **(I/C)** Observe an ESL/EFL class. The goal is to look specifically for any evidence of self- and peer-assessment. Assign some observers to note any instances of students' processing of the teacher's error treatment. Report findings to the class.
8. **(C)** Look at the self-assessments in Figures 6.3, 6.4, and 6.5. Evaluate their effectiveness in terms of the guidelines offered in this chapter.
9. **(G)** At the end of the chapter, Table 6.2 offers a broad estimate of the extent to which the alternatives to assessment in this chapter measure up to basic principles of assessment. In pairs or small groups, each assigned to one of the six alternatives, decide whether you agree with these evaluations. Defend your decisions and report them to the rest of the class.

FOR YOUR FURTHER READING

Brown, James Dean. (Ed.). (1998). *New ways of classroom assessment.* Alexandria, VA: Teachers of English to Speakers of Other Languages.

This volume in TESOL's "New Ways" series offers an array of nontraditional assessment procedures. Each procedure indicates its appropriate level, objective, class time required, and suggested preparation time. Included are examples of portfolios, journals, logs, conferences, and self- and peer-assessment. Alternatives to traditional assessment of listening, speaking, reading, and writing are also given. All techniques were contributed by teachers in a variety of levels, skill areas, and contexts around the world.

Law, Barbara, & Eckes, Mary. (2007). *Assessment and ESL:An alternative approach.* Winnipeg, Manitoba, Canada: Portage & Main Press.

This comprehensive resource provides accessible information on both research and practice in alternative assessment for learners of different ages (from elementary school to adult) and in a variety of contexts. One of its unique features is a number of stories of students and how they were able to make progress by using multiple alternative assessment techniques. The authors help teachers to look beneath the surface of traditional tests to document their students' progress.

CHAPTER 7

ASSESSING LISTENING

> **OBJECTIVES:** After reading this chapter, you will be able to
>
> - state a rationale for assessing listening as a separate skill as well as a skill that integrates with one or more of the other three skills
> - discern the overlap between assessing listening as an implicit, unanalyzed ability and its explicit, form-focused counterpart, namely grammar and vocabulary comprehension
>
> - incorporate performance-based assessment into your own assessment instruments
> - develop assessments that focus on one or several micro- and macroskills of listening performance
> - design assessments that target one or several of the modes of performance, ranging from intensive to extensive listening

In earlier chapters, a number of foundational principles of language assessment were introduced. Concepts such as practicality, reliability, validity, authenticity, washback, direct and indirect testing, and formative and summative assessment are by now part of your vocabulary. You have become acquainted with some tools for evaluating a "good" test, examined procedures for designing a classroom test, and explored the complex process of creating different kinds of test items. You have begun to absorb the intricate psychometric, educational, and political issues that intertwine in the world of standards-based and standardized testing.

Now our focus will shift away from standardized testing at the macro level of educational measurement in general to the context in which you will usually work: the day-to-day classroom assessment of the four skills of listening, speaking, reading, and writing. Because this is the level at which you will most frequently have the opportunity to apply principles of assessment, the next four chapters of this book provide guidelines and hands-on practice in testing within a curriculum of English as a second or foreign language.

Before directly discussing the assessment of the skills, and, in this chapter, listening, we will look at three introductory issues that will help you to put the separate skills into perspective: (a) Can you assess one skill in isolation, without the participation of at least one other skill? (b) How do grammar and vocabulary fit into the assessment of the skills? (c) Can we directly observe the performance of all four skills?

INTEGRATION OF SKILLS IN LANGUAGE ASSESSMENT

It's important to be crystal clear about the feasibility of ostensibly assessing just one skill at a time. Now you could argue that, in the real world, we do in fact use single skills in isolation. When we listen to a radio, read a book, deliver a speech, or write a letter, we're attending to one skill at those moments. So there are authentic manifestations of single skills in our everyday use of a language.

However, one could also easily argue that in the usual 16 or so waking hours of an adult user of a language, the overwhelming majority of that time involves integration of at least two skills. Conversations involve speaking and listening; writing can hardly be performed without reading; a good deal of computer use combines reading and writing (or at least keyboard production of some kind). Then, in the classroom, an even greater proportion of time is devoted to the integration of skills: discussions, asking questions, group work, responding to readings, problem solving—all of these require the language-user to engage in parallel processing of at least two skills at the same time. Every language teacher and researcher will tell you that *the integration of skills is of paramount importance in language learning* (see *TBP,* Chapter 15).

In assessing language, integration is even more of a certainty because assessment virtually always implies a "two-way street" between the teacher/tester and students: A set of questions or prompts is produced by the teacher and comprehended by the test-taker. Such integration is of course authentic in its simulation of real-world communication.

In this book, the four skills are treated in four different chapters. Despite that artificial division, no single skill is actually treated independently. In this chapter on listening, for instance, of the 20 example items used for illustration, only one of them tests listening in isolation (that one is a picture-cued item that requires identification of the correct picture). So do not let the separate treatment of the four language skills in this book predispose you to think that those skills are or should be assessed in isolation. The rationale for examining the skills in separate chapters is simply to provide clear organizers for you to identify principles, test types, tasks, and issues associated with each skill.

To cue the skills involved in each sample test item in the next four chapters, we provide a code consisting of the letters *L* (listening), *S* (speaking), *R* (reading), and/or *W* (writing). These serve to highlight the two or more skills that are integrated in a single item type.

ASSESSING GRAMMAR AND VOCABULARY

A second issue in the assessment of language skills is the age-old question of the role of grammar and vocabulary. We are all maybe too familiar with grammar and vocabulary tests from our own foreign-language classes. Perhaps you dreaded that daily or weekly "quiz," when the teacher told you to close your books and take out a blank sheet of paper, whereupon you were forced to identify grammar rules or define words from your lesson. Well, first we have to ask you if it's possible to assess one's knowledge of language forms *without* recourse to at least one of the skills? And of course your answer is, "Well, not really, since I might listen, speak, read, and/or write in order to understand and respond to the questions."

So let's be clear: There is no such thing as a test of grammar or vocabulary that does not invoke one or more of the separate skills of listening, speaking, reading, or writing. It's not uncommon to find "grammar tests" and "vocabulary tests" in textbooks, and these may be perfectly useful instruments. But responses on these quizzes are usually written, with multiple-choice selection or fill-in-the-blank items. In this book, we treat the various linguistic forms (phonology, morphology, lexicon, grammar, and discourse) within the context of skill areas. That way we don't perpetuate the myth that grammar and vocabulary and other linguistic forms can somehow be disassociated from a mode of performance.

Now in case you have noticed that Chapter 11 is a separate chapter on assessing grammar and vocabulary, let us explain. A communicative language-teaching approach emphasizes spontaneous communication in which **focus on form** is implicit for perhaps most of the minutes of a classroom hour. But in every effective communicative classroom, there is an appropriate and propitious time for explicit focus on form. Those are the moments and exercises when learners are asked to "zoom in" on the language they've been using and use form-focused exercises to cement phonological, grammatical, and lexical features into their competence.

A further complexity in this issue is the historical precedent of decades of testing in which focus on form (testing grammar and vocabulary) has all too often been the only criterion. To this day, many standardized tests ask test-takers to process explicit knowledge of formal aspects of the language in question, usually in the form of items that require the responder to identify correct grammar or a correct vocabulary item. Many such tests are so focused on form that little evidence of authenticity and real-world communication is incorporated into the test specifications.

With these complex issues in mind, we pay a good deal of attention to formal properties of language in the chapters on the four skills, but we will also devote a separate chapter (see Chapter 11) to assessing grammar and vocabulary. The former is to emphasize the inextricable partnership of meaning and form. The latter is to provide current perspectives on the myths and realities of form-focused assessment and to bring grammar and vocabulary tests more in line with current views of functional grammar and pragmatics.

OBSERVING THE PERFORMANCE OF THE FOUR SKILLS

A third factor to consider before focusing on listening itself is the relationship between the two interacting concepts of *performance* and *observation*. First, let's discuss performance. All language users perform the acts of listening and speaking, and many also read and write. They of course rely on their underlying competence to accomplish these performances. When you propose to assess someone's ability in one or a combination of the four skills, you assess that person's competence, but you observe the person's performance. Sometimes the performance does not indicate true competence: a bad night's rest, illness, an emotional distraction, test anxiety, a memory block, or other student-related reliability factors could affect performance, thereby providing an unreliable measure of actual competence.

Thus one important principle for assessing a learner's competence is to consider the fallibility of the results of a single performance, such as that produced in a test. As with any attempt at measurement, it is your obligation as a teacher to **triangulate** your measurements: Consider at least two (or more) performances and/or contexts before drawing a conclusion. This can take the form of one or more of the following designs:

- several tests that are combined to form an assessment
- a single test with multiple test tasks to account for learning styles and performance variables
- in-class and extra-class graded work
- alternative forms of assessment (e.g., journal, portfolio, conference, observation, self-assessment, peer-assessment)

Multiple measures will always give you a more reliable and valid assessment than a single measure.

A second principle is one that we teachers often forget. We must rely as much as possible on observable performance in our assessments of students. *Observable* means being able to see or hear the performance of the learner (the senses of touch, taste, and smell don't apply very often to language testing). What, then, is observable among the four skills of listening, speaking, reading, and writing? Table 7.1 offers an answer.

Table 7.1. Observable performance of the four skills

Can the teacher *directly* observe . . .		
	the process?	**the product?**
Listening	No	No
Speaking	Yes	No*
Reading	No	No
Writing	Yes	Yes

*Except in the case of an audio or video recording that preserves the output

Isn't it interesting that in the case of the receptive skills, we can observe neither the process of performing nor a product? I can hear your argument already: "But I can *see* that she's listening because she's nodding her head and frowning and smiling and asking relevant questions." Well, you're not observing the listening performance; you're observing the *result* of the listening. You can no more observe listening (or reading) than you can see the wind blowing. The process of the listening performance itself is the invisible, inaudible process of internalizing meaning from the auditory signals being transmitted to the ear and brain. Or you may argue that the product of listening is a spoken or written response from the student that indicates correct (or incorrect) auditory processing. Again, the product of listening and reading is not the spoken or written response. The product is within the structure of the brain, and until technology provides us with portable brain scanners to detect meaningful intake, it is impossible to observe the product. You observe only the result of the meaningful input in the form of spoken or written output, just as you observe the result of the wind by noticing the trees waving back and forth.

The productive skills of speaking and writing allow us to hear and see the process as it is performed. Writing gives a permanent product in the form of a written piece. But unless you have recorded speech, there is no *permanent* observable product for speaking performance, because all those words you just heard have vanished from your perception and (you hope) have been transformed into meaningful intake somewhere in your brain.

Receptive skills, then, are clearly the more enigmatic of the two modes of performance. You cannot observe the actual act of listening or reading, nor can you see or hear an actual product. You can observe learners only *while* they are listening or reading. The upshot is that all assessment of listening and reading must be made on the basis of observing the test-taker's speaking or writing (or nonverbal response), not on the listening or reading itself. Thus, basically, all assessment of receptive performance must be made by inference.

Discouraging, right? Well, not necessarily. We have developed reasonably good assessment tasks to make the necessary jump, through the process of inference, from unobservable reception to a conclusion about comprehension competence. All this is a good reminder not just of the importance of triangulation but of the potential fragility of assessing comprehension ability. The actual performance is made "behind the scenes," and those of us who propose to make reliable assessments of receptive performance need to be on our guard.

THE IMPORTANCE OF LISTENING

Listening has often played second fiddle to its counterpart, speaking. In the standardized testing industry, a number of separate oral production tests are available (see list of tests in the appendix at the back of this book), but it is rare to find just a listening test. One reason for this emphasis is that listening is often implied as a component of speaking. How could one speak a language without also listening? In addition, the overtly observable nature of speaking renders it more empirically measurable than listening. But perhaps a deeper cause lies in universal biases toward speaking. A good speaker is often (unwisely) valued more highly than a good listener. To determine if someone is a proficient user of a language, people customarily ask, "Do you speak Spanish?" People rarely ask, "Do you *understand* and speak Spanish?"

Every teacher of language knows that one's oral production ability—other than monologues, speeches, reading aloud, and the like—is only as good as one's listening comprehension ability. Of even further impact is the likelihood that input in the aural–oral mode accounts for a large proportion of successful language acquisition. In a typical day, we do measurably more listening than speaking (with the possible exception of one or two of your friends who never seem to stop talking!). Whether in the workplace, educational, or home context, aural comprehension far outweighs oral production in quantifiable terms of time, number of words, effort, and attention.

We therefore need to pay close attention to listening as a mode of performance for assessment in the classroom. In this chapter, we begin with the basic principles and types of listening and then move on to a survey of tasks that can be used to assess listening. (For a review of issues in teaching listening, see Chapter 16 of *TBP.*)

BASIC TYPES OF LISTENING

As with all effective tests, designing appropriate assessment tasks in listening begins with the specification of objectives or criteria. Those objectives may be classified in terms of several types of listening performance. Think about what you do when you listen. Literally in nanoseconds, the following processes flash through your brain:

1. You recognize speech sounds and hold a temporary "imprint" of them in short-term memory.
2. You simultaneously determine the type of speech event (monologue, interpersonal dialogue, transactional dialogue) that is being processed and attend to its context (who the speaker is, location, purpose) and the content of the message.
3. You use (bottom-up) linguistic decoding skills and/or (top-down) background schemata to bring a plausible interpretation to the message and assign a literal and intended meaning to the utterance.
4. In most cases (except for repetition tasks, which involve short-term memory only), you delete the exact linguistic form in which the message was originally received in favor of conceptually retaining important or relevant information in long-term memory.

Each of these stages represents a potential assessment objective:

- comprehending surface structure elements such as phonemes, words, into-nation, or a grammatical category
- understanding pragmatic context
- determining meaning of auditory input
- developing the gist, a global or comprehensive understanding

From these stages we can derive four commonly identified types of listening performance, each of which comprises a category within which to consider assess-ment tasks and procedures:

1. *Intensive:* listening for perception of the components (phonemes, words, intonation, discourse markers, etc.) of a larger stretch of language
2. *Responsive:* listening to a relatively short stretch of language (a greeting, ques-tion, command, comprehension check, etc.) in order to make an equally short response
3. *Selective:* processing stretches of discourse such as short monologues for sev-eral minutes in order to "scan" for certain information. The purpose of such performance is not necessarily to look for global or general meanings but to be able to comprehend designated information in a context of longer stretches of spoken language (such as classroom directions from a teacher, TV or radio news items, or stories). Assessment tasks in selective listening could ask students, for example, to listen for names, numbers, a grammatical cate-gory, directions (in a map exercise), or certain facts and events.
4. *Extensive:* listening to develop a top-down, global understanding of spoken language. Extensive performance ranges from listening to lengthy lectures to listening to a conversation and deriving a comprehensive message or pur-pose. Listening for the gist—or the main idea—and making inferences are all part of extensive listening.

For full comprehension, test-takers may at the extensive level need to invoke **interactive** skills (perhaps notetaking, questioning, discussion): listening that includes all four of the above types as test-takers actively participate in discussions, debates, conversations, role plays, and pair and group work. Their listening perfor-mance must be intricately integrated with speaking (and perhaps other skills) in the authentic give-and-take of communicative interchange.

MICRO- AND MACROSKILLS OF LISTENING

A useful way of synthesizing the above two lists is to consider a finite number of **microskills** and **macroskills** implied in the performance of listening comprehen-sion. Richards's (1983) list of microskills has proven useful in the domain of specifying objectives for learning and may be even more useful in forcing test designers to carefully identify specific assessment objectives. In the following box, the skills are subdivided into what we prefer to think of as microskills (attending to the smaller bits and chunks of language, in more of a bottom-up process) and macroskills (focusing on the larger elements involved in a top-down approach to a listening task). The micro- and macroskills provide 17 different objectives to assess in listening.

Micro- and macroskills of listening (adapted from Richards, 1983)

Microskills

1. Discriminate among the distinctive sounds of English
2. Retain chunks of language of different lengths in short-term memory
3. Recognize English stress patterns, words in stressed and unstressed positions, rhythmic structure, intonation contours, and their role in signaling information
4. Recognize reduced forms of words
5. Distinguish word boundaries, recognize a core of words, and interpret word order patterns and their significance
6. Process speech at different rates of delivery
7. Process speech containing pauses, errors, corrections, and other performance variables
8. Recognize grammatical word classes (nouns, verbs, etc.), systems (e.g., tense, agreement, pluralization), patterns, rules, and elliptical forms
9. Detect sentence constituents and distinguish between major and minor constituents
10. Recognize that a particular meaning may be expressed in different grammatical forms
11. Recognize cohesive devices in spoken discourse

Macroskills

12. Recognize the communicative functions of utterances, according to situations, participants, goals
13. Infer situations, participants, goals using real-world knowledge
14. From events and ideas described, predict outcomes, infer links and connections between events, deduce causes and effects, and detect such relations as main idea, supporting idea, new information, given information, generalization, and exemplification
15. Distinguish between literal and implied meanings
16. Use facial, kinesic, body language, and other nonverbal clues to decipher meanings
17. Develop and use a battery of listening strategies, such as detecting key words, guessing the meaning of words from context, appealing for help, and signaling comprehension or lack thereof

---

Implied in this taxonomy is a notion of what makes many aspects of listening difficult, or why listening is not simply a linear process of recording strings of language as they are transmitted into our brains. Developing a sense of which aspects of listening performance are predictably difficult will help you to challenge your students appropriately and assign weights to items. Consider the following list of what makes listening difficult (adapted from Dunkel, 1991; Jung, 2003, 2006; Richards, 1983; Ur, 1984):

1. *Clustering:* attending to appropriate "chunks" of language—phrases, clauses, constituents
2. *Redundancy:* recognizing the kinds of repetitions, rephrasing, elaborations, and insertions that unrehearsed spoken language often contains and benefiting from that recognition
3. *Reduced forms:* understanding the reduced forms that may not have been a part of an English-learner's past learning experiences in classes where only formal "textbook" language has been presented
4. *Performance variables:* being able to "weed out" hesitations, false starts, pauses, and corrections in natural speech
5. *Colloquial language:* comprehending idioms, slang, reduced forms, shared cultural knowledge
6. *Discourse markers:* understanding discourse markers such as "my first point," "secondly," "nevertheless," "next," "in conclusion," etc., which can be especially difficult in academic lectures (Jung 2003, 2006)
7. *Rate of delivery:* keeping up with the speed of delivery, processing automatically as the speaker continues
8. *Stress, rhythm, and intonation:* correctly understanding prosodic elements of spoken language, which is almost always much more difficult than understanding the smaller phonological bits and pieces
9. *Interaction:* managing the interactive flow of language from listening to speaking to listening, etc.

DESIGNING ASSESSMENT TASKS: INTENSIVE LISTENING

Once you have determined objectives, your next step is to design the tasks, including making decisions about how you will elicit performance and how you will expect the test-taker to respond. We will look at tasks that range from intensive listening performance, such as minimal phonemic pair recognition, to extensive comprehension of language in communicative contexts. The focus in this section is on the microskills of intensive listening.

Recognizing Phonological and Morphological Elements

A typical form of intensive listening at this level is the assessment of recognition of phonological and morphological elements of language. A classic test task gives a spoken stimulus and asks test-takers to identify the stimulus from two or more choices, as in the following two examples:

Phonemic pair, consonants [L, R]

Test-takers hear:	He's from California.
Test-takers read:	A. He's from California. B. She's from California.

Phonemic pair, vowels [L, R]

Test-takers hear:	Is he living?
Iest-takers read:	A. Is he leaving? B. Is he living?

In both cases above, minimal phonemic distinctions are the target. If you are testing recognition of morphology, you can use the same format:

Morphological pair, -ed ending [L, R]

Test-takers hear:	I missed you very much.
Test-takers read:	A. I missed you very much. B. I miss you very much.

Hearing the past-tense morpheme in this sentence challenges even advanced learners, especially if no context is provided. Stressed and unstressed words may also be tested with the same rubric. In the following example, the reduced form (contraction) of *cannot* is tested:

Stress pattern in can't *[L, R]*

Test-takers hear:	My girlfriend can't go to the party.
Test-takers read:	A. My girlfriend can't go to the party. B. My girlfriend can go to the party.

Because they are decontextualized, these kinds of tasks leave something to be desired in their authenticity. But they are a step better than items that simply provide a one-word stimulus:

One-word stimulus [L, R]

Test-takers hear:	vine
Test-takers read:	A. vine B. wine

Paraphrase Recognition

The next step up on the scale of listening comprehension microskills is words, phrases, and sentences, which are frequently assessed by providing a stimulus sentence and asking the test-taker to choose the correct paraphrase from a number of choices:

Sentence paraphrase [L, R]

Test-takers hear:	Hello, my name's Keiko. I come from Japan.
Test-takers read:	A. Keiko is comfortable in Japan. B. Keiko wants to come to Japan. C. Keiko is Japanese. D. Keiko likes Japan.

In the above item, the idiomatic *come from* is the phrase being tested. To add a little context, a conversation can be the stimulus task to which test-takers must respond with the correct paraphrase:

Dialogue paraphrase [L, R]

Test-takers hear:	Man:	Hi, Maria, my name's George.
	Woman:	Nice to meet you, George. Are you American?
	Man:	No, I'm Canadian.
Test-takers read:		A. George lives in the United States. B. George is American. C. George comes from Canada. D. Maria is Canadian.

Here, the criterion is recognition of the adjective form used to indicate country of origin: Canadian, American, Brazilian, Italian, etc.

DESIGNING ASSESSMENT TASKS: RESPONSIVE LISTENING

A question-and-answer format can provide some interactivity in these lower-end listening tasks. The test-taker's response is the appropriate answer to a question:

Appropriate response to a question [L, R]

Test-takers hear:	How much time did you take to do your homework?
Test-takers read:	A. In about an hour. B. About an hour. C. About $10. D. Yes, I did.

The objective of this item is recognition of the *wh-* question "how much?" and its appropriate response. Distractors are chosen to represent common learner errors: in distractor A, responding to "how much" versus "how much longer"; in distractor C, confusing "how much" in reference to time versus the more frequent reference to money; and in distractor D, confusing a *wh-* question with a yes/no question.

None of the tasks so far discussed have to be framed in a multiple-choice format. They can be offered in a more open-ended framework in which test-takers write or speak the response. The above item would then look like this:

Open-ended response to a question [L, S, W]

Test-takers hear:	How much time did you take to do your homework?
Test-takers write or speak:	_____.

If open-ended response formats gain a small amount of authenticity and creativity, they of course suffer some in their practicality, as teachers must then read students' responses and judge their appropriateness, which takes time.

DESIGNING ASSESSMENT TASKS: SELECTIVE LISTENING

A third type of listening performance is **selective** listening, in which the test-taker listens to a limited quantity of aural input and must discern within it some specific information. A number of techniques have been used that require selective listening.

Listening Cloze

Listening cloze tasks (sometimes called **cloze dictations** or **partial dictations**) require the test-taker to listen to a story, monologue, or conversation and simultaneously read the written text in which selected words or phrases have been deleted. **Cloze** procedure is most commonly associated with reading only (see Chapter 9). In its generic form, the test consists of a passage in which every *n*th word (typically every seventh word) is deleted and the test-taker is asked to supply an appropriate word. In a listening cloze task, test-takers see a transcript of the passage they are listening to and fill in the blanks with the words or phrases that they hear.

One potential weakness of listening cloze techniques is that they may simply become reading comprehension tasks. Test-takers who are asked to listen to a story with periodic deletions in the written version may not need to listen at all yet may still be able to respond with the appropriate word or phrase. You can guard against this eventuality if the blanks are items with high information load that cannot be easily predicted simply by reading the passage. In the example below (adapted from Bailey, 1998, p. 16), such a shortcoming was avoided by focusing only on the criterion of numbers. Test-takers hear an announcement from an airline agent and see the transcript with the underlined words deleted:

Listening cloze [L, R, W]

Test-takers hear:

Ladies and gentlemen, I now have some connecting gate information for those of you making connections to other flights out of San Francisco.

Test-takers read the sentences and write the missing words or phrases in the blanks.

Flight *seven-oh-six* to Portland will depart from gate *seventy-three* at *nine-thirty* P.M.
Flight *ten-forty-five* to Reno will depart at *nine-fifty* P.M. from gate *seventeen*.
Flight *four-forty* to Monterey will depart at *nine-thirty-five* P.M. from gate *sixty*.
And flight *sixteen-oh-three* to Sacramento will depart from gate *nineteen* at *ten-fifteen* P.M.

Other listening cloze tasks may focus on a grammatical category such as verb tenses, articles, two-word verbs, prepositions, or transition words/phrases. Notice two important structural differences between listening cloze tasks and a standard reading cloze. In a listening cloze, deletions are governed by the objective of the test, not by mathematical deletion of every *n*th word, and more than one word may be deleted, as in the above example.

Listening cloze tasks should normally use an **exact word** method of scoring, in which you accept as a correct response only the actual word or phrase that was spoken and consider other **appropriate words** as incorrect. (See Chapter 8 for further discussion of these two methods.) Such stringency is warranted; your objective is, after all, to test listening comprehension, not grammatical or lexical expectancies.

Information Transfer

Selective listening can also be assessed through an **information transfer** technique in which aurally processed information must be transferred to a visual representation, such as labeling a diagram, identifying an element in a picture, completing a form, or showing routes on a map.

At the lower end of the scale of linguistic complexity, simple **picture-cued items** are sometimes efficient rubrics for assessing certain selected information. Consider the following item:

Information transfer: multiple-picture-cued selection [L]

Test-takers hear:

Choose the correct picture. In my backyard I have a bird feeder. Yesterday, there were two birds and a squirrel fighting for the last few seeds in the bird feeder. The squirrel was on top of the bird feeder while the larger bird sat at the bottom of the feeder screeching at the squirrel. The smaller bird was flying around the squirrel, trying to scare it away.

Test-takers see:

The preceding example illustrates the need for test-takers to focus on just the relevant information. The objective of this task is to test prepositions and prepositional phrases of location ("at the bottom," "on top of," "around," along with "larger," "smaller"), so other words and phrases such as "backyard," "yesterday," "last few seeds", and "scare away" are supplied only as context and need not be tested. (The task also presupposes, of course, that test-takers are able to identify the difference between a bird and a squirrel!)

In another genre of picture-cued tasks, a number of people and/or actions are presented in one picture, such as a group of people at a party. Assuming that all the items, people, and actions are clearly depicted and understood by the test-taker, assessment may take the form of

- questions: "Is the tall man near the door talking to a short woman?"
- true/false: "The woman wearing a red skirt is watching TV."
- identification: "Point to the person who is standing behind the lamp." "Draw a circle around the person to the left of the couch."

In a third picture-cued option used by the Test of English for International Communication (TOEIC® Test), one single photograph is presented to the test-taker, who then hears four different statements and must choose one of the four to describe the photograph. Here is an example.

Information transfer: single-picture-cued verbal multiple-choice [L, R]

Test-takers see:

Test-takers hear:

    A. He's speaking into a microphone.
    B. He's putting on his glasses.
    C. He has both eyes closed.
    D. He's using a microscope.

Information transfer tasks may reflect greater authenticity by using charts, maps, grids, timetables, and other artifacts of daily life. In the example on the next page, test-takers hear a student's daily schedule, and the task is to fill in the partially completed weekly calendar.

Information transfer: chart-filling [L, R, W]

Test-takers hear:

Now you will hear information about Lucy's daily schedule. The information will be given twice. The first time just listen carefully. The second time, there will be a pause after each sentence. Fill in Lucy's blank daily schedule with the correct information. The example has already been filled in.

You will hear: Lucy gets up at eight o'clock every morning except on weekends.

You will <u>fill in the schedule</u> to provide the information.

Now listen to the information about Lucy's schedule. Remember, you will first hear all the sentences, then you will hear each sentence separately with time to fill in your chart.

Lucy gets up at eight o'clock every morning except on weekends. She has English on Monday, Wednesday, and Friday at ten o'clock. She has history on Tuesdays and Thursdays at two o'clock. She takes chemistry on Monday from two o'clock to six o'clock. She plays tennis on weekends at four o'clock. She eats lunch at twelve o'clock every day except Saturday and Sunday.

Now listen a second time. There will be a pause after each sentence to give you time to fill in the chart. *Lucy's schedule is repeated with a pause after each sentence.*

Test-takers see the following weekly calendar grid:

	Monday	Tuesday	Wednesday	Thursday	Friday	Weekends
8:00	get up	get up	get up	get up	get up	
10:00						
12:00						
2:00						
4:00						
6:00						

Such chart-filling tasks are good examples of aural *scanning* strategies. A listener must discern from a number of pieces of information which pieces are relevant. In the example on the previous page, virtually all of the stimuli are relevant, and very few words can be ignored. In other tasks, however, much more information might be presented than is needed (as in the birdfeeder item on page 169), forcing the test-taker to select the correct bits and pieces necessary to complete a task.

Chart-filling tasks increase in difficulty as the linguistic stimulus material becomes more complex. In one task described by Ur (1984, pp. 108–112), test-takers listen to a very long description of animals in various cages in a zoo. While they listen, they can look at a map of the layout of the zoo with unlabeled cages. Their task is to fill in the correct animal in each cage, but the complexity of the language used to describe the positions of cages and their inhabitants is very challenging. Similarly, Hughes (2003, p. 167) described a map-marking task in which test-takers must process around 250 words of colloquial language in order to complete the tasks of identifying names, positions, and directions in a car accident scenario on a city street.

Sentence Repetition [L, S]

The task of simply repeating a sentence or a partial sentence, or **sentence repetition**, is also used as an assessment of listening comprehension. As in a dictation (discussed below), the test-taker must retain a stretch of language long enough to reproduce it and then must respond with an oral repetition of that stimulus. Incorrect listening comprehension, whether at the phonemic or discourse level, may be manifested in the correctness of the repetition. A miscue in repetition is scored as a miscue in listening. In the case of somewhat longer sentences, one could argue that the ability to recognize and retain chunks of language as well as threads of meaning might be assessed through repetition.

Sentence repetition is far from a flawless listening assessment task. Buck (2001) noted that such tasks "are not just tests of listening, but tests of general oral skills" (p. 79). Further, this task may test only recognition of sounds, and it can easily be contaminated by lack of short-term memory ability, thus invalidating it as an assessment of comprehension alone. Also, the teacher may never be able to distinguish a listening comprehension error from an oral production error. Therefore, sentence repetition tasks should be used with caution.

DESIGNING ASSESSMENT TASKS: EXTENSIVE LISTENING

Drawing a clear distinction between any two of the categories of listening referred to here is problematic, but perhaps the fuzziest division is between selective and extensive listening. As we gradually move along the continuum from smaller to larger stretches of language, and from micro- to macroskills of listening, the probability of using more extensive listening tasks increases. Some important questions about designing assessments at this level emerge:

1. Can listening performance be distinguished from cognitive processing factors such as memory, associations, storage, and recall?
2. As assessment procedures become more communicative, does the task take into account test-takers' ability to use grammatical expectancies, lexical collocations, semantic interpretations, and pragmatic competence?
3. Are test tasks themselves correspondingly content valid and authentic—that is, do they mirror real-world language and context?
4. As assessment tasks become more and more open-ended, they more closely resemble pedagogical tasks, which leads one to ask, "What is the difference between assessment and teaching tasks?" The answer is scoring: The former imply specified scoring procedures, whereas the latter do not.

We address these questions as we look at a number of extensive or quasi-extensive listening comprehension tasks.

Dictation

Dictation is a widely researched genre of assessing listening comprehension. In a dictation, test-takers hear a passage, typically of 50 to 100 words, recited three times: first at normal speed; then with long pauses between phrases or natural word groups, during which time test-takers write down what they have just heard; and finally at normal speed once more so they can check their work and proofread. The following is a sample dictation at the intermediate level of English.

Dictation [L, W]

First reading (natural speed, no pauses, test-takers listen for gist):

The state of California has many geographical areas. On the western side is the Pacific Ocean with its beaches and sea life. The central part of the state is a large fertile valley. The southeast has a hot desert, and the north and west have beautiful mountains and forests. Southern California is a large urban area populated by millions of people.

Second reading (slowed speed, pause at each // break, test-takers write):

The state of California // has many geographical areas. // On the western side // is the Pacific Ocean // with its beaches and sea life. // The central part of the state // is a large fertile valley. // The southeast has a hot desert, // and the north and west // have beautiful mountains and forests. // Southern California // is a large urban area // populated by millions of people.

Third reading (natural speed, test-takers check their work).

Dictations have been used as assessment tools for decades. Some readers still cringe at the thought of having to render a correctly spelled, verbatim version of a paragraph or story recited by the teacher. Until research on integrative testing was published (see Oller, 1971), dictations were thought to be not much more than glorified spelling tests. However, the required integration of listening and writing in a dictation, along with its presupposed knowledge of grammatical and discourse expectancies, brought this technique back into vogue. Hughes (1989), Cohen (1994), Bailey (1998), and Buck (2001) all defended the plausibility of dictation as an integrative test that requires some sophistication in the language to process and write down all segments correctly. Thus I include dictation here under the rubric of extensive tasks, although I am more comfortable with labeling it quasi-extensive.

The difficulty of a dictation task can be easily manipulated by the length of the word groups (or **bursts**, as they are technically called); the length of the pauses; the speed at which the text is read; and the complexity of the discourse, grammar, and vocabulary used in the passage.

Scoring is another matter. Depending on your context and purpose in administering a dictation, you will need to decide on scoring criteria for several possible kinds of errors:

- spelling error only, but the word appears to have been heard correctly
- spelling and/or obvious misrepresentation of a word; illegible word
- grammatical or phonological error (e.g., "the southeast have a hot desert")
- skipped word or phrase
- permutation of words (e.g., "a fertile large valley"; "the part of the central state")
- additional words not in the original
- replacement of a word with an appropriate synonym

Determining the weight of each of these errors is a highly idiosyncratic choice; specialists disagree almost more than they agree on the importance of the above categories. They do agree (Buck, 2001) that a dictation is not a spelling test and that the first item in the list above should not be considered an error. They also suggest that point systems be kept simple (for maintaining practicality and reliability) and that a deductible scoring method, in which points are subtracted from a hypothetical total, is usually effective.

Dictation seems to provide a reasonably valid method for integrating listening and writing skills and for tapping into the cohesive elements of language implied in short passages. However, a word of caution lest you assume that dictation provides a quick and easy method of assessing extensive listening comprehension. If the bursts in a dictation are relatively long (more than five-word segments), this method places a certain amount of load on memory and processing of meaning (Buck, 2001, p. 78). However, only a moderate degree of cognitive processing is required, and claiming that dictation fully assesses the ability to comprehend pragmatic or illocutionary elements of language, context, inference, or semantics may be going too far.

Finally, one can easily question the authenticity of dictation: It is rare in the real world for people to write down more than a few chunks of information (e.g., addresses, phone numbers, grocery lists, directions) at a time.

Despite these disadvantages, the practicality of administration, a moderate degree of reliability in a well-established scoring system, and a strong correspondence to other language abilities speaks well for the inclusion of dictation among the possibilities for assessing extensive (or quasi-extensive) listening comprehension.

Communicative Stimulus-Response Tasks

Another—and more authentic—example of extensive listening is found in a popular genre of assessment task in which the test-taker is presented with a stimulus monologue or conversation and then is asked to respond to a set of comprehension questions. Such tasks (as you saw in Chapter 4 in the discussion of standardized testing) are commonly used in commercially produced proficiency tests. The monologues, lectures, and brief conversations used in such tasks are sometimes a little contrived—and certainly the subsequent multiple-choice questions don't mirror communicative, real-life situations—but with some care and creativity, one can create reasonably authentic stimuli, and in some rare cases the response mode (as shown in one example below) actually approaches complete authenticity. The following is a typical example of such a task.

Dialogue and multiple-choice comprehension items [L, R]

Test-takers hear:

Directions: Now you will hear a conversation between Lynn and her doctor. You will hear the conversation two times. After you hear the conversation the second time, choose the correct answer for questions 11 through 15 below. Mark your answers on the answer sheet provided.

Doctor:	Good morning, Lynn. What's the problem?
Lynn:	Well, you see, I have a terrible headache, my nose is running, and I'm really dizzy.
Doctor:	Okay. Anything else?
Lynn:	I've been coughing, I think I have a fever, and my stomach aches.
Doctor:	I see. When did this start?
Lynn:	Well, let's see, I went to the lake last weekend, and after I returned home I started sneezing.
Doctor:	Hmm. You must have the flu. You should get lots of rest, drink hot beverages, and stay warm. Do you follow me?
Lynn:	Well, uh, yeah, but . . . shouldn't I take some medicine?
Doctor:	Sleep and rest are as good as medicine when you have the flu.
Lynn:	Okay, thanks, Dr. Brown.

Test-takers read:

1. What is Lynn's problem?
   A. She feels horrible.
   B. She ran too fast at the lake.
   C. She's been drinking too many hot beverages.

2. When did Lynn's problem start?
   A. when she saw her doctor
   B. before she went to the lake
   C. after she came home from the lake

3. The doctor said that Lynn _____.
   A. flew to the lake last weekend
   B. must not get the flu
   C. probably has the flu

4. The doctor told Lynn _____.
   A. to rest
   B. to follow him
   C. to take some medicine

5. According to Dr. Brown, sleep and rest are _____ medicine when you have the flu.
   A. more effective than
   B. as effective as
   C. less effective than

Does this meet the criterion of authenticity? If you want to be painfully fussy, you might object that it is rare in the real world to eavesdrop on someone else's doctor–patient conversation. Nevertheless, the conversation itself is relatively authentic; we all have doctor–patient exchanges like this. Equally authentic, if you add a grain of salt, are monologues, lecturettes, and news stories, all of which are commonly utilized as listening stimuli to be followed by comprehension questions aimed at assessing certain objectives that are built into the stimulus.

Is the task itself (of responding to multiple-choice questions) authentic? It's plausible to assert that any task of this kind following a one-way listening to a conversation is artificial: We simply don't often encounter little quizzes about conversations we've heard (unless it's your parent, spouse, or best friend who wants to get in on the latest gossip!). The questions posed above, with the possible exception of question 14, are unlikely to appear in a lifetime of doctor visits. Yet the ability to respond correctly to such items can be construct validated as an appropriate measure of field-independent listening skills: the ability to remember certain details from a conversation. (As an aside here, many highly proficient native speakers of English might miss some of the above questions if they heard the conversation only once and had no visual access to the items until after the conversation was done.)

To compensate for the potential inauthenticity of poststimulus comprehension questions, you might, with a little creativity, be able to find contexts in which questions that probe understanding are more appropriate. Consider the following situation:

Dialogue and authentic questions on details [L, R]

Test-takers hear:

You will hear a conversation between a police detective and a man. The tape will play the conversation twice. After you hear the conversation a second time, choose the correct answers on your test sheet.

Detective:	Where were you last night at 11:00 P.M., the time of the murder?
Man:	Uh, let's see, well, I was just starting to see a movie.
Detective:	Did you go alone?
Man:	No, uh, well, I was with my friend, uh, Bill. Yeah, I was with Bill.
Detective:	What did you do after that?
Man:	We went out to dinner, then I dropped her off at her place.
Detective:	Then you went home?
Man:	Yeah.
Detective:	When did you get home?
Man:	A little before midnight.

Test-takers read:

1. Where was the man at 11:00 P.M.?
   A. in a restaurant
   B. in a theater
   C. at home

2. Was he with someone?
   A. He was alone.
   B. He was with his wife.
   C. He was with a friend.

3. Then what did he do?
   A. He ate out.
   B. He made dinner.
   C. He went home.

4. When did he get home?
   A. about eleven o'clock
   B. almost twelve o'clock
   C. right after the movie

5. The man is probably lying because (name two clues):
   A. _____
   B. _____

In this case, test-takers are brought into a scene in a crime story. The questions following are plausible questions that might be asked to review fact and fiction in the conversation. Question 11, of course, provides an extra shot of reality: The test-taker must name the probable lies told by the man (he referred to Bill as "her"; he saw a movie and ate dinner in the space of one hour), which requires the process of inference.

Authentic Listening Tasks

Ideally, the language assessment field would have a stockpile of listening test types that are cognitively demanding, communicative, and authentic, not to mention inter-active by means of an integration with speaking. However, the nature of a test as a sample of performance and a set of tasks with limited time frames implies an equally limited capacity to mirror all the real-world contexts of listening performance. According to Buck (2001), "There is no such thing as a communicative test. Every test requires some components of communicative language ability, and no test covers them all. Similarly, with the notion of authenticity, every task shares some character-istics with target-language tasks, and no test is completely authentic" (p. 92).

Having said that, we must note that recent technological developments have dramatically increased our capacity to create authentic assessments of listening ability. Computer technology offers a variety of situations and contexts in which the test-taker can participate interactively in a communicative exchange (Chapelle & Douglas, 2006). Video listening tests offer the advantage of simulating real-life situations, allowing test-takers to view body language and facial features and to "read the lips" of a speaker (Wagner, 2008).

Still, is it possible to say we can now assess aural comprehension in a truly com-municative context? Can we, at this end of the range of listening tasks, ascertain from test-takers that they have processed the main idea(s) of a lecture, the gist of a story, the pragmatics of a conversation, or the unspoken inferential data present in most authentic aural input? Can we assess a test-taker's comprehension of humor, idiom, and metaphor? The answer is a cautious yes, but not without some conces-sions to practicality. The answer is a more certain yes if we take the liberty of stretching the concept of assessment to extend beyond tests and into a broader framework of alternatives. Here are some possibilities:

1. *Notetaking* [L, W]. In the academic world, classroom lectures by professors are common features of a nonnative English-user's experience. One form of a midterm examination at the American Language Institute at San Francisco State University (Kahn, 2002) uses a 15-minute lecture as a stimulus. One among several response formats includes notetaking by the test-takers. These notes are evaluated by the teacher on a 30-point system, as follows:

Scoring system for lecture notes

0–15 points
Visual representation: Are your notes clear and easy to read? Can you easily find and retrieve information from them? Do you use the space on the paper to visually represent ideas? Do you use indentation, headers, numbers, etc.?

0–10 points
Accuracy: Do you accurately indicate main ideas from lectures? Do you note important details and supporting information and examples? Do you leave out unimportant information and tangents?

0–5 points
Symbols and abbreviations: Do you use symbols and abbreviations as much as possible to save time? Do you avoid writing out whole words, and do you avoid writing down every single word the lecturer says?

The process of scoring is time-consuming (a loss of practicality), and, because of the subjectivity of the point system, it lacks some reliability. But the gain is in offering students an authentic task that mirrors exactly what they have been focusing on in the classroom. The notes become an indirect but arguably valid form of assessing global listening comprehension. The task fulfills the criteria of cognitive demand, communicative language, and authenticity. On the other hand, although we might intuitively believe that taking notes on lectures is an aid to one's memory, Carrell, Dunkel, and Mollaun (2004) somewhat surprisingly found no significant differences in computer-based testing of listening comprehension when notetaking was allowed.

2. *Editing* [L, R, W] Another authentic task provides both a written and a spoken stimulus and requires the test-taker to listen for discrepancies. Scoring achieves relatively high reliability, as there are usually a small number of specific differences that must be identified. The task proceeds in this way:

Editing a written version of an aural stimulus

Test-takers read the written stimulus material (a news report, an e-mail from a friend, notes from a lecture, or an editorial in a newspaper)

Test-takers hear a spoken version of the stimulus that deviates, in a finite number of facts or opinions, from the original written form

Test-takers mark the written stimulus by circling any words, phrases, facts, or opinions that show a discrepancy between the two versions

---

One potentially interesting set of stimuli for such a task is the description of a political scandal first from a newspaper with perhaps a left-of-center political bias and then from a radio broadcast from another news station reflecting a right-of-center point of view. Test-takers are not only forced to listen carefully to differences but are subtly informed about biases in the news.

3. *Interpretive tasks* [L, R, S, W]. One of the intensive listening tasks described previously was paraphrasing a story or conversation. An interpretive task extends the stimulus material to a longer stretch of discourse and forces the test-taker to infer a response. Potential stimuli include

- song lyrics
- [recited] poetry
- radio/television news reports
- an oral account of an experience

Test-takers are then directed to interpret the stimulus by answering a few questions (in open-ended form). Questions might be:

- "Why was the singer feeling sad?"
- "What events might have led up to the reciting of this poem?"
- "What do you think the political activists might do next and why?"
- "What do you think the storyteller felt about the mysterious disappearance of her necklace?"

This kind of task moves us away from what might traditionally be considered a test toward an informal assessment, or possibly even a pedagogical technique or activity. But the task conforms to certain time limitations, and the questions can be quite specific, even though they ask the test-taker to use inference. Although reliable scoring may be an issue (there may be more than one correct interpretation), the authenticity of the interaction in this task and potential washback to the student surely give it some prominence among communicative assessment procedures.

4. *Retelling.* In a related task, test-takers listen to a story or news event and simply retell it, or summarize it, either orally (on an audiotape) or in writing. In so doing, test-takers must identify the gist, main idea, purpose, supporting points, and/or conclusion to show full comprehension. Scoring is partially predetermined by specifying a minimum number of elements that must appear in the retelling. Again, reliability may suffer, and the time and effort needed to read and evaluate the response lowers practicality. Validity, cognitive processing, communicative ability, and authenticity are all well incorporated into the task.

✫   ✫   ✫   ✫   ✫

A fifth category of listening comprehension was hinted at earlier in the chapter: **interactive** listening. Because such interaction presupposes a process of speaking in concert with listening, the interactive nature of listening is addressed in the next chapter. Don't forget that a significant proportion of real-world listening performance is interactive. With the exception of media input, speeches, lectures, and eavesdropping, many of our listening efforts are directed toward a two-way process of speaking and listening in face-to-face and/or real-time conversations.

EXERCISES

[Note: **(I)** Individual work; **(G)** Group or pair work; **(C)** Whole-class discussion.]

1. **(C)** In Table 7.1 on page 159, it is noted that one cannot actually observe listening and reading performance. It is also claimed that there isn't even a product to observe for speaking, listening, and reading. First, in a whole-class discussion, ascertain that these claims are understood. Then talk about how one can infer the competence of a test-taker to speak, listen, and read a language.

2. **(C)** Given that we spend much more time listening than we do speaking, why are there many more tests of speaking than listening?

3. **(G)** Look at the list of micro- and macroskills of listening on page 163. In pairs, each assigned to a different skill (or two), brainstorm some tasks that assess those skills. Present your findings to the rest of the class.

4. **(G)** Nine characteristics of listening that make listening "difficult" are listed on page 164. In pairs, each assigned to an assessment task itemized in this chapter, decide which of the nine factors, in order of significance, contribute to the potential difficulty of the items. Report back to the class.

5. **(G)** Assign the four basic types of listening (intensive, responsive, selective, extensive) to groups or pairs, one to each group. Look at the sample assessment techniques provided on pages 164–180 and evaluate them according to the five principles (practicality, reliability, validity, authenticity, and washback). Present your critique to the rest of the class.

6. **(G)** Try this one for a challenge: In the same groups as in no. 5 above and with the same type of listening, design some other item types, different from the one(s) provided here, that assess the same type of listening performance. Present those designs to the rest of the class.

7. **(G)** In pairs or groups, construct a listening cloze test. Each group should be assigned one grammatical category to work on: two-word verbs, verb tenses, prepositions, transition words, articles, and/or other grammatical categories. Present your findings to the class.

8. **(I/C)** On page 174; you are reminded that dictations are considered by some assessment specialists to be integrative (requiring the integration of listening, writing, and reading [proofreading], along with attendant grammatical and

discourse abilities). Looking back at the discussion at the beginning of the chapter on the integration of skills, do you think this a valid claim? Justify your response.

9. **(I/C)** Mentioned on page 178 is Buck's claim that "no test is completely authentic." Discuss the extent to which you agree or disagree with this assertion and justify your own conclusion.

FOR YOUR FURTHER READING

Buck, Gary. (2001). *Assessing listening.* Cambridge: Cambridge University Press.

One of a series of very useful reference books on assessing specific skill areas published by Cambridge University Press, Buck's volume gives an overview of research and pedagogy on listening comprehension and demonstrates many different assessment procedures in common use.

Rost, Michael. (2005). L2 listening. In E. Hinkel (Ed.), *Handbook of research in second language teaching and learning* (pp. 503–527). Mahwah, NJ: Lawrence Erlbaum Associates.

This is one of many excellent state-of-the-art articles in Hinkel's useful handbook. Although Rost doesn't focus explicitly on assessment in the chapter, he does provide a comprehensive look at teaching listening and by extension offers an indirect consideration of assessment. He discusses the roles of attention and perception in listening, the significance of vocabulary size, syntactic knowledge, paralinguistic cues, what we know about schemata activation, inferencing, memory, and how listener response is interwoven in the process of listening.

ASSESSING SPEAKING

From a pragmatic view of language performance, listening and speaking are almost always closely interrelated. As we mentioned in the last chapter, in the real world, skills are usually integrated in some combination of two or more skills. Whereas it is theoretically possible to isolate some listening performance tasks (see Chapter 7), it is very difficult to isolate oral production tasks that don't directly involve the interaction of aural comprehension. Only in limited contexts of speaking (monologues, speeches, telling a story, reading aloud, etc.) can we assess oral language without the aural participation of an interlocutor.

Also, although speaking is a productive skill that can be directly and empirically observed, those observations are invariably colored by the accuracy and effectiveness of a test-taker's listening skill, which necessarily compromises the reliability and validity of an oral production test. How do you know for certain that a speaking score is exclusively a measure of oral production without the potentially frequent clarifications of an interlocutor? This interaction of speaking and listening challenges the designer of an oral production test to tease apart, as much as possible, the factors accounted for by aural intake.

Another challenge is the design of elicitation techniques (see Fulcher, 2003; Luoma, 2004). Because most speaking is the product of creative construction, the speaker makes choices of lexicon, structure, and discourse. If your goal is to have test-takers demonstrate certain spoken grammatical categories, for example, the stimulus you design must elicit those grammatical categories in ways that prohibit the test-taker from avoiding or paraphrasing and thereby dodging production of the target form.

In the assessment of oral production, the more open-ended test tasks are, the greater the challenge in scoring due to the freedom of choice given to test-takers. In receptive performance, the elicitation stimulus can be structured to anticipate predetermined responses and only those responses. In productive performance, the oral or written stimulus must be specific enough to elicit output within an expected range of performance such that scoring or rating procedures apply appropriately. For example, in a picture-series task, the objective of which is to elicit a story in a sequence of events, test-takers could opt for a variety of plausible ways to tell the story, all of which might be equally accurate. How can such disparate responses be evaluated? One solution is to assign not one but several scores for each response, with each score representing one of several traits (pronunciation, fluency, vocabulary use, grammar, comprehensibility, etc.).

All of these issues are addressed in this chapter as we review types of spoken language and micro- and macroskills of speaking then outline numerous tasks for assessing speaking.

BASIC TYPES OF SPEAKING

In Chapter 7, we cited four categories of listening performance assessment tasks. A similar taxonomy emerges for oral production.

1. *Imitative.* At one end of a continuum of types of speaking, performance is the ability to simply parrot back (imitate) a word or phrase or possibly a sentence. Although this is a purely phonetic level of oral production, a number of prosodic (intonation, rhythm, etc.), lexical, and grammatical properties of language may be included in the performance criteria. We are interested only in what is traditionally labeled "pronunciation"; no inferences are made about the test-taker's ability to understand or convey meaning or to participate in an interactive conversation. The only role of listening here is in the short-term storage of a prompt, just long enough to allow the speaker to retain the short stretch of language that must be imitated.

2. *Intensive.* A second type of speaking frequently employed in assessment contexts is the production of short stretches of oral language designed to demonstrate competence in a narrow band of grammatical, phrasal, lexical, or phonological relationships (such as prosodic elements—intonation, stress, rhythm, juncture). The speaker must be aware of semantic properties to be able to respond, but interaction with an interlocutor or test administrator is minimal at best. Examples of intensive assessment tasks include directed response tasks (requests for specific production of speech), reading aloud, sentence and dialogue completion, limited picture-cued tasks including simple sequences, and translation up to the simple sentence level.

3. *Responsive.* Responsive assessment tasks include interaction and test comprehension but at the somewhat limited level of very short conversations, stan-

dard greetings and small talk, simple requests and comments, and the like. The stimulus is almost always a spoken prompt (to preserve authenticity), with perhaps only one or two follow-up questions or retorts:

   A. Mary: Excuse me, do you have the time?
          Doug: Yeah. Nine-fifteen.

   B. T: What is the most urgent environmental problem today?
          S: I would say massive deforestation.

   C. Jeff: Hey, Stef, how's it going?
          Stef: Not bad, and yourself?
          Jeff: I'm good.
          Stef: Cool. Okay, gotta go.

4. *Interactive.* The difference between responsive and interactive speaking is in the length and complexity of the interaction, which sometimes includes multiple exchanges and/or multiple participants. Interaction can be broken down into two types: (a) *transactional* language, which has the purpose of exchanging specific information, and (b) *interpersonal* exchanges, which have the purpose of maintaining social relationships. (In the three dialogues cited above, A and B are transactional, and C is interpersonal.) In interpersonal exchanges, oral production can become pragmatically complex with the need to speak in a casual register and use colloquial language, ellipsis, slang, humor, and other sociolinguistic conventions.

5. *Extensive (monologue).* Extensive oral production tasks include speeches, oral presentations, and storytelling, during which the opportunity for oral interaction from listeners is either highly limited (perhaps to nonverbal responses) or ruled out altogether. Language style is frequently more deliberative (planning is involved) and formal for extensive tasks, but we cannot rule out certain informal monologues such as casually delivered speech (e.g., recalling a vacation in the mountains, conveying a recipe for outstanding pasta primavera, recounting the plot of a novel or movie).

MICRO- AND MACROSKILLS OF SPEAKING

In Chapter 7, a list of listening micro- and macroskills enumerated the various components of listening that make up criteria for assessment. A similar list of speaking skills can be drawn up for the same purpose: to serve as a taxonomy of skills from which you can select one or several that become the objective(s) of an assessment task. The microskills refer to producing the smaller chunks of language such as phonemes, morphemes, words, collocations, and phrasal units. The macroskills imply the speaker's focus on the larger elements: fluency, discourse, function, style, cohesion, nonverbal communication, and strategic options. As shown on the next page, the micro- and macroskills total 16 different objectives to assess in speaking.

Micro- and macroskills of oral production

Microskills

1. Produce differences among English phonemes and allophones
2. Produce chunks of language of different lengths
3. Produce English stress patterns, words in stressed and unstressed positions, rhythmic structure, and intonation contours
4. Produce reduced forms of words and phrases
5. Use an adequate number of lexical units (words) to accomplish pragmatic purposes
6. Produce fluent speech at different rates of delivery
7. Monitor one's own oral production and use various strategic devices—pauses, fillers, self-corrections, backtracking—to enhance the clarity of the message
8. Use grammatical word classes (nouns, verbs, etc.), systems (e.g., tense, agreement, pluralization), word order, patterns, rules, and elliptical forms
9. Produce speech in natural constituents: in appropriate phrases, pause groups, breath groups, and sentence constituents
10. Express a particular meaning in different grammatical forms
11. Use cohesive devices in spoken discourse

Macroskills

12. Appropriately accomplish communicative functions according to situations, participants, and goals
13. Use appropriate styles, registers, implicature, redundancies, pragmatic conventions, conversation rules, floor-keeping and -yielding, interrupting, and other sociolinguistic features in face-to-face conversations
14. Convey links and connections between events and communicate such relations as focal and peripheral ideas, events and feelings, new information and given information, generalization and exemplification
15. Convey facial features, kinesics, body language, and other nonverbal cues along with verbal language
16. Develop and use a battery of speaking strategies, such as emphasizing key words, rephrasing, providing a context for interpreting the meaning of words, appealing for help, and accurately assessing how well your interlocutor is understanding you

---

As you consider designing tasks for assessing spoken language, these skills can act as a checklist of objectives. Although the macroskills have the appearance of being more complex than the microskills, both contain ingredients of difficulty, depending on the stage and context of the test-taker.

There is such an array of oral production tasks that a complete treatment is almost impossible within the confines of one chapter in this book. The following is a consideration of the most common techniques with brief allusions to related tasks. As already noted in the introduction to this chapter, consider three important issues as you set out to design tasks:

1. No speaking task is capable of isolating the single skill of oral production. Concurrent involvement of aural comprehension, and possibly reading, is usually necessary.
2. Eliciting the specific criterion you have designated for a task can be tricky because, beyond the word level, spoken language offers a number of productive options to test-takers. Make sure your elicitation prompt achieves its aims as closely as possible.
3. Because of these two characteristics of oral production assessment, it is important to carefully specify scoring rubrics for a response so that ultimately you achieve as high a reliability index as possible.

DESIGNING ASSESSMENT TASKS: IMITATIVE SPEAKING

You may be surprised to see the inclusion of simple phonological imitation in a consideration of assessment of oral production. After all, endless repeating of words, phrases, and sentences was the province of the long-since-discarded Audiolingual Method, and in an era of communicative language teaching, many believe that non-meaningful imitation of sounds is fruitless. Such opinions have faded in recent years as we discovered that an overemphasis on fluency can sometimes lead to the decline of accuracy in speech. So we have been paying more attention to pronunciation, especially suprasegmentals, in an attempt to help learners be more comprehensible.

An occasional phonologically focused repetition task is warranted as long as repetition tasks are not allowed to occupy a dominant role in an overall oral production assessment and as long as you artfully avoid a negative washback effect. Such tasks range from word level to sentence level, usually with each item focusing on a specific phonological criterion. In a simple repetition task, test-takers repeat the stimulus, whether it is a pair of words, a sentence, or perhaps a question (to test for intonation production).

Word and sentence repetition tasks [L, S]

Test-takers hear:	Repeat after me:
	beat *pause* bit *pause*
	bat *pause* vat *pause* etc.
	I bought a boat yesterday.
	The glow of the candle is growing. etc.
	When did they go on vacation?
	Do you like coffee? etc.
Test-takers repeat the stimulus.	

A variation on such a task prompts test-takers with a brief written stimulus which they are to read aloud. (In the following section on intensive speaking, some tasks are described in which test-takers read aloud longer texts.) Scoring specifications must be clear to avoid reliability breakdowns. A common form of scoring simply indicates a two- or three-point system for each response.

Scoring scale for repetition tasks

2	acceptable pronunciation
1	comprehensible, partially correct pronunciation
0	silence, seriously incorrect pronunciation

The longer the stretch of language, the more possibility for error and therefore the more difficult it becomes to assign a point system to the text. In such a case, it may be imperative to score only the criterion of the task. For example, in the sentence "When did they go on vacation?" because the criterion is falling intonation for *wh-* questions, points should be awarded regardless of any other mispronunciation.

Versant®

On the commercial market, one widely used oral production test that relies heavily on imitation tasks is Versant, formerly called PhonePass (see the appendix at the back of this book for a description). Among a number of speaking tasks on the test, repetition of sentences occupies a prominent role. It is remarkable that research on Versant has supported the construct validity of its repetition tasks not just for a test-taker's phonological ability but also for discourse and overall oral production ability (Balogh & Bernstein, 2007; Cascallar & Bernstein, 2000; Townshend, Bernstein, Todic, & Warren, 1998).

Of further interest is that scores for Versant are calculated by a computerized algorithm and reported back to the test-taker within minutes. The scoring procedure has been validated against human scoring on the same tasks with extraordinarily high reliabilities and correlation statistics (.94 overall). Further, this fifteen-minute test correlates with the much more elaborated Oral Proficiency Interview (OPI; described later in this chapter) at .75, indicating a very high degree of correspondence between the machine-scored Versant and human-scored speaking tests (Bernstein, DeJong, Pisoni, & Townshend, 2000; Farhady & Hedayati, 2008). However, some research questioned the authenticity of the test tasks in Phone Pass (Chun, 2005), sparking a bit of discussion with the Versant developers (Chun, 2008; Downey, Farhady, Present-Thomas, Suzuki, & Van Moere, 2008).

Those criticisms notwithstanding, further development of the Versant test could signal an increase in the future use of repetition and read-aloud procedures for the assessment of oral production. Because a test-taker's output is relatively predictable, scoring by means of speech-recognition technology becomes achievable and practical. As researchers uncover the constructs underlying both repetition/read-aloud tasks and oral production in all its complexities, we will have access to more comprehensive explanations of why such simple tasks appear to be reliable and valid indicators of very complex oral production proficiency.

DESIGNING ASSESSMENT TASKS: INTENSIVE SPEAKING

At the intensive level, test-takers are prompted to produce short stretches of discourse (no more than a sentence) through which they demonstrate linguistic ability at a specified level of language. Many tasks are "cued" in that they lead the test-taker into a narrow band of possibilities. Intensive tasks may also be described as **limited-response tasks** (Madsen, 1983), **mechanical tasks** (Underhill, 1987), or what classroom pedagogy would label **controlled responses**.

Directed Response Tasks

In this type of limited response task, the test administrator elicits a particular grammatical form or a transformation of a sentence. Such tasks are clearly mechanical and not communicative, but they do require minimal processing of meaning in order to produce the correct grammatical output.

Directed response [L, S]

Test-takers hear:	Tell me he went home.
	Tell me that you like rock music.
	Tell me that you aren't interested in tennis.
	Tell him to come to my office at noon.
	Remind him what time it is.

Read-Aloud Tasks

Intensive read-aloud tasks include reading beyond the sentence level up to a paragraph or two. This technique is easily administered by selecting a passage that incorporates test specs and by recording the test-taker's output; the scoring is relatively easy because all of the test-taker's oral production is controlled. Because of the results of research on the Versant test mentioned above, reading aloud may actually be a surprisingly strong indicator of overall oral production ability.

For many decades, foreign language programs have used reading passages to analyze oral production. Prator's (1972) *Manual of American English Pronunciation* included a "diagnostic passage" of about 150 words that students could read aloud into a tape recorder. Teachers listening to the recording would then rate students on

a number of phonological factors (vowels, diphthongs, consonants, consonant clusters, stress, and intonation) by completing a two-page diagnostic checklist on which
all errors or questionable items were noted. These checklists ostensibly offered direction to the teacher for emphases in the course to come.

An earlier form of the Test of Spoken English (TSE® Test) incorporated one
read-aloud passage of about 120 to 130 words with a rating scale for pronunciation
and fluency. The following passage is typical:

Read-aloud stimulus, paragraph length [R, S]

Despite the decrease in size—and, some would say, quality—of our cultural world,
there still remain strong differences between the usual British and American writing
styles. The question is, how do you get your message across? English prose conveys
its most novel ideas as if they were timeless truths, while American writing
exaggerates; if you believe half of what is said, that's enough. The former uses
understatement; the latter, overstatement. There are also disadvantages to each
characteristic approach. Readers who are used to being screamed at may not listen
when someone chooses to whisper politely. At the same time, the individual who is
used to a quiet manner may reject a series of loud imperatives.

The scoring scale for this passage provided a four-point scale for pronunciation
and for fluency, as shown in the following.

Test of Spoken English scoring scale (1987, p. 10)

Pronunciation:

Points:

0.0–0.4   Frequent phonemic errors and foreign stress and intonation
          patterns that cause the speaker to be unintelligible.
0.5–1.4   Frequent phonemic errors and foreign stress and intonation
          patterns that cause the speaker to be occasionally unintelligible.
1.5–2.4   Some consistent phonemic errors and foreign stress and
          intonation patterns, but the speaker is intelligible.
2.5–3.0   Occasional nonnative pronunciation errors, but the speaker is
          always intelligible.

Fluency:

Points:

0.0–0.4	Speech is so halting and fragmentary or has such a nonnative flow that intelligibility is virtually impossible.
0.5–1.4	Numerous nonnative pauses and/or a nonnative flow that interferes with intelligibility.
1.5–2.4	Some nonnative pauses but with a more nearly native flow so that the pauses do not interfere with intelligibility.
2.5–3.0	Speech is smooth and effortless, closely approximating that of a native speaker.

Such a rating list does not indicate how to gauge intelligibility, which is mentioned in both lists. Such slippery terms remind us that oral production scoring, even with the controls that reading aloud offers, is still an inexact science.

Underhill (1987, pp. 77–78) suggested some variations on the task of simply reading a short passage:

- reading a scripted dialogue, with someone else reading the other part
- reading sentences containing minimal pairs, for example:
    "Try not to heat/hit the pan too much."
    "The doctor gave me a bill/pill."
- reading information from a table or chart

If reading aloud shows certain practical advantages (predictable output, practicality, reliability in scoring), there are several drawbacks to using this technique for assessing oral production. Reading aloud is somewhat inauthentic in that we seldom read anything aloud to someone else in the real world, with the exception of a parent reading to a child, occasionally sharing a written story with someone, or giving a scripted oral presentation. Also, reading aloud calls on certain specialized oral abilities that may not indicate one's pragmatic ability to communicate orally in face-to-face contexts. You should therefore employ this technique with some caution and certainly supplement it as an assessment task with other, more communicative procedures.

Sentence/Dialogue Completion Tasks and Oral Questionnaires

Another technique for targeting intensive aspects of language requires test-takers to read dialogue in which one speaker's lines have been omitted. Test-takers are first given time to read through the dialogue to get its gist and to think about appropriate lines to fill in. Then as the tape, teacher, or test administrator produces one part orally, the test-taker responds. Here's an example:

Dialogue completion task [L, R, S]

Test-takers read (and then hear):

In a department store:

Salesperson:	May I help you?
Customer:	_____.
Salesperson:	Okay, what size do you wear?
Customer:	_____.
Salesperson:	Hmmm. How about this green sweater here?
Customer:	_____.
Salesperson:	Oh. Well, if you don't like green, what color would you like?
Customer:	_____.
Salesperson:	How about this one?
Customer:	_____.
Salesperson:	Great!
Customer:	_____.
Salesperson:	It's on sale today for $39.95.
Customer:	_____.
Salesperson:	Sure, we take Visa, MasterCard, and American Express.
Customer:	_____.

Test-takers respond with appropriate lines.

An advantage of this technique lies in its moderate control of the output of the test-taker. Although individual variations in responses are accepted, the technique taps into a learner's ability to discern expectancies in a conversation and to produce sociolinguistically correct language. One disadvantage of this technique is its reliance on literacy and an ability to transfer easily from written to spoken English. Another disadvantage is the contrived, inauthentic nature of this task; the same objective might be better accomplished using a role-play technique. Perhaps more useful is a whole host of shorter dialogues of two or three lines, each of which aims to elicit a specified target. In the following examples, somewhat unrelated items attempt to elicit the past tense, future tense, yes/no question formation, and asking for the time. Again, test-takers see the stimulus in written form.

Directed response tasks [R, S]

Test-takers see:

Interviewer:	What did you do last weekend?
Test-taker:	_____.
Interviewer:	What will you do after you graduate from this program?
Test-taker:	_____.
Test-taker:	_____?
Interviewer:	I was in Japan for two weeks.
Test-taker:	_____?
Interviewer:	It's ten-thirty.

Test-takers respond with appropriate lines.

One could contend that performance on these items is responsive rather than intensive. Although it is true that the discourse involves responses, there is a degree of control here that predisposes the test-taker to respond with certain expected forms. Such arguments underscore the fine lines of distinction between and among the selected five categories of speaking performance: imitative, intensive, responsive, interactive, and extensive.

It could also be argued that such techniques are nothing more than a written form of questions that might otherwise (and more appropriately) be part of a standard oral interview. This is also true, but the advantage that the written form offers is to provide a little more time for the test-taker to anticipate an answer, and it begins to remove the potential ambiguity created by aural misunderstanding. It helps to unlock the almost ubiquitous link between listening and speaking performance.

Underhill (1987) described yet another technique that is useful for controlling the test-taker's output: form-filling, or what I might rename "oral questionnaire." Here the test-taker sees a questionnaire that asks for certain categories of information (personal data, academic information, job experience, etc.) and supplies the information orally.

Picture-Cued Tasks

One of the more popular ways to elicit oral language performance at both intensive and extensive levels is a picture-cued stimulus that requires a description from the test-taker. Pictures may be very simple, designed to elicit a word or a phrase; somewhat more elaborate and "busy"; or composed of a series that tells a story or incident. The following is an example of a picture-cued elicitation of the production of a simple minimal pair.

Picture-cued elicitation of minimal pairs [L, S]

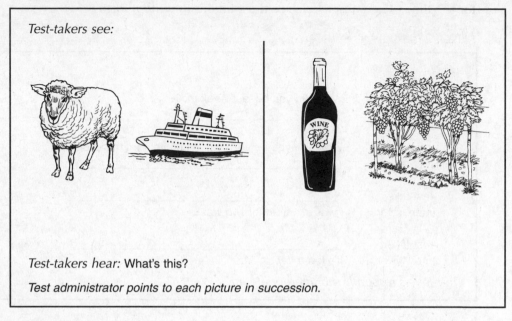

Test-takers see:

Test-takers hear: What's this?

Test administrator points to each picture in succession.

Grammatical categories may be cued by pictures. In the following sequences, comparatives are elicited:

Picture-cued elicitation of comparatives (Brown & Sahni, 1994, p. 135) [L, S]

Test-takers see:

APPLES
$1.99/b.

GRAPES
$2.48/b.

Test-takers hear: Use a comparative form to compare these objects.

The future tense is elicited with the following picture:

Picture-cued elicitation of future tense (Brown & Sahni, 1994, p. 145) [L, S]

Test-takers see:

Test-takers hear: This family is at an airport going on their vacation.

1. *Test administrator points to the picture in general.* Where are they going for their vacation?
2. *Test administrator points to the father.* What will he do in Hawaii?
3. *Test administrator points to the mother.* What will she do there?
4. *Test administrator points to the girl.* What is she going to do there?
5. *Test administrator points to the boy.* What is he going to do in Hawaii?

Notice that a little sense of humor is injected here: The family, bundled up in their winter coats, is looking forward to leaving the wintry scene behind them. A touch of authenticity is added in that almost everyone can identify with looking forward to a vacation on a tropical island.

Assessment of oral production may be stimulated through a more elaborate picture such as the following of a party scene.

Picture-cued elicitation of nouns, negative responses, numbers, and location (Brown & Sahni, 1994, p. 116) [L, S]

Test-takers see:

Test-takers hear:
1. *Test administrator points to the table.* What's this?
2. *Test administrator points to the end table.* What's this?
3. *Test administrator points to several chairs.* What are these?
4. *Test administrator points to the clock.* What's that?
5. *Test administrator points to both lamps.* What are those?
6. *Test administrator points to the table.* Is this a chair?
7. *Test administrator points to the lamps.* Are these clocks?
8. *Test administrator points to the woman standing up.* Is she sitting?
9. *Test administrator points to the whole picture.* How many chairs are there?
10. *Test administrator points to the whole picture.* How many women are there?
11. *Test administrator points to the TV.* Where is the TV?
12. *Test administrator points to the chair beside the lamp.* Where is this chair?
13. *Test administrator points to one person.* Describe this person.

In the first five questions, test-takers are asked to orally identify selected vocabulary items. In questions 6 through 13, assessment of the oral production of negatives, numbers, prepositions, and descriptions of people is elicited.

Moving into more open-ended performance, the following picture asks test-takers not only to identify certain specific information but also to elaborate with their own opinion, to accomplish a persuasive function, and to describe preferences in paintings.

Picture-cued elicitation of responses and description (Brown & Sahni, 1994, p. 162) [L, S]

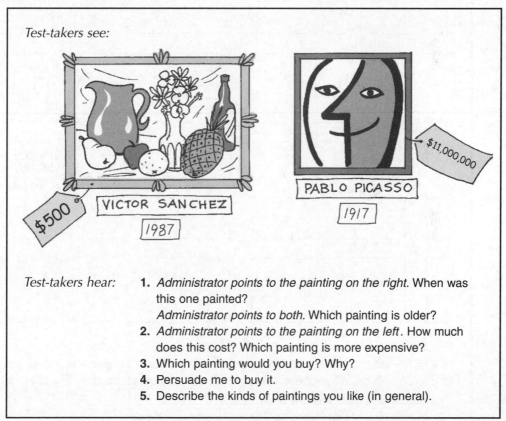

Test-takers see:

$500 VICTOR SANCHEZ *1987*

PABLO PICASSO *1917* $11,000,000

Test-takers hear:

1. *Administrator points to the painting on the right.* When was this one painted?
   Administrator points to both. Which painting is older?
2. *Administrator points to the painting on the left.* How much does this cost? Which painting is more expensive?
3. Which painting would you buy? Why?
4. Persuade me to buy it.
5. Describe the kinds of paintings you like (in general).

Maps are another visual stimulus that can be used to assess the language forms needed to give directions and specify locations. In the following example, the test-taker must provide directions to different locations.

Map-cued elicitation of giving directions (Brown & Sahni, 1994, p. 169) [L, S]

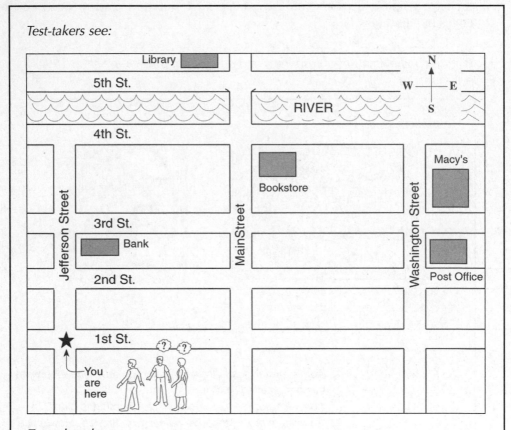

Test-takers see:

Test-takers hear:

You are at First and Jefferson Streets. *Administrator points to the spot.* People ask you for directions to get to five different places. Listen to their questions, then give directions.

1. Please give me directions to the bank.
2. Please give me directions to Macy's Department Store.
3. How do I get to the post office?
4. Can you tell me where the bookstore is?
5. Please tell me how to get to the library.

Scoring responses on picture-cued intensive speaking tasks varies, depending on the expected performance criteria. The tasks on page 194 that asked for just one-word or simple-sentence responses can be evaluated simply as "correct" or "incorrect." The three-point rubric (2, 1, and 0) suggested earlier may apply as well, with these modifications:

Scoring scale for intensive tasks

2	comprehensible; acceptable target form
1	comprehensible; partially correct target form
0	silence, or seriously incorrect target form

Opinions about paintings, persuasive monologue, and directions on a map create a more complicated problem for scoring. More demand is placed on the test administrator to make calculated judgments, in which case a modified form of a scale such as the one suggested for evaluating interviews (below) could be used:

- grammar
- vocabulary
- comprehension
- fluency
- pronunciation
- task (accomplishing the objective of the elicited task)

Each category may be scored separately, with an additional composite score that attempts to synthesize overall performance. To attend to so many factors, you probably need an audiotaped recording for multiple listening.

One moderately successful picture-cued technique involves a pairing of two test-takers. They are supplied with a set of four identical sets of numbered pictures, each minimally distinct from the others by one or two factors. One test-taker is directed by a cue card to describe one of the four pictures in as few words as possible. The second test-taker must then identify the picture. The four pictures on the next page is an example:

Picture-cued multiple-choice description for two test-takers [L, S]

Test-takers see:

Test-taker 1 describes (for example) picture C; test-taker 2 points to the correct picture.

The task here is simple and straightforward and clearly in the intensive category as the test-taker must simply produce the relevant linguistic markers. Yet it is still the task of the test administrator to determine a correctly produced response and a correctly understood response, because sources of incorrectness may not be easily pinpointed. If the pictorial stimuli are more complex than the above item, greater burdens are placed on both speaker and listener, with consequently greater difficulty in identifying which committed the error.

Translation (of Limited Stretches of Discourse)

Translation is a part of our tradition in language teaching that we tend to discount or disdain, if only because our current pedagogical stance plays down its importance. Translation methods of teaching are certainly passé in an era of direct approaches to creating communicative classrooms. But we should remember that in countries where English is not the native or prevailing language, translation is a meaningful communicative device in contexts in which the English-user is called on to be an interpreter. Also, translation is a well-proven communication strategy for learners of a second language.

Under certain constraints, then, it is not far-fetched to suggest translation as a device to check oral production. Instead of offering pictures or written stimuli, the test-taker is given a native-language word, phrase, or sentence and is asked to translate it. Conditions may vary from expecting an instant translation of an orally elicited linguistic target to allowing more thinking time before producing a translation of somewhat longer texts, which may optionally be offered to the test-taker in written form. (Translation of extensive texts is discussed at the end of this chapter.) As an assessment procedure, the advantages of translation lie in its control of the output of the test-taker, which of course means that scoring is more easily specified.

DESIGNING ASSESSMENT TASKS: RESPONSIVE SPEAKING

Assessment of responsive tasks involves brief interactions with an interlocutor, differing from intensive tasks in the increased creativity given to the test-taker and from interactive tasks by the somewhat limited length of utterances.

Question and Answer

Question-and-answer tasks can consist of one or two questions from an interviewer, or they can make up a portion of a whole battery of questions and prompts in an oral interview. They can vary from simple questions such as "What is this called in English?" to complex questions such as "What are the steps governments should take, if any, to stem the rate of deforestation in tropical countries?" The first question is intensive in its purpose; it is a *display question* intended to elicit a predetermined correct response. We have already looked at some of these types of questions in the previous section. Questions at the responsive level tend to be genuine *referential questions* in which the test-taker is given more opportunity to produce meaningful language in response.

In designing such questions for test-takers, it's important to make sure that you know *why* you are asking the question. Are you simply trying to elicit strings of language output to gain a general sense of the test-taker's discourse competence? Are you combining discourse and grammatical competence in the same question? Is each question just one in a whole set of related questions? Responsive questions may take the following forms:

Questions eliciting open-ended responses [L, S]

Test-takers hear:

1. What do you think about the weather today?
2. What do you like about the English language?
3. Why did you choose your academic major?
4. What kind of strategies have you used to help you learn English?
5. a. Have you ever been to the United States before?
   b. What other countries have you visited?
   c. Why did you go there? What did you like best about it?
   d. If you could go back, what would you like to do or see?
   e. What country would you like to visit next, and why?

Test-takers respond with a few sentences at most.

Notice that question 5 has five situationally linked questions that may vary slightly depending on the test-taker's response to a previous question.

Oral interaction with a test administrator often involves the latter forming all the questions. The flip side of this normal procedure of question-and-answer tasks, though possibly less reliable, is to elicit questions from the test-taker. To assess the test-taker's ability to produce questions, prompts such as the following can be used:

Elicitation of questions from the test-taker [L, S]

Test-takers hear:

- Do you have any questions for me?
- Ask me about my family or job or interests.
- If you could interview the president or prime minister of your country, what would you ask that person?

Test-takers respond with questions.

A potentially tricky form of oral production assessment involves more than one test-taker with an interviewer, which is discussed later in this chapter. With two students in an interview context, both test-takers can ask questions of each other.

Giving Instructions and Directions

We are all called on in our daily routines to read instructions on how to operate an appliance, how to put a bookshelf together, or how to create a delicious clam chowder. Somewhat less frequent is the mandate to provide such instructions orally, but this speech act is still relatively common. Using such a stimulus in an assessment context provides an opportunity for the test-taker to engage in a relatively extended stretch of discourse, to be very clear and specific, and to use appropriate discourse markers and connectors. The technique is simple: The administrator poses the problem, and the test-taker responds. Scoring is based primarily on comprehensibility and secondarily on other specified grammatical or discourse categories. Some possibilities follow.

Eliciting instructions or directions [L, S]

Test-takers hear:

- Describe how to make a typical dish from your country.
- What's a good recipe for making _____?
- How do you access e-mail on a PC?
- How would I make a typical costume for a _____ celebration in your country?
- How do you program telephone numbers into a cell phone?
- How do I get from _____ to _____ in your city?

Test-takers respond with appropriate instructions/directions.

Some pointers for creating such tasks: The test administrator needs to guard against test-takers knowing and preparing for such items in advance lest they simply parrot back a memorized set of sentences. An impromptu delivery of instructions is warranted here or, at most, a minute or so of preparation time. Also, the choice of topics needs to be familiar enough so that you are testing not general knowledge but linguistic competence; therefore, topics beyond the content schemata of the test-taker are inadvisable. Finally, the task should require the test-taker to produce at least five or six sentences (of connected discourse) to adequately fulfill the objective.

This task can be designed to be more complex, thus placing it in the category of extensive speaking. If your objective is to keep the response short and simple, then make sure your directive does not take the test-taker down a path of complexity that he or she is not ready to face.

Paraphrasing

Another type of assessment task that can be categorized as responsive asks the test-taker to read or hear a short story or description with a limited number of sentences (perhaps two to five) and produce a paraphrase of the story. For example:

Paraphrasing a story or description [L, R, S]

Test-takers hear: Paraphrase the following in your own words.

My weekend in the mountains was fabulous. The first day we backpacked into the mountains and climbed about 2,000 feet. The hike was strenuous but exhilarating. By sunset we found these beautiful alpine lakes and made camp there. The sunset was amazingly beautiful. The next two days we just kicked back and did little day hikes, some rock climbing, bird-watching, swimming, and fishing. The hike out on the next day was really easy—all downhill—and the scenery was incredible.

Test-takers respond with two or three sentences.

A more authentic context for paraphrase is aurally receiving and orally relaying a message. In the following example, the test-taker must relay information from a telephone call to an office colleague named Jeff.

Paraphrasing a phone message [L, S]

Test-takers hear:

Please tell Jeff that I'm tied up in traffic so I'm going to be about a half-hour late for the nine o'clock meeting. And ask him to bring up our question about the employee benefits plan. If he wants to check in with me on my cell phone, have him call 415-338-3095. Thanks.

Test-takers respond with two or three sentences.

The advantages of such tasks are that they elicit short stretches of output and perhaps tap into test-takers' ability to practice the conversational art of conciseness by reducing the output/input ratio. Yet you have to question the criterion being assessed. Is it a listening task more than production? Does it test short-term memory rather than linguistic ability? Is it testing the grammatical ability to produce reported speech? And how does the teacher determine scoring of responses? If you use short paraphrasing tasks as an assessment procedure, it's important to pinpoint the objective of the task clearly. In this case, the integration of listening and speaking is probably more at stake than simple oral production alone.

Test of Spoken English (TSE® Test)

Somewhere between responsive, interactive, and extensive speaking tasks lies another popular commercial oral production assessment, the Test of Spoken English (TSE), described in Chapter 5 and referenced in the appendix at the back of this book. More information is available at www.toefl.org.

The tasks on the TSE are designed to elicit oral production in various discourse categories rather than in selected phonological, grammatical, or lexical targets. Tasks include description, narration, summary, giving instructions, comparing and contrasting, etc. Lazaraton and Wagner (1996) examined 15 different specific tasks in collecting background data from native and nonnative speakers of English:

1. Giving a personal description
2. Describing a daily routine
3. Suggesting a gift and supporting one's choice
4. Recommending a place to visit and supporting one's choice
5. Giving directions
6. Describing a favorite movie and supporting one's choice
7. Telling a story from pictures
8. Hypothesizing about future action
9. Hypothesizing about a preventative action
10. Making a telephone call to the dry cleaner
11. Describing an important news event
12. Giving an opinion about animals in the zoo
13. Defining a technical term
14. Describing information in a graph and speculating about its implications
15. Giving details about a trip schedule

From their findings, the researchers were able to report on the validity of the tasks, especially the match between the intended task functions and the actual output of both native and nonnative speakers. For example, in one task test-takers see a map of a town and are directed to provide directions to a movie theater and to describe their favorite move that's playing at the theater. In another task, a series of events is pictured and test-takers must describe the "story" of the pictures. Other tasks are more complex and require test-takers to defend a point of view or interpret a graph.

The scoring rubric for the TSE gives you a good example of rating scales that are used to evaluate oral production (see Table 8.1 on the next page).

Table 8.1. Test of Spoken English scoring guide (1995)

TSE® Test Rating Scale

60 **Communication almost always effective: task performed very competently; speech almost never marked by nonnative characteristics**

Functions performed clearly and effectively
Appropriate response to audience/situation
Coherent, with effective use of cohesive devices
Almost always accurate pronunciation, grammar, fluency, and vocabulary

50 **Communication generally effective: task performed competently, successful use of compensatory strategies; speech sometimes marked by nonnative characteristics**

Functions generally performed clearly and effectively
Generally appropriate response to audience/situation
Coherent, with some effective use of cohesive devices
Generally accurate pronunciation, grammar, fluency, and vocabulary

40 **Communication somewhat effective: task performed somewhat competently, some successful use of compensatory strategies; speech regularly marked by nonnative characteristics**

Functions performed somewhat clearly and effectively
Somewhat appropriate response to audience/situation
Somewhat coherent, with some use of cohesive devices
Somewhat accurate pronunciation, grammar, fluency, and vocabulary

30 **Communication generally not effective: task generally performed poorly, ineffective use of compensatory strategies; speech very frequently marked by nonnative characteristics**

Functions generally performed unclearly and ineffectively
Generally inappropriate response to audience/situation
Generally incoherent, with little use of cohesive devices
Generally inaccurate pronunciation, grammar, fluency, and vocabulary

20 **No effective communication: no evidence of ability to perform task, no effective use of compensatory strategies; speech almost always marked by nonnative characteristics**

No evidence that functions were performed
Incoherent, with no use of cohesive devices
No evidence of ability to respond appropriately to audience/situation
Almost always inaccurate pronunciation, grammar, fluency, and vocabulary

Holistic scoring taxonomies such as these imply a number of abilities that comprise "effective" communication and "competent" performance of the task. The original version of the TSE (1987) specified three contributing factors to a final score on "overall comprehensibility": pronunciation, grammar, and fluency. The current scoring scale of 20 to 60 listed above incorporates task performance, function, appropriateness, and coherence as well as the form-focused factors. From reported scores, institutions are left to determine their own threshold levels of acceptability, but because scoring is holistic, they do not receive an analytic score of how each factor breaks down (see Douglas & Smith, 1997, for further information). Classroom teachers who propose to model oral production assessments after the tasks on the TSE must, in order to provide some washback effect, be more explicit in analyzing the various components of test-takers' output. Such scoring rubrics are presented in the next section.

DESIGNING ASSESSMENT TASKS: INTERACTIVE SPEAKING

The final two categories of oral production assessment (interactive and extensive speaking) include tasks that involve relatively long stretches of interactive discourse (interviews, role plays, discussions, games) and tasks of equally long duration but that involve less interaction (speeches, telling longer stories, and extended explanations and translations). The obvious difference between the two sets of tasks is the degree of interaction with an interlocutor. Also, interactive tasks are what some would describe as *interpersonal,* whereas the final category includes more *transactional* speech events.

Interview

When "oral production assessment" is mentioned, the first thing that comes to mind is an oral interview: A test administrator and a test-taker sit down in a direct face-to-face exchange and proceed through a protocol of questions and directives. The interview, which may be tape-recorded for relistening, is then scored on one or more parameters such as accuracy in pronunciation and/or grammar, vocabulary usage, fluency, sociolinguistic/pragmatic appropriateness, task accomplishment, and even comprehension.

Interviews can vary in length from perhaps 5 to 45 minutes, depending on their purpose and context. Placement interviews, designed to get a quick spoken sample from a student to verify placement into a course, may need only 5 minutes if the interviewer is trained to evaluate the output accurately. Longer comprehensive interviews such as the Oral Proficiency Interview (OPI; see the next section) are designed to cover predetermined oral production contexts and may require the better part of an hour.

Every effective interview contains a number of mandatory stages. Two decades ago, Michael Canale (1984) proposed a framework for oral proficiency testing that has withstood the test of time. He suggested that test-takers perform at their best if they are led through four stages:

1. *Warm-up.* In a minute or so of preliminary small talk, the interviewer directs mutual introductions, helps the test-taker become comfortable with the situation, apprises the test-taker of the format, and allays anxieties. No scoring of this phase takes place.

2. *Level check.* Through a series of preplanned questions, the interviewer stimulates the test-taker to respond using expected or predicted forms and functions. If, for example, from previous test information, grades, or other data, the test-taker has been judged to be a Level 2 (see below) speaker, the interviewer's prompts attempt to confirm this assumption. The responses may take a very simple or a very complex form, depending on the entry level of the learner. Questions are usually designed to elicit grammatical categories (such as past tense or subject–verb agreement), discourse structure (a sequence of events), vocabulary usage, and/or sociolinguistic factors (politeness conventions, formal/informal language). This stage could also give the interviewer a picture of the test-taker's extroversion, readiness to speak, and confidence, all of which may be of significant consequence in the interview's results. Linguistic target criteria are scored in this phase. If this stage is lengthy, a tape-recording of the interview is important.

3. *Probe.* Probe questions and prompts challenge test-takers to go to the heights of their ability, to extend beyond the limits of the interviewer's expectation through increasingly difficult questions. Probe questions may be complex in their framing and/or complex in their cognitive and linguistic demand. Through probe items, the interviewer discovers the ceiling or limitation of the test-taker's proficiency. This need not be a separate stage entirely but might be a set of questions that are interspersed into the previous stage. At the lower levels of proficiency, probe items may simply demand a higher range of vocabulary or grammar from the test-taker than predicted. At the higher levels, probe items will typically ask the test-taker to give an opinion or a value judgment, to discuss his or her field of specialization, to recount a narrative, or to respond to questions that are worded in complex form. Responses to probe questions may be scored, or they may be ignored if the test-taker displays an inability to handle such complexity.

4. *Wind-down.* This final phase of the interview is simply a short period of time during which the interviewer encourages the test-taker to relax with some easy questions, sets the test-taker's mind at ease, and provides information about when and where to obtain the results of the interview. This part is not scored.

The suggested set of content specifications for an oral interview (below) may serve as sample questions that can be adapted to individual situations.

Oral interview content specifications [L, S]

Warm-up:
1. Small talk

Level check:
The test-taker
2. answers *wh*-questions.
3. produces a narrative without interruptions.
4. reads a passage aloud.

5. tells how to make something or do something.

6. engages in a brief, controlled, guided role play.

Probe:

The test-taker

7. responds to interviewer's open-ended questions on possibly obscure topics intended to pose a challenge to the test-taker.

8. talks about his or her own field of study or profession.

9. engages in a longer, more open-ended role play (e.g., simulates a difficult or embarrassing circumstance) with the interviewer.

10. gives an impromptu presentation on some aspect of test-taker's field.

Wind-down:

11. Feelings about the interview, information on results, further questions

Some possible questions, probes, and comments that fit those specifications are as follows:

Sample questions for the four stages of an oral interview

1. Warm-up:

How are you?
What's your name?
What country are you from? What (city, town)?
Let me tell you about this interview.

2. Level check:

How long have you been in this (country, city)?
Tell me about your family.
What is your (academic major, professional interest, job)?
How long have you been working at your (degree, job)?
Describe your home (city, town) to me.
How do you like your home (city, town)?
What are your hobbies or interests? (What do you do in your spare time?)
Why do you like your (hobby, interest)?
Have you traveled to another country beside this one and your
    home country?
Tell me about that country.
Compare your home (city, town) to another (city, town).
What is your favorite food?
Tell me how to (make, do) something you know well.

What will you be doing ten years from now?

I'd like you to ask me some questions.

Tell me about an exciting or interesting experience you've had.

Read the following paragraph please. *Test-taker reads aloud.*

Pretend that you are _____ and I am a _____. *Guided role play follows.*

3. Probe:

What are your goals for learning English in this program?

Describe your [academic field, job] to me. What do you like and dislike about it?

What is your opinion of [a recent headline news event]?

Describe someone you greatly respect and tell me why you respect that person.

If you could redo your education all over again, what would you do differently?

How do eating habits and customs reflect the culture of the people of a country?

If you were [president, prime minister] of your country, what would you like to change about your country?

What career advice would you give to your younger friends?

Imagine you are writing an article on a topic you don't know very much about. Ask me some questions about that topic.

You are in a shop that sells expensive glassware. Accidentally you knock over an expensive vase, and it breaks. What will you say to the store owner? *Interviewer role plays the store owner.*

4. Wind-down:

Did you feel okay about this interview?

What are your plans for [the weekend, the rest of today, the future]?

You'll get your results from this interview [tomorrow, next week].

Do you have any questions you want to ask me?

It was interesting to talk with you. Best wishes.

The success of an oral interview will depend on

- clearly specifying administrative procedures of the assessment (practicality).
- focusing the questions and probes on the purpose of the assessment (validity)
- appropriately eliciting an optimal amount and quality of oral production from the test-taker (biased for best performance)
- minimizing the possibly harmful effect of the power relationship between interviewer and interviewee (biased for best performance)
- creating a consistent, workable scoring system (reliability)

The last two issues can be thorny. In every interview, the test-taker is put into the often uncomfortable situation of responding to, and interacting with, an "expert"—be that a teacher or a highly proficient user of the language (Plough & Bogart, 2008). The interviewer (the teacher, in a classroom context) needs to be aware of the power relationship that underlies the interview and do whatever possible to put the test-taker at ease, to lower his or her anxiety, and to draw out optimal performance.

Because of the potential, especially in the "level check" and "probe" stages, for open-ended creative responses from the test-taker, the interviewer may have to make judgments that are susceptible to some unreliability. The ability to make such judgments is acquired through experience, training, and careful attention to the linguistic criteria being assessed. Table 8.2 on pages 212–213 shows a set of descriptions for scoring open-ended oral interviews—descriptions that offer a little more detail than the TSE rubric (see page 206). These descriptions come from an earlier version of the OPI and are useful for classroom purposes.

The test administrator's challenge is to assign a score, ranging from 1 to 5, for each of the six categories indicated on the previous page. It may look easy to do, but in reality the lines of distinction between levels is quite difficult to pinpoint. Some training or at least a good deal of interviewing experience is required to make accurate assessments of oral production in the six categories. Usually the six scores are then amalgamated into one holistic score, a process that might not be relegated to a simple mathematical average if you wish to put more weight on some categories than you do on others.

This five-point scale, once known as "FSI levels" (because they were first advocated by the Foreign Service Institute in Washington, D.C.), is still in popular use among U.S. government State Department staff for designating proficiency in a foreign language. To complicate the scoring somewhat, the five-point holistic scoring categories have historically been subdivided into "pluses" and "minuses" as indicated in Table 8.3 on page 214. To this day, even though the official nomenclature has now changed (see OPI description below and in the appendix at the back of this book), in-group conversations refer to colleagues and coworkers by their FSI level: "Oh, Bob, yeah, he's a good 3-plus in Turkish—he can easily handle that assignment."

A variation on the usual one-on-one format with one interviewer and one test-taker is to place two test-takers at a time with the interviewer. An advantage of a two-on-one interview is the practicality of scheduling twice as many candidates in the same time frame, but more significant is the opportunity for student–student interaction. By deftly posing questions, problems, and role plays, the interviewer can maximize the output of the test-takers while lessening the need for his or her own output. A further benefit is the probable increase in authenticity when two test-takers can actually converse with each other. Disadvantages are equalizing the output between the two test-takers, discerning the interaction effect of unequal comprehension and production abilities, and scoring two people simultaneously.

Table 8.2. Oral proficiency scoring categories (H. D. Brown, 2001, pp. 406–407)

	Grammar	Vocabulary	Comprehension
I	Errors in grammar are frequent, but speaker can be understood by a native speaker used to dealing with foreigners attempting to speak his language.	Speaking vocabulary inadequate to express anything but the most elementary needs.	Within the scope of his very limited language experience, can understand simple questions and statements if delivered with slowed speech, repetition, or paraphrase.
II	Can usually handle elementary constructions quite accurately but does not have thorough or confident control of the grammar.	Has speaking vocabulary sufficient to express himself simply with some circumlocutions.	Can get the gist of most conversations of non-technical subjects (i.e., topics that require no specialized knowledge).
III	Control of grammar is good. Able to speak the language with sufficient structural accuracy to participate effectively in most formal and informal conversations on practical, social, and professional topics.	Able to speak the language with sufficient vocabulary to participate effectively in most formal and informal conversations on practical, social, and professional topics. Vocabulary is broad enough that he rarely has to grope for a word.	Comprehension is quite complete at a normal rate of speech.
IV	Able to use the language accurately on all levels normally pertinent to professional needs. Errors in grammar are quite rare.	Can understand and participate in any conversation within the range of his experience with a high degree of precision of vocabulary.	Can understand any conversation within the range of his experience.
V	Equivalent to that of an educated native speaker.	Speech on all levels is fully accepted by educated native speakers in all its features including breadth of vocabulary and idioms, colloquialisms, and pertinent cultural references.	Equivalent to that of an educated native speaker.

Fluency	Pronunciation	Task
(No specific fluency description. Refer to other four language areas for implied level of fluency.)	Errors in pronunciation are frequent but can be understood by a native speaker used to dealing with foreigners attempting to speak his language.	Can ask and answer questions on topics very familiar to him. Able to satisfy routine travel needs and minimum courtesy requirements. (Should be able to order a simple meal, ask for shelter or lodging, ask and give simple directions, make purchases, and tell time.)
Can handle with confidence but not with facility most social situations, including introductions and casual conversations about current events, as well as work, family, and autobiographical information.	Accent is intelligible though often quite faulty.	Able to satisfy routine social demands and work requirements; needs help in handling any complication or difficulties.
Can discuss particular interests of competence with reasonable ease. Rarely has to grope for words.	Errors never interfere with understanding and rarely disturb the native speaker. Accent may be obviously foreign.	Can participate effectively in most formal and informal conversations on practical, social, and professional topics.
Able to use the language fluently on all levels normally pertinent to professional needs. Can participate in any conversation within the range of this experience with a high degree of fluency.	Errors in pronunciation are quite rare.	Would rarely be taken for a native speaker but can respond appropriately even in unfamiliar situations. Can handle informal interpreting from and into language.
Has complete fluency in the language such that his speech is fully accepted by educated native speakers.	Equivalent to and fully accepted by educated native speakers.	Speaking proficiency equivalent to that of an educated native speaker.

Table 8.3. Subcategories of oral proficiency scores

Level	Description
0	Unable to function in the spoken language
0+	Able to satisfy immediate needs using rehearsed utterances
1	Able to satisfy minimum courtesy requirements and maintain very simple face-to-face conversations on familiar topics
1+	Can initiate and maintain predictable face-to-face conversations and satisfy limited social demands
2	Able to satisfy routine social demands and limited work requirements
2+	Able to satisfy most work requirements with language usage that is often, but not always, acceptable and effective
3	Able to speak the language with sufficient structural accuracy and vocabulary to participate effectively in most formal and informal conversations on practical, social, and professional topics
3+	Often able to use the language to satisfy professional needs in a wide range of sophisticated and demanding tasks
4	Able to use the language fluently and accurately on all levels normally pertinent to professional needs
4+	Speaking proficiency is regularly superior in all respects, usually equivalent to that of a well-educated, highly articulate native speaker
5	Speaking proficiency is functionally equivalent to that of a highly articulate, well-educated native speaker and reflects the cultural standards of the country where the language is spoken

Role Play

Role playing is a popular pedagogical activity in communicative language teaching classes. Within constraints set forth by the guidelines, it frees students to be somewhat creative in their linguistic output. In some versions, role play allows some rehearsal time so that students can map out what they are going to say. It also has the effect of lowering anxieties as students can, even for a few moments, take on the persona of someone other than themselves.

As an assessment device, role play opens some windows of opportunity for test-takers to use discourse that might otherwise be difficult to elicit. With prompts such as "Pretend that you're a tourist asking me for directions" or "You're buying a necklace from me in a flea market, and you want to get a lower price," certain personal, strategic, and linguistic factors come into the foreground of the test-taker's oral abilities. Although role play can be controlled or "guided" by the interviewer, this technique takes test-takers beyond simple intensive and responsive levels to a level of creativity and complexity that approaches real-world pragmatics. Scoring presents the usual issues in any task that elicits somewhat unpredictable responses from test-takers. The test administrator must determine the assessment objectives of the role play then devise a scoring technique that appropriately pinpoints those objectives.

Discussions and Conversations

As formal assessment devices, discussions and conversations with and among students are difficult to specify and even more difficult to score. However, as informal techniques to assess learners, they offer a level of authenticity and spontaneity that other assessment techniques may not provide. Discussions may be especially appropriate tasks through which to elicit and observe such abilities as

- topic nomination, maintenance, and termination
- attention getting, interrupting, floor holding, control
- clarifying, questioning, paraphrasing
- comprehension signals (nodding, "uh-huh," "hmm," etc.)
- negotiating meaning
- intonation patterns for pragmatic effect
- kinesics, eye contact, proxemics, body language
- politeness, formality, and other sociolinguistic factors

Assessing the performance of participants through scores or checklists (in which appropriate or inappropriate manifestations of any category are noted) should be carefully designed to suit the objectives of the observed discussion. Teachers also need to beware of the possibility that the presence of a checklist could make students feel some anxiety that could in turn negatively affect their performance. An additional complicating factor is the integrative nature of a discussion, making it advisable to assess comprehension—as well as production—in evaluating learners.

Games

Among informal assessment devices are a variety of games that directly involve language production. Consider the following types:

Assessment games [L, S, R, W]

---

1. "Tinkertoy" game: A Tinkertoy (or Lego block) structure is built behind a screen. One or two learners are allowed to view the structure. In successive stages of construction, the learners tell "runners" (who can't observe the structure) how to re-create the structure. The runners then tell "builders" behind another screen how to build the structure. The builders may question or confirm as they proceed but only through the two degrees of separation. The object is to re-create the structure as accurately as possible.
2. Crossword puzzles are created in which the names of all members of a class are clued by obscure information about them. Each class member must ask questions of others to determine who matches the clues in the puzzle.

3. Information gap grids are created such that class members must conduct mini-interviews of other classmates to fill in boxes (e.g., "born in July," "plays the violin," "has a two-year-old child," etc.).

4. City maps are distributed to class members. Predetermined map directions are given to one student who, with a city map in front of him or her, describes the route to a partner, who must then trace the route and get to the correct final destination.

Clearly, such tasks have strayed from the traditional notion of an oral production test and may even be well beyond assessments, but if you remember the discussion of these terms in Chapter 1 of this book, you can put the tasks into perspective. As assessments, the key is to specify a set of criteria and a reasonably practical and reliable scoring method. The benefit of such an informal assessment may not be its summative evaluation as much as its formative nature, with washback for the students.

ACTFL Oral Proficiency Interview (OPI)

The best-known oral interview format is one that has gone through a considerable metamorphosis over the last half-century, the Oral Proficiency Interview (OPI). The ACTFL OPI is currently used worldwide by academic institutions, government agencies, and private corporations for purposes such as academic placement, student assessment, program evaluation, professional certification, hiring, and promotional qualification. Originally known as the Foreign Service Institute (FSI) test, the OPI is the result of a historical progression of revisions under the auspices of several agencies, including the Educational Testing Service and the American Council on Teaching Foreign Languages (ACTFL). The latter, a professional society for research on foreign language instruction and assessment, has now become the principal body for promoting the use of the OPI. The OPI is widely used across dozens of languages around the world. Only certified examiners are authorized to administer the OPI; certification workshops are available, at costs of around $700 for ACTFL members, through ACTFL at selected sites and conferences throughout the year.

Specifications for the OPI approximate those delineated above under the discussion of oral interviews in general. In a series of structured tasks, the OPI is carefully designed to elicit pronunciation, fluency and integrative ability, sociolinguistic and cultural knowledge, grammar, and vocabulary. Performance is judged by the examiner to be at one of ten possible levels on the ACTFL-designated proficiency guidelines for speaking: Superior; Advanced—high, mid, low; Intermediate—high, mid, low; Novice—high, mid, low. A summary of those levels is provided in Table 8.4 on the next page.

The ACTFL Proficiency Guidelines may appear to be just another form of the FSI levels described earlier. Holistic evaluation is still implied, and in this case four levels are described. On closer scrutiny, however, they offer a markedly different set

Table 8.4. Summary highlights: ACTFL proficiency guidelines—speaking

Superior	Advanced	Intermediate	Novice
Superior-level speakers are characterized by the ability to • participate fully and effectively in conversations in formal and informal settings on topics related to practical needs and areas of professional and/or scholarly interests • provide a structured argument to explain and defend opinions and develop effective hypotheses within extended discourse • discuss topics concretely and abstractly • deal with a linguistically unfamiliar situation • maintain a high degree of linguistic accuracy • satisfy the linguistic demands of professional and/or scholarly life	Advanced-level speakers are characterized by the ability to • participate actively in conversations in most informal and some formal settings on topics of personal and public interest • narrate and describe in major time frames with good control of aspect • deal effectively with unanticipated complications through a variety of communicative devices • sustain communication by using, with suitable accuracy and confidence, connected discourse of paragraph length and substance • satisfy the demands of work and/or school situations	Intermediate-level speakers are characterized by the ability to • participate in simple, direct conversations on generally predictable topics related to daily activities and personal environment • create with the language and communicate personal meaning to sympathetic interlocutors by combining language elements in discrete sentences and strings of sentences • obtain and give information by asking and answering questions • sustain and bring to a close a number of basic, uncomplicated communicative exchanges, often in a reactive mode • satisfy simple personal needs and social demands to survive in the target language culture	Novice-level speakers are characterized by the ability to: • respond to simple questions on the most common features of daily life • convey minimal meaning to interlocutors experienced in dealing with foreigners by using isolated words, lists of words, memorized phrases, and some personalized recombinations of words and phrases • satisfy a very limited number of immediate needs

of descriptors. First, they are more reflective of a unitary definition of ability, as discussed earlier in this book (page 14). Instead of focusing on separate abilities in grammar, vocabulary, comprehension, fluency, and pronunciation, they focus more strongly on the overall task and on the discourse ability needed to accomplish the goals of the tasks. Second, for classroom assessment purposes, the six FSI categories more appropriately describe the components of oral ability than do the ACTFL holistic scores and therefore offer better washback potential. Third, the ACTFL requirement for specialized training renders the OPI less useful for classroom adaptation. Which form of evaluation is best is an issue that is still hotly debated (Reed & Cohen, 2001; Swendler, 2003).

We noted earlier that, for official purposes, the OPI relies on an administrative network that mandates certified examiners who pay a significant fee to achieve examiner status. This systemic control of the OPI adds test reliability to the procedure and assures test-takers that examiners are specialists who have gone through a rigorous training course. All these safeguards discourage the appearance of "outlaw" examiners who might render unreliable scores.

On the other hand, the whole idea of an oral interview under the control of an interviewer has come under harsh criticism from a number of language-testing specialists. Valdman (1988) summed up the complaint:

> The OPI forces test-takers into a closed system where, because the interviewer is endowed with full social control, they are unable to negotiate a social world. For example, they cannot nominate topics for discussion, they cannot switch formality levels, they cannot display a full range of stylistic maneuver. The total control the OPI interviewers possess is reflected by the parlance of the test methodology. . . . In short, the OPI can only inform us of how learners can deal with an artificial social *imposition* rather than enabling us to predict how they would be likely to manage authentic linguistic interactions with target-language native speakers. (p. 125)

Bachman (1988) also pointed out that the validity of the OPI simply cannot be demonstrated "because it confounds abilities with elicitation procedures in its design, and it provides only a single rating, which has no basis in either theory or research" (p. 149).

Meanwhile, a great deal of experimentation continues to be conducted to design better oral proficiency testing methods (Bailey, 1998; Bonk & Ockey, 2003; Halleck, 2007; Hughes, 2004; Jenkins & Parra, 2003; Young & He, 1998). With ongoing critical attention to issues of language assessment in the years to come, we may be able to solve some of the thorny problems of how best to elicit oral production in authentic contexts and create valid and reliable scoring methods.

DESIGNING ASSESSMENTS: EXTENSIVE SPEAKING

Extensive speaking tasks involve complex, relatively lengthy stretches of discourse. They are frequently variations on monologues, usually with minimal verbal interaction.

Oral Presentations

In the academic and professional arenas, it would not be uncommon to be called on to present a report, paper, marketing plan, sales idea, design of a new product, or method. A summary of oral assessment techniques would therefore be incomplete without some consideration of extensive speaking tasks. Once again the rules for effective assessment must be invoked: (a) specify the criterion, (b) set appropriate tasks, (c) elicit optimal output, and (d) establish practical, reliable scoring procedures. And once again scoring is the key assessment challenge.

For oral presentations, a checklist or grid is a common means of scoring or evaluation. Holistic scores are tempting to use for their apparent practicality, but they may obscure the variability of performance across several subcategories, especially the two major components of content and delivery. Following is an example of a checklist for a prepared oral presentation at the intermediate or advanced level of English.

Oral presentation checklist

Evaluation of oral presentation

Assign a number to each box according to your assessment of the various aspects of the speaker's presentation.

3	Excellent
2	Good
1	Fair
0	Poor

Content:
☐ The purpose or objective of the presentation was accomplished.
☐ The introduction was lively and got my attention.
☐ The main idea or point was clearly stated toward the beginning.
☐ The supporting points were
  • clearly expressed
  • supported well by facts, argument
☐ The conclusion restated the main idea or purpose.

Delivery:
☐ The speaker used gestures and body language well.
☐ The speaker maintained eye contact with the audience.
☐ The speaker used notes (and did not read a script verbatim).
☐ The speaker's language was natural and fluent.
☐ The speaker's volume of speech was appropriate.
☐ The speaker's rate of speech was appropriate.
☐ The speaker's pronunciation was clear and comprehensible.
☐ The speaker's grammar was correct and didn't prevent understanding.
☐ The speaker used visual aids, handouts, etc., effectively.
☐ The speaker showed enthusiasm and interest.
☐ (If appropriate) The speaker responded to audience questions well.

Such a checklist is reasonably practical. Its reliability can vary if clear standards for scoring are not maintained. Its authenticity can be supported in that all of the items on the list contribute to an effective presentation. The washback effect of such a checklist can be enhanced by written comments from the teacher, a conference with the teacher, peer evaluations using the same form, and self-assessment.

Picture-Cued Storytelling

One of the most common techniques for eliciting oral production is through visual pictures, photographs, diagrams, and charts. We have already looked at this elicitation device for intensive tasks, but at this level we consider a picture or a series of pictures as a stimulus for a longer story or description. Consider the following set of pictures:

Picture-cued story-telling task (H. D. Brown, 1999, p. 29) [L/R, S]

Test-takers see the following six-picture sequence:

Test-takers *hear or read:* Tell the story that these pictures describe.

Test-takers *use the pictures as a sequence of cues to tell a story.*

It's always tempting to throw any picture sequence at test-takers and have them talk for a minute or so about them. But as is true of every assessment of speaking ability, the objective of eliciting narrative discourse needs to be clear. In the above example (with a little humor added), are you testing for oral vocabulary ("girl," "alarm," "coffee," "telephone," "wet," "cat," etc.), for time relatives ("before," "after," "when"), for sentence connectors ("then," "and then," "so"), for past tense of irregular verbs ("woke," "drank," "rang"), and/or for fluency in general? If you are eliciting specific grammatical or discourse features, you might add to the directions specific instructions such as "Tell the story that these pictures describe. *Use the past tense of verbs.*" Your criteria for scoring need to make clear what it is you are hoping to assess. Refer back to some of the guidelines suggested under the section on oral interviews, above, or to the OPI for some general suggestions on scoring such a narrative.

Retelling a Story, News Event [L, R, S]

In this type of task, test-takers hear or read a story or news event that they are asked to retell. This differs from the paraphrasing task discussed on page 204 in that it is a longer stretch of discourse and, possibly, if it's a news article or presentation, a different genre. The objectives in assigning such a task vary from listening comprehension of the original to production of a number of oral discourse features (communicating sequences and relationships of events, stress and emphasis patterns, "expression" in the case of a dramatic story), fluency, and interaction with the hearer. Scoring should of course meet the intended criteria.

Translation (of Extended Prose)

Translation of words, phrases, or short sentences was mentioned under in the section on intensive speaking. Here, longer texts are presented for the test-taker to read in the native language and then translate into English. Those texts could come in many forms: dialogue; directions for assembly of a product; a synopsis of a story, play, or movie; directions on how to find something on a map; and other genres. The advantage of translation is in the control of the content, vocabulary, and, to some extent, the grammatical and discourse features. The disadvantage is that translation of longer texts is a highly specialized skill for which some individuals obtain post-baccalaureate degrees! To judge a nonspecialist's oral language ability on such a skill may be completely invalid, especially if the test-taker has not engaged in translation at this level. Criteria for scoring should therefore take into account not only the purpose in stimulating a translation but the possibility of errors that are unrelated to oral production ability.

☆   ☆   ☆   ☆   ☆

The evolution of human speech over hundreds of millennia has resulted in an extraordinarily complex system of vocal communication. This chapter has offered a relatively sweeping overview of some of the ways we have learned to assess our wonderful ability to produce sounds, words, and sentences and to string them together to communicate meaning. This chapter's limited number of assessment techniques may encourage your imagination to explore a potentially unlimited number of possibilities for assessing oral production.

EXERCISES

[Note: **(I)** Individual work; **(G)** Group or pair work; **(C)** Whole-class discussion.]

1. **(G)** In the introduction to the chapter, the unique challenges of testing speaking were described (interaction effect, elicitation techniques, and scoring). In pairs, offer practical examples of one of the challenges, as assigned to your pair. Explain your examples to the class.
2. **(C)** Review the five basic types of speaking that were outlined at the beginning of the chapter. Offer examples of each and pay special attention to distinguishing between imitative and intensive and between responsive and interactive.
3. **(G)** Look at the list of micro- and macroskills of speaking on page 186. In pairs, each assigned to a different skill (or two), brainstorm some tasks that assess those skills. Present your findings to the rest of the class.
4. **(C)** In Chapter 7, nine characteristics of listening (page 164) that make listening "difficult" were listed. What makes speaking difficult? Devise a similar list that could form a set of specifications to pay special attention to in assessing speaking.
5. **(G)** Divide the five basic types of speaking among groups or pairs, one type for each. Look at the sample assessment techniques provided and evaluate them according to the five principles (practicality, reliability, validity [especially face and content], authenticity, and washback). Present your critique to the rest of the class.
6. **(G)** In the same groups as in item 5 above, with the same type of speaking, design some other item types, different from the one(s) provided here, that assess the same type of speaking performance.
7. **(I)** Search for the Versant® test Web site. Try some of the sample practice exercises. Report back to the class on how valid, reliable, and authentic you felt the test was.
8. **(G)** Several scoring scales are offered in this chapter, ranging from simple (2–1–0) score categories to the more elaborate rubric used for the OPI. In groups, each assigned to a scoring scale, evaluate the strengths and weaknesses of each. Pay special attention to intra-rater and inter-rater reliability.

9. **(C)** If possible, role-play a formal oral interview in your class, with one student (with beginning to intermediate proficiency in a language) acting as the test-taker and another (with advanced proficiency) as the test administrator. Use the sample questions provided on pages 209–210 as a guide. This role play requires some preparation. The rest of the class can then evaluate the effectiveness of the oral interview. Finally, the test-taker and administrator can offer their perspectives on the experience.

FOR YOUR FURTHER READING

Luoma, Sari. (2004). *Assessing speaking.* Cambridge: Cambridge University Press.

This volume is one of a number of books in the Cambridge Language Assessment series. It targets language teachers wishing to evaluate their students' speaking abilities. It outlines current language assessment paradigms in an accessible manner, surveys research in the field, and provides teachers and test developers with practical guidelines to design and develop speaking tests and other assessment tools for their students.

Fulcher, Glenn. (2003). *Testing second language speaking.* London: Pearson Education.

Fulcher's book is a critical analysis of theoretical underpinnings, methods, and standards for assessing second language speaking ability. It contains task types that are commonly used in speaking tests; approaches to researching speaking tests; and specific methodologies that teachers, students, and test developers may use in their own projects. Annotated examples are presented to enhance understanding of practical testing projects.

Tarone, Elaine. (2005). Speaking in a second language. In E. Hinkel (Ed.), *Handbook of research in second language teaching and learning* (pp. 485–502). Mahwah, NJ: Lawrence Erlbaum Associates.

This handbook is an excellent authoritative source of surveys of more than 50 different subfields of second language acquisition and pedagogy. Tarone's chapter offers a wealth of information on issues and research on the oral production process, with an extensive bibliography. Her chapter describes both the functions of learner speech and formal characteristics and what it means to be competent in speaking a second language. All these issues are a necessary backdrop to tackling the assessment of spoken language ability.

CHAPTER 9

ASSESSING READING

OBJECTIVES: After reading this chapter, you will be able to

- state a rationale for assessing reading as a separate skill as well as a skill that integrates with one or more of the other three skills
- discern the overlap between assessing reading as an implicit, unanalyzed ability and its explicit, form-focused counterpart, namely grammar and vocabulary comprehension
- incorporate performance-based assessment into your own assessment instruments

- develop assessments that focus on one or several micro- and macroskills of reading performance, within a specified genre of written language
- design assessments that target one or several of the modes of performance, ranging from perceptive recognition of forms to extensive reading

With the technological boom of recent years, we have seen a burgeoning of visual and auditory media, filling our eyes and ears almost constantly. Nevertheless, the written word continues to play a vital role in conveying information; amusing and entertaining us; codifying our social, economic, and legal conventions; and fulfilling a host of other functions. In literate societies, most "normal" children learn to read by the age of five or six, and some even earlier. With the exception of a small number of people with learning disabilities, reading is a skill that is taken for granted.

In foreign language learning, reading is likewise a skill that teachers simply expect learners to acquire. Basic, beginning level textbooks in a foreign language presuppose a student's reading ability if only because it's a book that is the medium. Many formal tests use the written word as a stimulus for test-taker response; even oral interviews may require reading performance for certain tasks. Reading, arguably the most essential skill for success in all educational contexts, remains a skill of paramount importance as we create assessments of general language ability.

Is reading so natural and normal that learners should simply be exposed to written texts with no particular instruction? Will they just absorb the skills necessary to convert their perception of a handful of letters into meaningful chunks of information? Not necessarily. For learners of English, two primary hurdles must be cleared to become efficient readers. First, they need to be able to master fundamental **bottom-up** strategies for processing separate letters, words, and phrases as well as **top-down**, conceptually driven strategies for comprehension. Second, as

224

part of that top-down approach, second language readers must develop appropriate content and formal **schemata**—background information and cultural experience—to carry out those interpretations effectively.

The assessment of reading ability does not end with the measurement of comprehension. It is also important, especially in formative classroom assessment, to assess the strategies that readers use—or fail to use—to achieve ultimate comprehension of a text. For example, an academic technical report may be comprehensible to a student at the sentence level, but if the learner has not utilized certain strategies for noting the discourse conventions of that genre, misunderstanding may occur.

As we consider a number of different types or genres of written texts, the components of reading ability, and specific tasks that are commonly used in the assessment of reading, let's not forget the unobservable nature of reading. Like listening, one cannot see the **process** or observe a specific **product** of reading. Other than observing a reader's eye movements and page turning, there is no technology that enables us to "see" sequences of graphic symbols traveling from the pages of a book into compartments of the brain (in a possible bottom-up process). Even more outlandish is the notion that one might be able to watch information from the brain make its way down onto the page (in typical top-down strategies). Further, once something is read—information from the written text is stored—no technology allows us to empirically measure exactly what is lodged in the brain. All assessment of reading must be carried out by inference.

GENRES OF READING

Each **genre** of written text has its own set of governing rules and conventions. A reader must be able to anticipate those conventions to process meaning efficiently. With an extraordinary number of genres present in any literate culture, the reader's ability to process texts must be very sophisticated. Consider the following abridged list of common genres, which ultimately form part of the specifications for assessments of reading ability:

Genres of reading

---

1. Academic reading
   General interest articles (in magazines, newspapers, etc.)
   Technical reports (e.g., lab reports), professional journal articles
   Reference material (dictionaries, online encyclopedias, etc.)
   Textbooks, theses
   Essays, papers
   Test directions
   Editorials and opinion writing

2. Job-related reading

Messages (e.g., phone messages)
Letters/e-mails
Memos (e.g., interoffice)
Reports (e.g., job evaluations, project reports)
Schedules, labels, signs, announcements
Forms, applications, questionnaires
Financial documents (bills, invoices, etc.)
Directories (telephone, office, etc.)
Manuals, directions

3. Personal reading

Newspapers and magazines
Letters, e-mails, greeting cards, invitations
Messages, notes, lists, blogs
Schedules (train, bus, plane, etc.)
Recipes, menus, maps, calendars
Advertisements (commercials, want ads)
Novels, short stories, jokes, drama, poetry
Financial documents (e.g., checks, tax forms, loan applications)
Forms, questionnaires, medical reports, immigration documents
Comic strips, cartoons

When we realize that this list is only the beginning, it is easy to see how overwhelming it is to learn to read in a foreign language. The genre of a text enables readers to apply certain **schemata** that assists them in extracting appropriate meaning. If, for example, readers know that a text is a recipe, they will expect a certain arrangement of information (ingredients) and will know to search for a sequential order of directions. Efficient readers also must know what their purpose is in reading a text, the strategies for accomplishing that purpose, and how to retain the information.

The content validity of an assessment procedure is largely established through the genre of a text. For example, if learners in a program of English for tourism have been learning how to deal with customers needing to arrange bus tours, then assessments of their ability should include guidebooks, maps, transportation schedules, calendars, and other relevant texts.

MICROSKILLS, MACROSKILLS, AND STRATEGIES FOR READING

Aside from attending to genres of text, the skills and strategies for accomplishing reading emerge as a crucial consideration in the assessment of reading ability. The following micro- and macroskills represent the spectrum of possibilities for objectives in the assessment of reading comprehension.

Micro- and macroskills for reading comprehension

Microskills

1. Discriminate among the distinctive graphemes (letters or letter combinations that produce a phoneme) and orthographic patterns of English
2. Retain chunks of language of different lengths in short-term memory
3. Process writing at an efficient rate of speed to suit the purpose
4. Recognize a core of words and interpret word order patterns and their significance
5. Recognize grammatical word classes (nouns, verbs, etc.), systems (e.g., tense, agreement, pluralization), patterns, rules, and elliptical forms
6. Recognize that a particular meaning may be expressed in different grammatical forms
7. Recognize cohesive devices in written discourse and their role in signaling the relationship between and among clauses

Macroskills

8. Recognize the rhetorical conventions of written discourse and their significance for interpretation
9. Recognize the communicative functions of written texts, according to form and purpose
10. Infer context that is not explicit by activating schemata (using background knowledge)
11. From described events, ideas, etc., infer links and connections between events, deduce causes and effects, and detect such relations as main idea, supporting idea, new information, given information, generalization, and exemplification
12. Distinguish between literal and implied meanings
13. Detect culturally specific references and interpret them in a context of the appropriate cultural schemata
14. Develop and use a battery of reading strategies, such as scanning and skimming, detecting discourse markers, guessing the meaning of words from context, and activating schemata for the interpretation of texts

---

The assessment of reading can imply the assessment of a storehouse of reading strategies, as indicated in item 14. Aside from simply testing the ultimate achievement of comprehension of a written text, it may be important in some contexts to assess one or more of a storehouse of classic reading strategies. The following brief taxonomy of strategies is a list of possible assessment criteria.

Some principal strategies for reading comprehension

1. Identify your purpose in reading a text
2. Apply spelling rules and conventions for bottom-up decoding
3. Use lexical analysis (prefixes, roots, suffixes, etc.) to determine meaning
4. Guess at meaning (of words, idioms, etc.) when you aren't certain
5. Skim the text for the gist and for main ideas
6. Scan the text for specific information (names, dates, key words)
7. Use silent reading techniques for rapid processing
8. Use marginal notes, outlines, charts, or semantic maps for understanding and retaining information
9. Distinguish between literal and implied meanings
10. Use discourse markers (e.g., "in addition", "however," "nevertheless", etc.) to process relationships

TYPES OF READING

In the previous chapters we saw that both listening and speaking could be subdivided into at least five different types of performance. In the case of reading, variety of performance is derived more from the multiplicity of types of texts (the genres listed on pages 225–226) than from the variety of overt types of performance. Nevertheless, for considering assessment procedures, several types of reading performance are typically identified, and these serve as organizers of various assessment tasks.

1. *Perceptive.* In keeping with the set of categories specified for listening comprehension, similar specifications are offered here, except with some differing terminology to capture the uniqueness of reading. Perceptive reading tasks involve attending to the components of larger stretches of discourse: letters, words, punctuation, and other graphemic symbols. Bottom-up processing is implied.
2. *Selective.* This category is largely an artifact of assessment formats. To ascertain one's reading recognition of lexical, grammatical, or discourse features of language within a very short stretch of language, certain typical tasks are used: picture-cued tasks, matching, true/false, multiple-choice, etc. Stimuli

include sentences, brief paragraphs, and simple charts and graphs. Brief responses are intended as well. A combination of bottom-up and top-down processing may be used.

3. *Interactive.* Included among interactive reading types are stretches of language of several paragraphs to one page or more in which the reader must, in a psycholinguistic sense, interact with the text. That is, reading is a process of negotiating meaning; the reader brings to the text a set of schemata for understanding it, and intake is the product of that interaction. Typical genres that lend themselves to interactive reading are anecdotes, short narratives and descriptions, excerpts from longer texts, questionnaires, memos, announcements, directions, recipes, and the like. The focus of an interactive task is to identify relevant features (lexical, symbolic, grammatical, and discourse) within texts of moderately short length with the objective of retaining the information that is processed. Top-down processing is typical of such tasks, although some instances of bottom-up performance may be necessary.

4. *Extensive.* Extensive reading, as discussed in this book, applies to texts of more than a page, up to and including professional articles, essays, technical reports, short stories, and books. (It should be noted that reading research commonly refers to "extensive reading" as longer stretches of discourse, such as long articles and books that are usually read outside a classroom hour. Here that definition encompasses any text longer than a page.) The purposes of assessment usually are to tap into a learner's global understanding of a text, as opposed to asking test-takers to "zoom in" on small details. Top-down processing is assumed for most extensive tasks.

The four types of reading are demonstrated in Figure 9.1, which shows the relationships of length, focus, and processing mode among the four types.

	Length			Focus		Process	
	Short	**Medium**	**Long**	**Form**	**Meaning**	**Bottom-Up**	**Top-Down**
Perceptive	••			••		••	
Selective	•	•		••	•	•	•
Interactive		••		•	••	•	••
Extensive			••		••		••

• Moderate emphasis
•• Strong emphasis

Figure 9.1. Types of reading by length, focus, and process

Of further interest in assessing reading ability is the possibility of assessing reading independently of the other three skills. Granted, a significant portion of classroom time devoted to building reading skills integrates speaking and/or writing in the form of exercises, responding, and learner-centered interaction, but quite a number of common item formats for assessing reading, as you will see in this chapter, can be performed without recourse to listening, speaking, or writing. We can credit multiple-choice, matching, pointing, picture-cued, and other nonverbally-based formats for allowing us to capitalize on this uniqueness of reading.

DESIGNING ASSESSMENT TASKS: PERCEPTIVE READING

At the beginning level of reading a second language lies a set of tasks that are fundamental and basic: recognition of alphabetic symbols, capitalized and lowercase letters, punctuation, words, and grapheme–phoneme correspondences. Such tasks of perception are often referred to as **literacy** tasks, implying that the learner is in the early stages of becoming "literate." Some learners are already literate in their own native language, but in other cases the second language may be the first language that they have ever learned to read. This latter context poses cognitive and sometimes age-related issues that need to be considered carefully. Assessment of literacy is no easy assignment, and if you are interested in this particular challenging area, further reading beyond this book is advised (Barone & Xu, 2007; Cooper, 1997; Farr & Tone, 1994; Genesee, 1994; Harp, 1991; Hurley & Tinajero, 2000; Uribe & Nathenson-Mejía, 2008). Assessment of basic reading skills may be carried out in a number of different ways.

Reading Aloud [S, R]

The test-taker sees separate letters, words, and/or short sentences and reads them aloud, one by one, in the presence of an administrator. Because the assessment is of reading comprehension, any recognizable oral approximation of the target response is considered correct.

Written Response [R, W]

The same stimuli are presented, and the test-taker's task is to reproduce the probe in writing. Because of the transfer across different skills here, evaluation of the test-taker's response must be carefully treated. If an error occurs, you must determine its source; what might be assumed to be a writing error, for example, may actually be a reading error and vice versa.

Multiple-Choice

Multiple-choice responses are not only a matter of choosing one of four or five possible answers. Other formats, some of which are especially useful at the low levels of reading, include same/different, circle the answer, true/false, choose the letter, and matching. Some possibilities are as follows.

Minimal pair distinction [R]

Test-takers read:*		Circle S for same or D for different.		
1. led	let		S	D
2. bit	bit		S	D
3. seat	set		S	D
4. too	to		S	D

*In the case of very low-level learners, the teacher/administrator reads directions.

Grapheme recognition task [R]

Test-takers read:*	Circle the "odd" item, the one that doesn't "belong."	
1. piece	peace	piece
2. book	book	boot

*In the case of very low-level learners, the teacher/administrator reads directions.

Picture-Cued Items

Test-takers are shown a picture, such as the following, along with a written text and are given one of a number of possible tasks to perform.

Picture-cued word identification (Brown & Sahni, 1994, p. 124) [L, R]

Test-takers hear: Point to the word that you read here.

cat	clock	chair

With the same picture, the test-taker might read sentences and then point to the correct part of the picture:

Picture-cued sentence identification [L, R]

Test-takers hear: Point to the part of the picture that you read about here.

Test-takers see the picture and read each sentence written on a separate card.

The man is reading a book.

The cat is under the table.

A true/false procedure might also be presented with the same picture cue:

Picture-cued true/false sentence identification [R]

Test-takers read:

1. The pencils are under the table.   T   F
2. The cat is on the table.   T   F
3. The picture is over the couch.   T   F

Matching can be an effective method of assessing reading at this level. With objects labeled A, B, C, D, and E in the picture, the test-taker reads words and writes the appropriate letter beside the word:

Picture-cued matching word identification [R]

Test-takers read:

1. clock   _____
2. chair   _____
3. books   _____
4. cat   _____
5. table   _____

Finally, test-takers might see a word or phrase and then be directed to choose one of four pictures that is being described, thus requiring him or her to transfer from a verbal to a nonverbal mode. In the following item, test-takers choose the correct letter:

Multiple-choice picture-cued word identification [R]

Test-takers read: **Rectangle**

Test-takers see and choose the correct item:

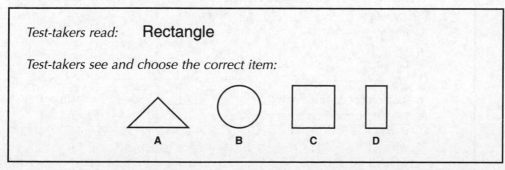

DESIGNING ASSESSMENT TASKS: SELECTIVE READING

Just above the rudimentary skill level of perception of letters and words is a category in which the test designer focuses on formal aspects of language (lexical, grammatical, and a few discourse features). This category includes what many incorrectly think of as testing "vocabulary and grammar." How many textbooks provide little tests and quizzes labeled "vocabulary and grammar" and never feature any other skill besides reading? Lexical and grammatical aspects of language are simply the forms we use to perform all four of the skills of listening, speaking, reading, and writing. (Notice that in all of these chapters on the four skills, formal features of language have become a potential focus for assessment.)

The following are some of the possible tasks you can use to assess lexical and grammatical aspects of reading ability.

Multiple-Choice (for Form-Focused Criteria)

By far the most popular method of testing a reading knowledge of vocabulary and grammar is the multiple-choice format, mainly for reasons of practicality: It is easy to administer and can be scored quickly. The most straightforward multiple-choice items may have little context but might serve as a vocabulary or grammar check. (See Chapter 11 for further discussion of form-focused assessment.)

Multiple-choice vocabulary/grammar tasks [R]

---

1. He's not married. He's _____.
   A. young
   B. single
   C. first
   D. a husband

2. If there's no doorbell, please _____ on the door.
   A. kneel
   B. type
   C. knock
   D. shout

3. The mouse is _____ the bed.
   A. under
   B. around
   C. between
   D. into

4. The bank robbery occurred _____ I was in the restroom.
   A. that
   B. during
   C. while
   D. which

---

5. Yeast is an organic catalyst _____ known to prehistoric humanity.
   A. was
   B. which was
   C. which it
   D. which

This kind of darting from one context to another to another in a test has become so commonplace that learners almost expect the disjointedness. Some improvement of these items is possible by providing some context within each item:

Contextualized multiple-choice vocabulary/grammar tasks [R]

1. Oscar: Do you like champagne?
   Lucy: No, I can't _____ it!
   A. stand
   B. prefer
   C. hate
   D. feel

2. Manager: Do you like to work by yourself?
   Employee: Yes, I like to work _____.
   A. independently
   B. definitely
   C. impatiently
   D. rapidly

3. Jack: Do you have a coat like this?
   John: Yes, mine is _____ yours.
   A. so same as
   B. the same like
   C. as same as
   D. the same as

4. Boss: Where did I put the Johnson file?
   Assistant: I think _____ is on your desk.
   A. you were the file looking at
   B. the you were looking at file
   C. the file you were looking at
   D. you were looking at the file

A better contextualized format is to offer a modified cloze test (see pages 241–244 for a treatment of cloze testing) adjusted to fit the objectives being assessed. In the following example, a few lines of English add to overall context.

Multiple-choice cloze vocabulary/grammar task [R]

I've lived in the United States **(21)** _____ three years. I **(22)** _____ live in Costa Rica. I **(23)** _____ speak any English. I used to **(24)** _____ homesick, but now I enjoy **(25)** _____ here. I have never **(26)** _____ back home **(27)** _____ I came to the United States, but I might **(28)** _____ to visit my family soon.

21. A. since
B. for
C. during

22. A. used to
B. use to
C. was

23. A. couldn't
B. could
C. can

24. A. been
B. be
C. being

25. A. live
B. to live
C. living

26. A. be
B. been
C. was

27. A. when
B. while
C. since

28. A. go
B. will go
C. going

The context of the story in this example may not specifically help the test-taker to respond to the items more easily, but it allows the learner to attend to one set of related sentences for eight items that assess vocabulary and grammar. Other contexts might involve some content dependencies, such that earlier sentences predict the correct response for a later item. Thus a pair of sentences in a short narrative might read as follows:

He showed his suitcase **(29)** _____ me, but it wasn't big **(30)** _____ to fit all his clothes. So I gave him my suitcase, which was **(31)** _____.

29. A. for
B. from
C. to

30. A. so
B. too
C. enough

31. A. larger
B. smaller
C. largest

To respond to item 31 correctly, the test-taker needs to be able to comprehend the context of needing a *larger* but not an equally grammatically correct *smaller* suitcase. Although such dependencies offer greater authenticity to an assessment (see Qian, 2008), they also add the potential problem of a test-taker's missing several later items because of an earlier comprehension error.

Matching Tasks

At this selective level of reading, the test-taker's task is simply to respond correctly, which makes matching an appropriate format. The most frequently appearing criterion in matching procedures is vocabulary. Following is a typical format:

Vocabulary matching task [R]

Write in the letter of the definition on the right that matches the word on the left.

_____	**1.** exhausted	a. unhappy
_____	**2.** disappointed	b. understanding of others
_____	**3.** enthusiastic	c. tired
_____	**4.** empathetic	d. excited

To add a communicative quality to matching, the first numbered list is sometimes a set of sentences with blanks and a list of words to choose from:

Selected response fill-in vocabulary task [R]

---

1. At the end of the long race, the runners were totally _____.
2. My parents were _____ with my bad performance on the final exam.
3. Everyone in the office was _____ about the new salary raises.
4. The _____ listening of the counselor made Christina feel well understood.

Choose from among the following:
disappointed
empathetic
exhausted
enthusiastic

Alderson (2000, p. 218) suggested matching procedures at an even more sophisticated level at which test-takers must discern pragmatic interpretations of certain signs or labels such as "Freshly made sandwiches" and "Use before 10/23/02." Matches for these are "We sell food" and "This is too old," which are selected from a number of other options.

Matching tasks have the advantage of offering an alternative to traditional multiple-choice or fill-in-the-blank formats and are sometimes easier to construct than multiple-choice items, as long as the test designer has chosen the matches carefully. Some disadvantages do come with this framework, however. They can become more of a puzzle-solving process—or a guessing game—than a genuine test of comprehension as test-takers struggle with the search for a match, possibly among 10 or 20 different items. Like other tasks in this section, they also are contrived exercises that are endemic to academia that are seldom found in the real world.

Editing Tasks

Editing for grammatical or rhetorical errors is a widely used test method for assessing linguistic competence in reading. The TOEFL® Test and many other tests employ this technique with the argument that it not only focuses on grammar but also introduces a simulation of the authentic task of editing, or discerning errors in written passages. Its authenticity may be supported if you consider proofreading a real-world skill that is being tested. Here is a typical set of examples of editing:

Multiple-choice grammar editing task (D. Phillips, 2001, p. 219) [R]

Test-takers read: Choose the letter of the underlined word that is not correct.

1. The <u>abrasively</u> action of the wind <u>wears</u> away <u>softer</u> <u>layers</u> of rock.
       A   B   C   D

2. There are two <u>way</u> of <u>making</u> a gas <u>condense</u>: cooling it or <u>putting</u> it under
                A   B   C   D

    pressure.

3. Researchers have <u>discovered</u> that the <u>application</u> of bright light can sometimes
                A   B

    be <u>uses</u> to <u>overcome</u> jet lag.
      C   D

The previous examples, with their disparate subject-matter content, are not as authentic as asking test-takers to edit a whole essay (see discussion, pages 247–249). Of course, if learners have never practiced error-detection tasks, the task itself is of some difficulty. Nevertheless, error detection has been shown to be positively correlated with both listening comprehension and reading comprehension results on the TOEFL, at $r < .58$ and $.76$, respectively (*TOEFL Score User Guide,* 2001). Despite some authenticity quibbles, this task maintains a construct validity that justifies its use.

Picture-Cued Tasks

In the previous section we looked at picture-cued tasks for perceptive recognition of symbols and words. Pictures and photographs may be equally well utilized for examining ability at the selective level. Several types of picture-cued methods are commonly used.

1. Test-takers read a sentence or passage and choose one of four pictures that is being described. The sentence (or sentences) at this level is more complex. A computer-based example follows:

Multiple-choice picture-cued response (D. Phillips, 2001, p. 276) [R]

> *Test-takers read a three-paragraph passage, one sentence of which is:*
>> During at least three-quarters of the year, the Arctic is frozen.
>
> Click on the chart that shows the relative amount of time each year that water is available to plants in the Arctic.
>
> *Test-takers see the following four pictures:*

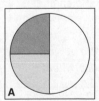 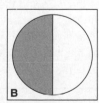 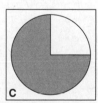

2. Test-takers read a series of sentences or definitions, each describing a labeled part of a picture or diagram. Their task is to identify each labeled item. In the following diagram, test-takers do not necessarily know each term, but by reading the definition they are able to make an identification. For example:

Diagram-labeling task [R]

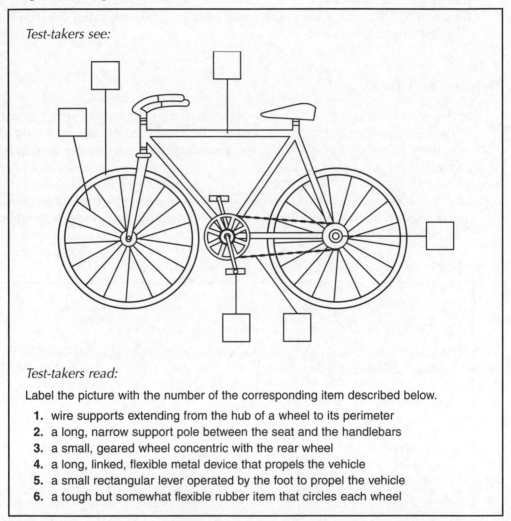

Test-takers see:

Test-takers read:

Label the picture with the number of the corresponding item described below.

   1. wire supports extending from the hub of a wheel to its perimeter
   2. a long, narrow support pole between the seat and the handlebars
   3. a small, geared wheel concentric with the rear wheel
   4. a long, linked, flexible metal device that propels the vehicle
   5. a small rectangular lever operated by the foot to propel the vehicle
   6. a tough but somewhat flexible rubber item that circles each wheel

The essential difference between the picture-cued tasks here and those that were outlined in the previous section is the complexity of the language.

Gap-Filling Tasks

Many of the multiple-choice tasks described on pages 234–237 can be converted into gap-filling, or "fill-in-the-blank," items in which the test-taker's response is to write a word or phrase. An extension of simple gap-filling tasks is to create sentence-completion items in which test-takers read part of a sentence and then complete it by writing a phrase.

Sentence completion tasks [R, W]

Oscar:	Doctor, what should I do if I get sick?
Doctor:	It is best to stay home and _____.
	If you have a fever, _____.
	You should drink as much _____.
	The worst thing you can do is _____.
	You should also _____.

The obvious disadvantage of this type of task is its questionable assessment of reading ability. The task requires both reading and writing performance, thereby rendering it of low validity in isolating reading as the sole criterion. Another drawback is scoring the variety of creative responses that are likely to appear. You will have to make a number of judgment calls on what comprises a correct response. In a test of reading comprehension only, you must accept as correct any responses that demonstrate comprehension of the first part of the sentence. This alone indicates that such tasks are better categorized as integrative procedures.

DESIGNING ASSESSMENT TASKS: INTERACTIVE READING

Tasks at this level, like selective tasks, have a combination of form-focused and meaning-focused objectives but with more emphasis on meaning. Interactive tasks may therefore imply a little more focus on top-down processing than on bottom-up. Texts are a little longer, from a paragraph to as much as a page or so in the case of ordinary prose. Charts, graphs, and other graphics may be somewhat complex in their format.

Cloze Tasks

One of the most popular types of reading assessment task is the **cloze** procedure. The word *cloze* was coined by educational psychologists to capture the Gestalt psychological concept of "closure," that is, the ability to fill in gaps in an incomplete image (visual, auditory, or cognitive) and supply (from background schemata) omitted details.

In written language, a sentence with a word left out should have enough context that a reader can close that gap with a calculated guess, using linguistic expectancies (formal schemata), background experience (content schemata), and some strategic competence. Based on this assumption, cloze tests were developed for native-language readers and defended as an appropriate gauge of reading ability. Some research (Oller, 1973, 1976, 1979; Jonz, 1991; Oller & Jonz, 1994) on second language acquisition vigorously defends cloze testing as an integrative measure not only of reading ability but also of other language abilities. It was argued that the ability to make coherent guesses in cloze gaps also taps into the ability to listen, speak, and write. With the decline in enthusiasm for the search for the ideal integrative test in recent years, cloze testing has returned to a more appropriate status as one of a number of assessment procedures available for testing reading ability.

Cloze tests are usually a minimum of two paragraphs in length to account for discourse expectancies. They can be constructed relatively easily as long as the specifications for choosing deletions and for scoring are clearly defined. Typically every seventh word (plus or minus two) is deleted (known as **fixed-ratio deletion**), but many cloze-test designers instead use a **rational deletion** procedure of choosing deletions according to the grammatical or discourse functions of the words. Rational deletion also allows the designer to avoid deleting words that would be difficult to predict from the context. For example, in the sentence "Everyone in the crowd enjoyed the gorgeous sunset," the seventh word is "gorgeous," but learners could easily substitute other appropriate adjectives. Traditionally, cloze passages have between 30 and 50 blanks to fill, but a passage with as few as half a dozen blanks can legitimately be labeled a cloze test.

Two approaches to the scoring of cloze tests are commonly used. The **exact word scoring** method gives credit to test-takers only if they insert the exact word that was originally deleted. The second method, **appropriate word scoring**, credits the test-taker for supplying any word that is grammatically correct and makes good sense in the context. In the sentence above about the "gorgeous sunset," the test-takers would get credit for supplying "beautiful," "amazing," and "spectacular." The choice between the two methods of scoring is one of practicality/reliability versus face validity. In the exact word approach, scoring can be done quickly (especially if the procedure uses a multiple-choice technique) and reliably. The second approach takes more time because the teacher must determine whether each response is indeed appropriate, but students will perceive the test as being fairer because they won't get "marked off" for appropriate, grammatically correct responses.

The following excerpts from a longer essay illustrate the difference between rational and fixed-ratio deletion and between exact word and appropriate word scoring.

Cloze procedure, fixed-ratio deletion (every seventh word) [R, W]

The recognition that one's feelings of (**1**) _____ and unhappiness can coexist much like (**2**) _____ and hate in a close relationship (**3**) _____ offer valuable clues on how to (**4**) _____ a happier life. It suggests, for (**5**) _____, that changing or avoiding things that (**6**) _____ you miserable may well make you (**7**) _____ miserable but probably no happier.

Cloze procedure, rational deletion (prepositions and conjunctions) [R,W]

The recognition that one's feelings (**1**) _____ happiness (**2**) _____
unhappiness can coexist much like love and hate (**3**) _____ a close
relationship may offer valuable clues (**4**) _____ how to lead a happier life. It
suggests, (**5**) _____ example, that changing (**6**) _____ avoiding things that
make you miserable may well make you less miserable (**7**) _____ probably no
happier.

In both versions there are seven deletions, but the second version allows the
test designer to tap into prediction of prepositions and conjunctions in particular.
The second version also provides more washback as students focus on targeted
grammatical features.

Both of these scoring methods could present problems, with the first version
presenting a little more ambiguity. Possible responses might include the following:

Fixed-ratio version, blank 3: *may, might, could, can*
                                4: *lead, live, have, seek*
                                5: *example, instance*

Rational deletion version, blank 4: *on, about*
                                    6: *or, and*
                                    7: *but, and*

Arranging a cloze test in a multiple-choice format allows even more rapid
scoring through hand-scoring with an answer key or hole-punched grid or
computer-scoring using scannable answer sheets. Multiple-choice cloze tests must
of course adhere to all the other guidelines for effective multiple-choice items that
were covered in Chapter 5, especially the choice of appropriate distractors; therefore they can take much longer to construct—possibly too long to pay off in a classroom setting.

Some variations on standard cloze testing have appeared over the years; two of
the better known are the C-test and the cloze-elide procedure. In the **C-test**
(Dörnyei & Katona, 1992; Klein-Braley, 1985; Klein-Braley & Raatz, 1984), the
second half (according to the number of letters) of every other word is obliterated
and the test-taker must restore each word. Although Klein-Braley and others have
vouched for its validity and reliability, many consider this technique to be "even
more irritating to complete than cloze tests" (Alderson, 2000, p. 225). Look at the
example on the next page and judge for yourself.

C-test procedure [R, W]

The recognition th_ _ one's feel_ _ _ _ of happ_ _ _ _ _ and unhap_ _ _ _ _ _ can coe_ _ _ _ much li_ _ love a_ _ hate i_ a cl_ _ _ relati_ _ _ _ _ _ may of_ _ _ valuable cl_ _ _ on h_ _ to le_ _ a hap_ _ _ _ life. I_ suggests, f_ _ example, th_ _ changing o_ avoiding thi_ _ _ that ma_ _ you mise_ _ _ _ _ may we_ _ make y_ _ less mise_ _ _ _ _ but prob_ _ _ _ no hap_ _ _ _.

The second variation, the **cloze-elide procedure**, inserts words into a text that don't belong. The test-taker's task is to detect and cross out the "intrusive" words. Look at the same passage:

Cloze-elide procedure [R]

The recognition that one's now feelings of happiness and unhappiness can under coexist much like love and hate in a close then relationship may offer valuable clues on how to lead a happier with life. It suggests, for example, that changing or avoiding my things that make you miserable may well make you less miserable ever but probably no happier.

Critics of this procedure (Davies, 1975) claimed that the cloze-elide procedure is actually a test of reading speed and not of proofreading skill, as its proponents asserted. Two disadvantages are nevertheless immediately apparent: (a) Neither the words to insert nor the frequency of insertion appears to have any rationale, and (b) fast and efficient readers are not adept at detecting the intrusive words. Good readers naturally weed out such potential interruptions.

Impromptu Reading Plus Comprehension Questions

If cloze testing is the most-researched procedure for assessing reading, the traditional "Read a passage and answer some questions" technique is undoubtedly the oldest and the most common. Virtually every proficiency test uses the format, and one would rarely consider assessing reading without some component of the assessment involving impromptu reading and responding to questions.

In the discussion on standardized testing in Chapter 5, we looked at a typical reading comprehension passage and a set of questions from the IELTS. Here's another such passage on the next page:

Reading comprehension passage (D. Phillips, 2001, pp. 421–422) [R]

Questions 1–10

The Hollywood sign in the hills that line the northern border of Los Angeles is a famous landmark recognized the world over. The white-painted, 50-foot-high, sheet metal letters can be seen from great distances across the Los Angeles basin.

The sign was not constructed, as one might suppose, by the movie business as a means of
(5) celebrating the importance of Hollywood to this industry; instead, it was first constructed in 1923 as a means of advertising homes for sale in a 500-acre housing subdivision in a part of Los Angeles called "Hollywoodland." The sign that was constructed at the time, of course, said "Hollywoodland." Over the years, people began referring to the area by the shortened version "Hollywood," and after the sign and its site were donated to the city in 1945, the last four
(10) letters were removed.

The sign suffered from years of disrepair, and in 1973 it needed to be completely replaced, at a cost of $27,700 per letter. Various celebrities were instrumental in helping to raise needed funds. Rock star Alice Cooper, for example, bought an O in memory of Groucho Marx, and Hugh Hefner of *Playboy* fame held a benefit party to raise the money for the Y. The construction of the new sign was finally completed in 1978.

1. What is the topic of this passage?
   (A) A famous sign
   (B) A famous city
   (C) World landmarks
   (D) Hollywood versus Hollywoodland

2. The expression "the world over" in line 2 could best be replaced by
   (A) in the northern parts of the world
   (B) on top of the world
   (C) in the entire world
   (D) in the skies

3. It can be inferred from the passage that most people think that the Hollywood sign was first constructed by
   (A) an advertising company
   (B) the movie industry
   (C) a construction company
   (D) the city of Los Angeles

4. The pronoun "it" in line 5 refers to
   (A) the sign
   (B) the movie business
   (C) the importance of Hollywood
   (D) this industry

5. According to the passage, the Hollywood sign was first built in
   (A) 1923
   (B) 1949
   (C) 1973
   (D) 1978

6. Which of the following is NOT mentioned about Hollywoodland?
   (A) It used to be the name of an area of Los Angeles.

   (B) It was formerly the name on the sign in the hills.
   (C) There were houses for sale there.
   (D) It was the most expensive area of Los Angeles.

7. The passage indicates that the sign suffered because
   (A) people damaged it
   (B) it was not fixed
   (C) the weather was bad
   (D) it was poorly constructed

8. It can be inferred from the passage that the Hollywood sign was how old when it was necessary to replace it completely?
   (A) Ten years old
   (B) Twenty-six years old
   (C) Fifty years old
   (D) Fifty-five years old

9. The word "replaced" in line 10 is closest in meaning to which of the following?
   (A) Moved to a new location
   (B) Destroyed
   (C) Found again
   (D) Exchanged for a newer one

10. According to the passage, how did celebrities help with the new sign?
    (A) They played instruments.
    (B) They raised the sign.
    (C) They helped get the money.
    (D) They took part in work parties to build the sign.

Notice that this set of questions, based on a 250-word passage, covers the comprehension of these features:

- main idea (topic)
- expressions/idioms/phrases in context
- inference (implied detail)
- grammatical features
- detail (scanning for a specifically stated detail)
- excluding facts not written (unstated details)
- supporting idea(s)
- vocabulary in context

These specifications, and the questions that exemplify them, are not just a string of "straight" comprehension questions that follow the thread of the passage. The questions represent a sample of the test specifications for TOEFL® Test reading passages, which are derived from research on a variety of abilities good readers exhibit. Notice that many of them are consistent with strategies of effective reading: skimming for main idea, scanning for details, guessing word meanings from context, inferencing, using discourse markers, etc. To construct your own assessments that involve short reading passages followed by questions, you can begin with TOEFL-like specs as a basis. Your focus in your own classroom will determine which of these—and possibly other specifications—you include in your assessment procedure, how you frame questions, and how much weight you give each item in scoring.

The technology of computer-based reading comprehension tests of this kind enables some additional types of items. Items such as the following are typical:

Computer-based TOEFL® Test reading comprehension item [R]

- Click on the word in paragraph 1 that means "subsequent work."
- Look at the word "they" in paragraph 2. Click on the word that "they" refers to.
- The following sentence could be added to paragraph 2:

  "Instead, he used the pseudonym Mrs. Silence Dogood."

  Where would it best fit into the paragraph? Click on the square ☐ to add the sentence to the paragraph.

- Click on the drawing that most closely resembles the prehistoric coelacanth. [*Four drawings are depicted on the screen.*]

Short-Answer Tasks

Multiple-choice items are difficult to construct and validate, and classroom teachers rarely have time in their busy schedules to design such a test. A popular alternative to multiple-choice questions following reading passages is the age-old short-answer format. A reading passage is presented, and the test-taker reads questions that must be answered, usually in written form, in a sentence or two. Questions might cover the same specifications indicated above for the TOEFL® Test reading but be worded in question form. For example, in a passage on the future of airline travel, the following questions might appear:

Open-ended reading comprehension questions [R, W]

---

1. What do you think the main idea of this passage is?
2. What would you infer from the passage about the future of air travel?
3. In line 6 the word "sensation" is used. From the context, what do you think this word means?
4. What two ideas did the writer suggest for increasing airline business?
5. Why do you think the airlines have recently experienced a decline?

Do not take lightly the design of questions. It can be difficult to make sure that they reach their intended criterion. You also need to develop consistent specifications for acceptable student responses and be prepared to take the time necessary to accomplish their evaluation. These rather predictable disadvantages may be outweighed by the face validity of offering students a chance to construct their own answers and by the washback effect of potential follow-up discussion.

Editing (Longer Texts)

The previous section of this chapter (on selective reading) described editing tasks, but there the discussion was limited to a list of unrelated sentences, each presented with an error to be detected by the test-taker. The same technique has been applied successfully to longer passages of 200 to 300 words. Several advantages are gained in the longer format.

First, authenticity is increased. The likelihood that students in English classrooms will read connected prose of a page or two is greater than the likelihood of their encountering the contrived format of unconnected sentences. Second, the task simulates proofreading one's own essay, where it is imperative to find and correct errors. Third, if the test is connected to a specific curriculum (such as placement into one of several writing courses), the test designer can draw up specifications for a number of grammatical and rhetorical categories that match the content of the courses. Content validity is thereby supported, and along with it the face validity of a task in which students are willing to invest.

Imao's (2001) test introduced one error in each numbered sentence. Test-takers followed the same procedure for marking errors as described in the previous section. Instructions to the student included a sample of the kind of connected prose that test-takers would encounter:

Contextualized grammar editing tasks (Imao, 2001) [R]

---

1. <u>Ever</u> since supermarkets first <u>appeared</u>, they have been <u>take</u> over <u>the</u> world.
   A   B   C   D

2. <u>Supermarkets</u> have changed people's <u>lifestyles</u>, yet <u>and</u> at the same time,
      A   B   C

changes in people's <u>lifestyles</u> have encouraged the opening of supermarkets. (**3**) As
                    D

a <u>result this</u>, many small <u>stores</u> have been <u>forced</u> out <u>of</u> business. (**4**) <u>Moreover</u>, some
      A   B   C   D   A

small stores <u>will</u> be able to survive <u>this</u> unfavorable <u>situation</u>.
           B   C   D

This can all be achieved in a multiple-choice format with computer scan scoring for a rapid return of results. Not only does an overall score provide a holistic assessment, but for the placement purposes that Imao's (2001) research addressed, teachers were given a diagnostic chart of each student's results within all of the specified categories of the test. For a total of 32 to 56 items in his editing test, Imao (p. 185) was able to offer teachers a computer-generated breakdown of performance in the following categories:

- sentence structure
- verb tense
- noun/article features
- modal auxiliaries
- verb complements
- noun clauses
- adverb clauses
- conditionals
- logical connectors
- adjective clauses (including relative clauses)
- passives

These categories were selected for inclusion from a survey of instructors' syllabuses in writing courses and proofreading workshops. This is an excellent example of the washback effect of a relatively large-scale, standardized multiple-choice test. Although one would not want to use such data as absolutely predictive of students' future work, these categories can provide guidelines to a teacher on areas of potential focus as the writing course unfolds.

Scanning [R]

Scanning is a strategy used by all readers to find relevant information in a text. Assessment of scanning is carried out by presenting test-takers with a text (prose or something in a chart or graph format) and requiring rapid identification of relevant bits of information. Possible stimuli include

- a one- to two-page news article
- an essay
- a chapter in a textbook
- a technical report
- a table or chart depicting some research findings
- a menu
- an application form

Among the variety of scanning objectives (for each of the genres named above), the test-taker must locate

- a date, name, or place in an article
- the setting for a narrative or story
- the principal divisions of a chapter
- the principal research finding in a technical report
- a result reported in a specified cell in a table
- the cost of an item on a menu
- specified data needed to fill out an application

Scoring of such scanning tasks can be reliable if the initial directions are specific ("How much does the dark chocolate torte cost?"). Because one of the purposes of scanning is to *quickly* identify important elements, timing may also be calculated into a scoring procedure.

Ordering Tasks

Students always enjoy the activity of receiving little strips of paper, each with a sentence on it, and assembling them into a story, sometimes called the "strip story" technique. Variations on this can serve as an assessment of overall global understanding of a story and the cohesive devices that signal the order of events or ideas. Alderson, Clapham, and Wall (1995, p. 53) warn, however, against assuming that there is only one logical order. They presented these sentences for forming a story.

Sentence-ordering task [R]

Put the following sentences in the correct order:

A   it was called "The Last Waltz"
B   the street was in total darkness
C   because it was one he and Richard had learned at school
D   Peter looked outside
E   he recognized the tune
F   and it seemed deserted
G   he thought he heard someone whistling

"D" was the first sentence, and test-takers were asked to order the sentences. It turned out that two orders were acceptable (DGECABF and DBFGECA), creating difficulties in assigning scores and leading the authors to discourage the use of this technique as an assessment device. However, if you are willing to place this procedure in the category of informal and/or formative assessment, you might consider the technique useful. Different acceptable sentence orders become an instructive point for subsequent discussion in class, and you thereby offer washback into students' understanding of how to connect sentences and ideas in a story or essay.

Information Transfer: Reading Charts, Maps, Graphs, Diagrams

Every educated person must be able to comprehend charts, maps, graphs, calendars, diagrams, and the like. Converting such nonverbal input into comprehensible intake requires not only an understanding of the graphic and verbal conventions of the medium but also a linguistic ability to interpret that information to someone else. Reading a map implies understanding the conventions of map graphics, but it is often accompanied by telling someone where to turn, how far to go, etc. Scanning a menu requires an ability to understand the structure of most menus as well as the capacity to give an order when the time comes. Interpreting the numbers on a stock market report involves the interaction of understanding the numbers and conveying that understanding to others.

All of these media presuppose the reader's appropriate schemata for interpreting them and often are accompanied by oral or written discourse to convey, clarify, question, argue, and debate, among other linguistic functions. Virtually every language curriculum, from rock-bottom beginning levels to high-advanced, utilizes this nonverbal, visual/symbolic dimension. It is therefore imperative that assessment procedures include measures of comprehension of nonverbal media.

To comprehend information in this medium (hereafter referred to simply as "graphics"), learners must be able to

- comprehend specific conventions of the various types of graphics
- comprehend labels, headings, numbers, and symbols
- comprehend the possible relationships among elements of the graphic
- make inferences that are not presented overtly

The act of comprehending graphics includes the linguistic performance of oral or written interpretations, comments, questions, etc. This implies a process of **information transfer** from one skill to another—in this case, from reading verbal and/or nonverbal information to speaking/writing. Assessment of these abilities covers a broad spectrum of tasks. Just some of the many possibilities follow:

Tasks for assessing interpretation of graphic information [R, S, W]

1. Read a graphic; answer simple, direct information questions. For example:
    map: "Where is the post office?"
    family tree: "Who is Tony's great grandmother?"
    statistical table: "What does p < .05 mean?"
    diagram of a steam engine: "Label the following parts."

2. Read a graphic; describe or elaborate on information.
    map: "Compare the distance between San Francisco and Sacramento to the distance between San Francisco and Monterey."
    store advertisements: "Who has the better deal on grapes, Safeway or Albertsons?"
    menu: "What comes with the grilled salmon entrée?"

3. Read a graphic; infer/predict information.
    stock market report: "Based on past performance, how do you think Macrotech Industries will do in the future?"
    directions for assembling a bookshelf: "How long do you think it will take to put this thing together?"

4. Read a passage; choose the correct graphic for it.
    article about the size of the ozone hole in the Antarctic: "Which chart represents the size of the ozone hole?"
    passage about the history of bicycles: "Click on the drawing that shows a penny-farthing bicycle."

5. Read a passage with an accompanying graphic; interpret both.

article about hunger and population, with a bar graph: "Which countries have
the most hungry people and why?"

article on number of automobiles produced and their price over a ten-year
period, with a table: "What is the best generalization you can make about
the production and cost of automobiles?"

6. Read a passage; create or use a graphic to illustrate.

directions from the bank to the post office: "On the map provided, trace the
route from the bank to the post office."

article about deforestation and carbon dioxide levels: "Make a bar graph to
illustrate the information in the article."

story including members of a family: "Draw Jeff and Christina's family tree."

description of a class schedule: "Fill in Mary's weekly class schedule."

All these tasks involve retrieving information from either written or graphic media and transferring that information to productive performance. It is sometimes too easy to simply conclude that reading must involve only 26 alphabetic letters, with spaces and punctuation, thus omitting a huge number of resources that we consult every day.

DESIGNING ASSESSMENT TASKS: EXTENSIVE READING

Extensive reading involves somewhat longer texts than we have been dealing with up to this point. Journal articles, technical reports, longer essays, short stories, and books fall into this category. The reason for placing such reading into a separate category is that reading this type of discourse almost always involves a focus on meaning using mostly top-down processing, with only occasional use of a targeted bottom-up strategy. Also, because of the extent of such reading, formal assessment is unlikely to be contained within the time constraints of a typical formal testing framework, which presents a unique challenge for assessment purposes.

Another complication in assessing extensive reading is that the expected response from the reader is likely to involve as much written (or sometimes oral) performance as reading. For example, in asking test-takers to respond to an article or story, one could argue that a greater emphasis is placed on writing than on reading. This is no reason to sweep extensive reading assessment under the rug; teachers should not shrink from the assessment of this highly sophisticated skill.

Before examining a few tasks that have proved to be useful in assessing extensive reading, it is essential to note that a number of the tasks described in previous categories can apply here. Among them are

- impromptu reading plus comprehension questions
- short-answer tasks
- editing
- scanning
- ordering
- information transfer
- interpretation (discussed under graphics)

In addition to those applications are tasks that are unique to extensive reading: skimming, summarizing, responding to reading, and notetaking.

Skimming Tasks

Skimming is the process of rapid coverage of reading matter to determine its gist or main idea. It is a prediction strategy used to give a reader a sense of the topic and purpose of a text, the organization of the text, the perspective or point of view of the writer, its ease or difficulty, and/or its usefulness to the reader. Of course skimming can apply to texts of less than one page, so it would be wise not to confine this type of task just to extensive texts.

Assessment of skimming strategies is usually straightforward: The test-taker skims a text and answers questions such as the following:

Skimming tasks [R, S/W]

- What is the main idea of this text?
- What is the author's purpose in writing the text?
- What kind of writing is this (newspaper article, manual, novel, etc.)?
- What type of writing is this (expository, technical, narrative, etc.)?
- How easy or difficult do you think this text will be?
- What do you think you will learn from the text?
- How useful will the text be for your (profession, academic needs, interests)?

Responses are oral or written, depending on the context. Most assessments in the domain of skimming are informal and formative: They are grist for an imminent discussion, a more careful reading to follow, or an in-class discussion, and therefore their washback potential is good. Insofar as the subject matter and tasks are useful to a student's goals, authenticity is preserved. Scoring is less of an issue than providing appropriate feedback to students on their strategies of prediction.

Summarizing and Responding

One of the most common means of assessing extensive reading is to ask the test-taker to write a summary of the text. The task that is given to students can be very simply worded:

Directions for summarizing [R, W]

> Write a summary of the text. Your summary should be about one paragraph in length (100–150 words) and should include your understanding of the main idea and supporting ideas.

Evaluating summaries is difficult: Do you give test-takers a certain number of points for targeting the main idea and its supporting ideas? Do you use a full/partial/no-credit point system? Do you give a holistic score? Imao (2001) used four criteria for the evaluation of a summary:

Criteria for assessing a summary (Imao, 2001, p. 184)

> 1. Expresses accurately the main idea and supporting ideas
> 2. Is written in the student's own words; occasional vocabulary from the original text is acceptable
> 3. Is logically organized
> 4. Displays facility in the use of language to clearly express ideas in the text

As you can readily see, a strict adherence to the criterion of assessing reading, and reading only, implies consideration of only the first factor; the other three pertain to writing performance. The first criterion is nevertheless a crucial factor; otherwise the reader/writer could pass all three of the other criteria with virtually no understanding of the text itself. Evaluation of the reading comprehension criterion of necessity remains somewhat subjective because the teacher will need to determine degrees of fulfillment of the objective (see below for more about scoring this task).

Of further interest in assessing extensive reading is the technique of asking a student to respond to a text. The two tasks should not be confused with each other: Summarizing requires a synopsis or overview of the text, whereas responding asks the reader to provide his or her own opinion on the text as a whole or on some statement or issue within it. Responding may be prompted by such directions as this:

Directions for responding to reading

> In the article "Poisoning the Air We Breathe," the author suggests that a global dependence on fossil fuels will eventually make air in large cities toxic. Write an essay in which you agree or disagree with the author's thesis. Support your opinion with information from the article and from your own experience.

One criterion for a good response here is the extent to which the test-taker accurately reflects the content of the article and some of the arguments therein. Scoring is difficult because of the subjectivity of determining an accurate reflection of the article itself. For the reading component of this task, as well as the summary task described above, a holistic scoring system may be feasible:

Holistic scoring scale for summarizing and responding to reading

> 3 Demonstrates clear, unambiguous comprehension of the main and supporting ideas
>
> 2 Demonstrates comprehension of the main idea but lacks comprehension of some supporting ideas
>
> 1 Demonstrates only a partial comprehension of the main and supporting ideas
>
> 0 Demonstrates no comprehension of the main and supporting ideas

The teacher or test administrator must still determine shades of gray between the point categories, but the descriptions help to bridge the gap between an empirically determined evaluation (which is impossible) and wild, impressionistic guesses.

An attempt has been made here to underscore the reading component of summarizing and responding to reading, but it is crucial to consider the interactive relationship between reading and writing that is highlighted in these two tasks. As you direct students to engage in such integrative performance, do not to treat it as a task for assessing reading alone.

Notetaking and Outlining [R, W]

Finally, a reader's comprehension of extensive texts may be assessed through an evaluation of a process of notetaking and/or outlining. Because of the difficulty of controlling the conditions and time frame for both these techniques, they rest firmly in the category of informal assessment. Their utility is in the strategic training that learners gain in retaining information through marginal notes that highlight key information or organizational outlines that put supporting ideas into a visually manageable framework. A teacher, perhaps in one-on-one conferences with students, can use student notes/outlines as indicators of the presence or absence of effective reading strategies and thereby point the learners in positive directions.

In his introduction to Alderson's (2000) book on assessing reading, Lyle Bachman observed, "Reading, through which we can access worlds of ideas and feelings, as well as the knowledge of the ages and visions of the future, is at once the most extensively researched and the most enigmatic of the so-called language skills" (p. x). It's the almost mysterious "psycholinguistic guessing game" (Goodman, 1970) of reading that poses the enigma. We still have much to learn about how people learn to read and especially about how the brain accesses, stores, and recalls visually represented language. This chapter has illustrated a number of possibilities for assessment of reading across the continuum of skills, from basic letter/word recognition to the retention of meaning extracted from vast quantities of linguistic symbols. We hope it will spur you to go beyond the confines of these suggestions and create your own methods of assessing reading.

EXERCISES

[Note: **(I)** Individual work; **(G)** Group or pair work; **(C)** Whole-class discussion.]

1. **(C)** Genres of reading are listed at the beginning of the chapter. Add other examples to each of the three categories. Among the listed examples and your additions, be specific in citing what makes certain genres more difficult than others. Select a few of the more difficult genres and discuss what you would assess (criteria) and how you would assess (some possible assessment techniques) them.
2. **(G)** Look at the list of micro- and macroskills of reading on page 227. In pairs, each assigned to a different skill (or two), brainstorm some tasks that assess those skills. Present your findings to the rest of the class.
3. **(C)** Critique Figure 9.1 on page 229. Do you agree with the categorizations of length, focus, and process for each of the four types of reading?
4. **(C)** Review the four basic types of reading that were outlined at the beginning of the chapter. Offer examples of each and pay special attention to distinguishing between perceptive and selective and between interactive and extensive.

5. **(C)** In Chapter 7, nine characteristics of listening were listed (page 164) that make listening "difficult." What makes reading difficult? As a whole class, brainstorm a similar list that could form a set of specifications to pay special attention to in assessing reading.

6. **(G)** Divide the four basic types of reading among groups or pairs, one type for each. Look at the sample assessment techniques provided and evaluate them according the five principles (practicality, reliability, validity [especially face and content], authenticity, and washback). Present your critique to the rest of the class.

7. **(G)** In the same groups as item 6 above, with the same type of reading, design some item types different from the one(s) provided here that assess the same type of reading performance.

8. **(G)** In the same groups as item 6, with the same type of reading, identify which of the 10 strategies for reading comprehension (page 228) are essential to perform the assessment task. Present those findings, possibly in a tabular format, to the rest of the class.

9. **(C)** In the concluding paragraph of this chapter, reference was made to the "enigmatic" nature of reading as a "psycholinguistic guessing game." Why is reading enigmatic? Why is it a "guessing game"? What does that say about the prospects of assessing reading?

FOR YOUR FURTHER READING

Alderson, J. Charles. (2000). *Assessing reading.* Cambridge: Cambridge University Press.

This volume in the Cambridge Language Assessment Series provides a comprehensive overview of the history and current state of the art of assessing reading. With an authoritative backdrop of research underlying the construct validation of techniques for the assessment of reading comprehension, a host of testing techniques are surveyed and evaluated.

Read, John. (2000). *Assessing vocabulary.* Cambridge: Cambridge University Press.

Another in the same Cambridge series, this book addresses issues in assessing vocabulary. Do not be misled by its placement in this chapter: Vocabulary can be assessed through performance in all four skills, not just reading. A good portion of this book centers on vocabulary knowledge for reading performance, however, and therefore is recommended here. Background research and practical techniques are explored.

Eskey, David. (2005). Reading in a second language. In E. Hinkel (Ed.), *Handbook of research in second language teaching and learning* (pp. 563-579). Mahwah, NJ: Lawrence Erlbaum Associates.

Although this chapter in the encyclopedic handbook of research doesn't focus explicitly on assessment, it provides the kind of backdrop to assessment that comes with a solid foundation in what it means to be a proficient reader of a second language. Eskey offers an overview of research on reading, including discussions of the role of vocabulary and grammar knowledge, reading rate, psycholinguistics considerations, and an overview of pedagogical issues.

CHAPTER 10

ASSESSING WRITING

OBJECTIVES: After reading this chapter, you will be able to

- state a rationale for assessing writing as a separate skill as well as a skill that integrates with reading and possibly other skills
- discern the overlap between assessing writing as an implicit, unanalyzed ability and its explicit, form-focused counterpart
- incorporate performance-based assessment into your own assessment instruments

- develop assessments that focus on one or several micro- and macroskills of writing within a specified genre
- design assessments that target one or more modes of performance, ranging from imitative production to extensive writing

Not many centuries ago, writing was a skill that was the exclusive domain of scribes and scholars in educational or religious institutions. Almost every aspect of everyday life for "common" people was carried out orally. Business transactions, records, legal documents, political and military agreements—all were written by specialists whose vocation it was to render language into the written word. Today, the ability to write is no longer the province of a special elite class of people. Writing skill, at least at rudimentary levels, is a necessary condition for achieving employment in many walks of life and is simply taken for granted in literate cultures.

In the field of second language teaching, only a half-century ago experts were saying that writing was primarily a convention for recording speech and reinforcing grammatical and lexical features of language. Now we understand the uniqueness of writing as a skill with its own features and conventions. We also fully understand the difficulty of learning to write "well" in any language, even in our own native language. Every educated child in developed countries learns the rudiments of writing in his or her native language, but very few learn to express themselves clearly with logical, well-developed organization that accomplishes an intended purpose. Yet we expect second language learners to write coherent essays with artfully chosen rhetorical and discourse devices!

With such a monumental goal, the job of teaching writing has occupied the attention of papers, articles, dissertations, books, and even separate professional journals exclusively devoted to writing in a second language, notably the *Journal of Second Language Writing*. (For further information on issues and practical techniques in teaching writing, refer to *TBP*, Chapter 21.)

It follows logically that the assessment of writing is no simple task. When you consider assessing students' writing ability, as usual you need to be clear about your objective or criterion. What is it you want to test: handwriting ability? correct spelling? sentences that are grammatically correct? paragraph construction? logical development of a main idea? All of these, and more, are possible objectives. In addition, each objective can be assessed through a variety of tasks, which we examine in this chapter.

Of further significance is the fact that the assessment of writing implies by definition the assessment of reading as well. After all, can one write a sentence in a language without being able to read the sentence just written? The testing of writing ability is very difficult to isolate. Moreover, as we discovered in the assessment of speaking, virtually all item formats for assessing writing rely on a written or oral prompt of some sort, and test-takers need to comprehend those prompts in order to respond appropriately. We can therefore safely say that assessing writing is virtually always integrated.

Before looking at specific tasks, we must scrutinize the different genres of written language (so that context and purpose are clear), types of writing (so that stages of the development of writing ability are accounted for), and micro- and macroskills of writing (so that objectives can be pinpointed precisely).

GENRES OF WRITTEN LANGUAGE

In Chapter 8, the discussion of assessment of reading listed more than 50 written language genres. The same classification scheme is reformulated here to include the most common genres that a second language writer might produce, within and beyond the requirements of a curriculum. Even though this list is slightly shorter, you should be aware of the surprising multiplicity of options of written genres that second language learners need to acquire.

Genres of writing

---

1. **Academic writing**
   Papers and general subject reports
   Essays, compositions
   Academically focused journals
   Short-answer test responses
   Technical reports (e.g., lab reports)
   Theses, dissertations

2. **Job-related writing**
   Messages (e.g., phone messages)
   Letters/e-mails

Memos (e.g., interoffice)
Reports (e.g., job evaluations, project reports)
Schedules, labels, signs
Advertisements, announcements
Manuals

3. Personal writing

Letters, e-mails, greeting cards, invitations
Messages, notes
Calendar entries, shopping lists, reminders
Financial documents (e.g., checks, tax forms, loan applications)
Forms, questionnaires, medical reports, immigration documents
Diaries, personal journals
Fiction (e.g., short stories, poetry)

TYPES OF WRITING PERFORMANCE

Four categories of written performance that capture the range of written production are considered here. Each category resembles the categories defined for the other three skills, but these categories, as always, reflect the uniqueness of the skill area.

1. *Imitative.* To produce written language, the learner must attain skills in the fundamental, basic tasks of writing letters, words, punctuation, and very brief sentences. This category includes the ability to spell correctly and to perceive phoneme–grapheme correspondences in the English spelling system. It is a level at which learners are trying to master the mechanics of writing. At this stage, form is the primary if not exclusive focus, whereas context and meaning are of secondary concern.

2. *Intensive (controlled).* Beyond the fundamentals of imitative writing are skills in producing appropriate vocabulary within a context, collocations and idioms, and correct grammatical features up to the length of a sentence. Meaning and context are of some importance in determining correctness and appropriateness, but most assessment tasks are more concerned with a focus on form and are rather strictly controlled by the test design.

3. *Responsive.* Here, assessment tasks require learners to perform at a limited discourse level, connecting sentences into a paragraph and creating a logically connected sequence of two or three paragraphs. Tasks relate to pedagogical directives, lists of criteria, outlines, and other guidelines. Genres of writing include brief narratives and descriptions, short reports, lab reports, summaries, brief responses to reading, and interpretations of charts or graphs. Under specified conditions, the writer begins to exercise some freedom of choice among alternative forms of expression of ideas. The writer has mastered the fundamentals of sentence-level grammar and is more focused on the discourse conventions that will achieve the objectives of the written text. Form-focused attention is mostly at the discourse level, with a strong emphasis on context and meaning.

4. *Extensive.* Extensive writing implies successful management of all the processes and strategies of writing for all purposes, up to the length of an essay, a term paper, a major research project report, or even a thesis. Writers focus on achieving a purpose, organizing and developing ideas logically, using details to support or illustrate ideas, demonstrating syntactic and lexical variety, and, in many cases, engaging in the **process** of multiple drafts to achieve a final product. Focus on grammatical form is limited to occasional editing or proofreading of a draft.

MICRO- AND MACROSKILLS OF WRITING

We turn once again to a taxonomy of micro- and macroskills that will assist you in defining the ultimate criterion of an assessment procedure. The earlier microskills apply more appropriately to imitative and intensive types of writing task, while the macroskills are essential for the successful mastery of responsive and extensive writing.

Micro- and macroskills of writing

Microskills

1. Produce graphemes and orthographic patterns of English
2. Produce writing at an efficient rate of speed to suit the purpose
3. Produce an acceptable core of words and use appropriate word order patterns
4. Use acceptable grammatical systems (e.g., tense, agreement, pluralization), patterns, and rules
5. Express a particular meaning in different grammatical forms
6. Use cohesive devices in written discourse

Macroskills

7. Use the rhetorical forms and conventions of written discourse
8. Appropriately accomplish the communicative functions of written texts according to form and purpose
9. Convey links and connections between events and communicate such relations as main idea, supporting idea, new information, given information, generalization, and exemplification
10. Distinguish between literal and implied meanings when writing
11. Correctly convey culturally specific references in the context of the written text

12. Develop and use a battery of writing strategies, such as accurately assessing the audience's interpretation, using prewriting devices, writing with fluency in the first drafts, using paraphrases and synonyms, soliciting peer and instructor feedback, and using feedback for revising and editing

DESIGNING ASSESSMENT TASKS: IMITATIVE WRITING

With the recent worldwide emphasis on teaching English at young ages, it is tempting to assume that every English-learner knows how to handwrite the Roman alphabet. Such is not the case. Many beginning-level English-learners, from young children to older adults, need basic training in and assessment of imitative writing: the rudiments of forming letters, words, and simple sentences. We examine this level of writing first.

Tasks in [Hand-] Writing Letters, Words, and Punctuation

First a comment on the increasing use of personal and laptop computers and hand-held instruments for creating written symbols: Handwriting has the potential of becoming a lost art as even very young children are more and more likely to use a keyboard to produce writing. Making the shapes of letters and other symbols is now more a question of learning typing skills than of training the muscles of the hands to use a pen or pencil. Nevertheless, for all practical purposes, handwriting remains a skill of paramount importance within the larger domain of language assessment.

A limited variety of types of tasks are commonly used to assess a person's ability to produce written letters and symbols. A few of the more common types are described here.

1. *Copying.* There is nothing innovative or modern about directing a test-taker to copy letters or words. The test-taker will see something like the following:

Handwriting letters, words, and punctuation marks [R, W]

Test-takers read: Copy the following words in the spaces given:

bit	Bet	bat	But	Oh?	Oh!
___	___	___	___	___	___
bin	Din	gin	Pin	Hello, John.	
___	___	___	___	___	

---

2. *Listening cloze selection tasks.* These tasks combine dictation with a written script that has a relatively frequent deletion ratio (every fourth or fifth word perhaps). The test sheet provides a list of missing words from which the test-taker must select. The purpose at this stage is not to test spelling but to give practice in writing. To increase the difficulty, the list of words can be deleted, but then spelling might become an obstacle. Probes look like this:

Listening cloze selection task [L, R, W]

Test-takers hear:
Write the missing word in each blank. Below the story is a list of words to choose from.

Have you ever visited San Francisco? It is a very nice city. It is cool in the summer and warm in the winter. I like the cable cars and bridges.

Test-takers see:

Have _____ ever visited San Francisco? It _____ a very

nice _____. It is _____ in _____ summer and _____

in the winter. I _____ the cable cars _____ bridges.

is	you	cool	city
like	and	warm	the

---

3. *Picture-cued tasks.* Familiar pictures are displayed, and test-takers are told to write the word that the picture represents. Assuming no ambiguity in identifying the picture (cat, hat, chair, table, etc.), no reliance is made on aural comprehension for successful completion of the task.

4. *Form completion tasks.* A variation on pictures is the use of a simple form (registration, application, etc.) that asks for name, address, phone number, and other data. Assuming, of course, that prior classroom instruction has focused on filling out such forms, this task becomes an appropriate assessment of simple tasks such as writing one's name and address.

5. *Converting numbers and abbreviations to words.* Some tests have a section on which numbers are written—for example, hours of the day, dates, or schedules—and test-takers are directed to write out the numbers. This task can serve as a reasonably reliable method to stimulate handwritten English. It lacks authenticity, however, in that people rarely write out such numbers (except in writing checks), and it is more of a reading task (recognizing numbers) than a writing task. If you plan to use such a method, be sure to specify exactly what the objective is and then proceed with some caution.

Converting abbreviations to words is more authentic: We actually do have occasions to write out days of the week, months, and words such as "street," "boulevard," "telephone," and "April" (months, of course, are often abbreviated with numbers). Test tasks may take this form:

Writing numbers and abbreviations [L, W]

Test-takers hear: Fill in the blanks with words.

Test-takers see:

9:00 _____ 5:45 _____

Tues. _____ 5/3 _____

726 S. Main St. _____

Spelling Tasks and Detecting Phoneme–Grapheme Correspondences

A number of task types are in popular use to assess the ability to spell words correctly and to process phoneme–grapheme correspondences.

1. *Spelling tests.* In a traditional, old-fashioned spelling test, the teacher dictates a simple list of words, one word at a time, followed by the word in a sentence, repeated again, with a pause for test-takers to write the word. Scoring emphasizes correct spelling. You can help to control for listening errors by choosing words that the students have encountered before—words that they have spoken or heard in their class.
2. *Picture-cued tasks.* Pictures are displayed with the objective of focusing on familiar words whose spelling may be unpredictable. Items are chosen according to the objectives of the assessment, but this format is an opportunity to present some challenging words and word pairs: "boot/book," "read/reed," "bit/bite," etc.
3. *Multiple-choice techniques.* Presenting words and phrases in the form of a multiple-choice task risks crossing over into the domain of assessing reading, but if the items have a follow-up writing component, they can serve as formative reinforcement of spelling conventions. They might be more challenging with the addition of homonyms. See the examples on the next page.

Multiple-choice reading-writing spelling tasks [R, W]

Test-takers read:

Choose the word with the correct spelling to fit the sentence, then write the word in the space provided.

1. He washed his hands with _____.
   A. soap
   B. sope
   C. sop
   D. soup

2. I tried to stop the car, but the _____ didn't work.
   A. braicks
   B. brecks
   C. brakes
   D. bracks

3. The doorbell rang, but when I went to the door, no one was _____.
   A. their
   B. there
   C. they're
   D. thair

---

4. *Matching phonetic symbols.* If students have become familiar with the phonetic alphabet, they could be shown phonetic symbols and asked to write the correctly spelled word alphabetically. This works best with letters that do not have one-to-one correspondence with the phonetic symbol (e.g., /æ/ and **a**). In the following sample, the answers, which of course do not appear on the test sheet, are included in brackets for your reference.

Converting phonetic symbols [R, W]

Test-takers read:

In each of the following words, a letter or combination of letters has been written in a phonetic symbol. Write the word using the regular alphabet.

1. tea /tʃ/ er   _____   [teacher]
2. d /e/   _____   [day]
3. /ð/ is   _____   [this]
4. n /au/   _____   [now]
5. l /aɪ/ k/   _____   [like]
6. c /æ/ t   _____   [cat]

Such a task risks confusing students who don't recognize the phonetic alphabet or use it in their daily routine. Opinion is mixed on the value of using phonetic symbols at the literacy level. Some claim it helps students perceive the relationship between phonemes and graphemes. Others caution against using yet another system of symbols when the alphabet already poses a challenge, especially for adults for whom English is the only language they have learned to read or write.

DESIGNING ASSESSMENT TASKS: INTENSIVE (CONTROLLED) WRITING

This next level of writing is what second language teacher training manuals have for decades called **controlled writing**. It may also be thought of as form-focused writing, grammar writing, or simply guided writing. A good deal of writing at this level is **display writing** as opposed to **real writing**: Students produce language to display their competence in grammar, vocabulary, or sentence formation and not necessarily to convey meaning for an authentic purpose. The traditional grammar/vocabulary test has plenty of display writing in it, because the response mode demonstrates only the test-taker's ability to combine or use words correctly. No new information is passed on from one person to the other.

Dictation and Dicto-Comp [L, W]

In Chapter 7, dictation was described as an assessment of the integration of listening and writing, but it is clear that the primary skill being assessed during dictation is listening. Because of its response mode, however, it deserves a second mention in this chapter. Dictation is simply the rendition in writing of what one hears aurally, so it could be classified as an imitative type of writing, especially since a proportion of the test-taker's performance centers on correct spelling. Also, because the test-taker must listen to stretches of discourse and in the process insert punctuation, dictation of a paragraph or more can arguably be classified as a controlled or intensive form of writing.

A form of controlled writing related to dictation is a **dicto-comp**. Here, a paragraph is read at normal speed, usually two or three times, then the teacher asks students to rewrite the paragraph from the best of their recollection. In one of several variations of the dicto-comp technique, the teacher, after reading the passage, distributes a handout with key words from the paragraph, in sequence, as cues for the students. In either case, the dicto-comp is genuinely classified as an intensive, if not a responsive, writing task. Test-takers must internalize the content of the passage, remember a few phrases and lexical items as key words, then recreate the story in their own words.

Grammatical Transformation Tasks [R, W]

In the heyday of structural paradigms of language teaching with slot-filler techniques and slot-substitution drills, the practice of making grammatical transformations—orally or in writing—was very popular. To this day, language teachers have also used this technique as an assessment task, ostensibly to measure grammatical competence. Numerous versions of the task are possible:

- Change the tenses in a paragraph.
- Change full forms of verbs to reduced forms (contractions).
- Change statements to yes/no or *wh-* questions.
- Change questions into statements.
- Combine two sentences into one using a relative pronoun.
- Change direct speech to indirect speech.
- Change from active to passive voice.

The list of possibilities is almost endless. The tasks are virtually devoid of any meaningful value. Sometimes test designers attempt to add authenticity by providing a context ("Today Doug is doing all these things. Tomorrow he will do the same things again. Write about what Doug will do tomorrow by using the future tense"), but this is just a backdrop for a written substitution task. On the positive side, grammatical transformation tasks are easy to administer and therefore practical, are quite high in scorer reliability, and arguably tap into a knowledge of grammatical forms that are performed through writing. If you are interested only in a person's ability to produce the forms, then such tasks may prove to be justifiable.

Picture-Cued Tasks

A variety of picture-cued controlled tasks have been used in English classrooms around the world. The main advantage in this technique is in detaching the almost ubiquitous reading and writing connection and offering instead a nonverbal means to stimulate written responses.

1. *Short sentences.* A drawing of some simple action is shown; the test-taker writes a brief sentence.

Picture-cued sentence writing (H. D. Brown, 1999, p. 40) [R, W]

Test-takers see the following pictures:

1.

2.

3.

Test-takers read: **1.** What is the woman doing?
   2. What is the man doing?
   3. What is the boy doing?

Test-takers write:

1. *She is eating. She is eating her dinner. She is holding a spoon.* etc.

---

2. *Picture description.* A somewhat more complex picture may be presented showing, say, a person reading on a couch, a cat under a table, books and pencils on the table, chairs around the table, a lamp next to the couch, and a picture on the wall over the couch (see Chapter 8, page 196). Test-takers are asked to describe the picture using four of the following prepositions: *on, over, under, next to, around.* As long as the prepositions are used appropriately, the criterion is considered to be met.

3. *Picture sequence description.* A sequence of three to six pictures depicting a story line can provide a suitable stimulus for written production. The pictures must be simple and unambiguous because an open-ended task at the selective level would give test-takers too many options. If writing the correct grammatical form of a verb is the only criterion, then some test items might include the simple form of the verb below the picture. The time sequence in the following task is intended to give writers some cues.

Picture-cued story sequence (H. D. Brown, 1999, p. 43) [R, W]

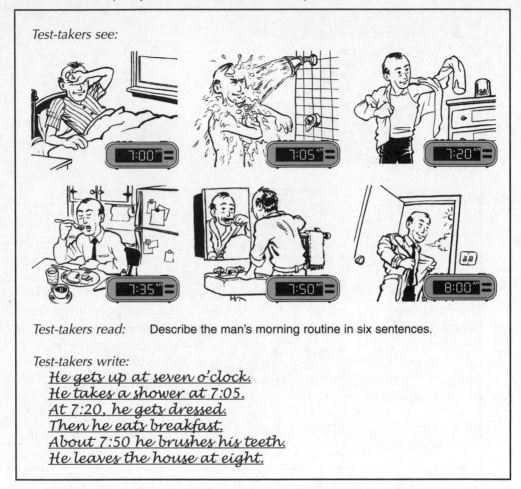

Test-takers see:

Test-takers read: Describe the man's morning routine in six sentences.

Test-takers write:
  He gets up at seven o'clock.
  He takes a shower at 7:05.
  At 7:20, he gets dressed.
  Then he eats breakfast.
  About 7:50 he brushes his teeth.
  He leaves the house at eight.

Although these kinds of tasks are designed to be controlled, even at this very simple level, a few different correct responses can be made for each item in the sequence. If your criteria in this task are both lexical and grammatical choice, then you need to design a rating scale to account for variations between completely right and completely wrong in both categories.

Scoring scale for controlled writing

2	grammatically and lexically correct
1	either grammar or vocabulary is incorrect, but not both
0	both grammar and vocabulary are incorrect

The following are some test-takers' responses to the first picture:

> He gets up at seven.
> He get up at seven.
> He is getting up at seven.
> He wakes seven o'clock.
> The man is arise at seven.
> He sleeps at seven o'clock.
> Sleeps on morning.

How would you rate each response? With the scoring scale above, the first response is a 2, the next five responses are a 1, and the last earns a zero.

Vocabulary Assessment Tasks

Most vocabulary study is carried out through reading. A number of assessments of reading recognition of vocabulary were discussed in the previous chapter: multiple-choice techniques, matching, picture-cued identification, cloze techniques, guessing the meaning of a word in context, etc. The major techniques used to assess vocabulary are (a) defining and (b) using a word in a sentence. The latter is the more authentic, but even that task is constrained by a contrived situation in which the test-taker, usually in a matter of seconds, has to come up with an appropriate sentence, which may or may not indicate that the test-taker "knows" the word.

Read (2000) suggested several types of items for assessment of basic knowledge of the meaning of a word, collocational possibilities, and derived morphological forms. His example centered on the word *interpret,* as follows:

Vocabulary writing tasks (Read, 2000, p. 179) [R, W]

Test-takers read:

1. Write two sentences, A and B. In each sentence, use the two words given.

   A. interpret, experiment _____.

   B. interpret, language _____.

2. Write three words that can fill in the blank.

   To interpret a(n) _____   i. _____

                                   ii. _____

                                   iii. _____

3. Write the correct ending for the word in each of the following sentences:

   Someone who interprets is an interpret _____.

   Something that can be interpreted is interpret _____.

   Someone who interprets gives an interpret _____.

Vocabulary assessment is clearly form-focused in the above tasks, but the procedures are creatively linked by means of the target word, its collocations, and its morphological variants. At the responsive and extensive levels, where learners are called on to create coherent paragraphs, performance obviously becomes more authentic, and lexical choice is one of several possible components of the evaluation of extensive writing.

Ordering Tasks

One task at the sentence level may appeal to those who are fond of word games and puzzles: ordering (or reordering) a scrambled set of words into a correct sentence. Here is the way the item format appears:

Reordering words in a sentence [R, W]

Test-takers read:
Put the words below into a possible order to make a grammatical sentence:

1. cold / winter / is / weather / the / in / the

2. studying / what / you / are

3. next / clock / the / the / is / picture / to

Test-takers write:

1. The weather is cold in the winter. (or) In the winter the weather is cold.

2. What are you studying?

3. The clock is next to the picture. (or) The picture is next to the clock.

Although this somewhat inauthentic task generates writing performance and may be said to tap into grammatical word-ordering rules, it presents a challenge to test-takers whose learning styles do not dispose them to logical-mathematical problem solving. If sentences are kept very simple (such as item 2) with perhaps no more than four or five words, if only one possible sentence can emerge, and if students have practiced the technique in class, then some justification emerges. However, once again, as in so many writing techniques, this task involves as much, if not more, reading performance as writing.

Short-Answer and Sentence-Completion Tasks

Some types of short-answer tasks were discussed in Chapter 9 because of the heavy participation of reading performance in their completion. Such items range from very simple and predictable to somewhat more elaborate responses. On the next page, look at the range of possibilities:

Limited response writing tasks [R, W]

Test-takers see:

1. Alicia: Who's that?
    Tony: _____ Gina.
    Alicia: Where's she from?
    Tony: _____ Italy.

2. Jennifer: _____?
    Kathy: I'm studying English.

3. Restate the following sentences in your own words, using the underlined word. You may need to change the meaning of the sentence a little.
    3a. I never miss a day of school.   <u>always</u>
    3b. I'm pretty healthy most of the time.   <u>seldom</u>
    3c. I play tennis twice a week.   <u>sometimes</u>

4. You are in the kitchen helping your roommate cook. You need to ask questions about quantities. Ask a question using *how much* (#4a) and a question using *how many* (#4b), using nouns like *sugar, pounds, flour, onions, eggs, cups.*
    4a. _____.
    4b. _____.

5. Look at the schedule of Roberto's week. Write two sentences describing what Roberto does, using the words *before* (#5a) and *after* (#5b).
    5a. _____.
    5b. _____.

6. Write three sentences describing your preferences: #6a: a big, expensive car or a small, cheap car; #6b: a house in the country or an apartment in the city; #6c: money or good health.
    6a. _____.
    6b. _____.
    6c. _____.

The reading-writing connection is apparent in the first three item types but has less of an effect in the last three, where reading is necessary to understand the directions but is not crucial in creating sentences. Scoring on a 2-1-0 scale (as described on page 270) may be the most appropriate way to avoid self-arguing about the appropriateness of a response.

ISSUES IN ASSESSING RESPONSIVE AND EXTENSIVE WRITING

Responsive writing creates the opportunity for test-takers to offer an array of possible creative responses within a pedagogical or assessment framework: Test-takers are "responding" to a prompt or assignment. Freed from the strict control of intensive writing, learners can exercise a number of options in choosing vocabulary, grammar, and discourse but with some constraints and conditions. Criteria now begin to include the discourse and rhetorical conventions of paragraph structure and of connecting two or three such paragraphs in texts of limited length. The learner is responsible for accomplishing a purpose in writing, developing a sequence of connected ideas, and empathizing with an audience.

The genres of text that are typically addressed here are

- short reports (with structured formats and conventions)
- responses to the reading of an article or story
- summaries of articles or stories
- brief narratives or descriptions
- interpretations of graphs, tables, and charts

It is here that writers become involved in the art (and science) of composing, or real writing, as opposed to display writing.

Extensive, or "free," writing, which is amalgamated into our discussion here, takes all the principles and guidelines of responsive writing and puts them into practice in longer texts such as full-length essays, term papers, project reports, and theses and dissertations. In extensive writing, however, the writer has been given even more freedom to choose: Topics, length, style, and perhaps even conventions of formatting are less constrained than in the typical responsive writing exercise. At this stage, all the rules of effective writing come into play, and the second language writer is expected to meet all the standards applied to native language writers.

Both responsive and extensive writing tasks are the subject of some classic, widely debated assessment issues that take on a distinctly different flavor from those at the lower-end production of writing.

1. *Authenticity.* Authenticity is a trait that is given special attention: If test-takers are being asked to perform a task, its face and content validity need to be assured in order to bring out the best in the writer. A good deal of writing performance in academic contexts is constrained by the pedagogical necessities of establishing the basic building blocks of writing; we have looked at assessment techniques that address those foundations. But once those fundamentals are in place, the would-be writer is ready to fly out of the protective nest of the writing classroom and assume his or her own voice. Offering that freedom to learners requires the setting of authentic real-world contexts in which to write. The teacher becomes less of an instructor and more of a coach or facilitator. Assessment therefore is typically formative, not summative, and positive washback is more important than practicality and reliability.

2. *Scoring.* Scoring is the thorniest issue at these final two stages of writing. With so many options available to a learner, each evaluation by a test administrator needs to be finely attuned not just to how the writer strings words together (the *form*) but also to what the writer is saying (the *function* of the

text). The quality of writing (its impact and effectiveness) becomes as important, if not more important, than all the nuts and bolts that hold it together. How are you to score such creative production, some of which is more artistic than scientific? A discussion of different scoring options continues below, followed by a reminder that responding and editing are nonscoring options that yield washback to the writer.

3. *Time.* Yet another assessment issue surrounds the unique nature of writing: It is the only skill in which the language producer is not necessarily constrained by time, which implies the freedom to process multiple drafts before the text becomes a finished product. Like a sculptor creating an image, the writer can take an initial rough conception of a text and continue to refine it until it is deemed presentable to the public eye. Virtually all real writing of prose texts presupposes an extended time period for it to reach its final form, and therefore the revising and editing processes are implied. Responsive writing, along with the next category of extensive writing, often relies on this essential drafting process for its ultimate success.

How do you assess writing ability within the confines of traditional, formal assessment procedures that are almost always, by logistical necessity, timed? We have a whole testing industry that has based large-scale assessment of writing on the premise that the **timed impromptu** format is a valid method of assessing writing ability. Is this an authentic format? Can a language learner—or a native speaker, for that matter—adequately perform writing tasks within the confines of a brief timed period of composition? Is that hastily written product an appropriate reflection of what that same test-taker might produce after several drafts of the same work? Does this format favor fast writers at the expense of slower but possibly equally good or better writers? Alderson & Banerjee (2002) and Weigle (2002) both cited this as one of the most pressing unresolved issues in the assessment of writing today. We return to this question later.

Because of the complexity of assessing responsive and extensive writing, this discussion has a different look from the one in the previous three chapters. Four major topics will be addressed: (a) a few fundamental task types at the lower (responsive) end of the continuum of writing at this level, (b) a description and analysis of the *Test of Written English* (TWE® Test) as a typical timed impromptu test of writing, (c) a survey of methods of scoring and evaluating writing production, and (d) a discussion of the assessment qualities of editing and responding to a series of writing drafts.

DESIGNING ASSESSMENT TASKS: RESPONSIVE AND EXTENSIVE WRITING

In this section we consider both responsive and extensive writing tasks. They are regarded here as a continuum of possibilities ranging from lower-end tasks whose complexity exceeds those in the previous category of intensive or controlled writing to more open-ended tasks such as writing short reports, essays, summaries, and responses, to texts of several pages or more.

Paraphrasing [R, L, W]

One of the more difficult concepts for second language learners to grasp is paraphrasing. The initial step in teaching paraphrasing is to ensure that learners understand the importance of paraphrasing: to say something in one's own words, to avoid plagiarizing, to offer some variety in expression. With those possible motivations and purposes in mind, the test designer needs to elicit a paraphrase of a sentence or paragraph, usually not more.

Scoring of the test-taker's response is a judgment call in which the criterion of conveying the same or similar message is primary, with secondary evaluations of discourse, grammar, and vocabulary. Other components of analytic or holistic scales (see later discussion, pages 283–285) might be considered as criteria for an evaluation. Paraphrasing is more often a part of informal and formative assessment than of formal, summative assessment, and therefore student responses should be viewed as opportunities for teachers and students to gain positive washback on the art of paraphrasing.

Guided Question and Answer

Another lower-order task in this type of writing, which has the pedagogical benefit of guiding a learner without dictating the form of the output, is a guided question-and-answer format in which the test administrator poses a series of questions that essentially serves as an outline of the emergent written text. In the writing of a narrative that the teacher has already covered in a class discussion, the following kinds of questions might be posed to stimulate a sequence of sentences.

Guided writing stimuli [R, W]

---

1. Where did this story take place? [setting]
2. Who were the people in the story? [characters]
3. What happened first? and then? and then? [sequence of events]
4. Why did _____ do _____? [reasons, causes]
5. What did _____ think about _____? [opinion]
6. What happened at the end? [climax]
7. What is the moral of this story? [evaluation]

Guided writing texts, which may be as long as two or three paragraphs, may be scored on either an analytic or a holistic scale (discussed on pages 283–285). Guided writing prompts such as these are less likely to appear on a formal test and more likely to serve as a way to prompt initial drafts of writing. This first draft can then undergo the editing and revising stages discussed in the next section of this chapter. A variation on using guided questions is to prompt the test-taker to write from an outline. The outline may be self-created from earlier reading and/or discussion or—less desirable—be provided by the teacher or test administrator. The outline helps to guide the learner through a presumably logical development of ideas that have been given some forethought. Assessment of the resulting text follows the same criteria listed below (item 3 in the next section, paragraph construction tasks).

Paragraph Construction Tasks [R, W]

The participation of reading performance is inevitable in writing effective paragraphs. To a great extent, writing is the art of emulating what one reads. You read an effective paragraph; you analyze the ingredients of its success; you emulate it. Assessment of paragraph development takes on a number of different forms:

1. *Topic sentence writing.* There is no cardinal rule that says every paragraph must have a topic sentence, but the stating of a topic through the lead sentence (or a subsequent one) has remained as a tried-and-true technique for teaching the concept of a paragraph. Assessment thereof consists of

   • specifying the writing of a topic sentence.
   • scoring points for its presence or absence.
   • scoring and/or commenting on its effectiveness in stating the topic.

2. *Topic development within a paragraph.* Because paragraphs are intended to provide a reader with "clusters" of meaningful, connected thoughts or ideas, another stage of assessment is development of an idea within a paragraph. Four criteria are commonly applied to assess the quality of a paragraph:

   • the clarity of expression of ideas
   • the logic of the sequence and connections
   • the cohesiveness or unity of the paragraph
   • the overall effectiveness or impact of the paragraph as a whole

3. *Development of main and supporting ideas across paragraphs.* As writers string two or more paragraphs together in a longer text (and as we move up the continuum from responsive to extensive writing), the writer attempts to articulate a thesis or *main idea* with clearly stated *supporting ideas*. These elements can be considered in evaluating a multiparagraph essay:

   • addressing the topic, main idea, or principal purpose
   • organizing and developing supporting ideas
   • using appropriate details to undergird supporting ideas
   • showing facility and fluency in the use of language
   • demonstrating syntactic variety

Strategic Options

Developing main and supporting ideas is the goal for the writer attempting to create an effective text, whether a short one- to two-paragraph one or an extensive one of several pages. A number of strategies are commonly taught to second language writers to accomplish their purposes. Aside from strategies of freewriting, outlining, drafting, and revising, writers need to be aware of the task that has been demanded and focus on the genre of writing and the expectations of that genre.

1. *Attending to task.* In responsive writing, the context is seldom completely open-ended: A task has been defined by the teacher or test administrator, and the writer must fulfill the criterion of the task. Even in extensive writing of longer texts, a set of directives has been stated by the teacher or is implied by the conventions of the genre. Four types of tasks are commonly addressed in academic writing courses: compare/contrast, problem/solution, pros/cons, and cause/effect. Depending on the genre of the text, one or more of these task types are needed to achieve the writer's purpose. If students are asked, for example, to "agree or disagree with the author's statement," a likely strategy would be to cite pros and cons and then take a stand. A task that asks students to argue for one among several political candidates in an election might be an ideal compare-and-contrast context, with an appeal to problems present in the constituency and the relative value of candidates' solutions. Assessment of the fulfillment of such tasks could be formative and informal (comments in marginal notes, feedback in a conference in an editing/revising stage), but the product might also be assigned a holistic or analytic score.

2. *Attending to genre.* The genres of writing that were listed at the beginning of this chapter provide some sense of the many varieties of text that may be produced by a second language learner in a writing curriculum. Another way of looking at the strategic options open to a writer is the extent to which both the constraints and the opportunities of the genre are exploited. Assessment of any writing necessitates attention to the conventions of the genre in question. Assessment of the more common genres may include the following criteria, along with chosen factors from the list in item 3 (main and supporting ideas) on the previous page:

Reports (lab reports, project summaries, article/book reports)
- conform to a conventional format (for this case, field)
- convey the purpose, goal, or main idea
- organize details logically and sequentially
- state conclusions or findings
- use appropriate vocabulary and jargon for the specific case

Summaries of readings/lectures/videos
- effectively capture the main and supporting ideas of the original
- maintain objectivity in reporting
- use writer's own words for the most part
- use quotations effectively when appropriate
- omit irrelevant or marginal details
- conform to an expected length

Responses to readings/lectures/videos
- accurately reflect the message or meaning of the original
- appropriately select supporting ideas to respond to
- express the writer's own opinion
- defend or support that opinion effectively
- conform to an expected length

Narration, description, persuasion/argument, and exposition
- follow expected conventions for each type of writing
- convey purpose, goal, or main idea
- use effective writing strategies
- demonstrate syntactic variety and rhetorical fluency

Interpreting statistical, graphic, or tabular data
- provide an effective global, overall description of the data
- organize the details in clear, logical language
- accurately convey details
- appropriately articulate relationships among elements of the data
- convey specialized or complex data comprehensibly to a lay reader
- interpret beyond the data when appropriate

Library research paper
- state purpose or goal of the research
- include appropriate citations and references in correct format
- accurately represent others' research findings
- inject writer's own interpretation, when appropriate, and justifies it
- include suggestions for further research
- sum up findings in a conclusion

Standardized Tests of Responsive Writing

A number of commercially available standardized tests include writing components: the TOEFL®, MELAB, IELTS® Tests, and others. Typically, such tests comprise a prompt, require the test-taker to respond within a time limit, and are scored by means of a rating scale. The *Test of Written English* (TWE®), for example, now incorporated into the Internet-based TOEFL® iBT, has gained a reputation as a well-respected measure of written English, and a number of research articles support its validity (Frase, Falettti, Ginther, & Grant, 1999; Hale, Taylor, Bridgeman, Carson, Kroll, & Cantor, 1996; Longford, 1996; Myford, Marr, & Linacre, 1996). The TWE is still offered as a separate test where only the paper-based TOEFL is available.

Sample prompts for the TWE® Test (Web site)

---

1. Some people say that the best preparation for life is learning to work with others and be cooperative. Others take the opposite view and say that learning to be competitive is the best preparation. Discuss these positions, using concrete examples of both. Tell which one you agree with and explain why.
2. Some people believe that automobiles are useful and necessary. Others believe that automobiles cause problems that affect our health and well-being. Which position do you support? Give specific reasons for your answer.
3. Do you agree or disagree with the following statement?

   Teachers should make learning enjoyable and fun for their students.

   Use reasons and specific examples to support your opinion.

The scoring guide for the TWE (see Table 10.1 on the next page) follows a widely accepted set of specifications for a holistic evaluation of an essay (see pages 283–284 for more discussion of holistic scoring). Each point on the scoring system is defined by a set of statements that address topic, organization and development, supporting ideas, facility (fluency, naturalness, appropriateness) in writing, and grammatical and lexical correctness and choice. Scoring is performed by two independent human evaluators.

It's important to put tests like the TWE in perspective. Timed impromptu tests have obvious limitations if you're looking for an authentic sample of performance in a real-world context. How many times in real-world situations (other than in academic writing classes) will you be asked to write an essay in 30 minutes? Probably never, but the TWE and other standardized timed tests are not intended to mirror the real world. Instead, they are intended to elicit a sample of writing performance that will be indicative of a person's writing ability in the real world. TWE designers sought to validate a feasible timed task that would be manageable within their constraints and at the same time offer useful information about the test-taker.

How does the Educational Testing Service justify the TWE as such an indicator? Research by Hale et al. (1996) showed that the prompts used in the TWE approximate writing tasks assigned in 162 graduate and undergraduate courses across several disciplines in eight universities. Another study (Golub-Smith, Reese, & Steinhaus,

Table 10.1. Test of Written English (TWE® Test) *scoring guide*

6   **Demonstrates clear competence in writing on both the rhetorical and syntactic levels, though it may have occasional errors**

A paper in this category
- effectively addresses the writing task.
- is well organized and well developed.
- uses clearly appropriate details to support a thesis or illustrate ideas.
- displays consistent facility in the use of language.
- demonstrates syntactic variety and appropriate word choice.

5   **Demonstrates competence in writing on both the rhetorical and syntactic levels, though it will probably have occasional errors**

A paper in this category
- may address some parts of the task more effectively than others.
- is generally well organized and developed.
- uses details to support a thesis or illustrate an idea.
- displays facility in the use of language.
- demonstrates some syntactic variety and range of vocabulary.

4   **Demonstrates minimal competence in writing on both the rhetorical and syntactic levels**

A paper in this category
- addresses the writing topic adequately but may slight parts of the task.
- is adequately organized and developed.
- uses some details to support a thesis or illustrate an idea.
- demonstrates adequate but possibly inconsistent facility with syntax and usage.
- may contain some errors that occasionally obscure meaning.

3   **Demonstrates some developing competence in writing, but it remains flawed on either the rhetorical or syntactic level, or both**

A paper in this category may reveal one or more of the following weaknesses:
- inadequate organization or development
- inappropriate or insufficient details to support or illustrate generalizations
- a noticeably inappropriate choice of words or word forms
- an accumulation of errors in sentence structure and/or usage.

2   **Suggests incompetence in writing**

A paper in this category is seriously flawed by one or more of the following weaknesses:
- serious disorganization or underdevelopment
- little or no detail, or irrelevant specifics
- serious and frequent errors in sentence structure or usage
- serious problems with focus

1   **Demonstrates incompetence in writing**

A paper in this category
- may be incoherent.
- may be undeveloped.
- may contain severe and persistent writing errors.

0   A paper is rated 0 if it contains no response, merely copies the topic, is off-topic, is written in a foreign language, or consists only of keystroke characters.

1993) ascertained the reliabilities across several types of prompts (e.g., compare/contrast vs. chart-graph interpretation). Both Myford et al. (1996) and Longford (1996) studied the reliabilities of judges' ratings. The question of whether a mere 30-minute time period is sufficient to elicit a sufficient sample of a test-taker's writing was addressed by Hale (1992). Henning and Cascallar (1992) conducted a large-scale study to assess the extent to which TWE performance taps into the communicative competence of the test-taker. The upshot of this research—which is updated regularly—is that the TWE (which adheres to a high standard of excellence in standardized testing) is, within acceptable standard error ranges, a remarkably accurate indicator of writing ability (Frase et al., 1999).

The flip side of this controversial coin reminds us that standardized tests are indicators, not fail-safe, infallible measures of competence. Even though we might need TWE scores for the administrative purposes of admissions or placement, we should not rely on such tests for instructional purposes (see Cohen, 1994). No one would suggest that such 30-minute writing tests offer constructive feedback (washback) to the student, nor do they provide the kind of formative assessment that a process approach to writing brings. Standardized impromptu writing tests are administrative necessities in a world where hundreds or thousands of applicants must be evaluated by some means short of calculating their performance across years of instruction in academic writing.

The convenience of standardized writing tests should not lull administrators into believing that they are the only measures that should be applied to students. It behooves users worldwide to offer secondary measures of writing ability to those test-takers who

- are on the threshold of a minimum score
- may be disabled by highly time-constrained or anxiety-producing situations
- could be culturally disadvantaged by a topic or situation
- (in the case of computer-based writing) have had few opportunities to compose on a computer

Although timed impromptu tests suffer from a lack of authenticity and put test-takers into an artificially time-constrained context, they nevertheless offer interesting, relevant information for an important but narrow range of administrative purposes. The classroom offers a much wider set of options for creating real-world writing purposes and contexts. The classroom becomes the locus of extended hard work and effort for building the skills necessary to create written production. The classroom provides a setting for writers, in a process of multiple drafts and revisions, to create a final, publicly acceptable product. The classroom is also a place where learners can take all the small steps, at their own pace, toward becoming proficient writers.

SCORING METHODS FOR RESPONSIVE
AND EXTENSIVE WRITING

At responsive and extensive levels of writing, three major approaches to scoring writing performance are commonly used by test designers: holistic, primary trait, and analytical. In the first method, a single score is assigned to an essay, which represents a reader's general overall assessment. Primary trait scoring is a variation of the holistic method in that the achievement of the primary purpose, or trait, of an essay is the only factor rated. Analytical scoring breaks a test-taker's written text down into a number of subcategories (organization, grammar, etc.) and gives a separate rating for each. Each of these scores are discussed below in more detail.

Holistic Scoring

The TWE® Test scoring scale on page 281 is a prime example of **holistic scoring**. In Chapter 8, a rubric for scoring oral production holistically was presented. Each point on a holistic scale is given a systematic set of descriptors, and the reader-evaluator matches an overall impression with the descriptors to arrive at a score. Descriptors usually (but not always) follow a prescribed pattern. For example, the first descriptor across all score categories may address the quality of task achievement, the second may deal with organization, the third with grammatical or rhetorical considerations, and so on. Scoring, however, is truly holistic in that those subsets are not quantitatively added up to yield a score.

Advantages of holistic scoring include

- fast evaluation
- relatively high inter-rater reliability
- the fact that scores represent "standards" that are easily interpreted by lay persons
- the fact that scores tend to emphasize the writer's strengths (Cohen, 1994, p. 315)
- applicability to writing across many different disciplines

Its disadvantages must also be weighed into a decision on whether to use holistic scoring:

- One score masks differences across the subskills within each score.
- No diagnostic information is available (no washback potential).
- The scale may not apply equally well to all genres of writing.
- Raters need to be extensively trained to use the scale accurately.

In general, teachers and test designers lean toward holistic scoring only when it is expedient for administrative purposes. As long as trained evaluators are in place, differentiation across six levels may be quite adequate for admission into an institution or placement into courses. For classroom instructional purposes, holistic scores provide very little information. In most classroom settings where a teacher wishes to adapt a curriculum to the needs of a particular group of students, much more differentiated information across subskills is desirable than is provided by holistic scoring.

Primary Trait Scoring

A second method of scoring, **primary trait**, focuses on "how well students can write within a narrowly defined range of discourse" (Weigle, 2002, p. 110). This type of scoring emphasizes the task at hand and assigns a score based on the effectiveness of the text's achieving that one goal. For example, if the purpose or function of an essay is to persuade the reader to do something, the score for the writing would rise or fall on the accomplishment of that function. If a learner is asked to exploit the imaginative function of language by expressing personal feelings, then the response would be evaluated on that feature alone.

For rating the primary trait of the text, Lloyd-Jones (1977) suggested a four-point scale ranging from 0 (no response or fragmented response) to 4 (the purpose is unequivocally accomplished in a convincing fashion). It almost goes without saying that organization, supporting details, fluency, syntactic variety, and other features will implicitly be evaluated in the process of offering a primary trait score. The advantage of this method is that it allows both writer and evaluator to focus on function. In summary, a primary trait score would assess

- the accuracy of the account of the original (summary)
- the clarity of the steps of the procedure and the final result (lab report)
- the description of the main features of the graph (graph description)
- the expression of the writer's opinion (response to an article)

Analytic Scoring

For classroom instruction, holistic scoring provides little washback into the writer's further stages of learning. Primary trait scoring focuses on the principal function of the text and therefore offers some feedback potential but no washback for any of the aspects of the written production that enhance the ultimate accomplishment of the purpose. Classroom evaluation of learning is best served through **analytic scoring**, in which as many as six major elements of writing are scored, thus enabling learners to hone in on weaknesses and capitalize on strengths.

Analytic scoring may be more appropriately called analytic assessment to capture its closer association with classroom language instruction than with formal testing. Brown and Bailey (1984) designed an analytical scoring scale that specified five major categories and a description of five different levels in each category, ranging from "unacceptable" to "excellent" (see Table 10.2 on pages 286–287).

At first glance, Brown and Bailey's (1984) scale may look similar to the TWE holistic scale discussed earlier: For each scoring category there is a description that encompasses several subsets. A closer inspection, however, reveals much more detail in the analytic method. Instead of just six descriptions, there are 25, each subdivided into a number of contributing factors.

The order in which the five categories (organization, logical development of ideas, grammar, punctuation/spelling/mechanics, and style and quality of expression) are listed may bias the evaluator toward the greater importance of organization and logical development as opposed to punctuation and style, but the mathematical assignment of the 100-point scale gives equal weight (a maximum of 20 points) to each of the five major categories. Not all writing and assessment specialists agree. You might, for example, consider the analytical scoring profile suggested by Jacobs, Zinkgraf, Wormuth, Hartfiel, and Hughey (1981), in which five slightly different categories were given the following point values:

Content	30
Organization	20
Vocabulary	20
Syntax	25
Mechanics	5
Total	**100**

As your curricular goals and students' needs vary, your own analytical scoring of essays may be appropriately tailored. Level of proficiency can make a significant difference in emphasis: At the intermediate level, for example, you might give more emphasis to syntax and mechanics, whereas advanced levels of writing may call for a strong push toward organization and development. Genre can also dictate variations in scoring. Would a summary of an article require the same relative emphases as a narrative essay? Most likely not. Certain types of writing, such as lab reports or interpretations of statistical data, may even need additional—or at least redefined— categories to capture the essential components of good writing within those genres.

Analytic scoring of compositions offers writers a little more washback than a single holistic or primary trait score. Scores in five or six major elements help call the writers' attention to areas of needed improvement. Practicality is lowered in that more time is required for teachers to attend to details within each of the categories to render a final score or grade, but ultimately students receive more information about their writing. Numerical scores alone, however, are still not sufficient for enabling students to become proficient writers, as we shall see in the next section.

BEYOND SCORING: RESPONDING TO EXTENSIVE WRITING

Formal testing carries with it the burden of designing a practical and reliable instrument that assesses its intended criterion accurately. To accomplish that mission, designers of writing tests are charged with the task of providing as "objective" a

Table 10.2. Analytic scale for rating composition tasks (Brown & Bailey, 1984, pp. 39–41)

	20–18 Excellent to Good	17–15 Good to Adequate	14–12 Adequate to Fair	11–6 Unacceptable–not college-level work	5–1
I. Organization: Introduction, Body, and Conclusion	Appropriate title, effective introductory paragraph, topic is stated, leads to body; transitional expressions used; arrangement of material shows plan (could be outlined by reader); supporting evidence given for generalizations; conclusion logical and complete	Adequate title, introduction, and conclusion; body of essay is acceptable, but some evidence may be lacking, some ideas aren't fully developed; sequence is logical but transitional expressions may be absent or misused	Mediocre or scant introduction or conclusion; problems with the order of ideas in body; the generalizations may not be fully supported by the evidence given; problems of organization interfere	Shaky or minimally recognizable introduction; organization can barely be seen; severe problems with ordering of ideas; lack of supporting evidence; conclusion weak or illogical; inadequate effort at organization	Absence of introduction or conclusion; no apparent organization of body; severe lack of supporting evidence; writer has not made any effort to organize the composition (could not be outlined by reader)
II. Logical development of ideas: Content	Essay addresses the assigned topic; the ideas are concrete and thoroughly developed; no extraneous material; essay reflects thought	Essay addresses the issues but misses some points; ideas could be more fully developed; some extraneous material is present	Development of ideas not complete or essay is somewhat off the topic; paragraphs aren't divided exactly right	Ideas incomplete; essay does not reflect careful thinking or was hurriedly written; inadequate effort in area of content	Essay is completely inadequate and does not reflect college-level work; no apparent effort to consider the topic carefully

III. Grammar	Native-like fluency in English grammar; correct use of relative clauses, prepositions, modals, articles, verb forms, and tense sequencing; no fragments or run-on sentences	Advanced proficiency in English grammar; some grammar problems don't influence communication, although the reader is aware of them; no fragments or run-on sentences	Ideas are getting through to the reader, but grammar problems are apparent and have a negative effect on communication; run-on sentences or fragments present	Numerous serious grammar problems interfere with communication of the writer's ideas; grammar review of some areas clearly needed; difficult to read sentences	Severe grammar problems interfere greatly with the message; reader can't understand what the writer was trying to say; unintelligible sentence structure
IV. Punctuation, spelling, and mechanics	Correct use of English writing conventions: left and right margins, all needed capitals, paragraphs indented, punctuation and spelling; very neat	Some problems with writing conventions or punctuation; occasional spelling errors; left margin correct; paper is neat and legible	Uses general writing conventions but has errors; spelling problems distract reader; punctuation errors interfere with ideas	Serious problems with format of paper; parts of essay not legible; errors in sentence punctuation and final punctuation; unacceptable to educated readers	Complete disregard for English writing conventions; paper illegible; obvious capitals missing, no margins, severe spelling problems
V. Style and quality of expression	Precise vocabulary usage; use of parallel structures; concise; register good	Attempts variety; good vocabulary; not wordy; register OK; style fairly concise	Some vocabulary misused; lacks awareness of register; may be too wordy	Poor expression of ideas; problems in vocabulary; lacks variety of structure	Inappropriate use of vocabulary; no concept of register or sentence variety

scoring procedure as possible and one that in many cases can be easily interpreted by agents beyond the learner. Holistic, primary trait, and analytic scoring all satisfy those ends. Yet beyond mathematically calculated scores lies a rich domain of assessment in which a developing writer is coached from stage to stage in a process of building a storehouse of writing skills. In the classroom, in the tutored relationship of teacher and student, and in the community of peer learners, most of the hard work of assessing writing is carried out. Such assessment is informal, formative, and replete with washback.

Most writing specialists agree that the best way to teach writing is a hands-on approach that stimulates student output and then generates a series of self-assessments, peer-editing and revision, and teacher response and conferencing (Ferris & Hedgcock, 2005; Raimes, 1991, 1998; Reid, 1993; Seow, 2002). It is not an approach that relies on a massive dose of lecturing about good writing or on memorizing a long list of rules on rhetorical organization, or on sending students home with an assignment to turn in a paper the next day. People become good writers by writing and seeking the facilitative input of others to refine their skills.

Assessment takes on a crucial role in such an approach. Learning how to become a good writer places the student in an almost constant stage of assessment. To give the student the maximum benefit of assessment, it is important to consider (a) earlier stages (from freewriting to the first draft or two) and (b) later stages (revising and finalizing) of producing a written text. A further factor in assessing writing is the involvement of self, peers, and teacher at appropriate steps in the process. (For further guidelines on the process of teaching writing, see *TBP*, Chapter 19.)

Assessing Initial Stages of the Process of Composing

Following are some guidelines for assessing the initial stages (the first draft or two) of a written composition. These guidelines are generic for self, peer, and teacher responding. Each assessor needs to modify the list according to the level of the learner, the context, and the purpose in responding.

Assessment of initial stages in composing

---

1. Focus your efforts primarily on meaning, main idea, and organization.
2. Comment on the introductory paragraph.
3. Make general comments about the clarity of the main idea and logic or appropriateness of the organization.
4. As a rule of thumb, ignore minor (local) grammatical and lexical errors.
5. Indicate what appear to be major (global) errors (e.g., by underlining the text in question) but allow the writer to make corrections.
6. Do not rewrite questionable, ungrammatical, or awkward sentences; rather, probe with a question about meaning.
7. Comment on features that appear to be irrelevant to the topic.

The teacher-assessor's role is as a guide, a facilitator, and an ally; therefore, assessment at this stage of writing needs to be as positive as possible to encourage the writer. An early focus on overall structure and meaning enables writers to clarify their purpose and plan and sets a framework for the writers' later refinement of the lexical and grammatical issues.

Assessing Later Stages of the Process of Composing

Once the writer has determined and clarified his or her purpose and plan and completed at least one or perhaps two drafts, the focus shifts toward "fine tuning" the expression with a view toward a final revision. Editing and responding assume an appropriately different character with these guidelines:

Assessment of later stages in composing

---

1. Comment on the specific clarity and strength of all main ideas and supporting ideas and on argument and logic.
2. Call attention to minor ("local") grammatical and mechanical (spelling, punctuation) errors but direct the writer to self-correct.
3. Comment on any further word choices and expressions that may not be awkward but are not as clear or direct as they could be.
4. Point out any problems with cohesive devices within and across paragraphs.
5. If appropriate, comment on documentation, citation of sources, evidence, and other support.
6. Comment on the adequacy and strength of the conclusion.

Through all these stages it is assumed that peers and teacher are both responding to the writer through conferencing in person, electronic communication, or, at the very least, an exchange of papers. The impromptu timed tests and the methods of scoring discussed earlier may appear to be only distantly related to such an individualized process of creating a written text, but are they in reality? All those developmental stages may be the preparation that learners need to both function in creative real-world writing tasks and successfully demonstrate their competence on a timed impromptu test. Those holistic scores are after all generalizations of the various components of effective writing. If the hard work of successfully progressing through a semester or two of a challenging course in academic writing ultimately means that writers are ready to function in their real-world contexts, *and* to get a 5 or 6 on the TWE® Test, then all the effort was worthwhile.

★　　★　　★　　★　　★

This chapter completes the cycle of considering the assessment of all of the four skills of listening, speaking, reading, and writing. As you contemplate using some of the assessment techniques that have been suggested, we think you can now fully appreciate three significant overarching guidelines for designing an effective assessment procedure:

1. It is virtually impossible to isolate any one of the four skills, perhaps with the exception of reading, without the involvement of at least one other mode of performance. Don't underestimate the power of the integration of skills in assessments designed to target a single skill area.

2. The variety of assessment techniques and item types and tasks is virtually infinite in that there is always some possibility for creating a unique variation. Explore those alternatives but with some caution lest your overzealous urge to be innovative distracts you from a focus on achieving the intended purpose and rendering an appropriate evaluation of performance.

3. Many item types that have been presented in these last four chapters target language forms as one of the possible assessment criteria. In many cases function and/or meaning is also being assessed. As you consider designing your own assessment instruments, make sure you're clear about the extent to which your objective is to assess form or function or both. To that end, we direct you to the next chapter to take a careful look at just what form-focused assessment is and how you can assess grammar and/or vocabulary within a communicative, task-based curriculum.

EXERCISES

[Note: (**I**) Individual work; (**G**) Group or pair work; (**C**) Whole-class discussion.]

1. (**C**) Genres of reading were listed at the beginning of Chapter 9 and genres of writing in this chapter, which is a shorter list. Why is the list for writing shorter? Add other examples to each of the three categories. Among the listed examples and new ones you come up with, be specific in citing what makes some genres more difficult than others. Select a few of the more difficult genres and discuss what you would assess (criteria) and how you would assess them (some possible assessment techniques).

2. (**C**) Review the four basic types of writing that were outlined at the beginning of the chapter. Offer examples of each and pay special attention to distinguishing between imitative and intensive and between responsive and extensive.

3. (**G**) Look at the list of micro- and macroskills of writing on pages 262–263. In pairs, each assigned to a different skill (or two), brainstorm some tasks that assess those skills. Present your findings to the rest of the class.

4. (**C**) In Chapter 7, nine characteristics of listening were listed (page 164) that make listening "difficult." What makes writing difficult? Devise a similar list,

which could form a set of specifications to pay special attention to in assessing writing.

5. **(G)** Divide the four basic types of writing among groups or pairs, one type for each. Look at the sample assessment techniques provided and evaluate them according to the five principles (practicality, reliability, validity [especially face and content], authenticity, and washback). Present your critique to the rest of the class.

6. **(G)** In the same groups as item 5 above, with one of the four basic types of writing assigned to your group, design some new items not described in this chapter. Present your items to the rest of the class.

7. **(I/C)** Visit the TOEFL® Test Web site and click on the description of the Test of Written English to familiarize yourself further with the TWE® Test. Then do the following: (a) Look at the TWE holistic scoring guide in this chapter (page 281) and evaluate its rater reliability; (b) discuss the validity of a timed impromptu test such as this for admission to an English-speaking university.

8. **(C)** Review the advantages and disadvantages of the three kinds of scoring presented in this chapter: holistic, primary trait, and analytic. Brainstorm a chart that shows how different contexts (types of test, objectives of a curriculum, proficiency levels, etc.) may benefit from each kind of scoring and what disadvantages may apply.

FOR YOUR FURTHER READING

Weigle, Sara Cushing. (2002). *Assessing writing.* Cambridge: Cambridge University Press.

This volume in the Cambridge Language Assessment Series provides a comprehensive overview of the history and current state of the art of assessing writing. With an authoritative backdrop of research underlying the construct validation of techniques for the assessment of written production, a host of actual testing techniques are surveyed and evaluated. A second and teacher-friendly article by Weigle (2007), "Teaching Writing Teachers about Assessment," is also a very useful reference that capsulizes a good deal of the substance of her 2002 book.

Ferris, Dana R., & Hedgcock, John S. (2005). *Teaching ESL composition: Purpose, process, and practice.* Mahwah, NJ: Lawrence Erlbaum Associates.

In the second edition of this widely used textbook on second language writing instruction, Ferris and Hedgcock update references and add new material. By synthesizing research findings and practical classroom instruction, the authors offer firmly grounded, hands-on examples, materials, and tasks in teaching writing. Chapter 8 provides a comprehensive overview of approaches to assessment of writing.

CHAPTER 11

ASSESSING GRAMMAR

AND VOCABULARY

OBJECTIVES: After reading this chapter, you will be able to

- state a rationale for treating form-focused assessment (of grammar and vocabulary) as a criterion that differs in purpose and context from assessing one or several of the four skills
- discern, through the backdrop of the nature of grammar, the purposes and contexts for assessing grammatical knowledge

- analyze the components of lexical ability and apply them to the assessment of vocabulary knowledge
- develop assessments that focus on specifically identified forms of language
- design assessments that target one or several of the modes of performance, ranging from perceptive recognition of forms to extensive reading

You have now had ample opportunities to examine many different assessment techniques in each of the four skills of listening, speaking, reading, and writing. Before that, we surveyed some of the so-called alternatives in assessment that are commonly used in language programs. Your head may be spinning with all the options that are possible to bring to bear to your language classroom. From intensive focus on the "bits and pieces" of language to extensive skills like listening to speeches and reading books, and from portfolios to self-assessment, the possibilities are limitless.

There is one more dominant "hot topic" in this field that we now turn to: assessing grammar and vocabulary, more technically known as **form-focused assessment**. One could argue that we've already discussed syntactic and lexical forms in the process of covering the four skills. After all, almost all of the microskills that you've been reading about in the previous four chapters are abilities that require a learner to focus on form. In assessing speaking, for example, you might be interested in a student's production of phonemes, stress patterns, or verb tenses. In our discussion of assessing writing, we called your attention to spelling, grammatical transformations, and vocabulary. All of this is form-focused assessment, and such a focus comprises important and legitimate criteria for language assessment, in the same way that form-focused instruction is also an integral aspect of communicative language-teaching methodology.

Now we know that the language-teaching field has been consumed—over perhaps centuries—with language forms, especially grammar and vocabulary. Across the globe, standardized tests typically manifest a strong emphasis on form, all of course in perfect harmony with classes and textbooks that continue to teach and test formal aspects of language. We know, too, that language learners worldwide are famous—or infamous—for spending months or even years acquiring knowledge *about* a language, in the form of its grammar rules, but gaining pitiful communicative ability to *use* the language. However, this "book-learned" knowledge of formal rules and paradigms is not to be confused with an informed approach to offering in our classrooms a reasonable intermingling of focus on form and focus on meaning (that is, communication for real-world pragmatic uses).

So within a paradigm of communicative methodology, what does it mean to "know" the grammar, vocabulary, phonology, and discourse rules of a language? How does that knowledge—whether explicit or implicit—influence the developing abilities of a learner to use language in the real world? These are questions that underlie our attention in this chapter to the place of form-focused assessment in all of the other aspects of language assessment that have already been considered in this book. How does one assess grammar? Is it appropriate to propose to test one's ability to comprehend or produce vocabulary? How can a teacher assess a student's implicit knowledge of forms? Must such knowledge be assessed through explicit focus on form? We now take a careful look at this often-misunderstood domain of language teaching and testing.

ASSESSING GRAMMAR

In the four skills of listening, speaking, reading, and writing, the knowledge of grammar is at the center of language use, so it isn't surprising that for many years we believed that knowing a language meant knowing the grammatical structures of that language. Although the importance of grammar in language learning hasn't changed, there has been a lot of debate about the place of teaching grammar in the language class. Over the years, the focus on grammar has changed, depending on the teaching method. For example, the Grammar Translation Method (see *TBP*, Chapter 2) was more about learning the structures of the language than using it for communicative purposes. In contrast, the Direct Method didn't focus on grammar teaching at all because it was thought that grammar would be learned through exposure and interaction, in much the same manner that native speakers acquire their first language.

The Communicative Language Teaching era of the 1980s and 1990s ushered in an approach to language teaching that emphasized meaning and fluency, and in some cases focus on form got lost in the shuffle. A few methods subscribed to the notion that students should pay no attention to grammar whatsoever and be allowed to "absorb" language (Krashen, 1997). Today, the goal of communicative language teaching is to help the language learner be able to communicate effectively in the real world; however, most communicative approaches recognize that grammatical competence is integral to language use, and therefore some attention to teaching grammar is advocated. Along with teaching grammar, what has been assessed as grammar has also changed over time. For example, in a Grammar Translation paradigm, tests consisted of the learners' ability to recite grammatical rules, provide an accurate translation of a text, or supply a grammatically accurate word. Today, the knowledge of grammar is evaluated by its correct use in communication through listening, speaking, reading, and writing in the second language.

In terms of assessment, "grammar is central to language description and test-taker performance" (Rimmer, 2006, p. 498), and therefore it's important to know how best to assess a learner's knowledge of grammar. To begin this discussion, we need to first understand what we mean by grammatical knowledge.

Defining Grammatical Knowledge

If you recall from Chapter 1, we discussed communicative competence (Canale & Swain, 1980) as consisting of four components: grammatical, sociolinguistic, discourse, and strategic competencies. In this model, grammatical competence was defined as knowledge of rules of phonology, lexis, syntax, and semantics, but the model did not clearly show us how these were associated. Larsen-Freeman (1991, 1997), influenced by the communicative competence model of language pedagogy, characterized grammatical knowledge to show the interrelatedness of phonology, lexis, syntax, and semantics. Her conceptualization of grammatical knowledge consisted of three interconnected elements:

1. *grammatical forms* or the structures of a language
2. the *grammatical meanings* of those forms
3. their *pragmatic meaning* or use in a given context

The elements above refer to the following: (1) Form is both morphology, or how words are formed, and syntax, how words are strung together; both morphology and syntax are concerned with the linguistic accuracy of language. (2) Grammatical meaning consists of both the literal and intended message that is conveyed by the form. It is concerned with the meaningfulness of the language used. (3) The pragmatic or implied meaning results from the appropriate language choices a learner makes in a given communicative event.

Grammatical knowledge of form, meaning, and use occurs at the sentence level and beyond the sentence or what is commonly called the discourse level. Discourse constraints include rules for cohesion (e.g., pronominal reference), information management (e.g., given/new information), and interactional knowledge (e.g., hedging devices to indicate disagreement), which identify relationships in language at the discourse level. Pragmatic meaning depends on the contextual, sociolinguistic, sociocultural, psychological, and rhetorical meanings of the given context and can occur at both the sentence and discourse level.

To assess this grammatical knowledge, we can target one or more of the features of form and meaning. Purpura's (2004, p. 91) framework, shown in Figure 11.1 on the next page, offers an excellent taxonomy of components of grammatical knowledge along with a list of possible grammar points that could be used to measure each of the points. Purpura suggested this framework be used as a guide to help define the ability or construct of grammatical knowledge, and we would add that you can use such a chart as a checklist of points to consider in your own form-focused assessment. Read Purpura's book for further explanations and a number of examples of components.

DESIGNING ASSESSMENT TASKS: SELECTED RESPONSE

With this brief summary of what grammar knowledge is, we can now more clearly examine different types of tests that can be used to measure this knowledge.

The input for selected response tasks can be language (or nonlanguage as in a gesture or picture) of any length from one word to several sentences of discourse. The test-taker is expected to select the correct response, which is meant to measure the knowledge of grammatical form and/or meaning. These responses are often scored dichotomously (0 or 1) although sometimes, depending on how the ability or construct is defined, partial credit scoring (e.g., 0, 1, or 2) may be used. Scoring is discussed in more detail in Chapter 12.

Multiple-Choice Tasks

The most common selected response task presents a blank or underlined word/words in a sentence and the test-taker must choose the correct response from options that are given. The advantages of the multiple-choice tasks are that they are easy to administer and score, and the disadvantages are that they are difficult to create, can promote guessing from test-takers, and are sometimes viewed as not being authentic language use. However, theses tasks are very popular, especially in standardized testing environments. Let's look at some examples of multiple-choice tasks for grammatical form and grammatical meaning:

Grammatical form

Carson: Did you see the movie *Titanic* last week?
Ethan: Yes, Mary loved it, and _____.
A. I loved too
B. I do
C. do did I
D. so do I

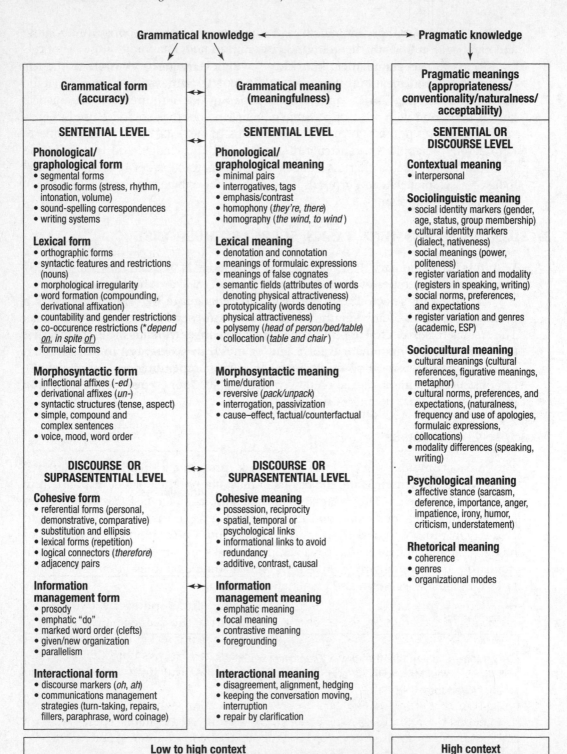

Figure 11.1. Components of grammatical and pragmatic knowledge (Purpura, 2004, p. 91)

The first part of this example provides the context for the response, but because all four responses convey the intended meaning, an understanding of the context is not essential to get the item correct. Thus the item is designed to assess only grammatical form and therefore the item would be scored either right or wrong.

Grammatical meaning

Yuko: Do you have plans for tonight?
Christina: Not really. _____
Yuko: Thanks, but I have a final paper to write.
A. How about you?
B. Need any help?
C. How about a movie?
D. Need to work?

In this example the first part asks a question about a future event. In the second part, the correct response could be any of the four options because they are all grammatically correct, but the third part of the dialogue provides the context that indicates the meaning of the correct response, which is a refusal to a suggestion. Thus the correct response is option C. Like the "grammatical form" example, the item is designed to assess only grammatical meaning and therefore would be scored either right or wrong.

Grammatical form and meaning

Jeff: Are you visiting your family this year?
Sonia: I don't know. _____; it depends on the airfares.
A. I didn't
B. I may be
C. I might
D. I had to

Here both the grammatical form and meaning of the options need to be considered for the correct response. As the second part of the dialogue indicates, there is a sense of uncertainty, and added to that is the indication that the visit is a future event. Thus the correct response is limited to one that shows both these aspects, which in this case is option C. Because both grammatical form and meaning are required, the item is scored either right or wrong.

Another multiple-choice task is error identification, where the input contains one incorrect or inappropriate grammatical feature in the item. These tasks are often used in grammar editing exercises (as illustrated in Chapter 9) and can also be used to test the knowledge of grammatical form and meaning.

Grammatical form and meaning

In America, most children <u>begin</u> to work at home, where they <u>are having</u> daily and /or
                                  A   B

weekly responsibilities such as <u>washing</u> the dishes and <u>feeding</u> the dog.
                                         C   D

In this example the item is designed to assess grammatical form, specifically the present tense form (*have*) that is needed to show habitual actions of most American children. These types of tasks are scored either right or wrong because the test-taker needs to identify only one error.

Discrimination Tasks

Discrimination tasks are another type of selected response task that ask the test-taker to attend to input that can be either language or nonlanguage and to respond in the form of a choice between or among contrasts or opposites, such as true/false, right/wrong, same/different, etc. Discrimination items are used to measure the difference between two similar areas of grammatical knowledge such as pronouns in subject and object position. In the following example, to test recognition of gender pronouns, the test-taker must be able to discriminate between two pictures, correctly choosing the picture that corresponds to the stimulus sentence. An alternative format could present one picture with two sentences, one of which correctly matches the picture.

Grammatical form and meaning

Directions: Choose the correct picture, A or B, to match the sentence below.

A   B

She delivered it to him.

Noticing Tasks or Consciousness-Raising Tasks

These tasks contain a wide range of input in the form of language or nonlanguage and are considered particularly helpful for learners. By attending consciously to form and/or meaning, learners become aware of the existence of specific language features in English (Ellis, 1997). In these types of tasks, test-takers are asked to indicate (underline or circle) that they have identified a specific feature in the language sample. In the following example, test-takers must distinguish between the two types of the modal *would*:

Grammatical meaning (Purpura, 2004, p. 134)

Directions: Circle *would* when it refers to the habitual past. Underline it when it refers to the present or future.

You know? You think you've got it bad. When I was kid a kid we would have to walk up hill to and from school every day. We would even do it when it snowed—winter or summer. And we would never even think of complaining. We would smile and go about our business. I wouldn't change those days for anything. Would you now please shut up and take out the garbage?

DESIGNING ASSESSMENT TASKS: LIMITED PRODUCTION

In limited production tasks, the input in the item is language (or nonlanguage) information. Like selected response tasks, the input could be a single sentence or a longer stretch of discourse. However, unlike selected response tasks, the test-taker's response represents only a limited amount of language production. This response can vary from a single word to a sentence depending on the grammatical ability or construct that is defined. Sometimes the range of possible correct answers for the response can be large. Scoring of these responses can be either dichotomous or partial credit. **Dichotomous scoring** means that there is only one criterion for correctness (form or meaning), and test-takers get it either right or wrong. **Partial credit scoring**, on the other hand, can be used with multiple criteria for correctness (form and meaning) and allows for adding up the scores for the item in terms of full (2), partial (1), or no credit (0). Limited responses can also be scored holistically or analytically. Among the most common limited production tasks are gap-fill, short-answer, and dialogue-completion tasks.

Gap-Filling Tasks

The language is presented in the form of a sentence, dialogue, or passage in which a number of words are deleted. The deletions are made to test one or more areas of grammatical knowledge, such as vocabulary knowledge and grammatical ability.

Test-takers must choose the appropriate response for the deletion or gap based on the context in which the language is presented. Consider the following examples:

Grammatical form

> I _____ a book right before I go to sleep. Recently, I have been reading biographies. I _____ the biographies of Charlie Chaplin and Mahatma Gandhi, and for the past few nights, I _____ about Oprah Winfrey.

In this example, the criteria for correctness are the grammatical forms (simple habitual present tense, "read"; past tense, "read"; present perfect, "have read"; and past perfect continuous tense, "have been reading").

Grammatical form and meaning

> The Mississippi River, also called the "Great River," is the longest river in the United States. The river _____ at Lake Itasca in the state of Minnesota. The river ends at the Gulf of Mexico where it _____ over half a million cubic feet of water into the gulf.

In this example, the criteria for correctness are both grammatical form and meaning in terms of simple habitual present tense verb forms and the lexical meaning of the words. So the first deleted word from the item is "originates" and thus the appropriate responses for the first deletion in addition to "originates" could be either "begins" or "starts" but not words such as "initiates" or "creates" because, although they have the same meaning as "originates," they are not meaningfully correct in the above context. Similarly, the next deleted word is "discharges," and other appropriate responses are "releases" or "expels" but not "dismisses" or "detonates" because, although they have the same lexical meaning as the original word, in the context of the sentences they are grammatically inappropriate.

Short-Answer Tasks

In some assessment tasks, the input is presented in the form of a question or questions following a reading passage or oral/visual stimulus. The expected test-taker response can vary from a single word to a sentence or two. These short answers can be scored dichotomously (right or wrong) for a single criterion for correctness or with partial credit for multiple criteria for correctness. Let's take a look at some example tasks on the next page.

Grammatical form and meaning

Directions: Read the following paragraph, then answer each question below in a sentence or two.

The Modern Olympics

The modern revival of the Olympic Games is due in a large measure to the efforts of Pierre, baron de Coubertin, of France. They were held, appropriately enough, in Athens in 1896, but that meeting and the ones that followed in Paris (1900) and St. Louis (1904) were hampered by poor organization and the absence of worldwide representation. The first successful meet was held at London in 1908; since then the games have been held in cities throughout the world. World War I prevented the Olympic meeting of 1916, and World War II the 1940 and 1944 meetings. The number of entrants, competing nations, and events has increased steadily since then. (*Columbia Electronic Encyclopedia,* 2008)

Question 1: What did Pierre, baron de Coubertin do?
Question 2: Why were the first few modern Olympic Games not successful?

Testing grammatical form and meaning

Directions: Look at the picture, then answer the question below.
Question: What is the woman doing?

In both of these examples, the test-taker must provide a response that is both grammatically correct and meaningful in terms of the question that is asked. In the first example, the response must be in the past tense and must show understanding of terms such as "poor organization" and the idea that the games lacked attendance. In the second example, the response must use the present continuous tense and must use appropriate vocabulary such as "using a computer," "surfing the Internet," or "sitting at a desk."

Dialogue-Completion Tasks

Here the input is presented in the form of a short conversation or dialogue in which a part of the exchange or the entire exchange is left blank and the expected response is meant to be grammatically correct. Like the other short-answer tasks, the criterion for correctness can be the form or form and meaning.

Testing grammatical form and meaning

Directions: Fill in the blanks in each conversation with one or more words that are grammatically correct in the context.

Conversation 1
Mayumi:　How was your trip to Los Angeles?
Karina:　It _____.
Mayumi:　I knew you would enjoy your visit! So, what did you do?
Karina:　I _____ Disneyland and Universal Studios.

Conversation 2
Server:　　What can I get you?
Customer: _____.
Server:　　That's a good choice—the pastrami sandwich is one of our most popular items.
Customer: I would also like a Coke.
Server:　　_____.
Customer: Okay, then I'll have lemonade.

In both examples, the correct response requires that the test-taker understand the information in the conversation that is provided by the other participant. Thus in the first of the two exchanges, the past tense marker "was" in "how was your trip to Los Angeles" indicates to the test-taker that the event is past and therefore the response must also be in the past tense. In addition, the test-taker must understand that the response must be positive because the next part of the dialogue indicates a pleasant trip. Likewise, in the second example, when the customer requests a certain beverage, the test-taker must provide the response of the server based on the next utterance of the customer.

DESIGNING ASSESSMENT TASKS: EXTENDED PRODUCTION

The input for extended tasks is usually presented in the form of a prompt. The input can vary in length and can be either language or nonlanguage (gesture or picture) information. The purpose of extended production is to obtain larger amounts of language from the test-taker and to allow for more creative construction; therefore these tasks are likely to elicit instances of authentic language use. On the other hand, because the responses of test-takers are usually open-ended with a number of possible correct options, these extended production tasks are often scored using rating scales. When constructing the rating scale, the test designer needs to first define the grammatical ability that will be assessed and the levels of ability, both of which must be able to be explicitly described in the scoring rubric. The following is a scoring rubric on a five-point scale for assessing the knowledge of syntax adapted from Bachman and Palmer (1996).

Table 11.1. Five-point scale for assessing syntactic knowledge (Bachman & Palmer, 1996, pp. 275–276)

Level of ability	Description
0 None	There is no evidence of knowledge of syntactic form or there is not enough information to judge the performance.
1 Limited	There is limited evidence of knowledge of syntactic form but range of use is small and the accuracy is poor.
2 Moderate	There is moderate evidence of knowledge of syntactic form; the range of use and accuracy is moderate.
3 Extensive	There is extensive evidence of knowledge of syntactic form; the range of use is large with few exceptions and the accuracy is good with few errors.
4 Complete	There is complete evidence of knowledge of syntactic form; the range of use is unlimited and the accuracy shows control.

Information Gap Tasks

This task, more commonly known as the info-gap task, presents the input in terms of incomplete information. That is, one test-taker is given half—or some—of the information and another test taker is given complementary information. Both test-takers then have to question each other to get all the information. The need for negotiation makes this type of task suitable for measuring a test-taker's grammatical knowledge to communicate functional meanings. The task can also be used to measure pragmatic knowledge because the reciprocal nature of the performance requires the language of the test-takers to display politeness, formality, appropriateness, and other conversational conventions. The following is an example of an info-gap task adapted from Purpura (2004). The task aims to measure test-takers' knowledge of question formation, other interactional form, and meaning and use such as request for clarification and repair. Each test-taker receives his or her own information along with a card with blanks for filling in information solicited from a partner.

Grammatical form, meaning, and pragmatic use

Working with a partner, ask questions to find out about the other painter. Then, using all your information, prepare a short report comparing the two famous painters.

Test-Taker A

Claude Monet

Nationality: French
Year of birth: 1840
Style of painting: Impressionist
Well-known paintings: *The Woman in the*
  Green Dress; *Water Lilies*
Year of death: 1926

Test-Taker B

Vincent van Gogh

Nationality: Dutch
Year of birth: 1853
Style of painting: Post-Impressionist
Well-known paintings: *The Starry Night*;
  Self Portrait
Year of death: 1890

In this example, Students A and B must pose questions to each other to gather information about the other painter. This requires the correct syntax of question formation such as in "What is Monet's nationality?" or "Is van Gogh Dutch?" Test-takers may also need to clarify information in the process and must use the correct form and meaning of the language for that purpose. For example, they might use modals for requests such as "Could you repeat that again please?"

Role-Play or Simulation Tasks

The input in role-play tasks present test-takers with a language or nonlanguage prompt that asks them to take on a role or simulate a situation to solve a problem, make a decision, or perform some transaction collaboratively. The expected response of a role-play or simulation task can contain a large amount of language, and therefore it can be used to measure a test-taker's knowledge of grammatical form, meaning, and pragmatic use.

An example of a problem-solving role play is given on the next page. The prompt describes an issue that needs to be resolved and suggests ways to solve the problem. The prompt also specifies three possible roles that test-takers could take on as part of the problem solving.

Grammatical form, meaning, and pragmatic use

Your state is facing a budget cut and the governor's finance committee has to decide how to allocate the limited amount of money. The mayor has called a town meeting to find out what the citizens think. You would like to see money given to an issue you support. Your job is to convince everyone to allocate money to the issue you support.

Each person must present his or her issue to the group, and then as a group you must decide which issue will be allocated money.

Member A: The streets in the old part of town need repair. It is important to restore the streets because many people who visit the city often go to the old part of town to see the historic homes. Tourism provides income.

Member B: The children's community center is going to close, which will leave many children with no place to go after school. If the place closes, parents will have to make changes in their work schedule to look after their children. In order to provide a safe place for children to meet, play, and interact, it is important we keep the children's community center open.

Member C: The local soccer team has been trying to make renovations to their soccer stadium for months. They need new seats and a new pitch if the soccer team is going to win games. In the past the soccer team was very successful and made the city very well known.

In this example, the test-takers must be able to provide responses that are grammatically correct in both form and meaning and that are appropriate for arguments and counterarguments—for example, "I think we should . . . because" or "Yes, but if we did that, we would . . ." or "I see your point, however . . ." In addition to the grammatical form and meaning, this type of task lends itself well to assessing pragmatic knowledge in terms of the role that the test-taker plays such as mayor, concerned citizen, mother, etc. Because the responses of the test-takers are extended and do not have one correct answer, they could be scored using a rating scale.

ASSESSING VOCABULARY

Words are the basic building blocks of a language; we use them to create sentences, larger paragraphs, and whole texts. As native speakers, we rapidly acquire vocabulary in childhood, and this development continues as we encounter new experiences and concepts, but for the second language learner the process is demanding, sometimes requiring a more conscious effort. Some second language learners make a studied attempt to enlarge their vocabulary, jotting down and memorizing lists of words or relying on their bilingual dictionaries to overcome the vocabulary or lexical gaps in their knowledge. For others, vocabulary acquisition seems to occur more naturally, the by-product of a knack for automatic language processing.

Language researchers and teachers recognize that vocabulary knowledge is integral to overall second language ability and are now focusing on ways to teach vocabulary and also assess the knowledge of vocabulary. To begin this discussion, let's look at what vocabulary is.

The Nature of Vocabulary

When we describe the nature of vocabulary we immediately think of "words." So what are words, and how do we define them for testing purposes? Consider the following paragraph adapted from a recent *Newsweek* magazine:

> There are big lies. And little lies. And somewhere in between there are the lies we tell our doctors. Even the most famous doctor of all, Hippocrates, knew that those pesky Greek patients might tell a fib or two. To find out if they were stretching the truth, Hippocrates measured their pulse rates.

First of all, we can identify words as tokens and types. **Tokens** are all the words in the paragraph, which in this case totals 53. **Types**, on the other hand, do not count words that are repeated, only words that are of different forms. So in the above paragraph, the word "lies" occurs three times but is counted only once. Both "doctor" and "doctors" appear, but they get counted as two types, even though they are in the same *word family*. Most vocabulary tests would not test two derivatives of the same family; otherwise one is most likely testing grammatical knowledge (e.g., "doctor" and its plural counterpart, "doctors").

Another set of categories that we need to consider when we talk about knowledge of words is the difference between **function words** and **content words**. Function words—prepositions, articles, conjunctions, and other "little" words—are seen as belonging more to the grammar of the language than vocabulary. In isolation, function words mostly show the association among content words in sentences. Content words are nouns, verbs, adjectives, and adverbs. Generally then, it's content words that we focus on in vocabulary tests.

Some vocabulary tests might focus on larger lexical items such as **phrasal verbs** ("put up with," "run into"), **compound nouns** ("personal computer," "fish tank"), or **idioms** ("a pretty penny," "against the clock," "actions speak louder than words"), which have meaning only as a whole unit.

Research (Moon, 1997; Nattinger & DeCarrico 1992; Pawley & Synder, 1983) has also identified **prefabricated language** that language users have at their disposal for communication. The prefabricated language or lexical phrases, as Nattinger and DeCarrico called them, are groups of words that seem to have a grammatical structure but operate as a single unit and have a particular function in communication. The authors identified four types of lexical phrases:

1. *Poly words* are short fixed phrases that perform a variety of functions such as qualifying, marking fluency, disagreement, etc. For example: *for the most part, so to speak,* and *wait a minute.*

2. ***Institutionalized expressions*** are longer utterances that are fixed in form such as proverbs and formulas for social interaction. For example: *pot calling the kettle black, nice to meet you, how's it going, see you later,* etc.
3. ***Phrasal constraints*** are medium-length phrases that have basic structure with one or two slots that can be filled by various words or phrases. For example: *yours truly/sincerely, as far as I know/can tell/am aware,* etc.
4. ***Sentence builders*** are phrases that provide the framework for a complete sentence with one or two slots where whole ideas can be expressed. For example: *that reminds me of X, on the other hand X,* and *not only X but also X,* etc. (Nattinger & DeCarrico, 1992, pp. 38–47).

In vocabulary testing, these larger lexical items have received less attention than single words, partly because traditional vocabulary tests have been discrete-type tests that lend themselves more easily to single-word test items. Single words are also easier to identify (from word lists and texts) as well as to score. In contrast, because larger lexical phrases can vary in grammatical form and have particular functions in spoken and written discourse, they are more open-ended, which makes them more difficult to identify and evaluate. However, larger lexical items can be used in vocabulary testing, especially when they are part of "embedded, comprehensive and context-dependent vocabulary measures" (Read, 2000, p. 24).

Defining Lexical Knowledge

So what does it mean to "know" a vocabulary item? One way to answer this question is to try to clarify everything a learner has to do to acquire a vocabulary item. Richards (1976, p. 83) outlined a series of assumptions about vocabulary ability that developed out of linguistic theory:

1. The native speaker of a language continues to expand his or her vocabulary in adulthood, whereas there is comparatively little development of syntax in adult life.
2. Knowing a word means knowing the degree of probability of encountering that word in speech or print. For many words we also "know" the sort of words most likely to be found associated with the word.
3. Knowing a word implies knowing the limitations imposed on the use of the word according to variations of function and situation.
4. Knowing a word means knowing the syntactic behavior associated with that word.
5. Knowing a word entails knowledge of the underlying form of a word and the derivations that can be made from it.
6. Knowing a word entails knowledge of the network of associations between that word and other words in language.

7. Knowing a word means knowing the semantic value of a word.
8. Knowing a word means knowing many of the different meanings associated with the word.

Nation (1990) took Richards's (1976) approach further by specifying the scope of the learner's task to include the distinction between *receptive* and *productive* vocabulary knowledge. We may be able to recognize a word when we see or hear it. But are we able to use it in our speech or writing? The production of a word requires a different (and perhaps more complex) set of abilities from those needed for reception of a word, so both modes of performance need to be taken into account in assessment.

To better understand the construct of vocabulary ability, let's go back to our discussion of communicative language testing in Chapter 1 (p. XX). Following Canale and Swain's (1980) model of communicative competence, Bachman (1990) and later Bachman and Palmer (1996) included not only language knowledge (grammatical and sociolinguistic competence) but also strategic competence, a set of "metacognitive strategies that provide language users with the ability to, or capacity to create or interpret discourse" (p. 67) as part of their model of communicative competence. Thus Bachman and Palmer's definition of language ability included both knowledge of language and the ability to put language to use in context. Other researchers (Chapelle, 1994) accounted for both the explicit knowledge of vocabulary and the ability (more implicitly) to put vocabulary knowledge to use in a given context. Three components make up Chapelle's definition of vocabulary ability:

1. the context of vocabulary use
2. vocabulary knowledge and fundamental processes
3. metacognitive strategies for vocabulary use

1. *Vocabulary in context.* Traditionally in testing, we view context as the sentence or environment in which the target word occurs. However, from a communicative language use position, context is more than just the linguistic environment in which a word occurs; it also includes different types of pragmatic knowledge. That is, the meaning of the target word has to be viewed within the social and cultural environment as well.

So when teenagers talk about a "babe" or describe an event as "da bomb," the context of the conversation should signal that the first case is not "a small baby" but rather a nice-looking girl and the second a description roughly equivalent to "awesome" or "great." Or consider Read's (2000) example of a British-American English confusion over the word "to table." In British English, the term *to table* means "to discuss now" (the issue is brought to the table), whereas in American English it means "to defer" (the issue is left on the table). In important business meetings, that difference could lead to some frustrating misunderstandings.

The context of vocabulary use may vary across generations, formal and informal language, and varieties and dialects of language as well as between non-specialized, everyday vocabulary and specialized or technical vocabulary. To understand context in a more social framework we should look at the type of activity the language user is engaged in, the social status of the participants in that activity, and finally the channel—whether written or spoken communication—in which the language will be used.

2. *Fundamental processes of vocabulary acquisition.* Another feature of vocabulary ability is the learner's knowledge of word characteristics, perceiving different forms of words, recognizing linguistic roots to decipher meaning, using context for guessing meaning, and even simply knowing the parts of speech to which words belong.

Related to vocabulary knowledge is how words or lexical items are organized in the brain of the learner and also how they gain access to their knowledge of vocabulary. Both of these are measurable. To understand lexical organization, researchers have looked at word-association or lexical network tasks, and for processes they have considered automaticity of word recognition.

3. *Metacognitive strategies.* The third component of Chapelle's (1994) definition of vocabulary ability is metacognitive strategies that all language users employ to manage communication. As Read (2000, p. 33) points out, we use a set of strategies in trying to read illegible handwriting, other strategies when we need to convey a sad message, and still others when we might be talking with a nonnative speaker of our language. Second language learners often use metacognitive strategies to overcome their lack of vocabulary knowledge when they are communicating. Most often they practice avoidance, such as using a lexical item because they don't know it or aren't sure of the correct pronunciation or grammatical form. Other times second language learners will paraphrase a word, fall back on their first language, use a superordinate term such as "musical instrument" for "trombone," or even appeal to authority when they are unsure of their knowledge of vocabulary.

These strategies are part of a learner's ability to use words, and although the strategies themselves are rarely assessed in a formal test, they figure largely into a student's level of success on a vocabulary test. At the very least, teachers can help students both to "remember" words as well as to produce them by using appropriate metacognitive strategies.

Perhaps you can now see that to "know" a word is not an easy matter to define. The prospect of assessing lexical ability becomes a little more complex than just asking students to choose a correct definition (out of maybe four or five) or to fill in a blank in a cloze test. Next, we'll take a closer look at how you can design tests to measure lexical ability.

SOME CONSIDERATIONS IN DESIGNING ASSESSMENT TASKS

You will remember that in Chapter 7, we advocate for assessing the various linguistic forms of grammar and vocabulary within the different skill areas, and therefore in general, for pedagogical purposes, integrated tests are appropriate for classroom assessment. However, as we have defined vocabulary knowledge as a separate ability in this chapter, our design of vocabulary tests, per se, will be more discrete than embedded tests that contribute to assessing a larger construct or ability than just vocabulary. Let's look at some steps you can take to design a vocabulary test.

1. *Clarify your purpose.* You are already aware that the first order of business in designing tests is to clarify the purpose of the test so that we can evaluate the results in relation to the intended use of the test. For example, a test of vocabulary can be used to assess how many high-frequency words a learner already knows before he or she begins a course of study; during the course of study a teacher can use vocabulary tests to assess learner progress or identify vocabulary that need further attention; and at the end of a course of study, the vocabulary test can provide information about the knowledge of lexical items a learner has studied.

2. *Define your construct.* Once we have clarified the intended purpose of the test we must next define the construct or the ability we're about to measure. The construct definition of vocabulary knowledge can be either syllabus-based or theory-based. For many of us as teachers, the syllabus-based approach to defining the construct is more appropriate because "the lexical items and the vocabulary skills to be assessed can be specified in relation to the learning objectives of the course" (Read, 2000, p. 153). The theory-based construct definition is applicable for research and for assessing vocabulary proficiency. So, for example, the previous discussion on Chapelle's (1994) model of vocabulary ability is one framework that can be used to define the construct a vocabulary test.

3. *Select your target words.* Next, in designing a vocabulary test it's important to consider the selection of target words. Consider the following categories for making your choices. Nation (1990) suggested that teaching and testing of vocabulary should be based on these **high-frequency words** (more often occurring) because these words are the basis for all proficient language users. Thus high-frequency words are generally the most useful in assessing the vocabulary ability of a learner. **Low-frequency words** (less often occurring) are much less valuable, and often learners pick them up based on how widely they read, their personal interests, their educational background, the society they live in, and the communication they engage in. In the case of low-frequency words, researchers focus more on how learners effectively use strategies to cope with these lexical items when they come across them in language use. Another category is **specialized vocabulary** (e.g., *membrane, molecule, cytoplasm* from biology), which figures more prominently in content-area instruction, and the assessment of these lexical items are more often found in subject-matter tests than in general language tests. The last category is **subtechnical words** (e.g., *cell, energy, structure*), which occur across registers or subject areas and thus can be used to assess different meanings and definitions. Academic word lists often contain subtechnical vocabulary.

4. *Determine mode of performance.* In designing vocabulary tests we must keep in mind two important features—*receptive* and *productive* vocabulary, a distinction presented earlier in our discussion of defining vocabulary ability. To have a better understanding of testing receptive and productive vocabulary, we need to clarify these terms further. We can receive and produce vocabulary in two ways. One is recognition or comprehension, whereby a learners are presented with a word and asked to show they know the meaning of that word. The following is a classic example of recognition:

Vocabulary recognition

Deviate means
A. to trick.
B. to hate.
C. to move away.
D. to go along.

The second mode of performance is recall and use, where the learner is not presented with the word but is provided with some sort of stimulus that is meant to draw out the target lexical item from the learner's memory; the learner is then asked to produce that word. The next test item of filling in the blank is an example of recall (plus production):

Vocabulary recall

That restaurant is so popular that you have to make a _____ if you want to eat there.

Once these four steps have been taken, you are then ready for the actual design of vocabulary items.

DESIGNING ASSESSMENT TASKS: RECEPTIVE VOCABULARY

Teachers often design vocabulary tests both to assess progress in vocabulary learning and to give learners feedback and encouragement to continue studying vocabulary. With classroom tests, practicality can be a significant concern, especially ease of construction and scoring. Thus many vocabulary tests are limited to single sentences. Let's begin by looking at vocabulary in the context of a single sentence.

First of all it is important to consider what role the context plays in the test item. One function of the context is to indicate a specific meaning of a high-frequency word. Second, the learner must be able to recognize the word based on the given context. Read (2000, p. 163) illustrates in the following item:

Vocabulary in a one-sentence context: High-frequency word

My grandfather is a very <u>independent</u> person.
A. never willing to give help
B. hard-working
C. not relying on other people
D. good at repairing things

In this example, the test-taker must be able to show understanding of the underlined adjective in the sentence. The options are all attributes of a person, and thus knowledge of the meaning of the word itself is needed to get the item correct.

In the case of low-frequency words, even a limited context can provide information that will enable the test-taker to recognize and infer the meaning of the lexical item. Items need to contain some amount of contextual information for the test-taker to get the item correct, as in the following:

Vocabulary in a one-sentence context: Low-frequency word

The <u>hazardous</u> road conditions were the cause of many fatal accidents over the weekend.
A. difficult
B. problematic
C. dangerous
D. complicated

Although all the above responses could be substituted for the underlined word, the information about the accidents being fatal implies the more serious state of being "dangerous."

Another type of receptive vocabulary assessment task is the well-known and widely used matching exercise. This type of recognition task requires test-takers to match the target word with its meaning or definition. Look at the example on the next page adapted from Read (2000, p. 172):

Vocabulary matching exercise

Find the meaning of following words. Write the corresponding number in the blank.

	1. to impose and collect by force
apathy _____	2. to be an agent of change
dearth _____	3. grain or seed
catalyst _____	4. a short time
kernel _____	5. to be insensitive to emotion or passionate feeling
plethora _____	6. excessively large quantity; overabundance
	7. lack, scarcity
	8. the act or process of change

In addition to assessing progress and giving feedback, teachers can also give vocabulary tests for proficiency purposes. In this case the most common approach is to investigate a learner's vocabulary size. One frequently used test to assess a learner's vocabulary size is word association. The procedure involves presenting the target word as a stimulus to test-takers and asking them to say the first word that comes to their mind. In recent years this methodology has seldom been used for second language learners because researchers (Meara, 1983, 1984; Read, 2000) found that second language learners produced varying word associations that were not helpful in determining their vocabulary size. So instead, the test method was changed from asking test-takers to supply the word to asking them to select a word. Here is an example taken from Read (2000, p. 181):

Word association

Edit

mathematics	film	pole	publishing
revise	risk	surface	text

Team

alternative	chalk	ear	group
orbit	scientists	sports	together

In both cases the test-taker is expected to choose the word that is closely associated with the target word. In the first example, although the word *edit* can collocate with words such as "film" or "text," the meaning of *edit* is revise. Likewise, the word *team* can be used as in a team of scientists or a sports team, but the meaning of "team" is found in the word *group.*

DESIGNING ASSESSMENT TASKS: PRODUCTIVE VOCABULARY

In the same way that context plays an important role in receptive vocabulary tasks, productive tasks, which involve recall and use, are also better performed within a context or situation. A common vocabulary test type is sentence completion, where the target vocabulary item is deleted from a sentence and the test-taker must understand the context in which the word occurs in order to produce the missing word. This methodology involves recall in that the test-taker must provide a lexical item from memory. Here are some examples:

Fill-in-the-blank

Write one word for each blank.

A swimmer kicks with his legs to _____ his body through the water.

That restaurant is so popular that you have to make a _____ or you'll be waiting two hours to get a table!

I needed some medicine, so my doctor wrote me a _____.

The recent rains have caused rivers to overflow and _____ many areas.

In the last item above, the information provided in the sentence context helps the test-taker to understand that the water in the river has spread beyond its banks, which then means "flood."

Going beyond a single sentence, longer passages provide opportunities to assess other aspects of vocabulary knowledge. Thus in addition to word meaning, the form and use of a lexical item can be assessed. The selective deletion cloze or gap-fill test is one type of test that draws on these aspects of word knowledge. For example:

Selective deletion cloze

The Montessori method of education, used worldwide today, was developed by Dr. Maria Montessori. She was the first woman in Italy to receive a medical degree, but found it difficult to practice _____ because Italians at that time were not ready to accept _____ doctors. So she turned to education, working with children who had been _____ away in mental _____ because they were considered _____ to learn. Through _____ thoughtful observations, and through her experience with these _____, she developed a _____ of educating them that was so _____ that they were able to pass reading and writing _____ designed for _____ children.

Here is the original text:

The Montessori method of education, used worldwide today, was developed by Dr. Maria Montessori. She was the first woman in Italy to receive a medical degree, but found it difficult to practice <u>medicine</u> because Italians at that time were not ready to accept <u>female</u> doctors. So she turned to education, working with children who had been <u>locked</u> away in mental <u>institutions</u> because they were considered <u>unable</u> to learn. Through <u>her</u> thoughtful observations, and through her experience with these <u>children</u>, she developed a <u>method</u> of educating them that was so <u>successful</u> that they were able to pass reading and writing <u>examinations</u> designed for <u>normal</u> children.

In this selective-deletion cloze or gap-fill test, the test-taker must be able to identify not only the meaning but also the form of the lexical item that is needed to fill in the blank. For example, for the deletions "working with children who had been _____ away in mental _____," the first deletion indicates that the vocabulary item required for the blank is a verb and that the form of that verb is the past participle form. For the next deletion, the word needs to be a noun and the noun needs to be plural. In addition to meaning and form, the pragmatic meaning of vocabulary items can also be assessed. Thus vocabulary choice can be dependent on the style and register of the language used. For example, for the following deletion, "and through her experience with these _____," the vocabulary item is a plural form noun, so both "kids" and "children" are suitable words, but the formality of the language found in the rest of the passage (because it is a written text) indicates that "children" rather than "kids" would be the better choice of a lexical item. If this were a spoken text then perhaps both "kids" and "children" would be equally acceptable.

It was noted at the beginning of this chapter that assessing grammar and vocabulary needs to be carefully understood in classroom contexts, especially within communicative methodology. In both teaching and assessment, focus on form has an important role to play in helping students "zoom in" on the bits and pieces of the language they are learning. Of course, these zoom lenses should not be overly utilized at the expense of appropriate, authentic wide-angle views of language as a tool for communicating meaning in the real world. So this chapter is best seen in the perspective of providing you with a further set of tools for assessment, those designed to examine the building blocks of language, which complement the tools that you use for assessing any or all of the four skills.

EXERCISES

[Note: (**I**) Individual work; (**G**) Group or pair work; (**C**) Whole-class discussion.]

1. (**C**) Look at Purpura's (2004) framework on page 296 that identifies components of grammatical knowledge and the list of possible grammar points that could be measured. As a class, brainstorm other grammar points that could be added to Purpura's taxonomy and list them on the board.

2. (**G**) Among the new grammar points added in item 1 above, assign one or two to a group, with different points for each group. In the group, design two or three items and show which type of task they belong to (selected, limited, or extended production) by describing the input and the scoring. Report back to the rest of the class.

3. (**G**) Divide the three types of tasks (selected, limited, and extended production) among groups or pairs, one type for each. Look at the sample assessment techniques provided and evaluate them according to the five principles (practicality, reliability, validity, authenticity, and washback). Present your critique to the rest of the class.

4. (**I/C**) After reading the introduction to the section on vocabulary, how would you define *vocabulary* for testing purposes? Share your answers with the class.

5. (**G**) Look at Richards's (1976) list on pages 307–308. In groups, each assigned to one of the items 3 through 8, brainstorm some examples or illustrations of each point. Then draft a test item or two that would take your assigned point into consideration. Share your results with the class.

6. (**G**) Consider the following learning scenarios:

    a vocational ESL class in Australia
    an elementary EFL class in Japan
    a test preparation (such as the TOEFL® or IELTS® Tests) school in China
    a college level ESL class (for biology majors) in the United States
    a high school EFL class in Brazil

    Divide the above scenarios among groups or pairs and identify the considerations you must take in designing a vocabulary test for that learning scenario. Consider purpose, objectives, and specifications in your discussion. Present a synopsis of your discussion to the class.

7. (**G**) Divide the receptive and productive assessment tasks (both recall and use) among groups or pairs, one type for each. Look at the sample assessment techniques provided and evaluate them according to the five principles (practicality, reliability, validity, authenticity, and washback). Present your critique to the rest of the class.

8. (**C**) Discuss when and how (context, purpose, objectives) you would assess grammar and vocabulary separately and when you would do so as part of any or all of the four skills.

FOR YOUR FURTHER READING

Pupura, James. E. (2004). *Assessing grammar*. Cambridge: Cambridge University Press.

One of several volumes in the series on language assessment by Cambridge University Press, this book provides a storehouse of information on form-focused assessment. From more theoretical research perspectives on defining grammatical ability and research on the role of grammar in communicative classrooms to practical steps toward designing tests and test tasks, Purpura helps readers to develop a backdrop for understanding form-focused assessment and confidently design their own tests.

Read, John. (2000). *Assessing vocabulary*. Cambridge: Cambridge University Press.

In the same series, this volume carefully examines the place of vocabulary in language assessment, the nature of vocabulary, and research on vocabulary assessment. Then Read provides steps for designing vocabulary tests, followed by some comments on future challenges in vocabulary assessment.

CHAPTER 12

GRADING AND

STUDENT EVALUATION

OBJECTIVES: After reading this chapter, you will be able to

- state a philosophy of grading that is contextualized to your institution and context
- communicate to students grading criteria that are both clear and an appropriate fit in your institutional context
- calculate grades based on a reliable system of scoring that is consistent with your institutional context and personal philosophy

- resolve in your context any cross-cultural dilemmas that might otherwise cause a mismatch between a teacher's and students' understanding of the meaning of a grade
- employ various alternatives to letter grading that will empower students and help them to use the feedback for further development

Grades must be the most-talked-about topic in anyone's school years.

"How'd you do, Jennifer?"
"Oh, pretty good. Got an A minus."
"Awesome! I did okay. Got a B."

"Ready for the test tomorrow?"
"No, gotta pull an all-nighter, I think."
"Oh, yeah, how've you been doing in the course?"
"Barely squeaking by with a C. You?"
"Not bad. Somewhere in the B range."

"Did you hear about Christina? Professor Kind gave her an A!"
"You're kidding. Christina? She was never in class."
"Yeah, maybe that winning smile helped some."

"Mr. Smart, I see that your overall GPA is a 4.3 out of 4."
"Well, uh, yes sir, I took quite a few advanced placement courses."
"Splendid work, Mr. Smart. Outstanding."
"Oh, thank you, Dr. Dean, thank you."
"Yes, we certainly would welcome you into the College of Hard Knocks!"

Isn't it ironic that untold hours of reading, listening to lectures, notetaking, writing papers, doing assignments, and going to classes are invariably reduced to one of five letters of the alphabet? And after all that grueling labor, the only thing that seems to really matter is that the letter goes onto a transcript? Even more mysterious is that those tiny little letters actually mean something: A person's whole sense of academic self-esteem is summed up and contained in one alphabetic symbol: A—"Wow, I'm awesome!"; C—"Ouch, not so good, I messed up big time"; F—"Oh, no, a complete, utter disaster; I'm done for."

If our lives are too often controlled by tests, as mentioned in the opening lines of this book, then our educational lives are certainly governed by the grades that are greatly determined by those tests. Educational systems define honors students, marginal students, college-bound students, exceptional students (on either end of the scale), failing students, and average students not so much by the quality of their performance(s) and not necessarily by demonstrated skills that have been observed but rather by grades.

Perhaps even more ironic is that the standards for assigning grades are extraordinarily variable across teachers, subject matter, courses, programs, institutions, school systems, and even cultures. Every institution from high school on up has its "easy" teachers and "tough" teachers who differ in their grading standards. Sometimes mathematics and science courses gain the reputation for being strict in assigning grades because one incorrect part of a complicated problem means a failing grade. Certain institutions are "known" by transcript evaluators to be stingy with high grades, and therefore a B in those places is equivalent to an A in others. American grading systems are demonstrably different from some systems in Europe and Asia; a course grade of 85 percent may be considered noteworthy in some countries, whereas in the United States the same percentage score is a B or possibly a B−.

Books and manuals on language assessment generally omit the topic of grading and student evaluation, and possibly for good reason. Focusing on the evaluation of a plethora of different separate assessment procedures may be sufficient for a course in language testing and assessment, without the complexity of tackling the summing up of all those assessments. On the other hand, every new teacher we know has questions about grading, and every experienced teacher has opinions, and therefore a book about language assessment would not be complete without discussing a few principles and practices of grading.

This chapter addresses topics such as these: What should grades reflect? How should different objectives, tasks, and components of a course figure into a formula for calculating grades? How do cultural and institutional philosophies dictate standards for grading? How can a teacher achieve reliability in grading students? What are some alternatives to letter grades? From this discussion, we can derive some generalizations about the nature of grading, some principles of grading, and some specific guidelines to follow in assigning grades.

THE PHILOSOPHY OF GRADING: WHAT SHOULD GRADES REFLECT?

You are teaching a course in English in a context of your choice (choose a country, institutional situation, course content, and proficiency level). You have been given a questionnaire to fill out. Complete the questionnaire now, before reading on.

Grading questionnaire

Directions: Look at the items below and circle the letters for all items that should be considered (however greatly or minimally) in a set of criteria for determining a final grade in a course.

_____ a. language performance of the student as formally demonstrated on tests, quizzes, and other explicitly scored procedures

_____ b. your intuitive, informal observation of the student's language performance

_____ c. oral participation in class

_____ d. improvement (over the entire course period)

_____ e. behavior in class ("deportment")—being cooperative, polite, disruptive, etc.

_____ f. effort

_____ g. motivation

_____ h. punctuality and attendance

Now look back at the items you circled. In the blank next to each, write a percentage that represents the weight that you would assign the item. Make sure your total percentages add up to 100. If they don't, adjust them until they do.

By completing this exercise, you have made a quick, intuitive allocation of factors that you think should be included in deciding the final grade for a course. In the second part of the exercise, you established a weighting system for each factor. You have essentially begun to articulate a philosophy of grading—at least for this (possibly hypothetical) course.

In a recent administration of this questionnaire to teachers at the American Language Institute at San Francisco State University, the item on which the teachers had the most agreement was item (a), which received percentage allocations from 50 percent to 75 percent. It is safe to assert that formal tests, quizzes, exercises, homework, essays, reports, presentations—all of which are usually marked in some way (with a grade, a "check" system [such as $\sqrt{+}$, $\sqrt{}$, or $\sqrt{-}$], a score, or a credit/no credit notation)—are universally accepted as primary criteria for determining grades. These tasks and assignments represent observable performance and can be conveniently recorded in a teacher's record book.

Items (b) and (c) also drew relatively strong support, but a word of caution is in order here. If intuitive, informal observations by the teacher figure into the final grade, it is very important to inform the students in advance how those observations and impressions will be recorded throughout the semester. Likewise, if oral participation is listed as one of the objectives of a course and as a factor in a final grade, the challenge to all teachers is to quantify that participation as clearly and directly as possible. Leaving either of these factors to a potentially whimsical or impressionistic evaluation at the end of the course not only risks unnecessary unreliability but leaves the student at the mercy of the teacher. Failure to decide *how* informal assessments and observations will be summed up risks confusing a student's "nice" cooperative behavior with actual performance.

On items (d) through (h) there was some disagreement and considerable discussion after the exercise, but all those items received at least a few votes for inclusion. How can those factors be systematically incorporated into a final grade? Some educational assessment experts state definitively that none of these items should ever be a factor in grading. Norman Gronlund (Gronlund & Waugh, 2008), a widely respected educational assessment specialist, gave the following advice:

> Base grades on student achievement, and achievement only. Grades should represent the extent to which the intended learning outcomes were achieved by students. They should *not* be contaminated by student effort, tardiness, misbehavior, and other extraneous factors. . . . If they are permitted to become part of the grade, the meaning of the grade as an indicator of achievement is lost. (p. 205)

Earlier in the same chapter, the authors specifically discouraged the inclusion of improvement in final grades, as it "distorts" the meaning of grades as indicators of achievement.

Perhaps their point is well worth considering as a strongly empirical philosophy of grading. However, before you rush to agree, examine points of view that consider other factors in assessing and grading. (Grove, 1998; Marzano, 2006; Power, 1998; Progosh, 1998; Smith, 2003). How many teachers do you know who are consistently impeccable in their objectivity as graders in the classroom?

To look at this issue in a broader perspective, think about some of the characteristics of assessment that have been discussed in this book. The importance of **triangulation** (multiple measures), for one, tells us that all abilities of a student may not be apparent on achievement tests and measured performances. One of the arguments for considering alternatives in assessment is that we may not be able to capture the totality of students' competence through formal tests; other observations are also significant indicators of ability. Nor should we discount most teachers' intuition, which enables them to form impressions of students that cannot easily be verified empirically. These arguments tell us that improvement, behavior, effort, motivation, and attendance might justifiably belong to a set of components that add up to a final grade.

Guidelines for Selecting Grading Criteria

If you are willing to include some nonachievement factors in your grading scheme, how do you incorporate them, along with the other more measurable factors? Consider the following guidelines.

1. It is essential for all components of grading to be consistent with an institutional philosophy and/or regulations (see pages 328–332 for a further discussion of this topic). Some institutions, for example, mandate deductions for unexcused absences. Others require that only the final exam determines a course grade. Still other institutions may implicitly dictate a relatively high number of As and Bs for each class of students. Embedded in institutional philosophies are the implicit expectations that students place on a school or program, and your attention to those impressions is warranted.

2. All of the components of a final grade need to be explicitly stated in writing to students at the beginning of a term of study, with a designation of percentages or weighting figures for each component.

3. If your grading system includes items (d) through (g) in the questionnaire on the previous page (improvement, behavior, effort, motivation), it is important for you to recognize their subjectivity, but this does not give you an excuse to avoid converting such factors into observable and measurable results. Challenge yourself to create checklists, charts, and note-taking systems that allow you to convey to the student the basis for your conclusions. It is further advisable to guard against final-week impressionistic, summative decisions by giving ongoing periodic feedback to students on such matters through written comments or conferences. By nipping potential problems in the bud, you may help students to change their attitudes and strategies early in the term.

4. Finally, consider allocating relatively small weights to items (c) through (h) so that a grade primarily reflects achievement. A designation of 5 percent to 10 percent of a grade to such factors will not mask strong achievement in a course. On the other hand, a small percentage allocated to these "fuzzy" areas can make a significant difference in a student's final course grade. For example, suppose you have a well-behaved, seemingly motivated and effort-giving student whose quantifiable scores put him or her at the top of the range of B grades. By allocating a small percentage of a grade to behavior, motivation, or effort (and by measuring those factors as empirically as possible), you can justifiably give this student a final grade of A−. Likewise, a reversal of this scenario may lead to a somewhat lower final grade.

Methods for Calculating Grades

I will never forget a university course I took in educational psychology for a teaching credential. There were regular biweekly multiple-choice quizzes, all of which were included in the final grade for the course. I studied hard for each test and consistently received percentage scores in the 90 to 95 range. I couldn't understand in the first few weeks of the course (a) why my scores warranted grades in the C range (I thought that scores in the low to mid-90s should have rated at least a B+, if not an A−) and (b) why students who were, in my opinion, not especially gifted were getting better grades.

In another course, Introduction to Sociology, there was no test, paper, or graded exercise until a midterm essay-style examination. The professor told the class nothing about the grading or scoring system, and we simply did the best we could. When the exams came back, I noted with horror that my score was a 47 out of 100. No grade accompanied this result, and I was convinced I had failed. After the professor handed back the tests, amid the audible gasps of others like me, he announced "good news": no one received an F! He then wrote on the blackboard his grading system for this 100-point test:

A   51 and above
B   42–50
C   30–41
D   29 and below

The anguished groans of students became sighs of relief.

These true stories illustrate a common philosophy in the calculation of grades. In both cases, the professors adjusted grades to fit the distribution of students across a continuum, and both, ironically, were using a form of relative grading (see below) based solely on the percentile ranking of students' scores:

A   Quartile 1 (the top 25 percent of scores)
B   Quartile 2 (the next 25 percent)
C   Quartile 3 (the next 25 percent)
D   Quartile 4 (the lowest 25 percent)

In the educational psychology course, many students got exceptionally high scores, and in the sociology course, almost everyone performed poorly according to an absolute scale. I later discovered, much to my chagrin, that in the ed psych course, more than half the class had access to quizzes from previous semesters, and the professor had simply administered the same series of quizzes! The sociology professor had a reputation for being "tough" and apparently demonstrated toughness by giving test questions that offered little chance of a student answering more than 50 percent correctly.

Among other lessons in the two stories is the importance of specifying your approach to grading. If you prespecify standards of performance on a numerical point system, you are using **absolute grading**. For example, having established points for a midterm test, points for a final exam, and points accumulated for the semester, you might adhere to the specifications in Table 12.1 on the next page.

There is no magic about specifying letter grades in differentials of 10 percentage points (such as some of those shown in Table 12.1). Many absolute grading systems follow such a model, but variations occur that range from establishing an A as 95 percent and above, all the way down to 85 percent and above. The decision is usually an institutional one.

The key to making an absolute grading system work is to be painstakingly clear on competencies and objectives and on tests, tasks, and other assessment techniques that will figure into the formula for assigning a grade. If you are unclear and haphazard in your definition of criteria for grading, the grades that are ultimately assigned are relatively meaningless.

Table 12.1. Absolute grading scale

	Midterm (50 points)	**Final Exam (100 points)**	**Other Performance (50 points)**	**Total No. of Points (200)**
A	45–50	90–100	45–50	180–200
B	40–44	80–89	40–44	160–179
C	35–39	70–79	35–39	140–159
D	30–34	60–69	30–34	120–139
F	below 30	below 60	below 30	below 120

Relative grading is more commonly used than absolute grading. It has the advantage of allowing your own interpretation and of adjusting for unpredicted ease or difficulty of a test. Relative grading is usually accomplished by ranking students in order of performance (percentile ranks) and assigning cut-off points for grades. An older, relatively uncommon method of relative grading is what has been called grading "on the curve," a term that comes from the normal bell curve of normative data plotted on a graph. Theoretically, in such a case one would simulate a normal distribution to assign grades such as the following: A = the top 10 percent; B = the next 20 percent; C = the middle 40 percent; D = the next 20 percent; F = the lowest 10 percent. In reality, virtually no one adheres to such an interpretation because it is too restrictive and usually does not appropriately interpret achievement test results in classrooms.

An alternative to conforming to a normal curve is to preselect percentiles according to an institutional expectation, as in the hypothetical distributions in Table 12.2 on the next page. In Institution X, the expectation is a curve that is slightly skewed to the right (higher frequencies in the upper levels), compared to a normal bell curve. The expectation in Institution Y is for virtually no one to fail a course and for a large majority of students to achieve As and Bs; here the skewness is more marked. The third institution may represent the expectations of a university postgraduate program where a C is considered a failing grade, a B is acceptable but indicates adequate work only, and an A is the expected target for most students.

Preselecting grade distributions, even in the case of relative grading, is still arbitrary and may not reflect what grades are supposed to "mean" in their appraisal of

Table 12.2. Hypothetical rank-order grade distributions

	Percentage of Students		
	Institution X	**Institution Y**	**Institution Z**
A	~15%	~30%	~60%
B	~30%	~40%	~30%
C	~40%	~20%	~10%
D	~10%	~ 9%	
F	~ 5%	~ 1%	

performance. A much more common method of calculating grades is what might be called *a posteriori* relative grading, in which a teacher exercises the latitude to determine grade distributions after the performances have been observed. Suppose you have devised a midterm test for your English class and you have adhered to objectives, created a variety of tasks, and specified criteria for evaluating responses. But when your students turn in their work, you find that they performed well below your expectations, with scores (on a 100-point basis) ranging from a high of 85 all the way down to a low of 44. Would you do what my sociology professor did and establish four quartiles and simply assign grades accordingly? That would be one solution to adjusting for difficulty, but another solution would be to adjust those percentile divisions to account for one or more of the following:

a. your own philosophical objection to awarding an A to a grade that is perhaps as low as 85 out of 100
b. your well-supported intuition that students really did not take seriously their mandate to prepare well for the test
c. your wish to include, after the fact, some evidence of great effort on the part of some students in the lower rank orders
d. your suspicion that you created a test that was too difficult for your students

One possible solution would be to assign grades to your 25 students as follows:

A	80–85	(3 students)
B	70–79	(7 students)
C	60–69	(10 students)
D	50–59	(4 students)
F	below 50	(1 student)

Such a distribution might confirm your appraisal that the test was too difficult and also that a number of students could have prepared themselves more adequately, therefore justifying the Cs, Ds, and F for the lower 15 students. The distribution is also faithful to the observed performance of the students and does not add unsubstantiated "hunches" into the equation.

Is there room in a grading system for a teacher's intuition, for your "hunch" that the student should get a higher or lower grade than is indicated by performance? Should teachers "massage" grades to conform to their appraisal of students beyond the measured performance assessments that have been stipulated as grading criteria? The answer is no, even though you may be tempted to embrace your intuition, and even though many of us succumb to such practice. We should strive in all of our grading practices to be explicit in our criteria and not yield to the temptation to "bend" grades one way or another. With so many alternatives to traditional assessments now available to us, we are capable of designating numerous observed performances as criteria for grades. In so doing we can strive to ensure that a final grade fully captures a summative evaluation of a student.

Teachers' Perceptions of Appropriate Grade Distributions

Most teachers bring to a test or a course evaluation an interpretation of estimated appropriate distributions, follow that interpretation, and make minor adjustments to compensate for such matters as unexpected difficulty. This prevailing attitude toward a relative grading system is well accepted and uncontroversial. What is surprising, however, is that teachers' preconceived notions of their own standards for grading often do not match their actual practice. Let me illustrate.

In a workshop with English teachers at the American Language Institute (ALI) at San Francisco State University, I (HDB) asked them to define a "great bunch" of students—a class that was exceptionally good—and to define another class of "poor performers"—a group of students who were quite unremarkable. Here was the way the task was assigned:

Grading distribution questionnaire

You have 20 students in your ALI class. You've done what you consider to be a competent job of teaching, and your class is what you would academically call a "great bunch of students." What would be an estimated number of students in each final grade category to reflect this overall impression of your students? Indicate such a distribution in the column on the left. Then do the same for what you would describe as a "poorly performing students" in a class in which you've done equally competent teaching. Indicate your distribution of the "poor performers" in the column on the right.

		"Great bunch"		"Poor performers"	
Number of	As	_____	As	_____	
	Bs	_____	Bs	_____	
	Cs	_____	Cs	_____	
	Ds	_____	Ds	_____	
	Fs	_____ (total no. = 20)	Fs	_____ (total no. = 20)	

When the responses were tabulated, the distribution for the two groups was as indicated in Figure 12.1. The workshop participants were not surprised to see the distribution of the "great bunch" but were quite astonished to discover that the "poor performers" actually conformed to a normal bell curve. Their conception of a disappointing group of students certainly did not look that bad on a graph. But their raised eyebrows turned to further surprise when the next graph was displayed, a distribution of the previous term's grades across the 420 grades assigned to students in all the courses of the ALI (see Figure 12.2 on the next page). The distribution was a virtual carbon copy of what they had just defined as a sterling group of students. They all agreed that the previous semester's students had not shown unusual excellence in their performance; in fact, a calculation of several prior semesters yielded similar distributions.

Two conclusions were drawn from this insight. First, teachers may hypothetically subscribe to a preselected set of expectations but in practice may not conform to those expectations. Second, teachers all agreed they were guilty of **grade inflation** at the ALI; their good nature and empathy for students predisposed them toward assigning grades that were higher than ALI standards and expectations. Over the course of a number of semesters, the implicit expected distribution of grades had soared to 62 percent of students receiving As and 27 percent Bs. It was then agreed that ALI students, who would be attending universities in the United States,

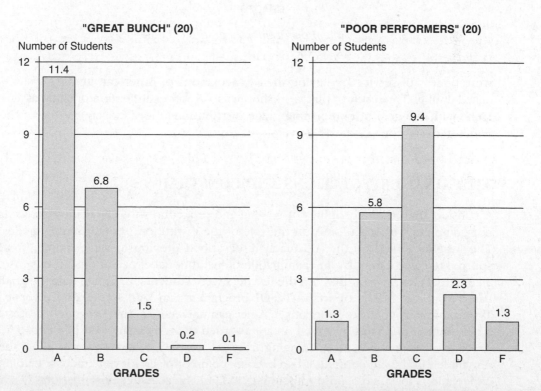

Figure 12.1. Projected distribution of grades for a "great bunch" and "poor performers"

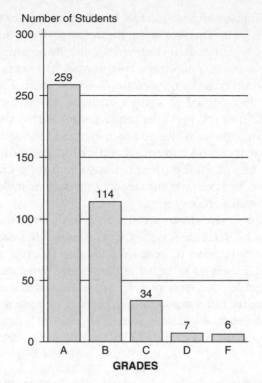

Figure 12.2. Actual distribution of grades, ALI, fall 1999

were done a disservice by having their expectations of American grading systems raised unduly. The result of that workshop was a closer examination of grade assignment with the goal of conforming grade distributions more closely to that of the undergraduate courses in the university at large.

INSTITUTIONAL EXPECTATIONS AND CONSTRAINTS

A consideration of philosophies of grading and procedures for calculating grades is not complete without a focus on the role of the institution in determining grades. The insights gained by the ALI teachers described previously, for example, were spurred to some extent by an examination of institutional expectations. In this case, an external factor was at play: All the teachers were students in, or had recently graduated from, the master of arts in TESOL program at San Francisco State University. Typical of many graduate programs in American universities, this program manifests a distribution of grades in which As are awarded to an estimated 60 percent to 70 percent of students, with Bs (ranging from B+ to B−) going to almost all of the remainder. In the ALI context, it had become commonplace for the graduate grading expectations to "rub off" onto ALI courses in ESL. The statistics bore that out.

Transcript evaluators at colleges and universities are faced with variation across institutions on what is deemed to be the threshold level for entry from a high school or another university. For many institutions around the world, the concept of letter grades is foreign. Point systems (usually 100 points or percentages) are more common globally than the letter grades used almost universally in the United States. Either way, we are bound by an established, accepted system. We have become accustomed in the United States to calculating grade point averages (GPAs) for defining admissibility: A = 4, B = 3, C = 2, D = 1. (Note: Some institutions use a five-point system and others use a nine-point system.) A student will be accepted or denied admission on the basis of an established criterion, often ranging from 2.5 to 3.5, which usually translates into the philosophy that a B student is admitted to a college or university.

Some institutions refuse to employ either a letter grade or a numerical system of evaluation and instead offer **narrative evaluations** of students (see the discussion on this topic on pages 334–335). This preference for more individualized evaluations is often a reaction to the overgeneralization of letter and numerical grading.

Being cognizant of an institutional philosophy of grading is an important step toward a consistent and fair evaluation of your students. If you are a new teacher in your institution, try to determine what its grading philosophy is. Sometimes it is not explicit; the assumption is simply made that teachers will grade students using a system that conforms to an unwritten philosophy. This has potentially harmful washback for students. A teacher in an organization who applies a markedly "tougher" grading policy than other teachers is likely to be viewed by students as being out of touch with the rest of the faculty. The result could be avoidance of the class and even mistrust on the part of students. Conversely, an "easy" teacher may become a favorite or popular teacher not because of what students learn but because students know they will get a good grade.

Cross-Cultural Factors and the Question of Difficulty

Of further interest, especially to those in the profession of English language teaching, is the question of cultural expectations in grading. Every learner of English comes from a native culture that may have implicit philosophies of grading at wide variance with those of an English-speaking culture. Granted, most English-learners worldwide are learning English within their own culture (say, learning English in Korea), but even in these cases it is important for teachers to understand the context in which they are teaching. A number of variables bear on the issue. In some cultures,

- it is unheard of to ask a student to self-assess performance.
- the teacher assigns a grade, and no one questions the teacher's criteria.
- the measure of a good teacher is one who can design a test that is so difficult that no student can achieve a perfect score. The fact that students fall short of such marks of perfection is a demonstration of the teacher's superior knowledge.

(continued)

- as a corollary, grades of A are reserved for a highly select few, and students are delighted with Bs.
- one single final examination is the accepted determinant of a student's entire course grade.
- the notion of a teacher's preparing students to do their best on a test is an educational contradiction.

As you bear in mind these and other cross-cultural constraints on philosophies of grading and evaluation, it is important to construct your own philosophy. This is an extra-sensitive issue for teachers from English-speaking countries (and educational systems) who take teaching positions in other countries. In such a case, you are a guest in that country, and it behooves you to tread lightly in your zeal for overturning centuries of educational tradition. You can be an agent for change, but do so tactfully and sensitively or you may find yourself on the first flight home!

Philosophies of grading, along with attendant cross-cultural variation, also must speak to the issue of gauging difficulty in tests and other graded measures. As noted above, in some cultures a "hard" test is a good test, but in others, a good test results in a distribution such as the one in the bar graph for a "great bunch" (Figure 12.1): a large proportion of As and Bs, a few Cs, and maybe a D or an F for very poor performers in the class. How do you gauge such difficulty as you design a classroom test that has not had the luxury of piloting and pre-testing? The answer is complex. It is usually a combination of a number of possible factors:

- experience as a teacher (with appropriate intuition)
- adeptness at designing feasible tasks
- special care in framing items that are clear and relevant
- mirroring in-class tasks that students have mastered
- variation of tasks on the test itself
- reference to prior tests in the same course
- a thorough review and preparation for the test
- knowledge of your students' collective abilities
- a little bit of luck

After mustering a number of the above contributors to a test that conforms to a predicted difficulty level, it is your task to determine, within your context, an expected distribution of scores or grades and to pitch the test toward that expectation. You will probably succeed most of the time, but every teacher knows the experience of evaluating a group of tests that turn out to be either too easy (everyone achieves high scores) or too hard. From those anomalies in your pedagogical life, you will learn something, and the next time you will change the test, prepare your students better, or predict your students' performance better.

What Do Letter Grades "Mean"?

An institutional philosophy of grading, whether it is explicitly stated or implicit, presupposes expectations for grade distribution and for a meaning or description of each grade. We have already looked at several variations on the mathematics of grade distribution. What has yet to be discussed is the meaning of letter grades. Typically, institutional manuals for teachers and students will list the following descriptors of letter grades:

A	excellent
B	good
C	adequate
D	inadequate/unsatisfactory
F	failing/unacceptable

Notice that the C grade is described as "adequate" rather than "average." The former term has in recent years been considered to be more descriptive, especially if a C is not mathematically calculated to be centered around the mean score.

Do these adjectives contain enough meaning to evaluate a student appropriately? What the letter grades ostensibly connote is a **holistic** score that sums up a multitude of performances throughout a course (or on a test, possibly consisting of multiple methods and traits). But do they? In the case of holistic scoring of writing or of oral production, each score category specifies as many as six different qualities or competencies that are being met. Can a letter grade provide such information? Does it tell a student about areas of strength and weakness, or about relative performance across a number of objectives and tasks? Or does a B just mean "better than most, but not quite as good as a few"? Even more complex—what does a GPA across four years of high school or college tell you about a person's abilities, skills, talents, and potential?

The overgeneralization implicit in letter grading underscores the meaninglessness of the adjectives typically cited as descriptors of those letters. Yet those letters have come to mean almost everything in their gate-keeping role in admissions decisions and employment acceptance. Is there a solution to this semantic conundrum? The answer is a cautious yes, with a twofold potential answer. First, every teacher who uses letter grades or a percentage score to provide an evaluation, whether a summative, end-of-course assessment or on a formal assessment procedure, should

- use a carefully constructed system of grading
- assign grades on the basis of explicitly stated criteria
- base the criteria on objectives of a course or assessment procedure(s)

Second, educators everywhere must work to persuade the gate-keepers of the world that letter/numerical evaluations are simply one side of a complex representation of a student's ability. Alternatives to letter grading are essential considerations.

Calculating Grades

One of the more common complaints uttered by teachers centers on the mundane task of simply calculating grades: adding up test and quiz results, factoring in other performance measures, and ultimately coming up with a final grade. For those who are mathematically minded, this is no doubt a simple mechanical task that is done with relative ease and quickness. For others the process is painstaking and time-consuming.

There are no doubt thousands of methods of arranging a grade book, whether it's a traditional paper-based one or a computer-based spreadsheet that is set up for you. Your own style, layout preferences, and predispositions toward this task will vary in many ways from another teacher's. If you're somewhat new at this business, you might want to consider consulting any of a plethora of Web resources available on the Internet. Here are just a few:

> www.classmategrading.com/
> www.teach-nology.com/downloads/grading/
> www.gradebooks4teachers.com/

A simple search with the key words "grading software" will ultimately yield dozens of possibilities.

A further bane of a teacher's life is the task of calculating—when necessary—means, medians, percentiles, and maybe even standard deviations of the results of term's grades for your classes. If this particular set of mathematical calculations is daunting for you, one way to resolve your dilemma would be to consult a classroom assessment textbook such as Marzano (2006), Popham (2007), or Gronlund and Waugh (2008). Another perhaps easier solution would be once again to turn to the Internet and search under "grading calculator," and you will find software that will perform all these calculations for you.

ALTERNATIVES TO LETTER GRADING

I can remember on occasion receiving from a teacher a term paper or a final examination with nothing on it but a letter grade or a number. My reaction was that I had put in hours and in some cases weeks of toil to create a product that had been reduced to a single symbol. It was a feeling of being demeaned, discounted, and unfulfilled. In terms of washback alone, a number or a grade provides absolutely no information to a student beyond a vague sense that he or she has pleased or displeased the teacher, or the assumption that some other students have done better or worse.

The argument for alternatives to letter grading can be stated with the same line of reasoning used to support the importance of alternatives in assessment in the previous chapter. Letter grades—and along with them numerical scores—are only one form of student evaluation. The principle of triangulation cautions us to provide as many forms of evaluation as are feasible.

For assessment of a test, paper, report, extra-class exercise, or other formal, scored task, the primary objective of which is to offer formative feedback, the possibilities beyond a simple number or letter include

- a teacher's marginal and/or end comments
- a teacher's written reaction to a student's self-assessment of performance
- a teacher's review of the test in the next class period
- peer-assessment of performance
- self-assessment of performance
- a teacher's conference with the student

For summative assessment of a student at the end of a course, those same additional assessments can be made, perhaps in modified forms:

- a teacher's marginal and/or end of exam/paper/project comments
- a teacher's summative written evaluative remarks on a journal, portfolio, or other tangible product
- a teacher's written reaction to a student's self-assessment of performance in a course
- a completed summative checklist of competencies, with comments
- narrative evaluations of general performance on key objectives
- a teacher's conference with the student

Most of the alternatives to grading for formative tests and other sets of tasks have been discussed in previous chapters. A more detailed look is now appropriate for a few of the summative alternatives to grading, particularly self-assessment, narrative evaluations, checklists, and conferences.

1. *Self-assessment.* A good deal was said in Chapter 10 about self-assessment. Here the focus is specifically on the feasibility of students' commenting on their own achievement in a whole course of study. Self-assessment of end-of-course attainment of objectives is recommended through the use of the following:

- checklists
- a guided journal entry that directs the student to reflect on the content and linguistic objectives
- an essay that self-assesses
- a teacher–student conference

In all of the above, the assessment should not simply end with the summation of abilities over the past term of study. The most important implication of reflective self-assessment is the potential for setting goals for future learning and development. The intrinsic motivation engendered through the autonomous process of reflection and goal-setting will serve as a powerful drive for future action.

2. *Narrative evaluations.* In protest against the widespread use of letter grades as exclusive indicators of achievement, a number of institutions have at one time or another required narrative evaluations of students. In some instances those narratives replaced grades, and in others they supplemented them. What do such narratives look like? Here are three narratives, all written for the same student by her three teachers in a preuniversity intensive English program in the United States. Notice the use of third-person singular, with the expectation that the narratives would be read by admissions personnel in the student's next program of study. Notice, too, that letter grades are also assigned.

Narrative evaluation

FINAL EVALUATION

COURSE: OCS/Listening   **Instructor:**   **Grade:** B+

Mayumi was a very good student. She demonstrated very good listening and speaking skills, and she participated well during class discussions. Her attendance was good. On tests of conversations skills, she demonstrated very good use of some phrases and excellent use of strategies she learned in class. She is skilled at getting her conversation partner to speak. On tape journal assignments, Mayumi was able to respond appropriately to a lecture in class, and she generally provided good reasons to support her opinions. She also demonstrated her ability to respond to classmates' opinions. When the topic is interesting to her, Mayumi is particularly effective in communicating her ideas. On the final exam, Mayumi was able to determine the main ideas of a taped lecture and to identify many details. In her final exam conversation, she was able to maintain a conversation with me and offer excellent advice on language learning and living in a new culture. Her pronunciation test shows that her stress, intonation, and fluency have improved since the beginning of the semester. Mayumi is a happy student who always is able to see the humor in a situation. I could always count on her smile in class.

COURSE: Reading/Writing   **Instructor:**   **Grade:** A-

Mayumi is a very serious and focused student. It was a pleasure having her in my class. She completed all of her homework assignments and wrote in her journal every day. Mayumi progressed a lot throughout the semester in developing her writing skills. Through several drafts and revision, she created some excellent writing products which had a main idea, examples, supporting details, and clear organization. Her second essay lacked the organization and details necessary for a good academic essay. Yet her third essay was a major improvement, being one of the best in the class. Mayumi took the opportunity to read a novel outside of class and wrote an extra-credit journal assignment about it. Mayumi has a good understanding of previewing, predicting, skimming, scanning, guessing vocabulary in context, reference words, and prefixes and suffixes. Her O. Henry reading presentation was very creative and showed a lot of effort; however, it was missing some parts. Mayumi was an attentive listener in class and an active participant who asked for clarification and volunteered answers.

COURSE: Grammar   **Instructor:**   **Grade:** A

Mayumi was an outstanding student in her grammar class this semester. Her attendance was perfect, and her homework was always turned in on time and thoroughly completed. She always participated actively in class, never hesitating to volunteer to answer questions. Her scores on the quizzes throughout the semester were consistently outstanding. Her test scores were excellent, as exemplified by the A+ she received on the final exam. Mayumi showed particular strengths in consistently challenging herself to learn difficult grammar; she sometimes struggled with assignments, yet never gave up until she had mastered them. Mayumi was truly an excellent student, and I'm sure she will be successful in all her future endeavors.

The arguments in favor of this form of evaluation are apparent: individualization, evaluation of multiple objectives of a course, face validity, and washback potential. But the disadvantages have worked in many cases to override such benefits: Narratives cannot be quantified easily by admissions and transcript evaluation offices; they take a great deal of time for teachers to complete; students have been found to pay little attention to them (especially if a letter grade is attached); and teachers have succumbed, especially in the age of computer-processed writing, to formulaic narratives that simply follow a template with interchangeable phrases and modifiers.

3. *Checklist evaluations.* To compensate for the time-consuming impracticality of narrative evaluation, some programs opt for a compromise: a checklist with brief comments from the teacher, ideally followed by a conference and/or a response from the student. The form on the next page is used for midterm evaluation in one of the high-intermediate listening-speaking courses at the American Language Institute.

Midterm evaluation checklist

MIDTERM EVALUATION FORM

Course _____   Tardies _____   Absences _____   Grade _____

Instructor _____   [signature] _____

	Excellent progress	Satisfactory improvement	Needs progress	Unsatisfactory progress
Listening skills				
Note-taking skills				
Public speaking skills				
Pronunciation skills				
Class participation				
Effort				

Comments: _____

_____

_____

_____

Goals for the rest of the semester: _____

_____

_____

_____

The advantages of such a form are increased practicality and reliability while maintaining washback. Teacher time is minimized; uniform measures are applied across all students; some open-ended comments from the teacher are available; and the student responds with his or her own goals (in light of the results of the checklist and teacher comments). When the checklist format is accompanied, as in this case, by letter grades as well, virtually none of the disadvantages of narrative evaluations remain, with only a small chance that some individualization may be slightly reduced. In the end-of-term chaos, students are also more likely to process checked boxes than to labor through several paragraphs of prose.

4. *Conferences.* Perhaps enough has been said about the virtues of conferencing. You already know that the impracticality of scheduling sessions with students is offset by its washback benefits. The end of a term is an especially difficult time to add more entries to your calendar, but with judicious use of classroom time (take students aside one by one while others are completing assigned work) and a possible office hour here and there, and with clear, concise objectives (to minimize time consumption and maximize feedback potential), conferences can accomplish much more than can a simple letter grade.

SOME PRINCIPLES AND GUIDELINES FOR GRADING AND EVALUATION

To sum up, I hope you have become a little better informed about the widely accepted practice of grading students, whether on a separate test or on a summative evaluation of performance in a course. You should now understand that

- grading is not necessarily based on a universally accepted scale
- grading is sometimes subjective and context-dependent
- grading of tests is often done on a "curve."
- grades reflect a teacher's philosophy of grading
- grades reflect an institutional philosophy of grading
- cross-cultural variation in grading philosophies needs to be understood
- grades often conform, by design, to a teacher's expected distribution of students across a continuum
- tests do not always yield an expected level of difficulty
- letter grades may not "mean" the same thing to all people
- alternatives to letter grades or numerical scores are highly desirable as additional indicators of achievement

With those characteristics of grading and evaluation in mind, the following principled guidelines should help you be an effective grader and evaluator of student performance:

Summary of guidelines for grading and evaluation

1. Develop an informed, comprehensive personal philosophy of grading that is consistent with your philosophy of teaching and evaluation.
2. Ascertain an institution's philosophy of grading and, unless otherwise negotiated, conform to that philosophy (so that you are not out of step with others).

4. Select appropriate criteria for grading and their relative weighting in calculating grades.
5. Communicate criteria for grading to students at the beginning of the course and at subsequent grading periods (midterm, final).
6. Triangulate letter grade evaluations with alternatives that are more formative and that give more washback.

This discussion of grading and evaluation brings us full circle to the themes presented in the first chapter of this book. There the interconnection of assessment and teaching was first highlighted; in contemplating grading and evaluating our students, that codependency is underscored. When you assign a letter grade to a student, that letter should be symbolic of your approach to teaching. If you believe that a grade should recognize only objectively scored performance on a final exam, it may indicate that your approach to teaching rewards end products only, not process. If you base some portion of a final grade on improvement, behavior, effort, motivation, and/or punctuality, it may say that your philosophy of teaching values those affective elements. You might be one of those teachers who feel that grades are a necessary nuisance and that substantive evaluation takes place through the daily work of optimizing washback in your classroom. If you habitually give mostly As, a few Bs, and virtually no Cs or below, it could mean, among other things, that your standards (and expectations) for your students are low. On the other hand, it could also mean that your standards are very high and that you put monumental effort into seeing to it that students are consistently coached throughout the term so that they are brought to their fullest possible potential.

As you develop your own philosophy of grading, make some attempt to conform that philosophy to your approach to teaching. In a communicative language classroom, that approach usually implies meaningful learning, authenticity, building of student autonomy, student–teacher collaboration, a community of learners, and the perception that your role is that of a facilitator or coach rather than a director or dictator. Let your grading philosophy be consonant with your teaching philosophy.

EXERCISES

[Note: **(I)** Individual work; **(G)** Group or pair work; **(C)** Whole-class discussion.]

1. **(G)** In pairs, check with each other on how you initially responded to the questionnaire on page 320. Now that you have read the rest of the chapter, how might you change your response, if at all? Defend your decisions and share the results with the rest of the class.

2. **(C)** Look again at the quote from Gronlund and Waugh (2008) on page 321. To what extent do you agree that grades should be based on student achievement and achievement only?

3. **(G)** In pairs or groups, each assigned to interview a different teacher in a number of different institutions, determine what that institution's philosophy of grading is. Start with questions about the customary distribution of grades; what teachers and student perceive to be "good," "adequate," and "poor" performance in terms of grades; absolute and relative grading; and what should be included in a final course grade. Report your findings to the class and compare different institutions.

4. **(C)** The cross-cultural interpretations of grades provide interesting contrasts in teacher and student expectations. With reference to a culture that you know fairly well, answer and discuss the following questions in regard to a midterm examination that counts for about 40 percent of a total grade in a course:

   a. Is it appropriate for students to assign a grade to themselves?
   b. Is it appropriate to ask the teacher to raise a grade?
   c. Consider these circumstances. You have a class of reasonably well-motivated students who have put forth an acceptable amount of effort and whose scores (out of 100 total points) are distributed as follows:

5 students:	90–94 (highest grade is 94)
10 students:	between 85 and 89
15 students:	between 80 and 84
5 students:	below 80

   Is it appropriate for you, the teacher, to assign these grades?

A	95 and above (0 students)
B	90–94 (5 students)
C	85–89 (10 students)
D	80–84 (15 students)
F	below 80 (5 students)

   d. How appropriate or feasible are the alternatives to letter grading that were listed on pages 333–337?

5. **(G)** In groups, each assigned to one of the four alternatives to letter grading (self-assessment, narrative evaluations, checklist evaluations, and conferences), evaluate the feasibility of your alternative in terms of a specific, defined context. Present your evaluation to the rest of the class.

(continued)

6. **(C)** Look at the summary of guidelines for grading and evaluation at the end of the chapter and determine the adequacy of each and whether other guidelines should be added to this list.

FOR YOUR FURTHER READING

Gronlund, Norman E., & Waugh, C. Keith. (2008). *Assessment of student achievement* (9th ed.). Boston: Allyn & Bacon.

In Chapter 11 of this classic book on assessment of various subject-matter content, the authors offer a substantive treatment of issues surrounding grading. The chapter deals with absolute and relative grading, mathematical considerations in grading, and six major guidelines for effective and fair grading. Their approach is rigorously empirical and offers a challenge to us all to be as clear and objective as possible in our assigning of grades.

Marzano, Robert. (2006). *Classroom assessment and grading that work.* Alexandria, VA: Association for Supervision and Curriculum Development.

This book offers a soundly based approach to grading that promises to enhance student achievement while adhering to curricular standards. The author notes that traditional point systems for grading often provide incorrect conclusions about students' actual competence and suggests alternative formative assessments, rubrics, and scoring/grading systems that are more appropriate for a diversity of students in the classroom and that offer some intrinsic motivation for students to keep pursuing goals.

APPENDIX

COMMERCIALLY PRODUCED TESTS OF ENGLISH AS A SECOND/FOREIGN LANGUAGE

Listed below is a selection of currently used tests that are produced by a variety of non-profit organizations. The list is not exhaustive, but it includes some of the more widely used tests. One test, the MLAT, is not a test of English but rather a test of overall language aptitude that is administered in English.

Consult the Internet for updated information on any of these tests.

International English Language Testing System (IELTS)	
Producer:	Jointly managed by the University of Cambridge Local Examinations Syndicate (UCLES), the British Council, and IDP Education Australia
Objective:	To test overall proficiency (language ability)
Primary market:	Australian, British, Canadian, and New Zealand academic institutions and professional organizations. American academic institutions are increasingly accepting IELTS for admissions purposes.
Type:	Computer-based (for the reading and writing sections), paper-based for the listening and speaking modules
Response modes:	Multiple-choice responses, essay, oral production
Time allocation:	2 hours, 45 minutes
Internet access:	http://www.ielts.org/
Description:	Reading: choice between academic reading or general training reading (60 minutes). Writing: the same option, academic writing or general training writing (60 minutes). Listening: four sections, for all candidates (30 minutes). Speaking: five sections, for all candidates (10 to 15 minutes)

Michigan English Language Assessment Battery (MELAB)	
Producer:	English Language Institute, University of Michigan
Objective:	To test overall proficiency (language ability)
Primary market:	Mostly U.S. and Canadian language programs and colleges; some worldwide educational settings as well
Type:	Paper-based
Response modes:	Multiple-choice responses, essay
Time allocation:	2 hours, 30 minutes to 3 hours, 30 minutes
Internet access:	www.lsa.umich.edu/eli/melab.htm
Description:	Impromtu essay (30 minutes). Listening: variety of item multiple-choice formats (25 minutes). Grammar, cloze reading, vocabulary, and reading comprehension (75 minutes). An oral interview (speaking test) is optional.

Modern Language Aptitude Test (MLAT)	
Producer:	Second Language Testing, Inc.
Objective:	To predict a student's likelihood of success and ease in learning a foreign language
Primary market:	Institutions and individuals wishing to measure foreign language learning aptitude
Type:	Paper-based and computer-based
Response mode:	Multiple-choice responses
Time allocation:	1 hour
Internet access:	http://www.2lti.com/htm/LangAptitudeTesting.htm#2
Description:	Five separate sections test (1) number learning, (2) phonetic script (sound–symbol association), (3) spelling clues, (4) words in sentences (sensitivity to grammatical structures), and (5) paired associates (rote memorization).

Oral Proficiency Interview (OPI)	
Producer:	American Council on Teaching Foreign Languages
Objective:	To test oral production skills of speakers in 60+ different foreign languages
Primary market:	Certification of speakers for government personnel and employees in the workplace; evaluation of students in language programs
Type:	Oral interview (telephone); computer-based (OPIc)
Response modes:	Oral production in a variety of genres and tasks
Time allocation:	20 to 30 minutes
Internet access:	http://www.actfl.org/
Description:	The telephonic version is an interactive interview between an ACTFL-certified tester and a candidate, adaptive to the experiences and linguistic competence of the candidate. The computer-based version (OPIc) is delivered electronically and on demand. This semidirect test is individualized to the test-taker. In both cases, digitally recorded speech is double-rated.

Test of English as a Foreign Language (TOEFL® iBT Test)	
Producer:	Educational Testing Service
Objective:	To test overall proficiency (language ability)
Primary market:	Almost exclusively U.S. universities and colleges for admission purposes
Type:	Internet-based
Response modes:	Multiple-choice responses, essay, spoken responses
Time allocation:	Up to 4 hours (iBT); 3 hours for paper-based test (PBT)
Internet access:	www.ets.org
Description:	Reading: three to five passages from academic texts (60 to 100 minutes). Listening: four to six lectures (60 to 90 minutes); Speaking: six tasks (20 minutes); Writing: two tasks (50 minutes)

Test of English for International Communication (TOEIC® Test)	
Producer:	Chauncey Group International, a subsidiary of Educational Testing Service
Objective:	To test overall proficiency (language ability)
Primary market:	Worldwide; business, commerce, and industry contexts (workplace settings)
Type:	Internet-based
Response modes:	Multiple-choice responses (listening and reading), speaking, writing
Time allocation:	2 hours (listening and reading sections), 20 minutes (speaking section), 60 minutes (writing section)
Internet access:	http://www.toeic.com
Description:	Listening tasks: statements, questions, short conversations, and short talks. Reading tasks: cloze sentences, error recognition, and comprehension. Speaking tasks: reading aloud, describing a picture, responding to questions, proposing a solution, and expressing an opinion. Writing tasks: writing a sentence based on a picture, responding to a written request, and writing an opinion essay

Test of Spoken English (TSE® Test)	
Producer:	Educational Testing Service
Objective:	To test oral production skills of nonnative English-speakers
Primary market:	Primarily used for employment, graduate assistantships, licensure, and certification purposes
Type:	Audio-delivered with written, graphic, and spoken stimuli
Response modes:	Oral tasks, connected discourse
Time allocation:	20 minutes
Internet access:	http://www.ets.org/
Description:	Oral production: Nine questions administered by audiocassette or telephone. Appropriate answers include narrating, recommending, persuading, and giving and supporting an opinion. The test-taker tells a story, describes a graph, and answers questions. The session is recorded, and trained raters determine an overall score for each test-taker.

Test of Written English (TWE® Test)

Producer:	Educational Testing Service
Objective:	To test written expression
Primary market:	Almost exclusively U.S. universities and colleges for admission purposes
Type:	In the TOEFL iBT, a computerized version of the TWE is a required component. In the TOEFL paper-based test (PBT), the TWE is the writing section.
Response modes:	Written essay
Time allocation:	30 minutes
Internet access:	http://www.ets.org/
Description:	One independent writing prompt, which the test-taker handwrites, scored on a scale of 0 to 6

Versant® Test

Producer:	Pearson Education
Objective:	To test oral production skills of nonnative English-speakers
Primary market:	Worldwide; primarily in workplace settings where employees require a comprehensible command of spoken English; secondarily in academic settings for placement and evaluation of students
Type:	Computer-assisted or telephone-mediated, with a test sheet. Versant also produces a Versant Spanish Test, Versant Arabic Test, and a lower-stakes Versant English Level Test. The English test is delivered in one of ten languages.
Response modes:	Oral, mostly constrained sentence-level tasks
Time allocations:	Approximately 15 to 17 minutes
Internet access:	www.versanttest.com
Description:	Test-takers respond to prompts that include reading aloud, repetition, short questions, sentence builds, story retelling, and open questions. An automated algorithm is used to calculate numeric scores ranging from 20 to 80.

GLOSSARY _____

absolute grading   see **grading**

achievement test   a test used to determine whether course objectives have been met—and appropriate knowledge and skills acquired—by the end of a given period of instruction

alternative assessment   various instruments that are less traditional and more authentic in their elicitation of meaningful communication

alternatives (in multiple-choice items)   see **options**

analytic scoring   an approach that separately rates a number of predetermined aspects (e.g., grammar, content, organization) of a test-taker's language production (e.g., writing); as opposed to **holistic scoring**

appropriate-word scoring   see **cloze**

aptitude test   a test designed to measure capacity or general ability *a priori* (e.g., before taking a foreign language course) to predict success in that undertaking

assessment   an ongoing process of collecting information about a given object of interest according to procedures that are systematic and substantively grounded

authenticity   the degree of correspondence of the characteristics of a given language test task to the features of a target language task

autonomy   the ability to set one's own goals and independently monitor success without the presence of an external stimulus

benchmarks   see **standards**

biased for best   providing conditions for a student's optimal performance on a test

bottom-up processing   comprehending language by first attending to the "smallest" elements (e.g., letters, syllables, words) of language and then combining them into increasingly larger elements; as opposed to **top-down processing**

bursts (in a dictation test)   the length of the word groups; see **dictation**

cloze   a text in which words are deleted and the test-taker must provide a word that fits the blank space

    appropriate-word scoring   a scoring method that accepts a suitable, grammatically and rhetorically acceptable word that fits the blank space in the original text

    exact-word scoring   a scoring method that is limited to accepting the same word found in the original text

    fixed ratio deletion   every n^{th} (e.g., sixth or seventh) word is deleted in a text

    listening cloze   a cloze test that requires the test taker to listen to a cloze passage while reading it; also known as **cloze dictation**, **partial dictation**

    rational deletion   words are deleted in a text on a rational basis (e.g., prepositions, sentence connectors) to assess specified grammatical or rhetorical categories

cloze-elide procedure   unnecessary words are inserted into a text and the test-taker must detect and eliminate those words

communicative test   a test that elicits a test-taker's ability to use language that is meaningful and authentic

competence   one's hypothesized (empirically unobservable) underlying ability to perform language

compound noun   a noun that is made up of two or more words; in English these are formed by nouns modified by other nouns or adjectives

computer-adaptive test (CAT)   instruments in which test-takers receive a set of questions that meet test specifications and that are generally appropriate for their performance level

computer-assisted language learning (CALL)   the application of computer technology to language learning and teaching

concurrent validity   see **validity**

consequential validity   see **validity**

construct   the specific definition of an ability, often not directly measurable (e.g., fluency) but which can be inferred from observation

construct validity   see **validity**

content word   a word that has meaning, such as a noun, main verb, adjective, and adverb; as opposed to **function word**

content-related validity   see **validity**

controlled-response task   a task that limits the amount of language that is produced; e.g., in a controlled writing task, a number of grammatical or lexical constraints apply

corpus linguistics   linguistic description or inquiry that utilizes computer-based corpora (large databases of real-world language) as its primary source, which in turn enables researchers to quantify frequencies, co-occurrences, collocations, etc.

criterion-referenced test   a test designed to give test-takers feedback, usually in the form of grades, on specific courses or lesson objectives; the distribution of students' scores across a continuum may be of little concern

criterion-related validity   see **validity**

critical language testing   a movement to expose possible covert social and political roles of language tests

critical pedagogy   an approach to learning and teaching that is motivated by beliefs about education and its place in society

C-test   a text in which the second half of every other word is eliminated and the test-taker must provide the whole word

diagnostic test   a test that is designed to diagnose specified aspects of a language

dialogue journal   a self-writing exercise in which a student records thoughts, feelings, and reactions which a teacher reads and responds to

dichotomous scoring   a method of scoring that allows only one correct response so that a test-taker's response is either right or wrong

dictation   a method of assessment in which test-takers listen to a text and write down what they hear

dicto-comp   a variant of dictation whereby test-takers listen to a relatively long text (e.g., a paragraph of several sentences or more) and try to internalize the content, some phrases, and/or key lexical items and then use them to recreate the text

direct testing   an assessment method in which the test-taker actually performs the target task; as opposed to **indirect testing**

discrete point test   assessments designed on the assumption that language can be broken down into its component parts and that those parts can be tested successfully

display writing   writing that is produced, usually in response to a prompt, to show competence in grammar, vocabulary, or sentence formation; as opposed to **real writing**

distractor efficiency   the effectiveness of the distractor to attract a test-taker away from the correct response

distractors   responses in a multiple-choice item used to divert or distract the test-taker from the correct response

equated forms   forms that are reliable across tests so that a score on a subsequent form of a test has the same validity and interpretability as the original test

evaluation   making decisions and/or value judgments based on the results of tests, other assessments, and/or teachers' reports

exact-word scoring   see **cloze**

face validity   see **validity**

focus on form   attention to the organizational structure (grammar, phonology, vocabulary, etc.) of a language

formal assessment   systematic, planned exercises or procedures constructed to give teacher and student an appraisal of student achievement

formative assessment   evaluating students in the process of "forming" their competencies and skills with the goal of helping them continue that growth process

form-focused assessment   assessment that focuses on the organizational components (e.g., grammar, vocabulary) of a language

frameworks of reference   see **standards**

function word   a word (e.g., preposition, pronoun, auxiliary verb, article, etc.) that has very little meaning but instead serves to express relationships among other words; as opposed to **content word**

gate-keeping   playing the role of allowing or denying someone passage into the next stage of an educational (or commercial, political, etc.) process

genre   type or category (e.g., academic writing, short story, pleasure reading) of a text

grade inflation   a phenomenon that shows a rise in the number of "high" grades assigned to students

grading   assigning a score to a test or a composite set of recorded assessments, usually by means of a letter (A through F)

> **absolute grading**   a score on a test-taker's performance is empirically calculated by predetermined measures of achievement of learning objectives
>
> **relative grading**   also known as "grading on the curve," in which a score on a test-taker's performance is compared to other test-takers and sometimes altered to suit instructional needs

high-frequency word   a word that appears most often in written and oral texts and is part of the foundation of vocabulary knowledge that proficient users of the language have acquired; as opposed to **low-frequency word**

high-stakes test   an instrument that provides information on the basis of which significant decisions are made about test-takers (e.g., admission to a course/school); see also **gate-keeping**

holistic scoring   an approach that uses a single general scale to give a global rating for a test-taker's language production; as opposed to **analytic scoring**

idiom   figure of speech whose meaning cannot be determined by the literal definition but whose metaphorical meaning is known through common use

impact   the effect of the use of a test on individual test-takers, institutions, and society

indirect testing   an assessment method in which the test-taker is not required to perform the target task; rather, inference is made from performance on non-target tasks; as opposed to **direct testing**

informal assessment   incidental, unplanned comments and responses, along with coaching and other impromptu feedback to the student

information transfer   a process in which information processed from one skill (e.g., listening to a telephone message) is used to perform another skill (e.g., writing down name/number to return a phone call)

institutionalized expression   a longer utterance that is fixed in form and used for social interaction (e.g., "how do you do?")

integrative test   a test that treats language competence as a unified set of interacting abilities of grammar, vocabulary, reading, writing, speaking, and listening

interactive (skills)   combining the use of more than one skill (reading, writing, speaking, and listening) in using language

inter-rater reliability   see **reliability**

interview   a context in which a teacher engages in a face-to-face question-and-answer dialogue with a student for a designated assessment purpose

intra-rater reliability   see **reliability**

intrinsic motivation   a self-propelled desire to excel

item discrimination   a statistic used to differentiate between high- and low-ability test-takers

item facility   a statistic used to examine the percentage of students who correctly answered a given test item

item response theory   a measurement approach that uses complex statistical modeling of test performance data to make generalizations about item characteristics

key   the correct response to a multiple-choice question

language ability   an individual's general or overall competence to perform in an acquired language; also less preferably referred to as *language proficiency*

limited-response task   a task that requires only a few words or a phrase as the answer

listening cloze   see **cloze**

low-frequency word   a word that seldom or rarely appears in written or spoken texts; as opposed to **high-frequency word**

macroskill   linguistic competencies that involve language competence beyond the sentence level (discourse, pragmatics, rhetorical devices); as opposed to **microskill**

measurement   a process of quantifying a test-taker's performance according to explicit procedures or rules

mechanical task   a task that determines in advance what the test-taker will produce (e.g., reading aloud or sentence repetition)

microskill   detailed specific linguistic competencies that involve processing up to and including the sentence-level (phonology, morphology, grammar, lexicon); as opposed to **macroskill**

multiple-choice test   an assessment instrument in which items offer the test-taker a choice among two or more listed options

multiple intelligences   types of intelligence that extend beyond traditional IQ-based concepts, such as spatial, musical, kinesthetic, naturalist, interpersonal, and intrapersonal intelligence

narrative evaluation   a form of individualized written feedback about a student's performance, sometimes used as an alternative or supplement to a letter grade

norm-referenced test   a test in which each test-taker's score is interpreted in relation to a mean (average score), median (middle score), standard deviation (extent of variance in scores), and/or percentile rank

objective tests   tests that have predetermined fixed responses

options   different responses from which a test-taker can choose in an item

partial credit scoring a method of scoring that permits multiple criteria for correctness so that a test-taker might get partial credit (a fraction of full credit) for a response to a test item

performance one's actual "doing" of language in the form of speaking and writing (production) and listening and reading (comprehension); as opposed to **competence**

performance-based assessment assessment that typically involves oral production, written production, open-ended responses, integrated performance (across skill areas), group performance, and other interactive tasks

performance levels see **standards**

phrasal constraint medium-length phrases that have a basic frame with one or two slots that can be filled with various words (e.g., "yours sincerely," "truly")

phrasal verb a combination of a verb with a preposition and/or adverb that often has a meaning that is different from the original verb (e.g., "look into")

picture-cued items test questions in which a visual stimulus serves to prompt a response or in which the test-taker chooses, among visuals, a response that correctly matches a spoken or written prompt

placement test a test meant to place a student into a particular level or section of a language curriculum or school

poly word a short, fixed phrase that performs a variety of functions (e.g., "hold your horses"); a disagreement marker

practicality the extent to which resources and time available to design, develop, and administer a test are manageable and feasible

predictive validity see **validity**

prefabricated language ready-made sentence stems and whole sentences or memorized chunks of sentences that provide models for the creation of new sentences

primary-trait scoring in a writing test, a single score indicating the effectiveness of the text in achieving its primary goal

process attending to the procedures (steps, strategies, tools, abilities) used to comprehend or produce language; as opposed to **product**

product attending to the end result of a linguistic action (e.g., in writing, the "final" paper, versus the various steps involved in composing the paper); as opposed to **process**

proficiency see **language ability**

proficiency test a test that is not limited to any one course, curriculum, or single skill in the language; rather, it tests overall global ability

psychometric structuralism a movement in language testing that seized the tools of the day to focus on issues of validity, reliability, and objectivity

real writing writing that is produced to convey meaning for an authentic purpose; as opposed to **display writing**

receptive response see **selective response**

relative grading see **grading**

reliability   the extent to which a test yields consistent and dependable results

    inter-rater   condition in which two or more scorers yield consistent scores for the same test

    intra-rater   condition in which the same scorer yields consistent scores across all tests

    student-related   a learner-related issue such as fatigue, anxiety, or physical or psychological factors which may make an "observed" score deviate from one's "true" score

    test   consistency of different facets of a test (e.g., instructions, item types, organization) in each test administration

    test administration   consistencies in conditions in which the test is administered

repetition   see **sentence repetition**

rubrics   statements that describe what a student can perform at a particular point on a rating scale; sometimes also called *band descriptors*

schemata   background knowledge; cultural or world knowledge

scoring, dichotomous   see **dichotomous scoring**

scoring, partial credit   see **partial credit scoring**

selective response   test items that require the test-taker to select rather than produce a response such as true/false or multiple-choice

sentence builder   a phrase with one or two slots that can be filled with whole ideas to make a complete sentence (e.g., "I think that X")

sentence repetition   the task of orally reproducing part of a sentence or a complete sentence that has been modeled by a teacher or test administrator

specialized vocabulary   technical terms or words that frequently occur in particular registers of language (e.g., legal language)

specifications (of a test)   planned objectives, features, methods, and structure of a test

standardized tests   tests that presuppose certain standard objectives or performance levels

standards   specifications of curricular objectives, criterion levels, and/or cut-off points against which a student's test performance is evaluated; also known as **benchmarks**, **frameworks of reference**, and **performance levels**

standards-based assessment   measures that are used to evaluate student academic achievement and to show that students have reached certain standards

stem   the stimulus or prompt for a multiple-choice question

strategic competence   the ability to employ communicative strategies to compensate for breakdowns as well as to enhance the rhetorical effect of utterances in the process of communication

student-related reliability   see **reliability**

subjective tests   tests in which the absence of predetermined or absolutely correct responses require the judgment of the teacher to determine correct and incorrect answers

subtechnical word   a word that occurs across a range of registers or subject areas

summative test   a test that aims to measure, or summarize, what a student has grasped and typically occurs at the end of a course or unit of instruction

supply items   options a test-taker can choose from for responses

task   a set or subset of linguistic actions that accomplish a real-world purpose, problem, or demand

task-based assessment   assessments that involve learners in actually performing the behavior that one purports to measure

test   a method or procedure for measuring a person's ability, knowledge, or performance in a given domain

test administration reliability   see **reliability**

test bias   a feature of the test that advantages or disadvantages one subgroup in comparison to another subgroup

test reliability   see **reliability**

test-wiseness   knowledge of strategies for guessing, maximizing the speed, or otherwise optimizing test task performance

tokens (in a reading passage) all the separate words; as opposed to **types**

top-down processing   comprehending language by first attending to the "larger" elements (e.g., paragraphs, discourse, pragmatics) of language and then possibly decomposing them into smaller units until the whole message has been processed; as opposed to **bottom-up processing**

triangulation (of assessments)   using two (or more) performances on an assessment, or two or more different assessments, to make a decision about a person's ability

types (in a reading passage)   repeated words that are not counted; as opposed to **tokens**

unitary trait hypothesis   the position that vocabulary, grammar, the "four skills," and other discrete points of language cannot be disentangled from each other in language performance

usefulness (of a test)   the extent to which a test accomplishes its intended objectives

validity   the extent to which inferences made from assessment results are appropriate, meaningful, and useful in terms of the purpose of the assessment

    concurrent   the extent to which results of a test are supported by other relatively recent performance beyond the test itself

    consequential   a test's impact, including such considerations as its accuracy in measuring intended criteria, its effect on the preparation of test-takers, and the (intended and unintended) social consequences of a test's interpretation and use

construct   any theory, hypothesis, or model that attempts to explain observed phenomena in one's universe of perceptions

content-related   the extent to which a test actually samples the subject matter about which conclusions are to be drawn

criterion-related   the extent to which the linguistic criteria of the test (e.g., specified classroom objectives) are measured and implied predetermined levels of performance are actually reached

face   the extent to which a test-taker views the assessment as fair, relevant, and useful for improving learning

predictive   the extent to which results of a test are used to gauge future performance

washback   the effect of assessments on classroom teaching and learning

BIBLIOGRAPHY

Acton, W. (1979). *Second language learning and the perception of difference in attitude.* Unpublished doctoral dissertation, University of Michigan.

Akiyama, T. (2004). *Introducing speaking tests into a Japanese senior high school entrance examination.* Unpublished doctoral dissertation, University of Melbourne.

Alderson, J. C. (2000). *Assessing reading.* Cambridge: Cambridge University Press.

Alderson, J. C. (2005). *Diagnosing language proficiency: The interface between learning and assessment.* London: Continuum Press.

Alderson, J. C., & Banerjee, J. (2001). Language testing and assessment (Part 1). *Language Teaching, 34,* 213–236.

Alderson, J. C., & Banerjee, J. (2002). Language testing and assessment (Part 2). *Language Teaching, 35,* 79–113.

Alderson, J. C., Clapham, C., & Wall, D. (1995). *Language test construction and evaluation.* Cambridge: Cambridge University Press.

Alderson, J.C. & Wall, D. (1993). Does washback exist? *Applied Linguistics, 14,* 115–129.

Alternative assessment [Special issue]. (1995). *TESOL Journal, 5*(1).

American Psychological Association. (2004). *Code of fair testing practices in education.* Washington, DC: Author.

Andrade, H. (2005). Teaching with rubrics: The good, the bad, and the ugly. *College Teaching, 53,* 27–31.

Andrade, H., & Du, Y. (2005). Student perspectives on rubric-referenced assessment. *Practical Assessment, Research & Evaluation, 10,* 1–11.

Armstrong, T. (1994). *Multiple intelligences in the classroom.* Philadelphia: Association for Curriculum Development.

Bachman, L. (1988). Problems in examining the validity of the ACTFL oral proficiency interview. *Studies in Second Language Acquisition, 10,* 149–164.

Bachman, L. (1990). *Fundamental considerations in language testing.* New York: Oxford University Press.

Bachman, L. (2002). Some reflections on task-based language performance assessment. *Language Testing, 19,* 453–476.

Bachman, L. (2005). Building and supporting a case for test use. *Language Assessment Quarterly, 2,* 1–34.

Bachman, L., & Palmer, A. S. (1996). *Language testing in practice.* New York: Oxford University Press.

Bachman, L., & Purpura, J. (2008). Language assessments: Gate-keepers or door openers? In B. Spolsky & F. Hult (Eds.), *The handbook of educational linguistics* (pp. 521–532). Hoboken, NJ: Wiley-Blackwell.

Bailey, A., Butler, F., & Sato, E. (2007). Standards-to-standards linkage under Title III: Exploring common language demands in ELD and science standards. *Applied Measurement in Education, 20*(1), 53–78.

Bailey, K. (1998). *Learning about language assessment: Dilemmas, decisions, and directions.* Cambridge, MA: Heinle and Heinle.

Balogh, J., & Bernstein, J. (2007). Workable models of standard performance in English and Spanish. In Y. Matsumoto, D. Oshima, O. Robinson, & P. Sells (Eds.), *Diversity in language: Perspectives & implications* (pp. 217–229). Stanford, CA: CSLI Publications.

Banerjee, J. (2003). Test review: The TOEFL CBT. *Language Testing, 20,* 111–123.

Barnett, J., & Antenucci, R. (2006). Language learner identities and professional standards for TESOL practitioners. *TESOL in Context, 16,* 129–146.

Barnwell, D. (1996). *A history of foreign language testing in the United States: From its beginnings to the present.* Tempe, AZ: Bilingual Press.

Barone, D., & Xu, S. (2007). *Literacy instruction for English language learners, pre-K–2.* New York: Guilford Press.

Barron, D., Henley, S., & Thompson, H. (2000). *Fostering information literacy: Connecting national standards, goals 2000, and the SCANS report.* Santa Barbara, CA: Libraries Unlimited.

Bernstein, J., DeJong, J., Pisoni, D., & Townshend, B. (2000). Two experiments on automatic scoring of spoken language proficiency. *Integrating Speech Technology in Learning,* 57–61.

Bishop, S. (2004). Thinking about professional ethics. *Language Assessment Quarterly, 1,* 109–122.

Black, P., & Wiliam, D. (1998). Assessment and classroom learning. *Assessment in Education, 5,* 7–74.

Blake, E. (2008). *No child left behind? The true story of a teacher's quest.* Poughkeepsie, NY: Hudson House Publishing.

Boldt, R. (1992). *Reliability of the Test of Spoken English™ revisited* (TOEFL Research Report No. RR-92-52). Princeton, NJ: Educational Testing Service.

Bonk, W., & Ockey, G. (2003). A many-faceted Rasch analysis of the second language group oral discussion task. *Language Testing, 20,* 89–110.

Brindley, G. (2001). Assessment. In R. Carter & D. Nunan (Eds.), *The Cambridge guide to teaching English to speakers of other languages* (pp. 137–143). Cambridge: Cambridge University Press.

Broadfoot, P. (2005). Dark alleys and blind bends: Testing the language of learning. *Language Testing, 22,* 123–141.

Brookhart, S. (2003). Developing measurement theory for classroom assessment purposes and uses. *Educational Measurement: Issues and Practices, 22,* 5–12.

Brown, H. D. (1999). *New vistas: An interactive course in English.* White Plains, NY: Pearson Education.

Brown, H. D. (2000). *Principles of language learning and teaching* (4th ed.). White Plains, NY: Pearson Education.

Brown, H. D. (2001). *Teaching by principles: An interactive approach to language pedagogy* (2nd ed.). White Plains, NY: Pearson Education.

Brown, H. D. (2002). *Strategies for success: A practical guide to learning English.* White Plains, NY: Pearson Education.

Brown, H. D. (2007a). *Principles of language learning and teaching* (5th ed.). White Plains, NY: Pearson Education.

Brown, H. D. (2007b). *Teaching by principles: An interactive approach to language pedagogy* (3rd ed.). White Plains, NY: Pearson Education.

Brown, H. D., & Sahni, S. (1994). *Vistas: An interactive course in English, student test package.* Englewood Cliffs, NJ: Prentice Hall Regents.

Brown, J. D. (1991). Do English faculties rate writing samples differently? *TESOL Quarterly, 25,* 587–603.

Brown, J. D. (1996). *Testing in language programs.* Upper Saddle River, NJ: Prentice Hall Regents.

Brown, J. D. (1998). *New ways of classroom assessment.* Alexandria, VA: Teachers of English to Speakers of Other Languages.

Brown, J. D. (2005). *Testing in language programs: A comprehensive guide to English language assessment* (2nd ed.). New York: McGraw-Hill.

Brown, J. D., & Bailey, K. M. (1984). A categorical instrument for scoring second language writing skills. *Language Learning, 34,* 21–42.

Brown, J. D., & Hudson, T. (1998). The alternatives in language assessment. *TESOL Quarterly, 32,* 653–675.

Brown, J. D., & Hudson, T. (2000). *Criterion-referenced language testing.* New York, NY: Cambridge University Press.

Brown, J. D., Hudson, T., Norris, J. M., & Bonk, W. (2002a). Examinee abilities and task difficulty in task-based second language performance assessment. *Language Testing, 19,* 395–418.

Brown, J. D., Hudson, T., Norris, J. M., & Bonk, W. (2002b). *Investigating second language performance assessments.* Honolulu, HI: University of Hawaii Press.

Buck, G. (2001). *Assessing listening.* Cambridge, MA: Cambridge University Press.

California Department of Education. (2002). *Listening and speaking standards for English language learners.* Sacramento, CA: Author.

Canale, M. (1984). Considerations in the testing of reading and listening proficiency. *Foreign Language Annals, 17,* 349–357.

Canale, M., & Swain, M. (1980). Theoretical bases of communicative approaches to second language teaching and testing. *Applied Linguistics, 1,* 1–47.

Carrell, P., Dunkel, P., & Mollaun, P. (2004). The effects of note-taking, lecture length, and topic on a computer-based test of ESL listening comprehension. *Applied Language Learning, 14,* 83–105.

Carroll, J. B. (1981). Twenty-five years of research on foreign language aptitude. In K. C. Diller (Ed.), *Individual differences and universals in language learning aptitude* (pp. 83–118). Rowley, MA: Newbury House.

Carroll, J. B. (1990). Cognitive abilities in foreign language aptitude: Then and now. In T. S. Parry & C. W. Stansfield (Eds.), *Language aptitude reconsidered* (pp. 11–29). Englewood Cliffs, NJ: Prentice Hall Regents.

Carroll, J. B., & Sapon, S. M. (1958). *Modern Language Aptitude Test.* New York, NY: The Psychological Corporation.

Carroll, J., & Sapon, S. M. (2000). *Modern Language Aptitude Test (MLAT): Manual.* San Antonio, TX: The Psychological Corp. Republished by Second Language Testing, Inc. Available: www.2LTI.com

Cascallar, E., & Bernstein, J. (2000, March). *The assessment of second language learning as a function of native language difficulty measured by an automated spoken English test.* Paper presented at the American Association of Applied Linguistics Conference, Vancouver, BC, Canada.

Celce-Murcia, M., Brinton, D., & Goodwin, J. (1996). *Teaching pronunciation: A reference for teachers of English to speakers of other languages.* Cambridge, MA: Cambridge University Press.

Chapelle, C. (1994). Are C-tests valid measures for L2 vocabulary research? *Second Language Research, 10,* 157–187.

Chapelle, C. (2005). Computer-assisted language learning. In E. Hinkel (Ed.), *Handbook of research in second language teaching and learning* (pp. 743–755). Mahwah, NJ: Lawrence Erlbaum Associates.

Chapelle, C., & Douglas, D. (2006). *Assessing language through computer technology.* New York, NY: Cambridge University Press.

Chapelle, C., Enright, M., & Jamieson, J. (2008). (Eds.) *Building a validity argument for the Test of English as a Foreign Language.* New York: Routledge.

Chapelle, C., & Jamieson, J. (2008). *Tips for teaching with CALL: Practical approaches to computer-assisted language learning.* White Plains, NY: Pearson Education.

Cheng, L. (2008). The key to success: English language testing in China. *Language Testing, 25,* 15–37.

Cheng, W., & Warren, M. (2005). Peer assessment of language proficiency. *Language Testing, 22,* 93–121.

Cheng, L., & Watanabe, Y. (Eds.). (2004). *Washback in language testing.* Mahwah, NJ: Lawrence Erlbaum Associates.

Cheng, L., Watanabe, Y., & Curtis, A. (Eds.). (2004). *Washback in language testing: Research contexts and methods.* Mahwah, NJ: Lawrence Erlbaum Associates.

Chinen, N. (2000, March). *Has CLT reached Japan?* Paper presented at the American Association of Applied Linguistics Conference, Vancouver, BC, Canada.

Choi, I. C. (2008). The impact of EFL testing on EFL education in Korea. *Language Testing, 25,* 39–62.

Christison, M. (2005). *Multiple intelligences and language learning.* San Francisco, CA: Alta Book Center Publishers.

Chun, C. (2005). An analysis of a language test for employment: The authenticity of the PhonePass test. *Language Assessment Quarterly, 3,* 295–306.

Chun, C. (2006). Commentary: An analysis of a language test for employment: The authenticity of the PhonePass Test. *Language Assessment Quarterly, 3,* 295–306.

Chun, C. (2008). Comments on "Evaluation of the Usefulness of the *Versant for English* Test: A Response": The author responds. *Language Assessment Quarterly, 5,* 168–172.

Clapham, C. (2000). Assessment and testing. *Annual Review of Applied Linguistics, 20,* 147–161.

Clark, J. L. D. (1983). Language testing: Past and current status—Directions for the future. *Modern Language Journal, 67,* 431–443.

Cloud, N. (2001). TESOL standards standing committee created. *Friends in TESOL, Fall,* 3.

Cohen, A. D. (1994). *Assessing language ability in the classroom* (2nd ed.). Boston: Heinle and Heinle.

Cohen, A. D. (2006). The coming of age of research on test-taking strategies. *Language Assessment Quarterly, 3,* 307–331.

Columbia Electronic Encyclopedia. (2008). New York, NY: Columbia University.

Conrad, S. (2005). Corpus linguistics and L2 teaching. In E. Hinkel (Ed.), *Handbook of research in second language teaching and learning* (pp. 393–409). Mahwah, NJ: Lawrence Erlbaum Associates.

Coombe, C., Folse, K., & Hubley, N. (2007). *A practical guide to assessing English language learners.* Ann Arbor, MI: University of Michigan Press.

Cooper, J. D. (1997). *Literacy: Helping children construct meaning* (3rd ed.). Boston: Houghton Mifflin.

Council of Europe. (2001). *Common European framework of reference for language learning, teaching, and assessment.* Cambridge: Cambridge University Press.

Cziko, G. A. (1982). Improving the psychometric, criterion-referenced, and practical qualities of integrative language tests. *TESOL Quarterly, 16,* 367–379.

Darling-Hammond, L. (2004). Standards, accountability, and school reform. *Teachers College Record, 106,* 1047–1085.

Davidson, F. (2006). World Englishes and test construction. In B. Kachru, Y. Kachru, & C. Nelson. (Eds.), *The handbook of world Englishes* (pp. 709–717). Malden, MA: Blackwell.

Davidson, F., Hudson, T., & Lynch, B. (1985). Language testing: Operationalization in classroom measurement and L2 research. In M. Celce-Murcia (Ed.), *Beyond basics: Issues and research in TESOL* (pp. 137–152). Rowley, MA: Newbury House.

Davidson, F., & Lynch, B. (2002). *Testcraft: A teacher's guide to writing and using language test specifications.* New Haven, CT: Yale University Press.

Davies, A. (1975). Two tests of speeded reading. In R. L. Jones & B. Spolsky (Eds.), *Testing language proficiency.* Washington, DC: Center for Applied Linguistics.

Davies, A. (2003). Three heresies of language testing research. *Language Testing, 20,* 355–368.

Davison, C. (2004). The contradictory culture of teacher-based assessment: ESL assessment practices in Australian and Hong Kong secondary schools. *Language Testing, 21,* 305–334.

de Szendeffy, J. (2005). *A practical guide to using computers in language teaching.* Ann Arbor: University of Michigan Press.

Dörnyei, Z., & Katona, L. (1992). Validation of the C-test amongst Hungarian EFL learners. *Language Testing, 9,* 187–206.

Douglas, D. (2000). *Assessing languages for specific purposes.* Cambridge: Cambridge University Press.

Douglas, D., & Hegelheimer, V. (2008). Assessing language using computer technology. *Annual Review of Applied Linguistics 2007, 27,* 115–132.

Douglas, D., & Smith, J. (1997). *Theoretical underpinnings of the Test of Spoken English revision project* (TOEFL Monograph Series RM-97-2). Princeton, NJ: Educational Testing Service.

Downey, R., Farhady, H., Present-Thomas, R., Suzuki, M., & Van Moere, A. (2008). Evaluation of the usefulness of the Versant for English test: A response. *Language Assessment Quarterly, 5,* 160–167.

Dunkel, P. (1991). Listening in the native and second/foreign language: Toward an integration of research and practice. *TESOL Quarterly, 25,* 431–457.

Duran, R., Canale, M., Penfield, J., Stansfield, C., & Liskin-Gasparo, J. (1985). *TOEFL from a communicative viewpoint on language proficiency: A working paper.* TOEFL Research Report #17. Princeton, NJ: Educational Testing Service.

Edgeworth, F. Y. (1888). The statistics of examinations. *Journal of the Royal Statistical Society, 51,* 599–635.

Ekbatani, G., & Pierson, H. (Eds.). (2000). *Learner-directed assessment in ESL.* Mahwah, NJ: Lawrence Erlbaum Associates.

Elder, C. (1997). What does test bias have to do with fairness? *Language Testing, 14,* 261–277.

Elder, C. (2001). *Experimenting with uncertainty: Essays in honour of Alan Davies* (Studies in Language Testing No. 11). Cambridge, MA: Cambridge University Press.

Ellis, R. (1997). *SLA research and language teaching.* Oxford, UK: Oxford University Press.

Epp, L., & Stawychny, M. (2001). Using the Canadian language benchmarks (CLB) to benchmark college programs/courses and language proficiency tests. *TESL Canada Journal, 18,* 32–47.

Eskey, D. (2005). Reading in a second language. In E. Hinkel (Ed.), *Handbook of research in second language teaching and learning* (pp. 563–579). Mahwah, NJ: Lawrence Erlbaum Associates.

Ethics in language testing [Special issue]. (1997). *Language Testing, 14* (3).

Farhady, H. (1982). Measures of language proficiency from the learner's perspective. *TESOL Quarterly, 16,* 43–59.

Farhady, H., & Hedayati, H. (2008, March. *Human operated, machine mediated, and automated tests of spoken English.* Paper presented at American Association of Applied Linguistics, Washington, DC.

Farr, R., & Tone, B. (1994). *Portfolio and performance assessment: Helping students evaluate their progress as readers and writers.* Orlando, FL: Harcourt Brace.

Ferris, D., & Hedgcock, J. (2005). *Teaching ESL composition: Purpose, process, and practice.* Mahwah, NJ: Lawrence Erlbaum Associates.

Fields, S. (2000). ELD test in the pipeline for 2000–2001 school year. *CATESOL News, 32,* 3.

Florida: Politically referenced tests? (2002). *Fair Test, 16,* 5–8.

Frase, L.T., Faletti, J., Ginther, A., & Grant, L. A. (1999). *Computer analysis of the TOEFL Test of Written English* (TOEFL Research Report No. RR-98-42). Princeton, NJ: Educational Testing Service.

Fulcher, G. (2000). The "Communicative" Legacy in Language Testing. *System, 28,* 483–497.

Fulcher, G. (2003). *Testing second language speaking.* London: Pearson Education.

Fulcher, G., & Davidson, F. (2007). *Language testing and assessment.* New York, NY: Routledge.

Gardner, D. (1996). Self-assessment for self-access learners. *TESOL Journal, 6,* 18–23.

Gardner, H. (1983). *Frames of mind: The theory of multiple intelligences.* New York, NY: Basic Books.

Gardner, H. (1999). *Intelligence reframed: Multiple intelligences for the 21st century.* New York, NY: Basic Books.

Gardner, H. (2000). *The disciplined mind: Beyond facts and standardized tests— The K–12 education that every child deserves.* New York, NY: Penguin Putnam.

Gasparro, J. E. (1985). *TOEFL from a communicative viewpoint on language proficiency: A working paper* (TOEFL Research Report No. RR-85-08). Princeton, NJ: Educational Testing Service.

Genesee, F. (Ed.). (1994). *Educating second language children: The whole child, the whole curriculum, the whole community.* New York, NY: Cambridge University Press.

Genesee, F., & Upshur, J. A. (1996). *Classroom-based evaluation in second language education.* Cambridge, MA: Cambridge University Press.

Gennaro, K. (2006). Fairness and test use: The case of the SAT and writing placement for ESL students. *Working Papers in TESOL & Applied Linguistics, 6.* Retrieved September 4, 2009, from http://journals.tc-library.org/index.php/tesol/issue/view/19

Gilfert, S. (1996). A review of TOEIC. *The Internet TESL Journal* [Online], *2.* Available: http://iteslj.org/Articles/Gilfert-TOEIC.html

Ginther, A. (2001). *Effects of the presence and absence of visuals on performance on TOEFL CBT listening-comprehensive stimuli* (TOEFL Research Report No. RR-01-16). Princeton, NJ: Educational Testing Service.

Goleman, D. (1995). *Emotional intelligence.* New York, NY: Bantam Books.

Golub-Smith, M., Reese, N., & Steinhaus, G. (1993). *Topic and topic type comparability on the Test of Written English* (TOEFL Research Report No. RR-93-10). Princeton, NJ: Educational Testing Service.

Goodman, K. (1970). Reading: A psycholinguistic guessing game. In H. Singer & R. B. Ruddell (Eds.), *Theoretical models and processes of reading* (pp. 497–508). Newark, DE: International Reading Association.

Gorman D., & Ernst, M. (2004). Test review: The Comprehensive Adult Student Assessment System (CASAS) Life Skills Reading Tests. *Language Assessment Quarterly, 1,* 73–84.

Gorsuch, G. J. (1998). Let them make quizzes: Student-created reading quizzes. In J. D. Brown (Ed.), *New ways of classroom assessment* (pp. 215–218). Alexandria, VA: Teachers of English to Speakers of Other Languages.

Gottlieb, M. (1995). Nurturing student learning through portfolios. *TESOL Journal, 5,* 12–14.

Gottlieb, M. (2000). Portfolio practices in elementary and secondary schools: Toward learner-directed assessment. In G. Ekbatani & H. Pierson (Eds.), *Learner-directed assessment in ESL* (pp. 89–104). Mahwah, NJ: Lawrence Erlbaum Associates.

Gottlieb, M., Carnuccio, L., Ernst-Slavit, G., & Katz, A. (2006). *PreK–12 English language proficiency standards.* Alexandria, VA: Teachers of English to Speakers of Other Languages.

Gronlund, N. E. (1998). *Assessment of student achievement* (6th ed.). Boston, MA: Allyn & Bacon.

Gronlund, N. E., & Waugh, C. K. (2008). *Assessment of student achievement* (9th ed.). Boston: Allyn & Bacon.

Grove, R. (1998). Getting the point(s): An adaptable evaluation system. In J. D. Brown (Ed.), *New ways of classroom assessment* (pp. 236–239). Alexandria, VA: Teachers of English to Speakers of Other Languages.

Hale, G. (1992). *Effects of amount of time allowed on the Test of Written English* (TOEFL Research Report No. RR-92-27). Princeton, NJ: Educational Testing Service.

Hale, G., Taylor, C., Bridgeman, B., Carson, J., Kroll, B., & Kantor, R. (1996). *A study of writing tasks assigned in academic degree programs* (TOEFL Research Report No. RR-95-44). Princeton, NJ: Educational Testing Service.

Halleck, G. (2007). Symposium article: Data generation through role-play: Assessing oral proficiency. *Simulation & Gaming, 38,* 91–106.

Hamp-Lyons, L. (2001). Ethics, fairness(es), and developments in language testing. In C. Elder (Ed.), *Experimenting with uncertainty: Essays in honour of Alan Davies* (Studies in Language Testing No. 11; pp. 222–227). Cambridge, MA: Cambridge University Press.

Hamp-Lyons, L., & Condon, W. (2000). *Assessing the portfolio: Principles for practice theory and research.* Cresskill, NJ: Hampton Press.

Harp, B. (1991). Principles of assessment in whole language classrooms. In B. Harp (Ed.), *Assessment and evaluation in whole language programs* (pp. 35–50). Norwood, MA: Christopher-Gordon.

Henning, G., & Cascallar, E. (1992). *A preliminary study of the nature of communicative competence* (TOEFL Research Report No. RR-92-17). Princeton, NJ: Educational Testing Service.

Hirvela, A., & Pierson, H. (2000). Portfolios: Vehicles for authentic self assessment. In G. Ekbatani & H. Pierson (Eds.), *Learner-directed assessment in ESL* (pp. 105–126). Mahwah, NJ: Lawrence Erlbaum Associates.

Holt, Rinehart, and Winston. (2003). *Alternative Assessment Guide.* New York, NY: Author.

Hosoya, M. (2001). *Is SFSU's Graduate Essay Test fair or unfair for international students?* Unpublished manuscript, San Francisco State University.

Huerta-Macías, A. (1995). Alternative assessment: Responses to commonly asked questions. *TESOL Journal, 5,* 8–11.

Hughes, A. (1989). *Testing for language teachers.* Cambridge, MA: Cambridge University Press.

Hughes, A. (2003). *Testing for language teachers* (2nd ed.). Cambridge, MA: Cambridge University Press.

Hughes R. (2004). Testing the visible: Literate biases in oral language testing. *Journal of Applied Linguistics, 1,* 295–309.

Hurley, S., & Tinajero, V. (2000). *Literacy assessment of second language learners.* Boston, MA: Allyn & Bacon.

International Language Testing Association. (2000). *Code of ethics for ILTA.* Available: http://www.iltaonline.com/index.php?option=com_content&view=article&id= 57&Itemid=47

Imao, Y. (2001). *Validating a new ESL placement test at SFSU.* Unpublished master's thesis, San Francisco State University.

Imao, Y., Castello, A., Kotani, A., Scarabelli, A., & Suk, N. (2000). *Toward a revision of the ESLPT at SFSU.* Unpublished manuscript, San Francisco State University.

Jacobs, H., Zinkgraf, S., Wormuth, D., Hartfiel, V., & Hughey, J. (1981). *Testing ESL composition: A practical approach.* Rowley, MA: Newbury House.

Jamieson, J. (1992). The cognitive styles of reflection/impulsivity and field independence and ESL success. *Modern Language Journal, 76,* 491–501.

Jamieson, J. (2005). Trends in computer-based second language assessment. *Annual Review of Applied Linguistics, 25,* 228–242.

Jenkins, S., & Parra, I. (2003). Multiple layers of meaning in an oral proficiency test: The complementary roles of non-verbal, paralinguistic, and verbal behaviors in assessment decisions. *Modern Language Journal, 87,* 90–107.

Jones, M., Jones, B., & Hargrove, T. (2003). *The unintended consequences of high-stakes testing.* Lanham, MD: Rowman & Littlefield.

Jonz, J. (1991). Cloze item types and second language comprehension. *Language Testing, 8,* 1–22.

Jung, E. (2003). The effects of organization markers on ESL learners' text understanding. *TESOL Quarterly, 37,* 749–759.

Jung, E. (2006). Misunderstanding of academic monologues by nonnative speakers of English. *Journal of Pragmatics, 38,* 1928–1942.

Kahn, R. (2002). *Revision of an ALI level 46 midterm exam.* Unpublished manuscript, San Francisco State University.

Klein-Braley, C. (1985). A cloze-up on the C-test: A study in the construct validation of authentic tests. *Language Testing, 2,* 76–104.

Klein-Braley, C., & Raatz, U. (1984). A survey of research on the C-test. *Language Testing, 2,* 134–146.

Kohn, A. (2000). *The case against standardized testing.* Westport, CT: Heinemann.

Krashen, S. (1997). *Foreign language education: The easy way.* Culver City, CA: Language Education Associates.

Kroll, B. (Ed.). (2003). *Exploring the dynamics of second language writing.* Cambridge, MA: Cambridge University Press.

Kuba, A. (2002). *Strategies-based instruction in Japanese high schools.* Unpublished master's thesis, San Francisco State University.

Kuhlman, N. (2001, April). *Standards for teachers, standards for children.* Paper presented at the California Teachers of English to Speakers of Other Languages Convention, Ontario, CA.

Kunnan, A. (2000). Fairness and justice for all. In A. Kunnan (Ed.), *Fairness and validation in language assessment* (pp. 1–13). Cambridge, MA: Cambridge University Press.

Larsen-Freeman, D. (1991). Teaching grammar. In M. Celce-Murcia (Ed.), *Teaching English as a second or foreign language* (pp. 279–296). Boston, MA: Heinle and Heinle.

Larsen-Freeman, D. (1997). Chaos/complexity science and second language acquisition. *Applied Linguistics, 48,* 141–165.

Lazaraton, A., & Wagner, S. (1996). *The Revised Test of Spoken English (TSE): Discourse analysis of native speaker and nonnative speaker data* (TOEFL Monograph Series RM-96-10). Princeton, NJ: Educational Testing Service.

Leacock, C., & Chodorow, M. (2001). *Automatic assessment of vocabulary usage without negative evidence* (TOEFL Research Report No. RR-01-21). Princeton, NJ: Educational Testing Service.

Leki, I. (2000). Writing, literacy, and applied linguistics. *Annual Review of Applied Linguistics, 20,* 99–115.

Leung, C., & Lewkowicz, J. (2006). Expanding horizons and unresolved conundrums: Language testing and assessment. *TESOL Quarterly, 40,* 211–234.

Lewkowicz, J. (2000). Authenticity in language testing: Some outstanding questions. *Language Testing, 17,* 43–64.

Liao, Y. (2006). Commentaries on the fairness issue in language testing. *Working Papers in TESOL & Applied Linguistics, 6.* Retrieved September 4, 2009, from http://journals.tc-library.org/index.php/tesol/issue/view/19

Linn, R. L. (2001). A century of standardized testing: Controversies and pendulum swings. *Educational Assessment, 7,* 29–38.

Llosa, L. (2007). Validating a standards-based classroom assessment of English proficiency: A multitrait–multimethod approach. *Language Testing, 24,* 489–515.

Lloyd-Jones, R. (1977). Primary trait scoring. In C. R. Cooper & L. Odell (Eds.), *Evaluating writing* (pp. 33–69). New York, NY: National Council of Teachers of English.

Longford, N. T. (1996). *Adjustment for reader rating behavior in the Test of Written English* (TOEFL Research Report No. RR-95-39). Princeton, NJ: Educational Testing Service.

Lowe, P. Jr. (1988). The unassimilated history. In P. Lowe & C. W. Stansfield (Eds.), *Second language proficiency assessment: Current issues* (pp. 11–51). Englewood Cliffs, NJ: Prentice-Hall.

Lowe, P. Jr., & Stansfield, C. W. (Eds.). (1988). *Second language proficiency assessment: Current issues.* Englewood Cliffs, NJ: Prentice Hall Regents.

Lumley, T. (2002). Assessment criteria in a large-scale writing test: What do they really mean to the raters? *Language Testing, 19,* 246–276.

Luoma, S. (2004). *Assessing speaking.* Cambridge, MA: Cambridge University Press.

Lynch, B. (2001). The ethical potential of alternative language assessment. In C. Elder (Ed.), *Experimenting with uncertainty: Essays in honour of Alan Davies* (Studies in Language Testing No. 11; pp. 228–239). Cambridge, MA: Cambridge University Press.

Lynch, B., & Davidson, F. (1994). Criterion-referenced language test development: Linking curricula, teachers, and tests. *TESOL Quarterly, 28,* 727–743.

Lynch, B., & Shaw, P. (2005). Portfolios, power, and ethics. *TESOL Quarterly, 39,* 263–297.

Madsen, H. (1983). *Techniques in testing.* New York, NY: Oxford University Press.

Marzano, R. (2006). *Classroom assessment and grading that work.* Alexandria, VA: Association for Supervision and Curriculum Development.

McKay, P. (2000). On ESL standards for school-age learners. *Language Testing, 17,* 185–214.

McNamara, M. (1998). Self-assessment: Keeping a language learning log. In J. D. Brown (Ed.), *New ways of classroom assessment* (pp. 38–41). Alexandria, VA: Teachers of English to Speakers of Other Languages.

McNamara, T. (2000). *Language testing.* Oxford, UK: Oxford University Press.

McNamara, T. (2006). Validity in language testing: The challenge of Sam Messick's legacy. *Language Assessment Quarterly, 3,* 31–51.

McNamara, T., & Roever, C. (2006). *Language testing: The social dimension.* Malden, MA: Blackwell Publishing.

McNamara, T., & Shohamy, E. (2008). Language tests and human rights. *International Journal of Applied Linguistics, 18,* 89–95.

Meara, P. (1983). Word associations in a foreign language. *Nottingham Linguistics Circular, 11,* 29–38.

Meara, P. (1984). The study of lexis in interlanguage. In A. Davies, C. Criper, & A. Howatt (Eds.), *Interlanguage* (pp. 225–235). Edinburgh: Edinburgh University Press.

Medina, N., & Neill, D. M. (1990). *Fallout from the testing explosion.* Cambridge, MA: National Center for Fair and Open Testing.

Meier, D., & Wood, G. (2006). *Many children left behind: How the No Child Left Behind Act is damaging our children and our schools.* Boston, MA: Beacon Press.

Mendelsohn, D. (1998). Teaching listening. *Annual Review of Applied Linguistics, 18,* 81–101.

Messick, S. (1989). Validity. In R. Linn (Ed.), *Educational measurement* (pp. 13–103). New York, NY: Macmillan.

Messick, S. (1996). Validity and washback in language testing. *Language Testing, 13,* 241–256.

Michigan English Language Assessment Battery. (2009). Ann Arbor: English Language Institute.

Moon, R. (1997). Vocabulary connections: Multiword items in English. In N. Schmitt & M. McCarthy (Eds.), *Vocabulary: Description, acquisition and pedagogy* (pp. 40–63). Cambridge, MA: Cambridge University Press.

Mosier, C. (1947). A critical examination of the concepts of face validity. *Educational and Psychological Measurement, 7,* 191–205.

Moskowitz, G. (1971). The classroom interaction of outstanding foreign language teachers. *Foreign Language Annals, 9,* 125–157.

Mousavi, S. A. (1999). *Dictionary of language testing* (2nd ed.). Tehran: Rahnama Publications.

Mousavi, S. A. (2002). *An encyclopedic dictionary of language testing* (3rd ed.). Taiwan: Tung Hua Book Company.

Mousavi, S. A. (2009). *An encyclopedic dictionary of language testing* (4th ed.). Tehran: Rahnama Publications.

Murphey, T. (1995). Tests: Learning through negotiated interaction. *TESOL Journal, 4,* 12–16.

Myford, C. M., Marr, D. B., & Linacre, J. M. (1996). *Reader calibration and its potential role in equating for the Test of Written English* (TOEFL Research Report No. RR-95-40). Princeton, NJ: Educational Testing Service.

Myford, C. M., & Wolfe, E. W. (2000). *Monitoring sources of variability within the Test of Spoken English assessment system* (TOEFL Research Report No. RR-00-66). Princeton, NJ: Educational Testing Service.

Nation, I. S. P. (1990). *Teaching and learning vocabulary*. New York, NY: Heinle and Heinle.

National Research Council. (2002). *Performance assessments for adult education: Exploring the measurement issues: Report of a workshop.* Washington, DC: National Academies Press.

National Research Council. (2005). *Measuring literacy: Performance levels for adults*. Washington, DC: National Academies Press.

Nattinger, J., & DeCarrico, J. (1992). *Lexical phrases and language teaching*. Oxford, UK: Oxford University Press.

Nichols, S., & Berliner, D. (2007). *Collateral damage: How high stakes testing corrupts America's schools.* Cambridge, MA: Harvard Education Press.

North, B. (2000). Defining a flexible common measurement scale: Descriptors for self and teacher assessment. In G. Ekbatani & H. Pierson (Eds.), *Learner directed assessment in ESL* (pp. 13–48). Mahwah, NJ: Lawrence Erlbaum Associates.

Norris, J. M., Brown, J. D., Hudson, T., & Yoshioka, J. (1998). *Designing second language performance assessments.* Honolulu: University of Hawaii Press.

Nuttall, C. (1996). *Teaching reading skills in a foreign language* (2nd ed.). Oxford, UK: Heinemann.

Oller, J. W. (1971). Dictation as a device for testing foreign language proficiency. *English Language Teaching, 25,* 254–259.

Oller, J. W. (1973). Cloze tests of second language proficiency and what they measure. *Language Learning, 23,* 105–119.

Oller, J. W. (1976). A program for language testing research. *Language Learning, 4,* 141–165.

Oller, J. W. (1979). *Language tests at school: A pragmatic approach.* London: Longman.

Oller, J. W. (1983). *Issues in language testing research.* Rowley, MA: Newbury House.

Oller, J. W., & Jonz, J. (1994). *Cloze and coherence.* Lewisburg, PA: Bucknell University Press.

O'Malley, J. M., & Valdez Pierce, L. (1996). *Authentic assessment for English language learners: Practical approaches for teachers.* White Plains, NY: Addison-Wesley.

Pawley, A., & Synder, F. (1983). Two puzzles for linguistic theory: Nativelike selection and nativelike fluency. In J. Richards & R. Schmidt (Eds.), *Language and communication* (pp. 191–226). London: Longman.

Peyton, J. K., & Reed, L. (1990). *Dialogue journal writing with nonnative English speakers: A handbook for teachers.* Alexandria, VA: Teachers of English to Speakers of Other Languages.

Phelps, R. (Ed.). (2005). *Defending standardized testing.* Mahwah, NJ: Lawrence Erlbaum Associates.

Phillips, D. (2001). *Longman introductory course for the TOEFL test.* White Plains, NY: Pearson Education.

Phillips, D. (2005). *Longman introductory course for the TOEFL test: Next generation (iBT).* White Plains, NY: Pearson Education.

Phillips, E. (2000). *Self-assessment of class participation.* Unpublished manuscript, San Francisco State University.

Pimsleur, P. (1966). *Pimsleur Language Aptitude Battery.* New York, NY: Harcourt, Brace & World.

Plough, I., & Bogart, P. (2008). Perceptions of examiner behavior modulate power relations in oral performance testing. *Language Assessment Quarterly, 5,* 195–217.

Popham, W. J. (1997). What's wrong—and what's right—with rubrics. *Educational Leadership, 55,* 72–75.

Popham, W. J. (2007). *Classroom assessment: What teachers need to know* (5th ed.). Boston: Allyn & Bacon.

Power, M. A. (1998). Developing a student-centered scoring rubric. In J. D. Brown (Ed.), *New ways of classroom assessment* (pp. 219–222). Alexandria, VA: Teachers of English to Speakers of Other Languages.

Powers, D. E., Albertson, W., Florek, T., Johnson, K., Malak, J., Nemceff, B., et al. (2002). *Influence of irrelevant speech on standardized test performance* (TOEFL Research Report No. RR-02-06). Princeton, NJ: Educational Testing Service.

Powers, D., Roever, C., Huff, K. L., & Trapani, C. S. (2003). *Validating LanguEdge courseware against faculty ratings and student self-assessments* (TOEFL Research Report RR-03-11). Princeton, NJ: Educational Testing Service.

Powers, D., Schedl, M., Wilson-Leung, S., & Butler, F. (1999*). Validating the revised Test of Spoken English against a criterion of communicative success* (TOEFL Research Report No. RR-99-05). Princeton, NJ: Educational Testing Service.

Prator, C. H. (1972). *Manual of American English pronunciation.* New York, NY: Holt, Rinehart & Winston.

Progosh, D. (1998). A continuous assessment framework. In J. D. Brown (Ed.), *New ways of classroom assessment* (pp. 223–227). Alexandria, VA: Teachers of English to Speakers of Other Languages.

Purpura, J. (2004). *Assessing grammar.* Cambridge: Cambridge University Press.

Qian, D. (2008). From single words to passages: Contextual effects on predictive power of vocabulary measures for assessing reading performance. *Language Assessment Quarterly, 5,* 1–19.

Raimes, A. (1991). Out of the woods: Emerging traditions in the teaching of writing. *TESOL Quarterly, 25,* 407–430.

Raimes, A. (1998). Teaching writing. *Annual Review of Applied Linguistics, 18,* 142–167.

Read, J. (2000). *Assessing vocabulary.* Cambridge: Cambridge University Press.

Reed, D. J., & Cohen, A. D. (2001). Revisiting raters and ratings in oral language assessment. In C. Elder (Ed.), *Experimenting with uncertainty: Essays in honour of Alan Davies* (Studies in Language Testing No. 11; pp. 82–96). Cambridge, MA: Cambridge University Press.

Reid, J. (1993). *Teaching ESL writing.* Englewood Cliffs, NJ: Prentice Hall Regents.

Richards, J. C. (1976). The role of vocabulary teaching. *TESOL Quarterly, 10, 77*–89.

Richards, J. C. (1983). Listening comprehension: Approach, design, procedure. *TESOL Quarterly, 17,* 219–239.

Rimmer, W. (2006). Measuring grammatical complexity: The Gordian knot. *Language Testing, 23,* 497–519.

Robinson, P. (2005). Aptitude and second language acquisition. *Annual Review of Applied Linguistics, 25,* 46–73.

Roever, C., & Powers, D. E. (2005). *Effects of language of administration on a self-assessment of language skills* (TOEFL Monograph MS-27). Princeton, NJ: Educational Testing Service.

Ross, S. (2005). The impact of assessment method on foreign language proficiency growth. *Applied Linguistics, 26,* 317–342.

Ross, S., & Okabe, J. (2006). The subjective and objective interface of bias detection on language tests. *International Journal of Testing, 6,* 229–253.

Rost, M. (2005). L2 listening. In E. Hinkel (Ed.), *Handbook of research in second language teaching and learning* (pp. 503–527). Mahwah, NJ: Lawrence Erlbaum Associates.

Rothstein, R. (2009). What's wrong with accountability by the numbers? *American Educator, 33,* 20–23.

Sakamoto, Y. (2002). *Japanese high school English teachers' attitudes toward communicative and traditional methodologies.* Unpublished master's thesis, San Francisco State University.

Savignon, S. J. (1982). Dictation as a measure of communicative competence in French as a second language. *Language Learning, 32,* 33–51.

Sawaki, Y., Stricker, L., & Oranje, A. (2008). *Factor structure of the TOEFL® Internet-based (iBT): Exploration in a field trial sample* (TOEFL Research Report No. RR-08-09). Princeton, NJ: Educational Testing Service.

Seow, A. (2002). The writing process and process writing. In J. C. Richards & W. A. Renandya (Eds.), *Methodology in language teaching: An anthology of current practice* (pp. 315–320). Cambridge, MA: Cambridge University Press.

Shepard, L., & Bliem, C. (1993). *Parent opinions about standardized tests, teacher's information, and performance assessments.* Los Angeles, CA: Center for Research on Evaluation, Standards, and Student Testing.

Shohamy, E. (1995). Performance assessment in language testing. *Annual Review of Applied Linguistics, 15,* 188–211.

Shohamy, E. (1997, March). *Critical language testing and beyond.* Paper presented at the American Association of Applied Linguistics Conference, Orlando, FL.

Shohamy, E. (2000). Fairness in testing. In A. J. Kunnan (Ed.), *Fairness and validation in language assessment: Selected papers from the 19th Language Testing Research Colloquium, Orlando, Florida* (pp. 15–19). Cambridge: Cambridge University Press.

Shohamy, E. (2001). *The power of tests: A critical perspective on the uses of language tests.* London: Pearson.

Short, D. (2000). The ESL standards: Bridging the academic gap for English language learners. *ERIC® Digest* (EDO-FL-00-13).

Silva, T., & Brice, C. (2004). Research in teaching writing. *Annual Review of Applied Linguistics, 24,* 70–106

Skehan, P. (1988). State of the art: Language testing (Part I). *Language Teaching, 21,* 211–221.

Skehan, P. (1989). State of the art: Language testing (Part II). *Language Teaching, 22,* 1–13.

Skehan, P. (2002). Theorising and updating aptitude. In P. Robinson (Ed.), *Individual differences and instructed language learning* (pp. 69-95). Amsterdam: Benjamins.

Smith, J. (2003). Reconsidering reliability in classroom assessment and grading. *Educational Measurement, 22,* 26-33.

Smolen, L., Newman, C., Wathen, T., & Lee, D. (1995). Developing student self-assessment strategies. *TESOL Journal, 5,* 22-27.

Spaan, M. (2006). Test and item specifications development. *Language Assessment Quarterly, 3,* 71-79.

Spada, N., & Frölich, M. (1995). *Communicative orientation of language teaching observation scheme.* Sydney, Australia: National Centre for English Language Teaching and Research, Macquarie University.

Spolsky, B. (1978). Introduction: Linguists and language testers. In B. Spolsky (Ed.), *Advances in language testing series: 2* (pp. v-x). Arlington, VA: Center for Applied Linguistics.

Spolsky, B. (1995). *Measured words: The development of objective language testing.* New York, NY: Oxford University Press.

Spolsky, B. (1997). The ethics of gatekeeping tests: What have we learned in a hundred years? *Language Testing, 14,* 242-247.

Spratt, M. (2005). Washback and the classroom: The implications for teaching and learning of studies of washback from exams. *Language Teaching Research, 19,* 5-29.

Stack, L., Stack, J., & Fern, V. (2002, April). *A standards-based ELD curriculum and assessment.* Paper presented at the Teachers of English to Speakers of Other Languages Convention, Salt Lake City, UT.

Stansfield, C., & Reed, D. (2004). The story behind the Modern Language Aptitude Test: An interview with John B. Carroll (1916-2003). *Language Assessment Quarterly, 1,* 43-56.

Staton, J., Shuy, R. W., Peyton, J. K., & Reed, L. (1987). *Dialogue journal communication: Classroom, linguistic, social and cognitive views.* Norwood, NJ: Ablex.

Sternberg, R. J. (1988). *The triarchic mind: A new theory of human intelligence.* New York, NY: Viking Press.

Sternberg, R. J. (1997). *Thinking styles.* Cambridge, MA: Cambridge University Press.

Stevenson, D. K. (1985). Authenticity, validity, and tea party. *Language Testing, 2,* 41-47.

Stites, R. (2004). A learner-centered approach to standards-based teaching and assessment: The EFF model. *CATESOL Journal, 16,* 161-178.

Stoynoff, S., & Chapelle, C. (2005). *ESOL tests and testing: A resource for teachers and administrators.* Alexandria, VA: Teachers of English to Speakers of Other Languages.

Strong-Krause, D. (2000). Exploring the effectiveness of strategies of self assessment in ESL placement. In G. Ekbatani & H. Pierson (Eds.), *Learner directed assessment in ESL* (pp. 49–74). Mahwah, NJ: Lawrence Erlbaum Associates.

Swain, M. (1984). Large scale communicative language testing. In S. Savignon & M. Berns (Eds.), *Initiatives in communicative language teaching: A book of readings* (pp. 185–201). Reading, MA: Addison-Wesley.

Swain, M. (1990). The language of French immersion students: Implications for theory and practice. In J. E. Alatis (Ed.), *Georgetown University round table on languages and linguistics* (pp. 401–412). Washington, DC: Georgetown University Press.

Swendler, E. (2003). Oral proficiency testing in the real world: Answers to frequently asked questions. *Foreign Language Annals, 36,* 520–526.

Tannenbaum, R., & Wylie, E. (2008). *Linking English-language test scores onto the Common European Framework of Reference: An application of standard-setting methodology* (TOEFL Research Report No. RR-08-34). Princeton, NJ: Educational Testing Service.

Tarone, E. (2005). Speaking in a second language. In E. Hinkel (Ed.), *Handbook of research in second language teaching and learning* (pp. 485–502). Mahwah, NJ: Lawrence Erlbaum Associates.

Taylor, L. (2004). Testing times: Research directions and issues for Cambridge ESOL examinations. *TESOL Quarterly, 38,* 141–151.

Test of Spoken English: Examinee handbook. (1987). Princeton, NJ: Educational Testing Service.

Test of English as a Foreign Language. (2009). Princeton, NJ: Educational Testing Service.

TOEFL score user guide. (2001). Princeton, NJ: Educational Testing Service.

TOEFL test and score manual. (2001). Princeton, NJ: Educational Testing Service.

Townshend, B., Bernstein, J., Todic, O., & Warren, E. (1998). Estimation of spoken language proficiency. *Proceedings of the ESCA Workshop on Speech Technology and Language Learning,* 179–182.

Underhill, N. (1987). *Testing spoken language: A handbook of oral testing techniques.* Cambridge: Cambridge University Press.

University of California. (2008). *California standards for the teaching profession.* Berkeley: Regents of the University of California.

Ur, P. (1984). *Teaching listening comprehension.* Cambridge, MA: Cambridge University Press.

Uribe, M., & Nathenson-Mejía, S. (2008). *Literacy essentials for English language learners.* New York, NY: Teachers College Press.

Valdez Pierce, L., & O'Malley, J. M. (1992). *Performance and portfolio assessments for language minority students.* Washington, DC: National Clearinghouse for Bilingual Education.

Valdman, A. (1988). The assessment of foreign language oral proficiency. *Studies in Second Language Acquisition, 10,* 121–128.

Wagner, E. (2006). Can the search for "fairness" be taken too far? *Working Papers in TESOL & Applied Linguistics, 6.* Retrieved September 4, 2009, from http://journals.tc-library.org/index.php/tesol/issue/view/19

Wagner, E. (2008). Video listening tests: What are they measuring? *Language Assessment Quarterly, 5,* 218–243.

Walker, B. (2004, October. *Success with instructional and evaluation rubrics.* Paper presented at Oregon Teachers of English to Speakers of Other Languages Convention, Portland.

Wang, L., Beckett, G., & Brown, L. (2006). Controversies of standardized assessment in school accountability reform: A critical synthesis of multidisciplinary research evidence. *Applied Measurement in Education, 19,* 305–328.

Weigle, S. C. (2002). *Assessing writing.* Cambridge, MA: Cambridge University Press.

Weigle, S. C. (2007). Teaching writing teachers about assessment. *Journal of Second Language Writing, 16,* 194–209.

Weir, C. J. (1990). *Communicative language testing.* London: Prentice Hall International.

Weir, C. J. (2001). The formative and summative uses of language test data: Present concerns and future directions. In C. Elder (Ed.), *Experimenting with uncertainty: Essays in honour of Alan Davies* (Studies in Language Testing No. 11; pp. 117–123). Cambridge, MA: Cambridge University Press.

Weir, C. J. (2005). Language testing and validation: An evidence-based approach. Basingstoke, England: Palgrave Macmillan.

White, J. (1998). *Do Howard Gardner's multiple intelligences add up?* London: University of London Institute of Education.

Wolcott, W. (1998). *An overview of writing assessment: Theory, research and practice.* Urbana, IL: National Council of Teachers of English.

Xi, X. (2008). *Investigating the criterion-related validity of the TOEFL speaking scores for ITA screening and setting standards for ITAs* (TOEFL Research Report No. RR-08-02). Princeton, NJ: Educational Testing Service.

Yoshida, K. (2001, March). *From the fishbowl to the open seas: Taking a step towards the real world of communication.* Paper presented at the Teachers of English to Speakers of Other Languages Convention, St. Louis, MO.

Young, R., & He, A. W. (1998, March). *Talking and testing: Discourse approaches to the assessment of oral proficiency.* Colloquium presented at the American Association of Applied Linguistics Conference, Seattle, WA.

NAME INDEX

Acton, W., 141
Akiyama, T., 87, 89, 103
Alderson, J. C., 16, 37, 118, 237, 243, 250, 256, 275
Andrade, H., 128
Antenucci, R., 94
Armstrong, T., 17, 18

Bachman, L., 3-5, 14-16, 27, 29, 31, 34-36, 72, 97, 108, 119, 218, 303, 308
Bachman, L.F., 84
Bailey, A., 88
Bailey, K., 18, 122, 145, 168, 174, 218, 284-286
Balogh, J., 188
Banerjee, J., 16, 275
Barnett, J., 94
Barnwell, D., 13
Barone, D., 230
Barron, D., 93
Beckett, G., 95
Berliner, D., 96, 99
Bernstein, J., 188
Black, P., 8
Blake, E., 88
Bliem, C., 126
Bogart, P., 211
Boldt, R., 117
Bonk, W., 126, 218
Bridgeman, B., 280
Brindley, G., 34
Brinton, D., 10
Broadfoot, P., 30
Brookhart, S., 128

Brown, H. D., 12, 17, 19, 137, 149, 150, 195-198, 212, 220, 232, 269, 270
Brown, J. D., 8, 18, 27-29, 68, 69, 84, 123, 126, 127, 131, 145, 154, 155, 284-286
Brown, L., 95
Brown, S., 92
Buck, G., 172, 174, 178, 182
Butler, F., 88, 117

Canale, M., 14, 15, 34, 207, 294, 308
Carnuccio, L., 87, 102
Carrell, P., 179
Carroll, J. B., 11, 12
Carson, J., 280
Cascallar, E., 95, 96, 105, 188, 282
Celce-Murcia, M., 10
Chapelle, C., 19, 21, 38, 178, 308-310
Cheng, L., 38, 85
Cheng, W., 145
Chinen, N., 89
Choi, I. C., 34, 98
Christison, M., 17, 97
Chun, C., 36, 188
Clapham, C., 6, 250
Clark, J.L.D., 13
Cloud, N., 93
Cohen, A. D., 218, 282, 283
Condon, W., 132
Conrad, S., 21

Cooper, J. D., 230
Council of Europe, 87
Curtis, A., 38
Cziko, G.A., 13

Darling-Hammond, L., 95
Davidson, F., 8, 27, 29, 33, 34, 36, 59
Davies, A., 34, 244
Davison, C., 92
DeCarrico, J., 306, 307
DeJong, J., 188
De Szendeffy, J., 19
Dörnyei, Z., 243
Douglas, D., 19-21, 178, 207
Downey, R., 188
Du, Y., 128
Dunkel, P., 164, 179
Duran, R., 34

Eckes, M., 155
Ekbatani, G., 144
Elder, C., 89
Ellis, R., 299
Enright, M., 38
Ernst, M., 93
Ernst-Slavit, G., 87, 102

Faletti, J., 280
Farhady, H., 14, 188
Farr, R., 230
Fern, V., 90
Ferris, D., 288
Ferris, D. R., 291
Fields, S., 88

SUBJECT INDEX

ELD. *See* English Language
Development (ELD)
Elicitation, 2
Elicitation techniques, 183
Emotional quotient (EQ), 17
England, standard-setting in, 87
English as a second language
(ESL)
assessment of curriculum for,
93
standards for, 87–88, 90. *See
also* Standards
English as a Second Language
Placement Test (ESLPT)
design of, 113
explanation of, 107, 108
web site for, 107
English for speakers of other
languages (ESOL). *See* English
as a second language (ESL)
English language, 89
English language development
(ELD), 87, 92. *See also* English
as a second language (ESL)
English language learners
(ELLs). *See* English as a
second language (ESL)
Error identification, 297
ESLPT. *See* English as a Second
Language Placement Test
(ESLPT)
Ethical issues, 98–100
Europe, standards-setting in, 87
European Association for
Language Testing and
Assessment, 87
Evaluation. *See also* Grading;
Scoring
checklist, 335–336
explanation of, 5
narrative, 329, 334–335
principles and guidelines for
test, 40–47
Exact word scoring method,
168–169, 242
Extended production tasks,
303–305
Extensive listening
authentic listening tasks and,
178–180
communicative stimulus-
response tasks and,
175–178
designing tasks for,
172–173

dictation and, 173–175
explanation of, 162
Extensive reading
explanation of, 229, 252–253
notetaking and outlining
tasks for, 255–256
skimming tasks for, 253
summarizing and responding
tasks for, 254–255
Extensive speaking
explanation of, 185, 218–219
oral presentations and,
219–220
picture-cued storytelling and,
220–221
retelling stories and, 221
translations and, 221
Extensive writing
assessment tasks for, 275–279
explanation of, 262
guided question and answer
and, 276–277
issues in assessing, 273–275
paragraph construction tasks
and, 277
paraphrasing and, 276
responding to, 285, 288–290
scoring for, 274–275,
283–285
strategic options and, 278–279

Face validity, 35–36
Fair Test, 96
Feedback
to enhance washback, 38–39
to journals, 138
test design and, 80–81
Fill-in-the blank task, 314
Fixed-ratio deletion, 242, 243
Foreign Service Institute (FSI),
211
Formal assessment, 7
Formative assessment
appeal of, 8
explanation of, 7
washback in, 39
Form completion tasks, 264
Form-focused assessment, 293
Frameworks of reference, 21
FSI levels, 211
Function words, 306

Games, 215–216
Gap-filling tasks, 240–241,
299–300

Gate-keeping function, 11, 95
Grade inflation, 327
Grade point average (GPA), 331
Grading. *See also* Scoring
absolute, 323–324
alternatives to letter, 332–337
cultural expectations in,
329–330
institutional views of,
328–329
letter, 331
method to calculate,
322–326, 332
overview of, 318–319
philosophy of, 20–321, 330
principles of, 337–338
relative, 324, 325
selecting criteria for, 322
teacher perceptions of,
326–328
test design and, 79–80
Grading distribution
questionnaire, 326
Grading questionnaire, 320
Graduate Management
Admission Test (GMAT®), 194
Graduate Record Exam (GRE®),
8, 95, 104
Grammar assessment
background of, 293–294
dialogue-completion tasks
and, 302
discrimination tasks and, 298
function of, 158
gap-filling tasks and, 299–300
information gap tasks and,
303–304
multiple-choice tasks and,
295, 297–298
noticing tasks or
consciousness-raising tasks
and, 299
role play or simulation tasks
and, 304–305
short-answer tasks and,
300–302
Grammar journals, 137
Grammar tasks, 235, 236, 248
Grammar translation method,
293
Grammar unit test
determining objectives for,
57–58
feedback to, 81
test design for, 54